JavaScript
Introductory

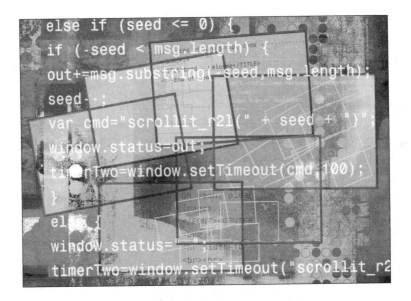

Don Gosselin

COURSE
TECHNOLOGY

Thomson Learning™

ONE MAIN STREET, CAMBRIDGE, MA 02142

Australia • Canada • Denmark • Japan • Mexico • New Zealand • Philippines
Puerto Rico • Singapore • South Africa • Spain • United Kingdom • United States

JavaScript: Introductory is published by Course Technology.

Associate Publisher	Kristen Duerr
Product Manager	Jennifer Muroff
Production Editor	Ellina Beletsky
Developmental Editor	Marilyn Freedman
Marketing Manager	Susan Ogar
Associate Product Manager	Tricia Coia
Editorial Assistant	Jennifer Adams
Cover Designer	Sue Yee, Black Fish Design Company, Inc.

Disclaimer

Course Technology reserves the right to revise this publication and make changes from time to time in its content without notice.

Cartoon characters referenced in Tutorial 4 are registered trademarks of the Walt Disney, Warner Brothers, and Viacom corporations.

The Web addresses in this book are subject to change from time to time as necessary without notice.

For more information, contact Course Technology, One Main Street, Cambridge, MA 02142; or find us on the World Wide Web at *www.course.com*.

For permission to use material from this text or product, contact us by

- ■ Web: www.thomsonrights.com
- ■ Phone: 1-800-730-2214
- ■ Fax: 1-800-730-2215

ISBN 0-619-00048-1

Printed in Canada

Preface

JavaScript: Introductory is designed to provide a guide for the beginning programmer to develop Web applications using the JavaScript programming language. This textbook focuses on JavaScript code that is compatible with Netscape JavaScript 1.2, which is supported by Navigator 4 and Internet Explorer 4. This textbook assumes that students have no programming language experience or knowledge of HTML.

Organization and Coverage

JavaScript: Introductory introduces users to basic JavaScript programming concepts along with the syntax to implement them. The World Wide Web, HTML, and JavaScript are introduced in Tutorial 1, along with programming logic and debugging. Variables, functions, objects, and events are discussed in Tutorial 2. This early introduction of variables, functions, objects, and events gives users a framework for better understanding more advanced concepts and techniques later in the text and allows them to work on more comprehensive projects from the start. Tutorials 3 and 4 teach users the fundamentals of data types and operators, and structured logic using control structures and statements. Tutorial 5 introduces window and frame concepts, and Tutorial 6 explains how to use JavaScript to create and manipulate forms. In Tutorial 7, users learn about dynamic HTML through animation.

JavaScript: Introductory combines text explanation with step-by-step exercises that illustrate the concepts being explained, reinforcing understanding and retention of the material presented. Throughout the book, HTML tags and syntax are introduced as necessary.

The individual using *JavaScript: Introductory* builds applications from the bottom up rather than using pre-written code. This technique facilitates a deeper understanding of the concepts used in Web programming with JavaScript. When individuals complete this book, they will know how to create and modify simple JavaScript language applications, and they will have the tools to create more complex applications. Users will also have a fundamental knowledge of programming concepts that will be useful whether they continue to learn more about the JavaScript language or go on to learn other scripting languages or object-oriented languages, such as C++ and Visual Basic.

JavaScript: Introductory distinguishes itself from other JavaScript language books in the following ways:

- It is written and designed specifically for individuals without previous programming experience or knowledge of HTML.

- The code examples are short; one concept is featured in each code example.
- Variables, functions, objects, and events are covered earlier than in many other texts, giving users a better understanding of the more advanced concepts and techniques that occur later in the text, and allowing them to work on significant projects from the start.
- Text explanation is interspersed with step-by-step exercises.
- HTML tags and syntax are introduced throughout the text, as necessary.
- JavaScript applications are built from the bottom up; the user gains a clear picture of how complex programs are built.
- Programming techniques are presented in easy-to-understand lessons.

Features

JavaScript: Introductory is a superior textbook because it also includes the following features:

- **"Read This Before You Begin" Page** This page is consistent with Course Technology's unequaled commitment to helping instructors introduce technology into the classroom. Technical considerations and assumptions about hardware, software, and default settings are listed in one place to help instructors save time and eliminate unnecessary aggravation.
- **Case Approach** Each chapter addresses programming-related problems that individuals could reasonably expect to encounter in business. All of the cases are followed by a demonstration of an application that could be used to solve the problem. Showing users the completed application before they learn how to create it is motivational and instructionally sound. By allowing users to see the type of application they will create after completing the chapter, users will be more motivated to learn because they can see how the programming concepts that they are about to learn can be used and, therefore, why the concepts are important.
- **Step-by-Step Methodology** The unique Course Technology methodology keeps users on track. They write program code always within the context of solving the problems posed in the tutorial. The text constantly guides users and lets them know where they are in the process of solving the problem. The numerous illustrations guide individuals to create useful, working programs.
- **Tips** These notes provide additional information—for example, an alternate method of performing a procedure, background information on a technique, a commonly-made error to watch out for, debugging techniques, or the name of a Web site the user can visit to gather more information.
- **Summaries** Following each chapter is a Summary that recaps the programming concepts and commands covered in each section.

- **Review Questions** Each tutorial concludes with meaningful, conceptual Review Questions that test users' understanding of what they learned in the tutorial.
- **Exercises** Programming Exercises users with additional practice of the skills and concepts they learned in the lesson. These exercises increase in difficulty and are designed to allow the user to explore the language and programming environment independently.

Web Browser Environments

Individuals can use either Netscape Navigator 4, Internet Explorer 4, or Internet Explorer 5 to create the exercises in this text. This text focuses on JavaScript code that is compatible with Netscape JavaScript 1.2, which all three browsers support.

CT Teaching Tools

All the teaching tools for this text are found in the Instructor's Resource Kit, which is available from the Course Technology Web site (www.course.com) and on CD-ROM.

- **Instructor's Manual**

  The Instructor's Manual has been quality assurance tested. It is available on CD-ROM and through Course Technology Faculty Online Companion on the World Wide Web. The Instructor's Manual contains the following items:

  - Answers to all the review questions and solutions to all the programming exercises in the book.
  - Technical Notes that include troubleshooting tips.
  - **Course Test Manager Version 1.2 Engine and Test Bank** Course Test Manager (CTM) is a cutting-edge Windows-based testing software program, developed exclusively for Course Technology, that helps instructors design and administer examinations and practice tests. This full-featured program allows instructors to randomly generate practice tests that provide immediate on-screen feedback and detailed study guides for incorrectly answered questions. Instructors can also use CTM to create printed and online tests over the network. Tests on any or all tutorials of this textbook can be created, previewed, and administered entirely over a local area network. CTM can grade the tests automatically at the computer and can generate statistical information on individual as well as group performance. A CTM test bank has been written to accompany this text and is included on the CD-ROM. The test bank includes multiple-choice, true/false, short answer, and essay questions.

- **Solution Files** Solution files contain possible solutions to all the problems users are asked to create or modify in the tutorials and cases. (Due to the nature of software development, user solutions might differ from these solutions and still be correct.)
- **Data Files** Data files, containing all data that readers will use for the tutorials and exercises in this textbook, are provided through Course Technology's Online Companion on the Instructor's Resource Kit CD-ROM. A Help file includes technical tips for lab management. See the inside front cover of this textbook and the "Read This Before You Begin" page preceding Tutorial 1 for more information on data files.

Acknowledgments

A text such as this represents the hard work of many people, not just the author. I would like to thank all of the people who helped make this book a reality. First and foremost, I would like to thank Marilyn Freedman, Developmental Editor, for her outstanding work and for making me a better writer. I would also like to thank Nan Fritz and her staff at nSight; Kristen Duerr, Associate Publisher; Jennifer Muroff, Product Manager; Ellina Beletsky, Production Editor; and Brendan Taylor, Jonathan Greacen, and Nicole Ashton, Quality Assurance testers. Thanks to Mary Ann O'Brien and Ellie Lottero of Harvard University and Peggy Beckley of RWD Technologies for giving me the time off to write.

Many, many thanks to the reviewers for their invaluable comments and suggestions, including Raymond Calvert, Manatee Community College; Jim Dunne, Arapahoe Community College; Ed Kaplan, Bentley College; Catherine Leach, Henderson State University; Le Nguyen, Parker Compumotor; Dave Reed, Dickinson College; Mildred Tassone, The Chase Manhattan Bank; and Rod Tosten, Gettysburg College.

As always, thanks to my friend and colleague, George T. Lynch, for getting me started. Most important, thanks to my wonderful wife, Kathy, for her eternal patience. Thanks also go to my cat, Mabeline, for keeping me company; to my dog, Noah, for taking me out for a walk on those rare occasions when I unchain myself from my computer; and to all of my friends and family for their understanding when I disappear for days and weeks on end.

Don Gosselin
Spencer, Massachusetts

Contents

t u t o r i a l   2

VARIABLES, FUNCTIONS, OBJECTS, AND EVENTS 41

t u t o r i a l   3

DATA TYPES AND OPERATORS 93

tutorial 4

DECISION MAKING WITH CONTROL STUCTURE AND STATEMENTS 145

t u t o r i a l   5

WINDOWS AND FRAMES 201

t u t o r i a l   7

DYNAMIC HTML AND ANIMATION 323

Appendix

JAVASCRIPT REFERENCE A-1

Read This Before You Begin

To the User

Data disks

To complete the tutorials and exercises in this book, you need Data disks. Your instructor will provide you with Data disks or ask you to make your own.

If you are asked to make your own Data disks, you will need three blank, formatted high-density disks. You will need to copy a set of folders from a file server or standalone computer onto your disks. Your instructor will tell you which computer, drive letter, and folders contain the files you need. The following table shows you which folders go on each of your disks, so that you will have enough disk space to complete all the tutorials and exercises:

Student Disk	Write this on the disk label	Put these folders on the disk
1	Tutorials 1, 2, and 3	Tutorial.01, Tutorial.02, and Tutorial.03
2	Tutorials 4, 5, and 6	Tutorial.04, Tutorial.05, and Tutorial.06
3	Tutorial 7	Tutorial.07

When you begin each tutorial, make sure you are using the correct Data disk. See the inside front or inside back cover of this book for more information on Data disk files, or ask your instructor or technical support person for assistance.

Using Your Own Computer

You can use your own computer to complete the Tutorials and exercises in this book. To use your own computer, you will need the following:

- **Web Browser Software.** You can download a copy of Netscape Navigator 4 from the Netscape Products home page at http://home.netscape.com/download/index.html. You can download a copy of Internet Explorer 4 or 5 from the Internet Explorer home page at http://www.microsoft.com/windows/ie/; click Download from the menu near the top of the Web page.

■ **Text Editor or HTML Editor** You will need a text editor or an HTML editor in order to create the exercises. You can use Notepad, WordPad, or any word processing program capable of creating simple text files. You can also use an HTML editor, such as Microsoft FrontPage or Adobe PageMill, with a graphical interface that allows you to create Web pages and immediately view the results.

■ **Data Files** You can get the Data files from your instructor. You will not be able to complete all the tutorials and exercises in this book using your own computer until you have the Data files. The user files may also be obtained electronically through the World Wide Web.

Visit Our World Wide Web Site

Additional materials designed especially for you might be available for your course on the World Wide Web. Go to **www.course.com**. Search for this book title periodically on the Course Technology Web site for more details.

To the Instructor

To complete all the exercises and tutorials in this book, your users must use a set of user files. These files are included in the Instructor's Resource Kit. They may also be obtained electronically through the Course Technology Web site at **www.course.com**. Follow the instructions in the Help file to copy the user files to your server or standalone computer. You can view the Help file using a text editor, such as WordPad or Notepad.

Once the files are copied, you can make Data disks for the users yourself, or tell them where to find the files so they can make their own Data disks. Make sure the files get copied correctly onto the Data disks by following the instructions in the Data disks section, which will ensure that users have enough disk space to complete all the tutorials and exercises in this book.

Course Technology Data Files

You are granted a license to copy the Data files to any computer or computer network used by individuals who have purchased this book.

TUTORIAL

Introduction to JavaScript

1

case ▶ WebAdventure, Inc., a Web site design firm, has recently hired you in an entry-level position. You are excited about working for a Web site design firm since, like many other people today, you spend a lot of time surfing the Internet. You know that Web pages consist of different types of information formatted in various ways. You have also noticed that some Web sites are more interactive than others and have different types of features that were not available several years ago. Games, order forms, animation, and various visual effects now seem to be part of almost every Web page you visit. You are excited about learning how to develop these types of Web pages. Your first challenge at WebAdventure is to gain an understanding of Web development and programming and find out where JavaScript fits in.

In this section you will learn:

- About the World Wide Web
- What JavaScript is used for
- About Hypertext Markup Language
- How to create an HTML document
- About the JavaScript programming language
- About logic and debugging

Programming, HTML, and JavaScript

The World Wide Web

JavaScript lives and works within Web pages on the World Wide Web. To understand how JavaScript functions, it helps to know a little about how the World Wide Web operates.

The **World Wide Web** (the "Web") was created in 1989 at the European Laboratory for Particle Physics in Geneva, Switzerland, as a way to easily access cross-referenced documents that exist on the Internet. Documents are located and opened using **hypertext links**, which contain a reference to a specific document. **Hypertext Markup Language** (**HTML**) is a simple language used to design the Web pages that appear on the World Wide Web. A **Web browser** is a program that displays HTML documents on your computer screen. Currently, the two most popular Web browsers are Netscape Navigator and Microsoft Internet Explorer.

tip

This textbook uses the terms HTML documents and Web pages interchangeably.

Every Web page or document has a unique address known as a **Uniform Resource Locator** (URL). You can think of a URL as a Web page's telephone number. Each URL consists of four parts: a protocol (usually HTTP), a service, either the domain name for a Web server or a Web server's Internet Protocol address, and a file name. **Hypertext Transfer Protocol** (HTTP) manages the hypertext links that are used to navigate the Web; you can think of HTTP as driving the Web. HTTP ensures that Web browsers correctly process and display the various types of information contained in Web pages (text, graphics, and other information). The protocol portion of a URL is followed by a colon, two forward slashes, and the service, which is usually *www* for "World Wide Web." A **domain name** is a unique address used for identifying a computer, often a Web server, on the Internet. The domain name consists of two parts separated by a period. The first part of a domain name is usually composed of text that easily identifies a person or an organization, such as DonGosselin or Course. The last part of a domain name identifies the type of institution or organization. For instance, com (for *company*) represents private companies, gov (for *government*) represents government agencies, and edu (for *educational*) represents educational institutions. For example, course.com is the domain name for Course Technology. Examples of entire URLs include http://www.DonGosselin.com and http://www.course.com.

An **Internet Protocol**, or **IP address**, is another way to uniquely identify computers or devices connected to the Internet, using a series of four groups of numbers separated by periods. All Internet domain names are associated with a unique IP address.

In a URL, a specific filename, or a combination of directories and a filename, can follow a domain name or IP address. If the URL does not specify a filename, the requesting Web server looks for a file named INDEX.HTML in the root or specified directory. Figure 1-1 points out the parts of a sample URL that opens an HTML document named `html_ref.html`.

Sample URL: http://www.sandia.gov/sci_compute/html_ref.html

Protocol

Domain name

Directory

Filename

Figure 1-1: Sample URL

JavaScript's Role on the Web

The original purpose of the World Wide Web was locating and displaying information. Once the Web grew beyond a small academic and scientific community, people began to recognize that greater interactivity would make the Web more useful. As commercial applications of the Web grew, the demand for more interactive and visually appealing Web sites also grew. Documents created using basic HTML, however, are static; the main purpose of HTML is to tell a browser how the document should appear. You can think of an HTML document as being approximately equivalent to a document created in a word-processing or desktop publishing program—the only thing you can do with it is view or print it. In response to the demand for greater interactivity, Netscape developed the JavaScript programming language for use in Navigator Web browsers.

JavaScript brings HTML to life and makes Web pages dynamic. Instead of HTML documents being static, JavaScript can turn them into applications, such as games or order forms. You can use JavaScript to change the contents of a Web page after it has been rendered by a browser, to interact with a user through forms and controls, to create visual effects such as animation, and to control the Web browser window itself. None of these things was possible before the creation of JavaScript.

Thanks in large part to JavaScript, the Web today is used for many different purposes, including advertising and entertainment. Many businesses today (and probably most in the future) have a Web site. To attract people to a Web site, and keep them there, a business's Web site must be exciting, interactive, and visually stimulating. Business Web sites use "flashing signs" that advertise specials, animation, interactivity, intuitive navigation controls, and many other types of effects to help sell their products. It is also easy to find games, animation, and other forms of entertainment on the Web. All of these types of applications and effects can be created with JavaScript.

To gain a better idea of what you can do with JavaScript, examine Figures 1-2, 1-3, and 1-4. You will be creating these programs in later tutorials. The map displayed in Figure 1-2 is an image map. Passing your mouse over a country on the map highlights the country and displays its name at the bottom of the Web page. You will create the image map in Tutorial 2. Figure 1-3 displays an online calculator you will create in Tutorial 3. The last program, in Figure 1-4, is an online product registration form that you will create in Tutorial 6. These are just some of the examples of the programs you will create with JavaScript in this textbook.

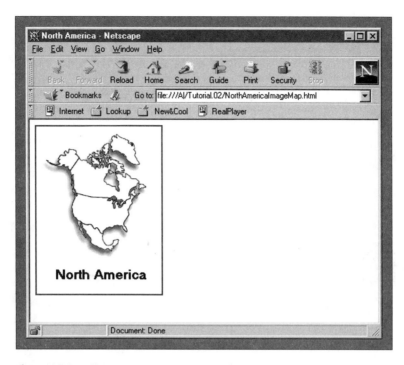

Figure 1-2: Image map

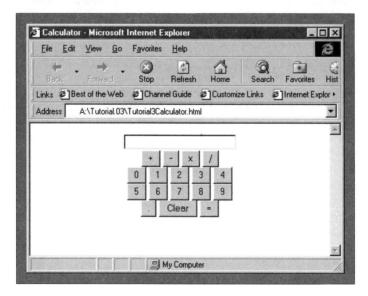

Figure 1-3: Online calculator

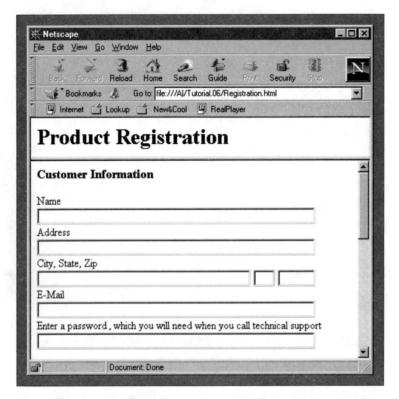

Figure 1-4: Product registration form

Hypertext Markup Language

To work with JavaScript, you must understand Hypertext Markup Language and how to construct Web pages, because JavaScript exists within Web pages. This section explains the basic principles of HTML that you will need to know to work with JavaScript. Throughout this text, additional HTML will be introduced as necessary. You can skip this section if you are already familiar with HTML.

HTML documents must be text documents that contain formatting instructions, called **tags**, along with the text that is to be displayed on a Web page. HTML tags range from formatting commands that boldface and italicize text to controls that allow user input, such as radio buttons and check boxes. Other HTML tags allow you to display graphic images and other objects in a document or Web page.

When you open an HTML document in a Web browser, the document is assembled and formatted according to the instructions contained in its tags. A Web browser's process of assembling and formatting an HTML document is called **parsing** or **rendering**. Tags are enclosed in brackets (< >), and most consist of a starting tag and an ending tag that surround the text or other items they are formatting or controlling. For example, the starting tag to boldface a line of text is <B> and the ending tag is </B>. Any text contained between this pair of tags appears boldfaced when you open the HTML document in a Web browser. The following line is an example of how to boldface text in an HTML document:

```
<B>This text will be boldfaced in a Web browser.</B>
```

All HTML documents begin with <HTML> and end with </HTML>. These tags tell a Web browser that the instructions between them are to be assembled into an HTML document. The opening and closing <HTML>...</HTML> tags are required and contain all the text and other tags that make up the HTML document. HTML contains many tags for creating HTML documents. Some of the more common tags are listed in Figure 1-5.

You use various parameters, called **attributes**, to configure many HTML tags. Attributes are placed before the closing bracket of the starting tag. For example, the <IMG> tag that embeds an image or video clip in an HTML document can be configured with a number of attributes, including the SRC attribute, which specifies the filename of the image file or video clip. To include the SRC attribute within the <IMG> tag, you type <IMG SRC="mygraphic.gif">. You must enclose the value of the attribute in double quotation marks.

HTML Tag	Description
<B></B>	Formats enclosed text in a bold typeface
<BODY></BODY>	Encloses the body of the HTML document
 	Inserts a line break
<CENTER></CENTER>	Centers text within the browser window and according to the width of the page

Figure 1-5: Common HTML tags (continued)

HTML Tag	Description
<HEAD></HEAD>	Encloses the page header and contains information about the entire page
<Hn></Hn>	Heading level tags, where n represents a number from 1 to 6
<HR>	Inserts a horizontal rule
<HTML></HTML>	Required tags that start and end an HTML document
<I></I>	Formats enclosed text in an italic typeface
<IMG src="...">	Inserts an image file
<P>	Begins a new paragraph
<STRONG></STRONG>	Formats enclosed text in a strong typeface, similar to bold
<TABLE></TABLE>	Creates a table. Each table row is defined by <TR>, and each table cell is defined by <TD>.
<TITLE></TITLE>	Encloses the page title, which is the text that appears in the browser's title bar—this tag must appear between the <HEAD> tags
<U></U>	Underlines enclosed text

Figure 1-5: Common HTML tags (continued)

Two important HTML tags are the <HEAD> tag and the <BODY> tag. The <HEAD> tag contains information that is used by the Web browser and is placed at the start of an HTML document, after the opening <HTML> tag. Several tags are placed within the <HEAD>...</HEAD> tag pair to help manage a document's content. The <TITLE> tag contains text that is displayed in a browser's title bar and is the only required element for the <HEAD> tag. With the exception of the <TITLE> tag, elements contained in the <HEAD> tag do not affect the rendering of the HTML document. When JavaScript programs are included in an HTML document, they often appear within the <HEAD>...</HEAD> tag pair. Figure 1-6 lists the tags placed within the <HEAD>...</HEAD> tag pair.

HTML Tag	Description
<TITLE>...</TITLE>	Contains the document's title, which appears in a browser's title bar
<STYLE>...</STYLE>	Identifies a style sheet

Figure 1-6: HTML tags placed within the <HEAD>...</HEAD> tag pair (continued)

Attribute	Description
\<LINK>	Specifies an external link between the HTML document and an external source
\<SCRIPT>...\</SCRIPT>	References embedded scripts
\<ISINDEX>	Creates a one-field search form
\<BASE>	Identifies the document's base URL
\<META>	Contains document properties

Figure 1-6: HTML tags placed within the \<HEAD>...\</HEAD> tag pair (continued)

Following the \<HEAD> tag is the \<BODY> tag, which contains the body of the HTML page. The attributes of the \<BODY> tag determine the appearance of an HTML document. Figure 1-7 lists the attributes of the \<BODY> tag.

Attribute	Determines
ALINK	The color of an active link
BACKGROUND	The background image
BGCOLOR	The background color
LINK	The color of an unvisited link
TEXT	Text color
VLINK	The color of a visited link

Figure 1-7: \<BODY> tag attributes

When a Web browser parses or renders an HTML document, it ignores non-printing characters such as spaces, tabs, and carriage returns in the code; only recognized HTML tags and text are included in the final document that appears in the Web browser. You cannot use carriage returns in the body of an HTML document to insert spaces before and after a paragraph; the browser recognizes only paragraph \<P> and \
 tags for this purpose. If you use paragraph \<P> tags to create blank lines in an HTML document, be aware that certain Web browsers, such as Internet Explorer, ignore tags that do not contain content. If you use the tag \<P> to create an empty line in an HTML document, the Web browser may completely ignore it. To prevent this from happening, include a **non-breaking space** code   and an ending tag so that the paragraph tag reads \<P> \</P>. Figure 1-8 shows an HTML document, while Figure 1–9 shows how it appears in a Web browser.

```
<HTML>
<HEAD>
<TITLE>Hello World</TITLE>
</HEAD>
<BODY>
<H1>Hello World (this is the H1 tag)</H1>
<H2>This line is formatted with the H2 tag</H2>
<P>This body text line contains several character formatting
tags including <I>italics</I>, <B>bold</B>, <U>underline</U>,
and <STRIKE>strikethrough</STRIKE>. The following code line
creates a line break followed by a horizontal rule.<BR>
<HR>
<IMG src="Checkmrk.jpg">This line contains an image.
</BODY>
</HTML>
```

Figure 1-8: An HTML document

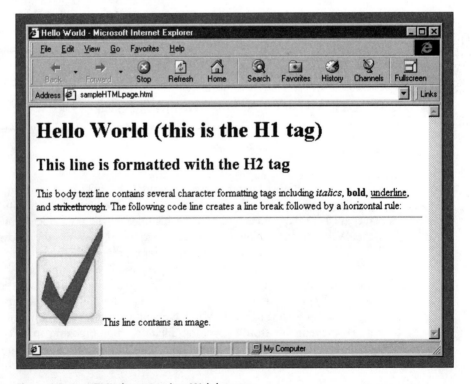

Figure 1-9: An HTML document in a Web browser

Some HTML tags, such as the paragraph tag <P>, do not necessarily require ending tags. In addition, different browsers have different requirements as to when an ending tag is required.

Creating an HTML Document

Since HTML documents are text files, you can create them in any text editor such as Notepad, WordPad, or any word-processing program capable of creating simple text files. If you use a text editor to create an HTML document, you cannot view the final result until you open the document in a Web browser. However, many applications (called HTML editors) are designed specifically for creating HTML documents. Some popular HTML editors, such as Microsoft FrontPage and Adobe PageMill, have graphical interfaces that allow you to create Web pages and immediately view the results, similar to the WYSIWYG (what-you-see-is-what-you-get) feature in word-processing programs. In addition, many current word-processing applications, including Microsoft Word and WordPerfect, allow you to save files as HTML documents. All these HTML editors still create simple text files, but they automate the process of applying tags. For example, if you create a document in Word that contains boldface text, then save it as an HTML document, the bold <B> tag is automatically added to the text in the HTML text file that is created.

Be aware that different Web browsers render HTML documents in different ways. For example, an HTML document displayed in Internet Explorer can appear differently in Navigator.

Next, you will create an HTML document containing some of the tags you have seen in this section. You can use any text editor, such as Notepad or WordPad, or an HTML editor.

To create an HTML document:

1 Start your text editor or HTML editor and create a new document.

2 Type **<HTML>** to begin the HTML document. Remember that all HTML documents should begin and end with the <HTML>...</HTML> tag pair.

3 Press **Enter** and add the following <HEAD> and <TITLE> to the document.

The title will appear in your Web browser's title bar. Remember that the <HEAD>...</HEAD> tag pair must include the <TITLE>...</TITLE> tag pair. The <TITLE>...</TITLE> tag pair cannot exist outside of the <HEAD>...</HEAD> tag pair.

```
<HEAD>
<TITLE>Web Page Example</TITLE>
</HEAD>
```

4 Press **Enter** and type **<BODY>** to begin the body section of the HTML document.

5 Press **Enter** and type the following tags and text to create the body of the HTML document.

```
<H1>Hello World</H1>
<P>This is my first Web page.</P>
<HR>
<H2>This line is H2</H2>
<H3>This line is H3</H3>
<P>The following line is empty.</P>
<P> </P>
<P><B>bold</B>, <I>italic</I>, <U>underline</U></P>
```

6 Press **Enter**, then finish the document by typing the following tags to close the <BODY>...</BODY> and <HTML>...</HTML> tag pairs:

```
</BODY>
</HTML>
```

7 Save the file as **HelloWorld.html** in the **Tutorial.01** folder on your Student Disk.

> Some Web servers do not correctly interpret spaces within the name of HTML files. For example, a file name of *Hello World.html* (with a space between *Hello* and *World*) may not be interpreted correctly on some servers. For this reason, filenames in this text do not include spaces.

8 Start Navigator, Internet Explorer, or another Web browser. Then open the **HelloWorld.html** file in your Web browser. Figure 1-10 displays the HelloWorld.html file as it appears in Navigator 4.0.

9 Close your Web browser by clicking the **Close** button ⊠.

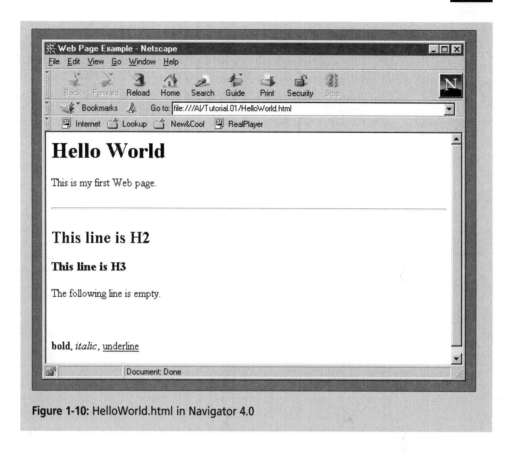

Figure 1-10: HelloWorld.html in Navigator 4.0

The JavaScript Programming Language

JavaScript is a scripting language. The term **scripting language** refers to programming languages that are executed by an interpreter from within a Web browser. An **interpreter** translates programming code into an executable format *each time* the program is run—one line at a time. Programs written in scripting languages, such as JavaScript, are interpreted when a scripting engine loads an HTML page. A **scripting engine** is an interpreter that is part of the Web browser. A Web browser that contains a scripting engine to translate scripts is called a **scripting host**. Navigator and Internet Explorer are both examples of scripting hosts for JavaScript programs.

The JavaScript language was first introduced in Navigator and was originally called LiveScript. With the release of Navigator 2.0, the name was changed to JavaScript 1.0. Subsequently, Microsoft released its own version of JavaScript in Internet Explorer 4.0 and named it JScript. The most current versions of each implementation are JavaScript 1.3 in Navigator and JScript 3.0 in Internet Explorer. However, these two implementations are not entirely compatible with each other. The goal of this text is to create JavaScript programs that can run on either Navigator or Internet Explorer. Therefore, this text focuses on JavaScript code that is compatible with Netscape JavaScript 1.2, which is supported by Navigator 4 and Internet Explorer 4. Netscape JavaScript 1.2 is considered the current JavaScript standard and is roughly compatible with JScript 2.0.

The European Computer Manufacturer's Association, or ECMA, produced an international, standardized version of JavaScript called ECMAScript. ECMAScript is roughly compatible with JavaScript 1.1. Future versions of Netscape JavaScript are expected to completely conform to ECMAScript. Microsoft claims that JScript 3.0 is already 100% compliant with ECMAScript.

Many people think that JavaScript is related to or is a simplified version of the Java programming language. They are, however, entirely different languages. Java is a compiled, object-oriented programming language that was created by Sun Microsystems and is considerably more difficult to master than JavaScript. JavaScript is an interpreted scripting language that was created by Netscape. Although Java is often used to create programs that can run from a Web page, Java programs are external programs that execute independently of a browser. In contrast, JavaScript programs run within a Web page and control the browser.

JavaScript is available in two formats: client-side JavaScript and server-side JavaScript. The standardized **client-side JavaScript** is the format available to HTML pages displayed in Web browsers (the *client*). JavaScript version 1.2 in Navigator 4.0 and ECMAScript are client-side versions of JavaScript. Server-side JavaScript is used with Web servers to access file systems, communicate with other applications, access databases, and perform other tasks. Currently, server-side JavaScript is proprietary and vendor-specific. You must know a slightly different version of the language for each vendor's Web server; there is no server-side standard similar to ECMAScript. Client-side and server-side JavaScript share the same basic programming features. Figure 1-11 illustrates how client-side and server-side JavaScript are related.

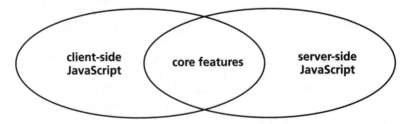

Figure 1-11: Relationship of client-side and server-side JavaScript

Logic and Debugging

All programming languages, including JavaScript, have their own **syntax,** or rules of the language. To write a program, you must understand a given programming language's syntax. You must also understand computer programming logic. The **logic** underlying any program involves executing the various parts of the program in the correct order to produce the desired results. For example, although you know how to drive a car well, you may not reach your destination if you do not follow the correct route. Similarly, you might be able to use a programming language's syntax correctly, but be unable to execute a logically constructed, workable program. Examples of logical errors include multiplying two values when you meant to divide them, or producing output prior to obtaining the appropriate input. The following JavaScript code contains another example of a logic error:

```
var count = 1
while (count <= 10) {
    alert("The number is " + count);
}
```

The code in the example uses a while statement, which is used to repeat a command or series of commands based on the evaluation of certain criteria. The criterion in the example is the value of a variable named count (you will learn about variables in Tutorial 2). The while statement is supposed to execute until the count variable is less than or equal to 10. However, there is no code within the while statement's body that changes the count variable's value. The count variable will continue to have a value of 1 through each iteration of the loop. In this case, an alert dialog box containing the text string *The number is 1* will be displayed over and over again, no matter how many times you press the OK button. This type of logical error is called an infinite loop.

Do not worry about how the JavaScript code in the example is constructed. The example is only meant to give you a better understanding of a logical error.

Any error in a program that causes it to function incorrectly, whether due to incorrect syntax or flaws in logic, is called a bug. **Debugging** describes the act of tracing and resolving errors in a program. Legend has it that the term *debugging* was first coined by Grace Murray Hopper, a mathematician who was instrumental in developing the COBOL programming language. As the story from the 1940s goes, a moth short-circuited a primitive computer that Hopper was using. Removing the moth from the computer *debugged* the system and resolved the problem. Today, a bug refers to any sort of problem in the design and operation of a program.

Do not confuse bugs with computer viruses. Bugs are problems within a program that occur because of syntax errors, design flaws, or run-time errors. Viruses are self-contained programs designed to "infect" a computer system and cause mischievous or malicious damage. Actually, virus programs themselves can contain bugs if they contain syntax errors or do not perform (or do damage) as their creators envisioned.

Many programming languages include commands and other features to assist in locating bugs in a program. However, the version of JavaScript covered in this textbook does not contain any useful debugging tools. Future versions of JavaScript are expected to include debugging features. To provide you with some debugging skills, debugging suggestions are offered in the Tips feature throughout this book.

However, as you read the debugging tips, keep in mind that debugging is not an exact science—every program you write is different and requires different methods of debugging. Your own logical and analytical skills are the best debugging resources you have.

In the next section you will start learning how to create JavaScript programs.

 # S U M M A R Y

- Hypertext Markup Language (HTML) is a simple protocol used to design Web pages that appear on the World Wide Web.

- The World Wide Web is driven by Hypertext Transfer Protocol (HTTP), which manages the hypertext links that are used to navigate the Web.

- Every Web document has a unique address known as a Uniform Resource Locator (URL).

- JavaScript brings HTML to life and makes Web pages dynamic, turning them into applications, such as games or order forms.

- HTML documents must be text documents that contain formatting instructions, called **tags**, along with the text that is to be displayed on a Web page.

- HTML tags range from formatting commands to controls that allow user input, to tags that allow the display of graphic images and other objects.

- A Web browser's process of assembling and formatting an HTML document is called parsing or rendering.

- An interpreter translates programming code into an executable format each time the program is run—one line at a time.

- JavaScript is an interpreted programming language.

- A scripting engine is an interpreter that is part of the Web browser. A Web browser that contains a scripting engine to translate scripts is called a scripting host.

- Standardized client-side JavaScript is the JavaScript format available to HTML pages displayed in Web browsers.

- All programming languages, including JavaScript, have their own syntax, or rules of the language.

- The logic behind any program involves executing the various parts of the program in the correct order to produce the desired results.

- Debugging describes the act of tracing and resolving errors in a program.

QUESTIONS

1. _____ manages the hypertext links that are used to navigate the Web.
   a. Netscape Navigator
   b. The European Laboratory for Particle Physics
   c. Hypertext Transfer Protocol
   d. Internet Explorer

2. Every Web document has a unique address known as _____.
   a. its IP address
   b. a hyperlink
   c. a Uniform Resource Locator
   d. its domain name

3. HTML elements _____.
   a. must include a starting tag and an ending tag
   b. only include a starting tag
   c. may contain an ending tag, depending on the HTML element
   d. do not contain starting or ending tags

4. HTML is _____.
   a. case-sensitive
   b. not case-sensitive
   c. must be created using initial caps
   d. must be created using uppercase letters

5. HTML documents start and end with the _____ tag pairs.
   a. <BODY>...</BODY>
   b. <HEAD>...</HEAD>
   c. <HTML>...</HTML>
   d. <WEB>...</WEB>

6. HTML attributes are placed within the _____.
   a. opening bracket of the starting tag
   b. opening bracket of the ending tag
   c. closing bracket of the starting tag
   d. closing bracket of the ending tag

7. The rules of a programming language are known as its _____.
   a. procedures
   b. assembly
   c. syntax
   d. logic

8. Executing the various statements and procedures of a program in the correct order to produce the desired results is called _____.
   a. reasoning
   b. directional assembly
   c. syntax
   d. logic

9. The term _____ language is used to refer to interpreted languages that run from within a Web browser.
    a. Internet programming
    b. machine
    c. assembly
    d. scripting

10. The version of JavaScript that is the format available to HTML pages in a Web browser is called _____ JavaScript.
    a. precompiled
    b. server-side
    c. embedded
    d. client-side

E X E R C I S E S

1. Design an HTML document that will be used as the home page for a company that sells sporting goods. If you have access to clip art, include pictures of sports equipment that the company sells, such as basketballs, baseball gloves, and tennis rackets. For each item, include information such as the manufacturer and sales price. Include <HEAD> and <BODY> sections in your document. In the <HEAD> section, include a <TITLE>. Use at least five different HTML elements to format the <BODY> section. Save the HTML document as SportsCompany.html in the **Tutorial.01** folder on your Student Disk. Although you are only using static HTML elements to create the Web page (that is, you cannot yet include any dynamic JavaScript elements such as order forms), make a list of dynamic elements you would like to add to your Web page, such as a catalog request form.

2. Search the Internet using Yahoo! or another search engine for information on the History of the World Wide Web, and write a one-page paper explaining what you have learned.

3. Visit the Web site of the World Wide Web Consortium (W3C) at http://www.w3.org, and read about the latest HTML specifications. Write a summary of the improvements being made to the HTML language and explain how the improvements will affect the design of Web pages.

4. Search the Web for three examples of complete programs or effects created with JavaScript. Describe the programs and effects in a one-page paper, and state whether you think they were effective.

5. Jakob Nielsen writes a popular Internet column called Alertbox at http://www.useit.com/alertbox/. Read the following three columns from Alertbox and write a brief description of what you learned: "The Top Ten New Mistakes of Web Design" (May 30, 1999), "Who commits the Top Ten Mistakes in Web design?" (May 16, 1999), and "'Top Ten Mistakes' revisited three years later" (May 2, 1999).

6. Visit your local library or bookstore, or search the Internet, for information on programming logic and debugging. Write a one-page paper on what you learned.

7. Search the Internet for information on Internet protocols, domain names, and IP addresses. Write a brief summary describing how these items interact.

In this section you will learn:
- About the <Script> tag
- How to create a JavaScript source file
- How to add comments to a JavaScript Program
- How to hide JavaScript from incompatible browsers
- About placing JavaScript in HEAD or BODY section of HTML documents

A First JavaScript Program

The <SCRIPT> Tag

JavaScript programs run from within an HTML document. The statements that make up a JavaScript program in an HTML document are contained between the <SCRIPT>...</SCRIPT> tag pairs. The **<SCRIPT>** tag is used to notify the Web Browser that the commands that follow it need to be interpreted by a scripting engine. The **LANGUAGE** attribute of the <SCRIPT> tag tells the browser which scripting language and which version of the scripting language is being used. To tell the Web browser the statements that follow need to be interpreted by the JavaScript scripting engine, you include the following code in your HTML document:

```
<SCRIPT LANGUAGE="JavaScript">
JavaScript statements;
</SCRIPT>
```

tip

Although this text covers JavaScript, you can use other types of scripting languages with Web pages. Microsoft's VBScript is another type of scripting language, which is based on the Visual Basic programming language. To use VBScript in your HTML document, you would use the code <SCRIPT LANGUAGE="VBScript">VBScript statements</SCRIPT>. Do not confuse JScript with VBScript. JScript is Microsoft's version of the JavaScript scripting language. To specify the JScript language, you specify *JavaScript* as the LANGUAGE attribute.

JavaScript is the default scripting language for most Web browsers. If you omit the LANGUAGE attribute from the <SCRIPT> tag, your JavaScript program should still run. However, the Internet is always changing. New technologies, including new scripting languages, are being introduced constantly. It is difficult to determine whether competing scripting languages, such as VBScript, will become dominant. Therefore, it is advisable that you always use the LANGUAGE attribute of the <SCRIPT> tag to tell the browser which scripting language you are using.

You also use the LANGUAGE attribute to specify which version of JavaScript you are using. Certain Web browsers support only certain versions of JavaScript.

For example, Navigator 3.0 supports only JavaScript versions 1.1 and lower. When you specify a JavaScript version number using the LANGUAGE attribute of the <SCRIPT> tag, you remove the space between the word *JavaScript* and the appropriate version number. If you include a space between the scripting language name and the version number, the browser will not interpret your code. A Web browser cannot interpret *JavaScript 1.1* because there is a space between JavaScript and the version number. The following code specifies that the JavaScript code to follow is compatible with JavaScript versions 1.1 and lower:

```
<SCRIPT LANGUAGE="JavaScript1.1">
JavaScript statements
</SCRIPT>
```

Figure 1-12 lists the versions of Navigator, along with the versions of JavaScript they support and the appropriate code to include in the <SCRIPT> tag.

Netscape Version	JavaScript Compatibility	Code
Navigator earlier than 2.0	not supported	—
Navigator 2.0	JavaScript 1.0	<SCRIPT LANGUAGE="JavaScript">...</SCRIPT>
Navigator 3.0	JavaScript 1.1 and lower	<SCRIPT LANGUAGE="JavaScript1.1">...</SCRIPT>
Navigator 4.0 - 4.05	JavaScript 1.2 and lower	<SCRIPT LANGUAGE="JavaScript1.2">...</SCRIPT>
Navigator 4.06 - 4.5	JavaScript 1.3 and lower	<SCRIPT LANGUAGE="JavaScript1.3">...</SCRIPT>

Figure 1-12: JavaScript versions supported in Navigator

When an HTML document is being loaded, the Web browser checks the JavaScript version number that is specified by the LANGUAGE attribute of the <SCRIPT> tag. If the Web browser you are using does not support the specified JavaScript version, it ignores all statements between the <SCRIPT>...</SCRIPT> tag pairs. If you want your Web page to be compatible with older versions of Web browsers, then you should specify the JavaScript version number that is supported by those older browsers. For example, if you want your Web page to be displayed in Navigator version 3.0, then the <SCRIPT> tag in your HTML code should read <SCRIPT LANGUAGE="JavaScript1.1">...</SCRIPT> since Navigator 3.0 only supports JavaScript versions 1.1 and earlier. Later in this section, you will learn how to completely hide JavaScript statements from incompatible browsers.

When you notify a Web browser that your JavaScript code is for an earlier version of JavaScript, the syntax of your program must conform to the earlier version. Code in this text is compatible with JavaScript version 1.2, which is supported by Navigator 4.0 and Internet Explorer 4.0.

In addition to being an interpreted scripting language, JavaScript is an object-oriented programming language. An **object** is programming code and data that can be treated as an individual unit or component. Individual lines in a programming language are called **statements**. Groups of related statements associated with an object are called **methods.** JavaScript treats many things as objects. One of the most commonly used objects in JavaScript programming is the Document object. The **Document object** represents the content of a browser's window. Any text, graphics, or other information displayed in a Web page is part of the Document object. One of the most common uses of the Document object is to add new text to a Web page. You create new text on a Web page with the **write() method** or the **writeln() method** of the Document object.

To execute, or call, an object's method, you append the method to the object with a period, and include any required arguments or parameters between the method's parentheses. An **argument** is any type of information that can be passed to a method. The write() and writeln() methods of the Document object require a text string as an argument. A **text string**, or **literal string,** is text that is contained within double quotation marks. The text string that is passed as an argument to the write() and writeln() methods of the Document object is the text that the Document object uses to create new text on a Web page. For example, `document.write("this is a text string");` writes the text *this is a text string* to the HTML document. When you want to include a quoted string within a literal string, you surround the quoted text with single quotation marks. For example, `document.write("this is a 'text' string");` writes the text *this is a 'text' string* to the HTML document.

The write() and writeln() methods perform essentially the same function that you perform when you manually add text to the body of a standard HTML document. Whether you add text to an HTML document using standard HTML tags or using the write() or writeln() methods, the text is added according to the order in which the statement is encountered in the HTML file. Unlike standard HTML text, the write() and writeln() methods can add new text to an HTML document after a browser has rendered the document.

The only difference between the write() and writeln() methods is that the writeln() method adds a carriage return after the line of text. Carriage returns, however, are only recognized inside of the HTML <PRE>...</PRE> tag pair. The <PRE>...</PRE> tag pair is short for preformatted text. This tag pair tells a Web browser that any text and line breaks contained between the opening and closing tag are to be rendered exactly as they appear. The <PRE>...</PRE> tag pair is known as a **container element** because it contains text and other HTML tags. For a Web browser to recognize the line break following the writeln() method, you must enclose the <SCRIPT>...</SCRIPT> tag pairs within the <PRE>...</PRE> tag pairs.

Figure 1-13 contains a script that prints *Hello World* to a Web browser using the writeln() method of the Document object. Notice that the <SCRIPT>...</SCRIPT> tag pairs are enclosed in the <PRE>...</PRE> tag pairs. Figure 1-14 shows the output.

```
<PRE>

<SCRIPT LANGUAGE="JavaScript1.2">

document.writeln("Hello World");

document.writeln(
"This line is printed below the 'Hello World' line.");

</SCRIPT>

</PRE>
```

Figure 1-13: Hello World script using the writeln() method of the Document object

••

tip

For simple JavaScript files such as the Hello World script, you can omit the <HTML>, <HEAD>, and <BODY> tags.

••

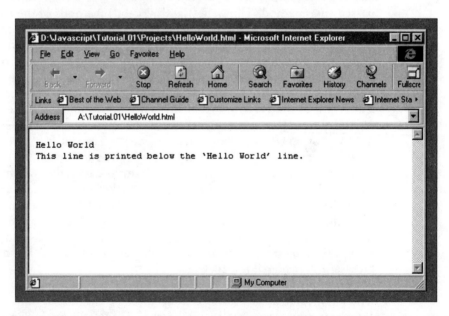

Figure 1-14: Output of the Hello World script using the writeln() method of the Document object

••

tip

While the two document.writeln() statements in Figure 1-13 are placed on their own lines, you can include JavaScript statements on the same line if they are separated by semi-colons. Since the statements in Figure 1-13 are on separate lines, the semicolons at the end of each statement are not actually necessary. However, it is considered good JavaScript programming practice to end any statement with a semicolon.

••

Objects that are part of the JavaScript programming language itself, such as the Document object, are commonly referred to with an initial cap to distinguish them as "top-level" objects. However, unlike HTML, JavaScript is case-sensitive. Although we refer to the Document object in the course of this text with an uppercase *D*, you must use a lowercase *d* when referring to the Document object in a script. The statement `Document.write("Hello World");` will cause an error message since the JavaScript interpreter does not recognize an object named Document with an uppercase *D*. Similarly, the following misspelled statements will cause an error:

```
DOCUMENT.write("Hello World");
Document.Write("Hello World");
document.WRITE("Hello World");
```

Figure 1-15 shows the error message that appears when you attempt to execute an invalid statement in Navigator, and Figure 1-16 shows the error message that appears when you attempt to execute this statement in Internet Explorer.

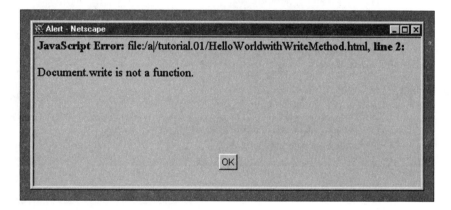

Figure 1-15: Error message in Navigator

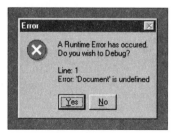

Figure 1-16: Error message in Internet Explorer

Next, you will create a simple JavaScript document.

To create a JavaScript document:

1   Start your text editor or HTML editor and create a new document.

2   Type **<PRE>** to start a preformatted text container.

3   Press **Enter** and type **<SCRIPT LANGUAGE="JavaScript1.2">** to begin the JavaScript document.

4   Press **Enter** and type `document.writeln("This is the first line in my JavaScript file.");`.

5   Press **Enter** again and type `document.writeln("This is the second line in my JavaScript file.");`.

6   Press **Enter** one more time and type **</SCRIPT>** to close the **<SCRIPT>...</SCRIPT>** tag pair.

7   Type **</PRE>** to close the preformatted text container.

8   Save the file as **MyFirstJavaScript.html** in the **Tutorial.01** folder on your Student Disk.

9   Open the **MyFirstJavaScript.html** file in your Web browser. If you receive one of the error messages displayed in Figure 1-15 or 1-16, check the case of the object and the writeln() method in the `document.writeln()` statements. Figure 1-17 displays the MyFirstJavaScript.html file as it appears in Internet Explorer.

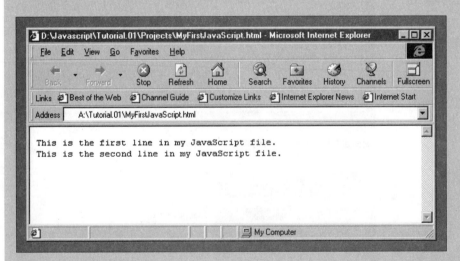

Figure 1-17: MyFirstJavaScript.html in Internet Explorer

Creating a JavaScript Source File

JavaScript is often incorporated directly into an HTML document. However, you can also save JavaScript code in an external file called a source file. A JavaScript source file is usually designated with the file extension .js and contains only JavaScript statements; it does not contain the HTML <SCRIPT>...</SCRIPT> tag pair. Instead, the <SCRIPT>...</SCRIPT> tag pair is located within the HTML document that calls the source file. To access JavaScript code that is saved in an external file, you use the SRC attribute of the <SCRIPT> tag. The **SRC attribute** accepts a text string that specifies the URL or directory location of a JavaScript source file. For example, to load a JavaScript source file named SampleSourceFile.js located in the C:\javafiles directory, you include the following code in an HTML document:

```
<SCRIPT LANGUAGE="JavaScript1.2"
SRC="c:\javafiles\samplesourcefile.js">
</SCRIPT>
```

JavaScript source files cannot include HTML tags. If you include HTML tags in a JavaScript source file, you will receive an error message. Also, when you specify a source file in your HTML document using the SRC attribute, the browser will ignore any other JavaScript code located between the <SCRIPT>...</SCRIPT> tag pairs. For example, consider the following JavaScript code. The JavaScript source file specified by the SRC attribute of the <SCRIPT> tag executes properly, but the document.write() statement is ignored.

```
<SCRIPT LANGUAGE="JavaScript1.2"
SRC="c:\javafiles\samplesourcefile.js">
document.write("this JavaScript statement will be ignored");
</SCRIPT>
```

Certain older Web browsers, such as Navigator 2.0, do not recognize the SRC attribute of the <SCRIPT> tag.

If the JavaScript code you intend to use in an HTML document is fairly short, then it is usually easier to include JavaScript code in an HTML document. However, for longer JavaScript code it is easier to include the code in a .js source file. There are several reasons you may want to use .js source files instead of adding the code to an HTML document:

- Your HTML document will be neater. Lengthy JavaScript code in an HTML document can be confusing—you may not be able to tell at a glance where the HTML code ends and the JavaScript code begins.
- The JavaScript code can be shared among multiple HTML documents. For example, your Web site may contain pages that allow users to order an item. Each Web page displays a different item, but uses the same JavaScript code to gather order information. Instead of recreating the JavaScript order information code within each HTML document, the Web pages can share a central JavaScript source file. Sharing a single source file among multiple HTML documents reduces disk space. In addition, when you share a source file among multiple HTML documents, a Web browser only needs to keep one copy of the file in memory, which reduces system overhead.

- JavaScript source files hide JavaScript code from incompatible browsers. If your HTML document contains JavaScript code, instead of calling an external JavaScript source file, an incompatible browser will display the code as if it were standard text.
- JavaScript source files help hide your JavaScript code. When you spend significant amounts of time writing code, you do not necessarily want other programmers to be able to copy the code and claim it as their own—particularly if your code is copyrighted or if you sell JavaScript programming solutions. When your JavaScript is embedded in an HTML document, other programmers can easily copy your code by viewing the source of your HTML document—unless your JavaScript code is contained in a source file.

You can use a combination of embedded JavaScript code and JavaScript source files in your HTML documents. The ability to combine embedded JavaScript code and JavaScript source files in a single HTML document is advantageous if you have multiple HTML documents, each of which requires individual JavaScript code statements, but all of which also share a single JavaScript source file. Suppose you have a Web site with multiple Web pages. Each page displays a product that your company sells. You may have a JavaScript source file that collects order information, such as a person's name and address, that is shared by all the products you sell. Each individual product may also require other types of order information that you need to collect using JavaScript code. For example, one of your products may be a shirt, for which you need to collect size and color information. On another Web page, you may sell jellybeans, for which you need to collect quantity and flavor information. Each of these products can share a central JavaScript source file to collect standard information, but can also include embedded JavaScript code to collect product-specific information.

When you include multiple JavaScript sections in an HTML document, you must include the <SCRIPT>...</SCRIPT> tag pair for each section. Each JavaScript section in an HTML document is executed in the order in which it appears. Figure 1-18 displays an HTML document that calls an external source file and includes embedded JavaScript.

```
<HTML>

<HEAD>

<TITLE>HTML Document with Two JavaScript Sections</TITLE>

</HEAD>

<BODY>

The following two lines call an external
JavaScript source file.<BR>

<SCRIPT LANGUAGE="JavaScript1.2"
SRC="c:\javafiles\samplesourcefile.js">

</SCRIPT>
```

Figure 1-18: HTML document that calls an external source file and includes embedded JavaScript

The following section executes embedded JavaScript code that is contained in a preformatted text section.

```
<PRE>
<SCRIPT LANGUAGE="JavaScript1.2">
document.writeln("Your order has been confirmed.");
document.writeln("Thank you for your business.");
</SCRIPT>
</PRE>
</BODY>
</HTML>
```

Next you will create an HTML document that calls an external JavaScript source file and that includes embedded JavaScript. First you will create the main HTML document.

To create the main HTML document:

1 Start your text editor or HTML editor and create a new document.

2 Type the opening <HTML> and <HEAD> tags:

```
<HTML>
<HEAD>
```

3 Press **Enter** and add the title: **<TITLE>Multiple JavaScript Calls</TITLE>**.

4 Press **Enter** and type **</HEAD>** to close the <HEAD>...</HEAD> tag pair.

5 Press **Enter** and add the following code to begin the body of the HTML document and to call an external JavaScript source file:

```
<BODY>
<SCRIPT LANGUAGE="JavaScript1.2"
SRC="javascriptsource.js">
</SCRIPT>
```

6 Press **Enter** and type the following code that executes embedded JavaScript code in a preformatted text container:

```
<PRE>
<SCRIPT LANGUAGE="JavaScript1.2" >
document.writeln(
"This line was created with embedded JavaScript code.");
document.writeln(
"This line was also created with embedded JavaScript code.");
</SCRIPT>
</PRE>
```

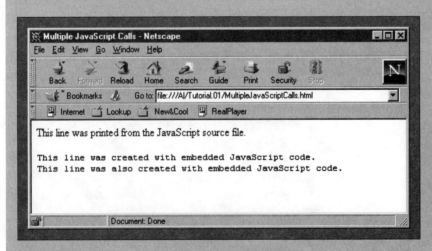

> **▶ help**
>
> Literal strings such as the text in the preceding writeln ( ) statements must be on a single line. If you include a line break within a literal string you will receive an error message.

7 Press **Enter** and add the following code to close the <HTML> and <BODY> tags:

```
</BODY>
</HTML>
```

8 Save the file as **MultipleJavaScriptCalls.html** in the **Tutorial.01** folder on your Student Disk.

Next you will create the JavaScript source file, then open MultipleJavaScript Calls.html.

To create the JavaScript source file and open MultipleJavaScriptCalls.html:

1 Create a new document in your text editor or HTML editor.

2 Type **document.write("This line was printed from the JavaScript source file.")**. This will be the only line in the document. Remember that you do not include the <SCRIPT> tag within a source file.

3 Save the file as **javaScriptSource.js** in the **Tutorial.01** folder on your Student Disk.

4 Open the **MultipleJavaScriptCalls.html** file in your Web browser. Figure 1-19 displays the MultipleJavaScriptCalls.html file as it appears in Navigator 4.0.

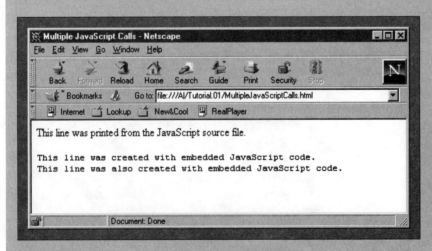

Figure 1-19: MultipleJavaScriptCalls.html in Navigator 4.0

Adding Comments to a JavaScript Program

When you create a program, whether it is with JavaScript or any other programming language, it is considered good programming practice to add comments to your code. **Comments** are nonprinting lines that you place in your code to contain various types of remarks, including the name of the program, your name and the date you created the program, notes to yourself, or instructions to future programmers who may need to modify your work. When you are working with long scripts, comments make it easier to decipher how a program is structured.

JavaScript supports two types of comments: line comments and block comments. **Line comments** are created by adding two slashes // before the text you want to use as a comment. The // characters instruct the JavaScript interpreter to ignore all text to the end of the line. Line comments can appear at the end of a line of code, or they can exist on an entire line by themselves. **Block comments** span multiple lines and are created by adding /* to the first line that is to be included in the block. You close a comment block by typing */ after the last text to be included in the block. Any text or lines between the opening /* characters and the closing */ characters is ignored by the JavaScript interpreter. Figure 1-20 displays a JavaScript file containing line and block comments.

▶ **tip**

Comments in JavaScript use the same syntax as comments created in C++ and Java.

```
<SCRIPT LANGUAGE="JavaScript1.2" >

/*

This line is part of the block comment.

This line is also part of the block comment.

*/

document.writeln("Comments Example");  // Line comments can follow
code statements

// This line comment takes up an entire line.

/* This is another way of creating a block comment. */

</SCRIPT>
```

Figure 1-20: JavaScript file with line and block comments

Next you will add comments to the MyFirstJavaScript.html file.

1   Open the **MyFirstJavaScript.html** file in your text editor or HTML editor.

2   Place your cursor at the end of the line containing the opening <SCRIPT> tag, press **Enter**, and add the following comment block:

```
/*
JavaScript code for MyFirstJavaScript.html
your name
today's date
*/
```

> When you create comments in your JavaScript programs, be sure to use a forward slash (/) and not a backward slash (\). People often confuse these two characters. If you include a backward slash instead of a forward slash when creating a comment, you will receive an error when you attempt to open the file in a Web browser.

3   Place your cursor at the end of the line that reads `document.writeln("This is the first line in my JavaScript file.");`, press **Tab**, then type `// Line 1`.

4   Place your cursor at the end of the line that reads `document.writeln("This is the second line in my JavaScript file.");` and type `// Line 2`.

5   Save the **MyFirstJavaScript.html** file, then open it in your Web browser to confirm that the comments are not displayed.

Hiding JavaScript from Incompatible Browsers

Creating JavaScript source files hides JavaScript code from incompatible browsers. However, if your HTML document contains embedded JavaScript codes instead of calling an external .js source file, then an incompatible browser will display the codes as if they were standard text. To hide embedded JavaScript code from incompatible browsers, you enclose the code between the <SCRIPT>...</SCRIPT> tag pair in an HTML comment block. HTML comments are different from JavaScript comments. HTML comment blocks begin with <!-- and end with -->. Any text located between the opening and closing comment tags is not rendered by the browser. For example, Figure 1-21 displays an HTML document containing comments. Figure 1-22 shows the output. The text located between the comment tags is not rendered by the browser.

```
<HTML>

<HEAD>

<TITLE></TITLE>

</HEAD>

<BODY>

This line is rendered normally since it is located before the opening
comment tag.<BR>

<!--Text on this line is not displayed

Text on this line is not displayed

This line is not displayed either -->

This line is rendered normally since it is located after the closing
comment tag. <BR>

</BODY>

</HTML>
```

Figure 1-21: HTML document with comments

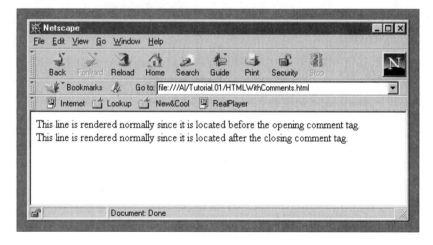

Figure 1-22: Output of HTML document with comments

Most Web browsers do not display lines that are set off with an HTML comment tag. However, browsers compatible with JavaScript ignore the HTML comment tags and execute the JavaScript code normally. Remember that JavaScript-compatible browsers never display JavaScript code. Instead, the code is interpreted by the browser's scripting engine. Only JavaScript comment tags can be used to hide JavaScript code from the interpreter. Figure 1-23 shows an example of JavaScript code that is hidden from incompatible browsers, using HTML comments, but that would be executed by compatible browsers.

```
<SCRIPT LANGUAGE="JavaScript1.2">

<!--  This line starts the HTML comment block

document.writeln("Your order has been confirmed.");

document.writeln("Thank you for your business.");

This line ends the HTML comment block -->

</SCRIPT>
```

Figure 1-23: JavaScript code hidden from incompatible browsers, using HTML comments

When your HTML document is displayed by a browser that is incompatible with JavaScript, you usually want to display some sort of message to tell users that their browser is not compatible with your program. You can display an alternate message to users of incompatible browsers by using the <NOSCRIPT>...</NOSCRIPT> tag pair. The <NOSCRIPT>...</NOSCRIPT> tag pair usually follows the <SCRIPT>...</SCRIPT> tag pair. Figure 1-24 illustrates how to use the <NOSCRIPT> tag.

```
<SCRIPT LANGUAGE="JavaScript1.2">
<!--  This line starts the HTML comment block
document.writeln("Your order has been confirmed.");
document.writeln("Thank you for your business.");
This line ends the HTML comment block -->
</SCRIPT>
<NOSCRIPT>
This line is displayed if a browser does not support JavaScript<BR>
</NOSCRIPT>
```

Figure 1-24: JavaScript code with <NOSCRIPT> tag

> Alternate text in the <NOSCRIPT> tag is also displayed if a user has disabled JavaScript support in their Web browser.

Next you will modify the MyFirstJavaScript.html file so that it is hidden from incompatible browsers and displays an alternate message using the <NOSCRIPT> tag.

To modify the MyFirstJavaScript.html file so that it is hidden from incompatible browsers and displays an alternate message using the <NOSCRIPT> tag:

1 Open the **MyFirstJavaScript.html** file in your text editor or HTML editor.

2 Place your cursor at the end of the line containing the opening <SCRIPT> tag, press **Enter**, and then type **<!--** to start the HTML comment block that hides the JavaScript code from incompatible browsers.

3 Place your cursor at the end of the line that reads **document.writeln("This is the second line in my JavaScript file."); // Line 2**, press **Enter**, and then type **-->** to close the HTML comment block.

4 Place your cursor at the end of the line that reads **</PRE>**, press **Enter** to insert a new line, and type the following code to display a message to browsers that do not support JavaScript:

```
<NOSCRIPT>
Your browser does not support JavaScript.<BR>
</NOSCRIPT>
```

5 Save the **MyFirstJavaScript.html** file and open it in your Web browser. If you are using a recent version of Navigator or Internet Explorer, the JavaScript section should execute normally. However, if you are using a browser that does not support JavaScript, you will see the message *Your browser does not support JavaScript.*

Placing JavaScript in HEAD or BODY sections

A Web browser renders tags in an HTML document in the order in which they are encountered. When you have multiple JavaScript code sections in an HTML document, each section is also executed in the order in which it appears. For example, in the following code, the embedded JavaScript code executes before the call to the JavaScript source file since the embedded code appears first.

```
The following embedded JavaScript code executes first. <BR>
<SCRIPT LANGUAGE="JavaScript1.2">
document.writeln("First JavaScript code section in document");
</SCRIPT> <BR>
The following JavaScript source file executes after the embedded
JavaScript code. <BR>
<SCRIPT LANGUAGE="JavaScript1.2" SRC="javascriptsource.js">
</SCRIPT>
```

The order in which a browser executes JavaScript code also depends on which section of the HTML document the JavaScript code is placed in. HTML documents usually consist of a <HEAD> section and a <BODY> section. The <HEAD> section contains information that is used by the Web browser and is rendered before the <BODY> section. The <BODY> section usually contains the content of a Web page that will be displayed. JavaScript code can be placed in either section or between the two sections. Where you place your JavaScript code will vary, depending on the program you are writing.

It is a good idea to place as much of your JavaScript code as possible in the <HEAD> section, since the <HEAD> section of an HTML document is rendered before the <BODY> section. When placed in the <HEAD> section, JavaScript code will be processed before the main body of the HTML document is displayed. You may want to place JavaScript code in the <HEAD> section when your code performs behind-the-scenes tasks that are required by JavaScript code sections located in the <BODY> section.

S U M M A R Y

- The statements that make up a JavaScript program in an HTML document are contained between the <SCRIPT>...</SCRIPT> tag pairs.

- The LANGUAGE attribute of the <SCRIPT> tag specifies which scripting language is being used and the scripting language's version.

- JavaScript is the default scripting language for most Web browsers.

- If the Web browser you are using does not support the specified JavaScript version, all statements between the <SCRIPT>...</SCRIPT> tag pairs are ignored.

- If you anticipate that your Web page will be displayed on older versions of Web browsers, then you should specify the JavaScript version number for the version of JavaScript that is supported by that browser.

- The Document object represents the content of a browser's window.

- You can create new text on a Web page using the write() method or the writeln() method of the Document object.

- An argument is any type of information that can be passed to a method.

- A text string, or literal string, is text that is contained within quotation marks.

- The write() and writeln() methods perform essentially the same function as adding text directly to the body of a standard HTML document. The only difference between the write() and writeln() methods is that the writeln() method adds a carriage return after the line.

- Unlike HTML, JavaScript is case-sensitive.

- You can save JavaScript code in an external file called a source file. A JavaScript source file is usually designated with the file extension .js and contains only JavaScript statements; it does not contain the <SCRIPT>...</SCRIPT> tag pair.

- You use the SRC attribute of the <SCRIPT> tag to access JavaScript code that is saved in an external file. The SRC attribute accepts a text string that specifies the URL or directory location of a JavaScript source file.

- JavaScript source files cannot include HTML tags.

- HTML documents can use a combination of embedded JavaScript code and JavaScript source files.

- When you include multiple JavaScript sections in an HTML document, you must include the <SCRIPT>...</SCRIPT> tag pair for each section.

- Comments are nonprinting lines that you place in your code to contain various types of remarks.

- You create line comments by adding two slashes // before the text you want to use as a comment.

- Block comments span multiple lines. You create a block comment by adding /* to the first line that is to be included in the block. You close a comment block by typing */ after the last text to be included in the block.

- To hide embedded JavaScript code from incompatible browsers, you enclose the code between the <SCRIPT>...</SCRIPT> tag pair in an HTML comment block (<!-- ... -->).

- Most Web browsers do not display lines that appear between HTML comment tags (<!--...-->). However, browsers compatible with JavaScript ignore the HTML comment tags and execute the JavaScript code normally.

- You display an alternate message to users of incompatible browsers with the <NOSCRIPT>...</NOSCRIPT> tag pair. The <NOSCRIPT>...</NOSCRIPT> tag pair usually follows the <SCRIPT>...</SCRIPT> tag pair.

- When you have multiple JavaScript code sections in an HTML document, each section is executed in the order in which it appears.

- It is a good idea to place as much of your JavaScript code as possible in the <HEAD> section, since the <HEAD> section of an HTML document is rendered before the <BODY> section.

 **Q U E S T I O N S**

1. Scripting code in an HTML document is located _____.
   a. inside the closing bracket of the <SCRIPT> tag
   b. between the <SCRIPT>...</SCRIPT> tag pairs
   c. before the opening <SCRIPT> tag
   d. after the closing <SCRIPT> tag

2. The <SCRIPT> tag _____.
   a. is only used with JavaScript
   b. is only used with VBScript
   c. can be used with both JavaScript and VBScript
   d. is not used with either JavaScript or VBScript

3. Which of the following is not valid with the LANGUAGE attribute of the <SCRIPT> tag?
   a. JavaScript1.2
   b. JAVASCRIPT1.2
   c. javascript1.2
   d. JavaScript 1.2

4. If a Web browser does not support the version of JavaScript specified by the LAN-GUAGE attribute, then the JavaScript statements contained in the <SCRIPT>...</SCRIPT tag pairs _____.
   a. are converted to a supported version
   b. close the Web browser
   c. are ignored
   d. are displayed as text

5. A(n) _____ refers to programming code and data that can be treated as an individual unit or component.
   a. icon
   b. procedure
   c. concealed unit
   d. object

6. The JavaScript object that represents the contents of a browser's window is called the _____ object.
   a. Document
   b. HTML
   c. Browser
   d. Contents

7. With JavaScript, new text is created on a Web page using the write() method or the _____ method.
   a. output()
   b. writeln()
   c. print()
   d. println()

8. Which of the following is the correct syntax for including a quoted string within a literal string?
   a. "this is a ""quoted"" string"
   b. 'this is a 'quoted' string'
   c. "this is a "quoted" string"
   d. "this is a 'quoted' string"

9. The _____ tag pair tells a Web browser that any text and line breaks it contains are to be rendered as is.
   a. <FORMAT>...</FORMAT>
   b. <CONTAINER>...</CONTAINER>
   c. <COMPOSE>...</COMPOSE>
   d. <PRE>...</PRE>

10. Which of the following statements is correct?
    a. DOCUMENT.write("Hello World")
    b. Document.Write("Hello World")
    c. document.write("Hello World")
    d. document.WRITE("Hello World")

11. A JavaScript source file is called using the _____ attribute of the <SCRIPT> tag.
    a. LANGUAGE
    b. FILE
    c. SOURCE
    d. SRC

12. JavaScript source files _____.
    a. can include HTML tags
    b. cannot include HTML tags
    c. can include certain types of HTML tags
    d. cannot include JavaScript statements

13. When an HTML document calls a JavaScript source file, the <SCRIPT>...</SCRIPT> tag pairs are _____.
    a. located in the HTML document
    b. located in the JavaScript source file
    c. located in both the HTML document and the JavaScript source file
    d. not necessary

14. When would you not use a JavaScript source file?
    a. when you will use the JavaScript code with incompatible browsers
    b. when the JavaScript source file is shared by multiple HTML documents
    c. when the JavaScript code is fairly short and is not shared
    d. when you do not want to share your code with other programmers

15. HTML documents can contain _____.
    a. embedded JavaScript code but not JavaScript source files
    b. JavaScript source files but not embedded JavaScript code
    c. either JavaScript code or JavaScript source files
    d. both embedded JavaScript code and JavaScript source files

16. You create line comments in JavaScript code by adding _____ to a line you want to use as a comment.
   a. ||
   b. **
   c. //
   d. \\

17. Block comments begin with /* and end with _____.
   a. */
   b. /*
   c. //
   d. **

18. You hide JavaScript code from incompatible browsers by using _____.
   a. an HTML filter
   b. the <MASK> tag
   c. JavaScript comment tags
   d. HTML comment tags

19. You display alternate text to users of incompatible browsers by using the _____ tag pair.
   a. <NOSCRIPT>...</NOSCRIPT>
   b. <SUBMESSAGE>...</SUBMESSAGE>
   c. <MESSAGEBOX>...</MESSAGEBOX>
   d. <NOJAVASCRIPT>...</NOJAVASCRIPT>

20. How are JavaScript code sections executed in an HTML document?
   a. All embedded JavaScript code is executed first.
   b. All JavaScript source files are executed first.
   c. Each JavaScript code section is executed according to the sequence in which you added it to the HTML document.
   d. Each JavaScript code section is executed in the order in which it appears.

21. JavaScript _____ of an HTML document.
   a. cannot be placed in either the <HEAD> or <BODY> sections
   b. can be placed in either the <HEAD> or <BODY> sections
   c. can only be placed in the <HEAD> section
   d. can only be placed in the <BODY> section

E X E R C I S E S

1. Explain when you should use embedded JavaScript and when you should use a JavaScript source file.

2. Create an HTML document, using the following instructions. Create the document header using an HTML tag. Add the first text line using embedded JavaScript code and add the second line using a JavaScript source file. Be sure to include the LANGUAGE attribute in the <SCRIPT> tags. Include a <HEAD> section with a <TITLE>; use *Tutorial 1 Exercise 2* for the title text. Add an HTML comment with your name and the date.

Add the same comment information to the embedded JavaScript and the JavaScript source file, using JavaScript comments. Hide the JavaScript code from incompatible browsers by using HTML comment tags, and create a <NOSCRIPT> section that says *Your browser does not support JavaScript.* Save the file as Tut1Ex2.html in the Tutorial.01 folder on your Student Disk. An example of how your document should look appears in Figure 1-25.

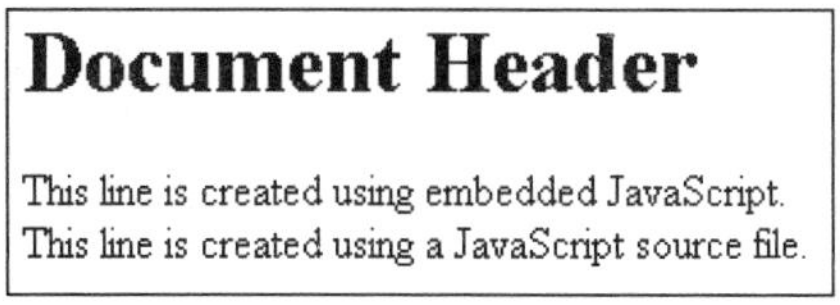

Document Header

This line is created using embedded JavaScript.
This line is created using a JavaScript source file.

Figure 1-25: Tutorial 1 Exercise 2

3. Create an HTML document that prints the names of the continents. Create the document header using an HTML tag. Create the numbers in each line using standard HTML tags, but create the continent names using embedded JavaScript. (You will need to use multiple JavaScript sections.) Be sure to include the LANGUAGE attribute in the <SCRIPT> tags. Include a <HEAD> section with a <TITLE>; use *Tutorial 1 Exercise 3* for the title text. Add an HTML comment with your name and the date. Add the same information to the first embedded JavaScript section, using JavaScript comments. Hide the JavaScript code from incompatible browsers by using HTML comment tags, and create a <NOSCRIPT> section that says *Your browser does not support JavaScript.* Save the file as Tut1Ex3.html in the Tutorial.01 folder on your Student Disk. Your HTML document should look similar to Figure 1-26.

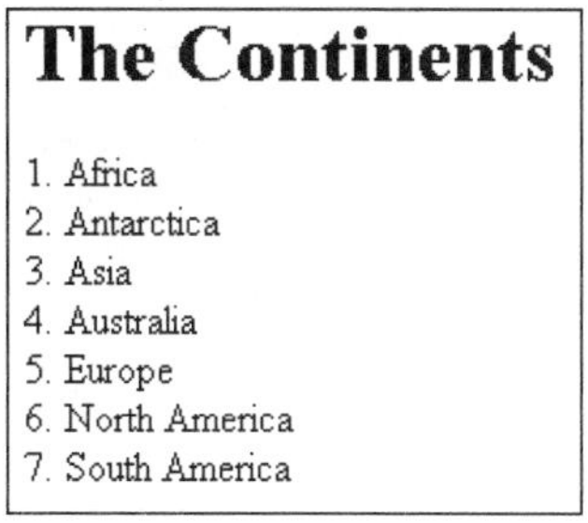

The Continents

1. Africa
2. Antarctica
3. Asia
4. Australia
5. Europe
6. North America
7. South America

Figure 1-26: Tutorial 1 Exercise 3

4. Create an HTML document that prints the preamble to the Constitution. Build the paragraph and its formatting using a combination of JavaScript code and HTML tags. Be sure to include the LANGUAGE attribute in the <SCRIPT> tags. Include a <HEAD> section with a <TITLE>; use *Tutorial 1 Exercise 4* for the title text. Add an HTML comment with your name and the date. Add the same information to the first JavaScript section, using JavaScript comments. Hide the JavaScript code from incompatible browsers by using HTML comment tags, and create a <NOSCRIPT> section that says *Your browser does not support JavaScript.* Save the file as Tut1Ex4.html in the Tutorial.01 folder on your Student Disk. Your HTML document should resemble the sample document in Figure 1-27.

The Preamble of the Constitution

*We, **the people of the United States**, in order to form a more perfect **Union**, establish <u>justice</u>, insure <u>domestic tranquility</u>, provide for the <u>common defense</u>, promote the <u>general welfare</u>, and secure the blessings of liberty to ourselves and our posterity, do ordain and establish this **Constitution** for the **United States of America**.*

Figure 1-27: Tutorial 1 Exercise 4

Variables, Functions, Objects, and Events

case ▶ Image maps are very popular features on Web sites. They consist of an image that is divided into regions, and each region is associated with a URL. You can open each region's associated URL by clicking the region. You can use JavaScript code to perform various tasks when a user's mouse passes over or moves off a region in an image map.

One of WebAdventure's clients, a car rental agency, wants an image map to be the centerpiece of its home page. They want to let their customers know that they can use the Web site to find the closest location for car pickup and drop-off anywhere in North America. Your task is to create an image map that displays the name of a country and changes the color of the country when the mouse passes over it.

Previewing the NorthAmericaImageMap.html file

In this tutorial, you will create an HTML document named NorthAmericaImage Map.html that uses JavaScript to display the name of each North American country and change the country's color when a mouse passes over it.

To preview the NorthAmericaImageMap.html file:

1 In your Web browser, open the **NorthAmericaImageMap.html** file from the Tutorial.02 folder on your Student Disk. An image of North America appears. Figure 2-1 displays an example of the program in a Web browser.

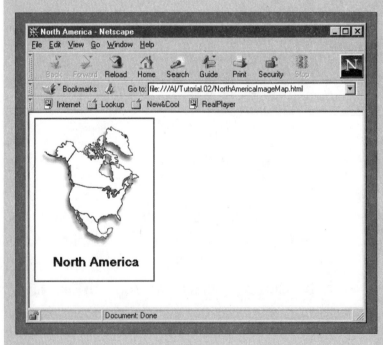

Figure 2-1: NorthAmericaImageMap.html

2 Move your mouse over each of the countries on the map. As your mouse enters a country, the country is highlighted and the text at the bottom of the map changes to display the country name. When you move your mouse off a highlighted country, the original image of North America reappears.

3 When you are finished, close your browser window.

4 Next, open the **NorthAmericaImageMap.html** file in your text editor or HTML editor and examine the code. Notice the statements that start with "function". The functions contain the code that changes the highlighted country on the image map. The image map itself is created with the <IMG>, <MAP>, and <AREA> tags in the body section.

5 Close your text editor or HTML editor when you are finished examining the code.

In this lesson you will learn:

- How to declare and use variables
- How to define functions
- How to call functions
- How to use JavaScript objects
- How to use object inheritance and prototypes
- How to use object methods
- About variable scope

Working with Variables, Functions, and Events

Variables

One of the most important aspects of programming is the ability to store and manipulate values in computer memory locations. The values stored in computer memory locations are called **variables**. Data contained in a specific variable often change. For example, you may have a program that creates a variable with the current time. Each time the program runs, the time is different, so the value *varies*. Another example is a payroll program that assigns employee names to a variable named `employeeName`. The memory location referenced by the variable `employeeName` might contain different values (a different value for every employee of the company) at different times.

In JavaScript, you use the reserved keyword `var` to create variables. **Reserved words**, or **keywords**, are part of the JavaScript language syntax. Reserved words cannot be used for variable names. Figure 2-2 lists the JavaScript reserved words.

abstract	char	do	finally
boolean	class	double	float
break	const	else	for
byte	continue	extends	function
case	default	false	goto
catch	delete	final	if

Figure 2-2: JavaScript reserved words

implements	new	static	true
import	null	super	try
in	package	switch	typeof
instanceof	private	synchronized	var
int	protected	this	void
interface	public	throw	while
long	return	throws	with
native	short	transient	

Figure 2-2: JavaScript reserved words (continued)

....

Some reserved words in Figure 2-2 are not currently used, but are reserved for future use.

....

When you use the reserved word **var** to create a variable, you **declare** the variable. You can assign a value to a variable at declaration using the syntax **var** *variable_name* **= value;**. The equal sign in a variable declaration assigns a value to the variable. This use is different from the standard use of the equal sign in an algebraic formula.

The value you assign a variable can be a literal string or a numeric value. For example, the statement **var myVariable = "Hello";** assigns the literal string Hello to the variable myVariable. The statement **var myVariable = 100;** assigns the numeric value 100 to the variable myVariable.

....

You are not required to use the **var** keyword to declare a variable. However, omission of the **var** keyword can change where a variable can be used in a program. Regardless of where in your program you intend to use a variable, it is good programming practice to use the **var** keyword when declaring a variable.

....

You can declare multiple variables in the same statement using a single **var** keyword followed by a series of variable names and assigned values separated by commas. For example, the following statement creates several variables using a single **var** keyword:

```
var firstVar = "text", secondVar = 100, thirdVar = 2.5;
```

Notice in the preceding example that each variable is assigned a value. Although you can assign a value when a variable is declared, you are not required to do so. Your program may assign the value later, or you may use a variable to store user input. When you declare a variable without assigning it a value, you must use the **var** keyword.

Regardless of whether you assign a value to a variable when it is declared, you change the variable's value at any point in a program by using a statement that includes the variable's name, followed by an equal sign, followed by the value you want to assign to the variable. The following code declares a variable named myDog, assigns it an initial value of *Golden Retriever*, and prints it using the document.writeln() function. The third statement changes the value of the myDog variable to *Irish Setter*, and the fourth statement prints the new value. The myDog variable is declared with the `var` keyword only once.

```
var myDog = "Golden Retriever";
document.writeln(myDog);
mydog = "Irish Setter";
document.writeln(myDog);
```

The name you assign to a variable is an identifier. Identifiers must begin with an uppercase or lowercase ASCII letter, dollar sign ($), or underscore (_). You can use numbers in an identifier, but not as the first character.

There are some rules and conventions you need to follow when naming a variable. Reserved words cannot be used for variable names, and you cannot use spaces within a variable name. Common practice is to use an underscore (_) character to separate individual words within a variable name, as in my_variable_name. Another common practice is to use a lowercase letter for the first letter of the first word in a variable name, with subsequent words starting with an initial cap, as in myVariableName. Figure 2-3 lists examples of some legal variable names, and Figure 2-4 lists examples of some illegal variable names.

```
my_variable

$my_variable

_my_variable

my_variable_example

myVariableExample
```

Figure 2-3: Examples of legal variable names

```
%my_variable

1my_variable

#my_variable

@my_variable

~my_variable

+my_variable
```

Figure 2-4: Examples of illegal variable names

 tip

Some versions of Web browsers, including Navigator 2.02 and Internet Explorer 3.02, do not recognize the dollar sign in variable names. If you want your JavaScript programs to operate with older Web browsers, avoid using the dollar sign in variable names.

Variable names, like other JavaScript code, are case-sensitive. Therefore, the variable name myVariable contains different values than variables named myvariable, MyVariable, or MYVARIABLE. If you receive an error when running a JavaScript program, be sure that you are using the correct case when referring to any variables you have declared.

Defining Functions

Individual statements used in a computer program are often grouped into logical units called procedures. In JavaScript programming, procedures are called functions. A **function** allows you to treat a related group of JavaScript statements as a single unit. Functions, like all JavaScript code, must exist within the <SCRIPT>...</SCRIPT> tag pair. Before you can use a function in a JavaScript program, you must first create, or define, it. The lines that compose a function within an HTML document are called the **function definition**. The syntax for defining a function is:

```
function name_of_function(parameters) {
statements;
}
```

A function definition consists of three parts:

- The reserved word `function` followed by the function name. The reserved word `function` notifies the JavaScript interpreter that the code that follows is a function. As with variables, the name you assign to a function is called an identifier. The same rules and conventions that apply to variable names apply to function names.
- Any parameters required by the function, contained within parentheses following the function name
- The function's statements, enclosed in curly braces { }

Parameters are placed within the parentheses that follow a function name. A **parameter**, or **argument**, is a variable that will be used within a function. For example, you may write a function named calculate_square_root() that calculates the square root of a number contained in a variable named number. The function name would be written as calculate_square_root(number). Functions can contain multiple arguments separated by commas. To add three separate number arguments to the calculate_square_root() function, you write the function name as calculate_square_root(number1, number2, number3).

●●

Functions are not required to contain arguments. Many functions only perform a task and do not require external data. For example, you may have a function that displays the same message each time a user visits your Web site; this type of function only needs to be executed and does not require any other information.

●●

Following the parentheses containing a function's arguments are a set of curly braces containing the function's statements. A function's statements must be contained within the function's braces. Figure 2-5 displays an example of a function that prints the names of multiple companies.

```
function print_company_name(company1, company2, company3) {

    document.writeln(company1);

    document.writeln(company2);

    document.writeln(company3);

}
```

Figure 2-5: Function that prints the name of multiple companies

Notice how the function in Figures 2-5 is structured. The opening curly brace is on the same line as the function name, and the closing curly brace is on its own line following the function statements. Each statement between the curly braces is indented one-half inch. This structure is the preferred format among many JavaScript programmers. However, for simple functions it is sometimes easier to include the function name, curly braces, and statements on the same line. Recall that JavaScript ignores line breaks, spaces, and tabs. The only syntax requirement for spacing in JavaScript is that a semi-colon separate statements on the same line.

Calling Functions

A function definition does not execute automatically. Creating a function definition only names the function, specifies its arguments, and organizes the statements it will execute. To execute a function, you must invoke, or **call**, it from elsewhere in your program. To call a function, you create a statement that includes the function name followed by parentheses containing any variables or values to be assigned to the function's arguments. Sending variables or values to a called function's arguments is called **passing arguments**. The argument takes on the value of the variable that is passed.

Always create functions within the <HEAD> section, and place calls to a function within the <BODY> section. The <HEAD> section of an HTML document is always rendered before the <BODY> section. Placing functions in the <HEAD> section and function calls in the <BODY> section ensures that functions will be created before they are actually called. If your program does attempt to call a function before it has been created, you will receive an error. Figure 2-6 shows a JavaScript program that prints the name of a company. Figure 2-7 shows the output. Notice that the function is defined in the <HEAD> section of the HTML document and is called from the <BODY> section.

```
<HTML>

<HEAD>

<TITLE>Print Company Name Function</TITLE>

<SCRIPT LANGUAGE="JavaScript1.2">

<!-- HIDE FROM INCOMPATIBLE BROWSERS

function print_company_name(company_name) {

    document.writeln(company_name);

}

// STOP HIDING FROM INCOMPATIBLE BROWSERS -->

</SCRIPT>

</HEAD>

<BODY>

<SCRIPT LANGUAGE="JavaScript1.2">

<!-- HIDE FROM INCOMPATIBLE BROWSERS

print_company_name("My Company");

// STOP HIDING FROM INCOMPATIBLE BROWSERS -->

</SCRIPT>

</BODY>

</HTML>
```

Figure 2-6: JavaScript function being called from the <BODY> section

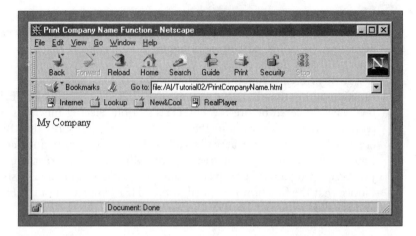

Figure 2-7: Output of the JavaScript function being called from the <BODY> section

In the program in Figure 2-6, the statement that calls the function passes the literal string *My Company* to the function. When the print_company_name() function receives the literal string, it assigns it to the company_name argument variable.

A JavaScript program is composed of all the <SCRIPT> sections within an HTML document; each individual <SCRIPT> section is not necessarily its own individual JavaScript program (although it could be if there are no other <SCRIPT> sections in the HTML document).

In many instances, you may want one function to receive a value from another function that you can then use in other code. For instance, if you have a function that performs a calculation on a number that is passed to it, you would want to receive the result of the calculation. Consider a function that calculates the average of a series of numbers that you pass to it—the function would be useless if you never saw the result. To return a value to a calling statement, you assign the calling statement to a variable. The following statement calls a function named average_numbers() and assigns any return value to a variable named returnValue. The statement also passes three literal values to the function.

```
var returnValue = average_numbers(1, 2, 3);
```

To actually return a value to a returnValue variable, you must include the return statement within the average_numbers() function. The following code contains the average_numbers() function, which calculates the average of three numbers and returns the value contained in the result variable to the calling statement using the return statement:

```
function average_numbers(a, b, c) {
    var sum_of_numbers = a + b + c;
    var result = sum_of_numbers / 3;
    return result;
}
```

You are not required to return a value from a function.

You will learn more about performing calculations in Tutorial 3.

The variable name that is returned from a function and the variable name that receives the returned value can be the same. For instance, in the preceding examples, the variable name in the `return` statement in the function and the variable name in the calling statement could both be returnValue. Also, when you pass variables as arguments to a function, the passed variables and the argument names within the function itself can also be the same. If you pass variables to the average_numbers() function, instead of literal values you can use the statement `average_numbers(a, b, c);`, even though the argument names within the function itself are *a*, *b*, and *c*. However, most programmers usually use unique names to identify specific variables in their code.

Using unique names to identify specific variables makes it easier to understand a program's logic and assists in the debugging process.

You do not need to receive return values from all functions. For example, you would not need to receive a return value from a function that changes the background color of an HTML document or performs some other task that does not create or return a useful value. If you do not need to receive a return value from a function, then you are not required to assign the calling statement to a variable. For instance, if you want to call the average_numbers() function to calculate the average of the three literal values 2, 3, and 4, but do not require a return value, you type `average_numbers(2, 3, 4);` without assigning the statement to the returnValue variable.

When a function performs a calculation such as an average, you normally want to receive a return value.

Next you will create a JavaScript program that contains two functions. The first function will print a message when it is called, and the second function will return a value that is printed after the calling statement.

To create a JavaScript program that contains two functions:

1   Create a new document in your text editor or HTML editor.

2   Type the opening <HTML> and <HEAD> tags along with the <TITLE>...</TITLE> tag pair, as follows:

```
<HTML>
<HEAD>
<TITLE>Two Functions Program</TITLE>
```

3 Type the opening <SCRIPT> tag and HTML comments to hide the code from incompatible browsers:

```
<SCRIPT LANGUAGE="JavaScript1.2">
<!-- HIDE FROM INCOMPATIBLE BROWSERS
```

4 Type the first function, which writes a message to the screen using an argument that is passed from the calling statement:

```
function print_message(first_message) {
    document.writeln(first_message);
}
```

5 Type the second function that displays the second message. The only purpose of this function is to return the literal string *This message was returned from a function* to the calling statement.

```
function return_message(second_message) {
    return "This message was returned from a function";
}
```

6 Type the following lines to close the <SCRIPT> section:

```
// STOP HIDING FROM INCOMPATIBLE BROWSERS -->
</SCRIPT>
```

7 Add **</HEAD>** to close the <HEAD>...</HEAD> tag pair.

8 Add the following code to begin the body of the HTML document and to create a preformatted text container:

```
<BODY>
<PRE>
```

9 Add the opening statements for the JavaScript section that calls the functions in the <HEAD> section:

```
<SCRIPT LANGUAGE="JavaScript1.2">
<!-- HIDE FROM INCOMPATIBLE BROWSERS
```

10 Type the following two statements to call the functions in the <HEAD> section. The first statement sends the text string *This text was printed from a function* and does not receive a return value. The second statement assigns the function call to a variable named return_value, but does not send the function any arguments.

```
print_message("This text was printed from a function");
var return_value = return_message();
```

11 Write the value of the return_value variable to the screen by adding **document.writeln(return_value);**.

12 Add the following code to end the HTML comments and close the <SCRIPT> tag pair:

```
// STOP HIDING FROM INCOMPATIBLE BROWSERS -->
</SCRIPT>
```

13 Close the <PRE>, <BODY>, and <HTML> tags:

```
</PRE>
</BODY>
</HTML>
```

14 Save the file as **TwoFunctionsProgram.html** in the **Tutorial.02** folder on your Student Disk. Open the **TwoFunctionsProgram.html** file in your Web browser. Figure 2-8 displays the TwoFunctionsProgram.html file.

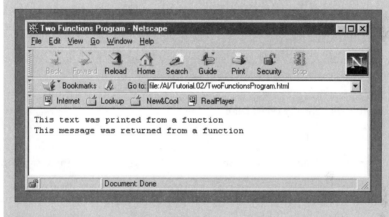

Figure 2-8: TwoFunctionsProgram.html

help

If you receive error messages, make sure that all of your JavaScript code is in the correct case—remember that JavaScript is case-sensitive. Also check to see that you have entered all of the opening and closing HTML tags.

15 Close the Web browser window and the text editor.

Understanding JavaScript Objects

Traditional object-oriented programming languages, such as C++ and Java, create objects through which you access procedures and data. Objects are based on classes. In object-oriented programming, data, procedures, and other attributes are contained in a structure known as a **class**. Objects are instances of classes and inherit all the class's procedures and data; you do not access a class directly. Objects can also be based on other objects. Objects based on another class or object are said to *descend* from the object. Similarly, a class or object from which an object descends is called an ancestor class or object.

In comparison, JavaScript objects are based on functions called constructor functions. A function that is used as the basis for an object is called an object definition, or a **constructor function**. When you create a new object from a constructor function, you are said to be instantiating a new object or extending the old object. As with the inheritance found in traditional class-based objects, JavaScript objects inherit all the data and procedures of the constructor function on which they are based. Any JavaScript function can serve as a constructor.

▶ **tip**

A constructor function is more like a template on which an object is based than a class from which an object is instantiated.

Constructor functions have two types of elements: properties and methods. A **property** is a variable within a constructor function. These variables, or properties, are considered to be the data of any objects that are created from the constructor function. A **method** is a function—whether a built-in JavaScript function or a function you create—that is called from within an object.

▶ **tip**

Properties are also called fields.

The following code is a constructor function named Animal and contains three properties: animal_type, animal_sound, and animal_transport_mode:

```
function Animal(type, sound, transport_mode) {
    this.animal_type = type; // dog, cat, etc.
    this.animal_sound = sound;     // woof, meow, etc.
    this.animal_transport_mode = transport_mode;
        // walk/run, fly, swim
}
```

▶ **tip**

Class names in traditional object-oriented programming languages usually begin with an uppercase letter. Since constructor functions are the equivalent of classes, it is customary to begin the name of constructor functions with an uppercase letter, to differentiate constructor functions in your code from regular functions.

Notice the this keyword in the preceding example. The this keyword refers to the current object that called the constructor function. The three statements assign the three arguments, type, sound, and transport_mode to the animal_type, animal_sound, and animal_transport_mode properties (which are variables) of whichever object (this) is instantiated from the constructor function. The use of the this reference is one of the primary differences between standard functions and constructor functions. Standard functions do not include a this reference, since they are not used as the basis of objects.

tip

The this reference is also used with the <FORM> tag to refer to a form that contains an object. You will learn about forms in Tutorial 6.

Objects are created from constructor functions using the new keyword. The following code creates a new object named pet from the animal constructor function and passes the appropriate arguments, which are assigned to the object's properties:

```
pet = new Animal("dog", "woof", "walk/run");
```

The pet object now has three properties: type, sound, and transport_mode. To access an object's property, you add a period and the property name to the object. For example, to access the sound property of the pet object you type pet.sound. Unlike methods, such as document.write(), a property is not followed by parentheses. If you add parentheses to a property, JavaScript will attempt to locate a method (or function) by that name. For example, if you wrote pet.sound() instead of pet.sound, JavaScript assumes you are running the sound() method of the pet object instead of accessing the sound property of the pet object.

Object Inheritance and Prototypes

Objects inherit the properties and methods of the constructor functions from which they are instantiated. When you instantiate a new object named cat based on the Animal constructor function, the new object includes the animal_type, animal_sound, and animal_transport_mode properties. After instantiating a new object, you can assign additional properties to the object, using a period. The following code creates a new object named cat based on the Animal constructor function, then assigns to the cat object a new property named size.

```
cat = new Animal("feline", "meow", "walk/run");
cat.size = "fat";
```

Constructor functions do not require arguments, such as the type, sound, and transport_mode arguments in the Animal constructor function. You are also not required to pass arguments to a constructor function when you instantiate an object. For instance, you can instantiate the cat object using the statement cat = new Animal();, then assign the property values later. However, if you attempt to use a property that does not have an assigned value, you will receive a special value of *undefined*. If you add the size property to the cat object, then attempt to print the property using the statement document.write(cat.size); without assigning the size property a value, the value *undefined* will print instead.

When you add a new property to an object that has been extended from a constructor function, the new property is only available to that specific object; the property is not available to the constructor function or to any other objects that were extended from the same constructor function. However, if you use the prototype property, any new properties you create will also be available to the constructor function and any objects that extend it. The **prototype property** is a built-in property that specifies the constructor from which an object was extended. The following code adds the size property, which is a prototype of the cat object, to the Animal constructor function. By using a prototype property, all objects that extend the Animal constructor function will also have access to the size property.

```
cat = new Animal("feline", "meow", "walk/run");
cat.prototype.size = "fat";
```

In this case, all Animal objects would have a size of *fat*. Since not all animals can be described as fat, you can assign an empty value to the size property using the statement `cat.prototype.size = "";`. You can then assign the size property to each individual object. The statement to assign a size property to the cat object would be `cat.size = "fat";`.

Object definitions can extend other object definitions. Consider the Animal constructor function that contains three generic properties that can be applied to all animals. You may need to create additional object definitions that extend Animal and that contain properties specific to certain types of animals. To extend one object definition from another object definition, you use the prototype property, followed by the new keyword and the name of the object definition to extend. Figure 2-9 shows two additional object definitions, WildAnimal and FarmAnimal, both of which extend Animal and that include properties specific to each animal type.

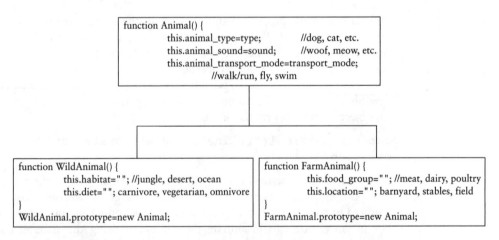

Figure 2-9: Two object definitions extending another object definition

Objects instantiated from either WildAnimal or FarmAnimal will include the three properties from the Animal constructor function, along with the properties specific to each individual object. For example, the following code instantiates an object from FarmAnimal and assigns the object's properties:

```
chicken = new FarmAnimal();
// Animal object definition
```

```
chicken.animal_type = "chicken";
// Animal object definition
chicken.animal_sound = "cluck";
// Animal object definition
chicken.animal_transport_mode = "walk/fly";
// FarmAnimal object definition
chicken.location = "barnyard";
// FarmAnimal object definition
chicken.food_group = "poultry"
// FarmAnimal object definition
```

••

Some object-oriented programming languages allow objects to inherit from more than one object definition. JavaScript, however, only allows objects to inherit from a single object definition.

••

Next you will create a JavaScript program that demonstrates objects and inheritance. The program will contain a Company object definition. The Company object definition contains several properties that apply to all departments within the company. You will also create two object definitions, Sales and Production, which extend Company. The Sales and Production object definitions include properties unique to each department. After you create the object definitions, you will create instances of each object and print the associated properties.

To create a JavaScript program that demonstrates objects and inheritance:

1 Start your text editor or HTML editor and create a new document. If your text editor is still open, create a new document.

2 Type the opening <HTML>, <HEAD>, and <TITLE> tags:

```
<HTML>
<HEAD>
<TITLE>Company Objects Program</TITLE>
```

3 Type the opening <SCRIPT> tag, and HTML comments to hide the code from incompatible browsers:

```
<SCRIPT LANGUAGE="JavaScript1.2">
<!-- HIDE FROM INCOMPATIBLE BROWSERS
```

4 Type the first constructor function, which creates the properties that apply to all departments within the company:

```
function Company() {
    this.company_name = "WebAdventure, Inc.";
    this.company_products = "Internet services";
}
```

5   Next, create the constructor function for the Sales department, which extends the Company object definition:

```
function Sales() {
    this.territory = "North America";
    this.sales_reps = "50";
}
Sales.prototype = new Company();
```

6   Now, create the constructor function for the Production department, which also extends the Company object definition:

```
function Production() {
    this.facilities = "New York, Chicago, and Los Angeles";
    this.personnel = "100";
}
Production.prototype = new Company();
```

7   Type the following lines to close the <SCRIPT> and <HEAD> sections.

```
// STOP HIDING FROM INCOMPATIBLE BROWSERS -->
</SCRIPT>
</HEAD>
```

8   Add the following code to begin the body of the HTML document and to create a preformatted text container.

```
<BODY>
<PRE>
```

9   Add the opening statements for the JavaScript section that calls the constructor functions in the <HEAD> section:

```
<SCRIPT LANGUAGE="JavaScript1.2">
<!-- HIDE FROM INCOMPATIBLE BROWSERS
```

10   Add the following code to instantiate a new Sales object and write its properties to the screen. Notice that the document.write() and document.writeln() methods use a plus sign (+) to combine literal strings with properties.

▶ **tip**

In Tutorial 3, you will learn more about operations that you can perform in JavaScript.

```
sales_object = new Sales();
document.writeln(sales_object.company_name);
document.writeln("Producer of " +
        sales_object.company_products);
document.write("With " + sales_object.sales_reps +
    " sales reps");
document.writeln(" in " + sales_object.territory);
```

11   Next, add the following code to instantiate a new Production object and write its properties to the screen.

```
production_object = new Production();
document.write(production_object.company_name);
document.writeln(" has " + production_object.personnel +
    " production personnel");
document.write("with facilities in " +
    production_object.facilities);
```

12   Add the following lines to close the HTML comments and <SCRIPT> tag:

```
// STOP HIDING FROM INCOMPATIBLE BROWSERS -->
</SCRIPT>
```

13   Close the <PRE>, <BODY>, and <HTML> tags:

```
</PRE>
</BODY>
</HTML>
```

14   Save the file as **CompanyObjects.html** in the **Tutorial.02** folder on your Student Disk, then open it in your Web browser. Figure 2-10 displays the CompanyObjects.html file as it appears in a web browser.

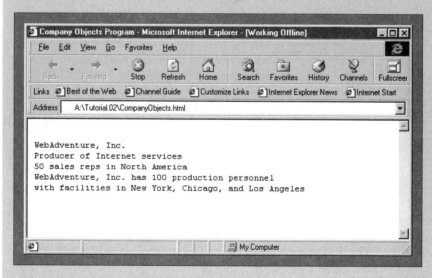

Figure 2-10: CompanyObjects.html

15   Close the Web browser window and the text editor.

Object Methods

Object methods are functions associated with a particular object. When you create a function that will be used as an object's method, you use the `this` reference in the same manner as you do when creating a constructor function. Consider the Animal object definition. To create a method that prints the three object properties (animal_type, animal_sound, animal_transport_mode), you write a function as follows:

```
function displayAnimalProperties() {
    document.write(this.animal_type + "<BR>");
    document.write(this.animal_sound + "<BR>");
    document.write(this.animal_transport_mode + "<BR>");
}
```

 tip

Since the displayAnimalProperties() method is not a constructor function, the first letter of the method name is not capitalized.

Recall that you must place the writeln() method within a <PRE>...</PRE> tag pair for it to work. There may be times, however, when it is easier not to include the <PRE>...</PRE> tag pair. Notice that the code in the preceding example does not use a <PRE>...</PRE> tag pair. Instead, each document.write() method contains a literal string that includes a <BR> tag. Using the <BR> tag as a literal value inside the <SCRIPT>...</SCRIPT> tag pair is an alternative to using the <PRE>...</PRE> tag pairs required for document.writeln() methods.

After a method is created, it must be added to the constructor function, using the syntax `this.methodName = functionName;`. The *methodName* following the `this` reference is the name that is being assigned to the function within the object. Be sure not to include the parentheses following the function name, as you would when calling a function in JavaScript. The statement `this.methodName = functionName();` is incorrect, because it includes parentheses. To add the displayAnimalProperties() method to the Animal function definition, you include the statement `this.displayAnimalProperties = displayAnimalProperties;` within the function definition's braces.

After you instantiate an object based on an object definition, you call the object's methods by adding a period and the method name to the object name, followed by parentheses containing any arguments that need to be passed to the method. The syntax for calling an object method is `objectName.methodName(arguments);`. The following statements instantiate a new object based on the Animal object definition and call the object's displayAnimalProperties() method.

```
guppy = new Animal("fish", "blub", "swim");
guppy.displayAnimalProperties();
```

Next you will modify the CompanyObjects program so that the document.write() and document.writeln() functions for the Sales and Production objects are contained within their own methods.

To modify the CompanyObjects program so that the document.write() and document.writeln() functions for the Sales and Production objects are contained within their own methods:

1   Open the **CompanyObjects.html** file in your text editor or HTML editor, then immediately save it as **CompanyObjectsWithMethods.html**.

2   Just before the statement that reads `// STOP HIDING FROM INCOMPATIBLE BROWSERS -->` in the <SCRIPT> section between the <HEAD>...</HEAD> tag pair, add the following function that will be used as a method of the Sales object. Notice that the function uses <BR> tags to add line breaks, since the <SCRIPT> section is not located between a <PRE>...</PRE> tag pair.

```
function displaySalesInfo() {
    document.write(this.company_name + "<BR>");
    document.write("Producer of " + this.company_products
        + "<BR>");
    document.write("With " + this.sales_reps + "
        sales reps");
    document.write(" in " + this.territory + "<BR>");
}
```

3   Immediately after the displaySalesInfo() function, add the following displayProductionInfo() function:

```
function displayProductionInfo() {
    document.write(this.company_name);
    document.write(" has " + this.personnel + " production
        personnel"+ "<BR>");
    document.write("with facilities in " + this.facilities);
}
```

4   Add the statement `this.displaySalesInfo = displaySalesInfo` just before the closing brace for the Sales() function definition.

5   Add the statement `this.displayProductionInfo = display ProductionInfo;` just before the closing brace for the Production() function definition.

6   Delete the seven document.write() and document.writeln() methods located in the <SCRIPT> section within the <BODY>...</BODY> tag pair. The <SCRIPT> section should now only contain the two lines that instantiate the sales_object and production_object.

7   Insert a line after the statement that instantiates the sales_object and add the statement `sales_object.displaySalesInfo();`.

8   Insert a line after the statement that instantiates the production_object and add the statement `production_object.displayProductionInfo();`.

9 Save the **CompanyObjectsWithMethods.html** file, then open it in your Web browser. The file should appear the same as Figure 2-10.

10 Close the Web browser window.

Variable Scope

When you use a variable in a Java Script program, particularly a complex JavaScript program, you need to be aware of the variable's scope. **Variable scope** refers to where in your program a declared variable can be used. A variable's scope can be either global or local. A **global variable** is one that is declared outside of a function and is available to all parts of your program. A **local variable** is declared inside a function and is only available within the function in which it is declared. Local variables cease to exist when the function ends. If you attempt to use a local variable outside of the function in which it is declared, you will receive an error message.

The arguments within the parentheses of a function declaration are considered to be local variables.

When you declare a global variable, the use of the `var` keyword is optional. For example, you can write the statement `var myVariable = "This is a variable.";` as `myVariable = "This is a variable.";`. However, it is considered good programming technique to always use the `var` keyword when declaring variables.

The following code includes a global variable and a function containing a local variable. Both the global variable and the function are contained in the <SCRIPT>...</SCRIPT> tag pair in the <HEAD> section. When the function is called from the <BODY> section, the global variable and the local variable print successfully from within the function. After the call to the function, the global variable again prints successfully from the <BODY> section. However, when the program tries to print the local variable from the <BODY> section, an error message is generated since the local variable ceases to exist when the function ends.

```
<HTML>
<HEAD>
<TITLE>Variable Scope</TITLE>
<SCRIPT LANGUAGE="JavaScript1.2">
<!--HIDE FROM INCOMPATIBLE BROWSERS
```

```
var firstGlobalVariable = "First global variable";
function scopeExample() {
    secondGlobalVariable = "Second global variable";
    var localVariable = "Local variable";
    document.writeln(firstGlobalVariable); // prints
    successfully
    document.writeln(secondGlobalVariale); // prints
    successfully
    document.writeln(localVariable);          // prints
    successfully
}
// STOP HIDING FROM INCOMPATIBLE BROWSERS -->
</SCRIPT>
</HEAD>
<BODY>
<PRE>
<SCRIPT LANGUAGE="JavaScript1.2">
<!--HIDE FROM INCOMPATIBLE BROWSERS
scopeExample();
document.writeln(firstGlobalVariable);    // prints
successfully
document.writeln(secondGlobalVariable);   // prints
successfully
document.writeln(localVariable);             // error message
// STOP HIDING FROM INCOMPATIBLE BROWSERS -->
</SCRIPT>
</PRE>
</BODY>
</HTML>
```

When a program contains a global variable and a local variable with the same name, the local variable takes precedence when its function is called. After a function assigns a new value to a local variable, that value also becomes the global variable's value. In the following code, the global variable showDog is assigned a value of *Golden Retriever* before the function that contains a local variable of the same name is called. Once the function is called, the local showDog variable is assigned a value of *Irish Setter*. After the function ends, *Irish Setter* is still the value of the showDog variable.

```
var showDog = "Golden Retriever";
function duplicateVariableNames() {
    var showDog = "Irish Setter";
}
duplicateVariableNames();
document.writeln(showDog);      // value printed is Irish
Setter
```

SUMMARY

- The values stored in computer memory locations are called variables.

- You use the reserved word `var` to declare a variable.

- Words that are part of the JavaScript language syntax are called reserved words, or keywords. Reserved words cannot be used for function names or variable names in a JavaScript program.

- A function allows you to treat a related group of JavaScript statements as a single unit. Functions, like all JavaScript code, must exist between the <SCRIPT>...</SCRIPT> tag pair.

- Before you can use a function in a JavaScript program, you must first create, or define, the function. The statements that compose a function are called the function definition.

- A parameter, or argument, is a variable that will be used within a function. Arguments are contained in parentheses following the function name.

- Sending variables or values to a called function's arguments is called passing arguments.

- To return a value to the calling statement, you include the `return` statement within the called function.

- A function that is used as the basis for an object is called an object definition, or a constructor function.

- Two types of elements are found within constructor functions: properties and methods. A property is a variable within a constructor function that is considered to be the data of any objects that are created from the constructor function. A method is a function— whether a built-in JavaScript function or a function you create—that is called from within an object.

- The `this` keyword refers to the current object that called the constructor function. Standard functions do not include a `this` reference, since they are not used as the basis of objects.

- The prototype property is a built-in property that specifies the constructor from which an object was extended.

- Object definitions can extend other object definitions.

- Object methods are essentially functions associated with a particular object.

- The syntax for calling an object method is `objectName.methodName(arguments);`.

- Variable scope refers to where in your program a declared variable can be used. A variable's scope can be either global or local. Global variables are declared outside of functions and are available to all parts of your program. Local variables are declared inside functions and are available only within the functions in which they are declared.

Q U E S T I O N S

1. Which is the correct syntax for declaring a variable and assigning it a string?
   a. `var myVariable = "Hello";`
   b. `var myVariable = Hello;`
   c. `"Hello" = var myVariable;`
   d. `var "Hello" = myVariable;`

2. Which of the following is a legal name for a variable?
   a. %variable_name
   b. 1variable_name
   c. variable_name
   d. +variable_name

3. Identifiers in JavaScript cannot begin with _____.
   a. an uppercase or lowercase ASCII letter
   b. the dollar sign ($)
   c. an underscore character (_)
   d. a number

4. A(n) _____ allows you to treat a related group of JavaScript commands as a single unit.
   a. statement
   b. variable
   c. function
   d. event

5. The lines that compose a function within an HTML document are called the function _____.
   a. section
   b. unit
   c. container
   d. definition

6. Which item is *not* part of a function definition?
   a. the reserved word `function` followed by the function name
   b. the opening <SCRIPT>...</SCRIPT> tag pair
   c. any parameters required by the function, contained within parentheses following the function name
   d. the function's statements enclosed in braces { }

7. JavaScript reserved words can be used as _____.
   a. function names
   b. variables
   c. both of these
   d. neither of these

8. A variable that is contained within a function's parentheses is called a parameter or a(n) _____.

a. field
b. routine
c. method
d. argument

9. A function's statements are located between which characters?

a. { }
b. [ ]
c. < >
d. ( )

10. Sending arguments to a called function is called _____ arguments.

a. generating
b. passing
c. routing
d. submitting

11. Why should JavaScript functions be placed within an HTML document's <HEAD> section?

a. You are not allowed to create functions within the <BODY> section.
b. Doing so ensures that each function will be created before it is called.
c. They are not used as often as other types of JavaScript code.
d. You are less likely to forget to create each function.

12. A function that is used as the basis for an object is called an object definition or a(n) _____.

a. method
b. class
c. constructor function
d. object variable

13. Variables found within a constructor function that are considered to be the data of any objects that are created from the constructor function are called _____.

a. properties
b. methods
c. object files
d. bits

14. Any functions, whether built-in JavaScript functions or functions you create, are called _____ when they are called from within an object.

a. procedures
b. methods
c. constructors
d. statements

15. The this keyword refers to _____.

a. the HTML document
b. the Web browser window
c. the currently executing JavaScript statement
d. the current object that called the constructor function

16. What is the correct syntax for creating an object named my_car from a constructor function named Chevrolet that requires two arguments: color and engine?

a. `my_car() = new Chevrolet "red", "V8";`

b. `my_car = new Chevrolet("red", "V8");`

c. `new Chevrolet("red", "V8") = my_car;`

d. `my_car("red", "V8") = new Chevrolet;`

17. When you create an object from a constructor function that includes two arguments in the function definition, you

a. must pass both arguments to the constructor function.

b. must pass at least one of the arguments to the constructor function.

c. are not required to pass the arguments to the constructor function.

d. pass the arguments to the constructor function prior to creating the object.

18. The built-in property that specifies the constructor from which an object was extended is called the _____ property.

a. origination

b. default

c. source

d. prototype

19. What is the correct syntax for adding a new property named sales to the prototype of an object named company?

a. `company.prototype.sales = "";`

b. `prototype.company.sales = "";`

c. `sales.company.prototype = "";`

d. `company.prototype = sales("");`

20. What is the correct syntax for adding a method named myMethod to a constructor function named myConstructorFunction?

a. `myConstructorFunction = new myMethod();`

b. `myMethod = this.myMethod;`

c. `this.myMethod = myMethod();`

d. `this.myMethod = myMethod;`

21. A variable that is declared outside a function is called a(n) _____ variable.

a. local

b. class

c. program

d. global

22. A local variable must be declared _____.

a. before a function

b. with the `var` keyword

c. within a function definition's braces

d. with the local keyword

EXERCISES

1. Create an HTML document named PersonalInfo.html with a function in the <HEAD> section named printPersonalInfo. Within the printPersonalInfo function, use the document.write() and document.writeln() methods to print your name, address, date of birth, and Social Security number to the screen. Call the function from the <BODY> section of the document.

2. Create an HTML document named FavoriteFoods.html. Within the <HEAD> section, create four functions that print the names of your favorite foods. For example, you may have a function named *chinese* that contains the statement `document.writeln("Chinese");`. Call each of the functions from the <BODY> of the HTML document, starting with your favorite type of food. Combine the document.write() and document.writeln() methods with strings to describe the order of your favorite food. For example, to print the line *My favorite food is Chinese*, the JavaScript statement would read `document.write("My favorite food is " + chinese());`.

3. Create an HTML document named CarObject.html that includes a constructor function in the <HEAD> section named Automobile. Include four properties in the Automobile object definition: make, model, color, and engine. Instantiate a new Automobile object in the <BODY> of the HTML document, then assign the values of your car to each of the Automobile properties. Print each of the properties to the screen.

4. Create an HTML document named CompanyInfo.html that includes a constructor function in the <HEAD> section named Company. Include four properties in the Company object definition: name, products, motto, and employees. Also create a method named Employees() that prints the number of employees. Instantiate a new Company object in the <BODY> of the HTML document, then assign values to each of the properties. Print the name, products, and motto properties to the screen using writeln() methods. Print the number of employees using the Employees() method. Combine each printed property with a descriptive string. For example, when you print the company name, it should read something like *The company name is MyCompany*.

5. Create an HTML document that prints the names of your favorite movies. The document should contain two functions: one that prints your three favorite comedies and one that prints your three favorite dramas. Name one function comedy and the other function drama. Assign each of the movie titles to a local variable within the comedy or drama function, then print each variable. Also create a global variable that will hold the name of your absolute favorite movie. Call the comedy and drama functions from a <SCRIPT>...</SCRIPT> tag pair in the body of the HTML document, then print the name of your absolute favorite movie after the two functions are called. Save the document as FavoriteMovies.html.

In this section you will learn:
- About events
- About HTML tags and events
- How to use event handlers
- About links
- How to use link events
- How to create an image map

Using Events

Understanding Events

One of the primary ways in which JavaScript makes HTML documents dynamic is through events. You can use JavaScript events to add interactivity between your Web pages and users. An **event** is a specific circumstance that is monitored by JavaScript. The most common events are actions that users take. For example, when a user clicks a button, a *click* event is generated. You can think of an event as a trigger that fires specific JavaScript code in response to a given situation.

One common use of events is to run some sort of code in response to a user request. For example, one type of JavaScript program found on the Web today is a calculator program, such as a mortgage calculator. Once users enter the required information for a mortgage, such as the interest rate, number of years, and amount of the loan, they may click a Calculate button that calculates the amount of a monthly mortgage payment. Calculation of the monthly mortgage payment is executed by the event that occurs when a user clicks the Calculate button. The image map you will create in this tutorial relies on an event that occurs when users pass their mice over a portion of the map. This type of event is called a *mouseover* event; it executes code that changes the highlighted portion of the map.

User-generated events, however, are not the only types of events monitored by JavaScript. Events that are not direct results of user actions, such as the *load* event, are also monitored. The load event, which is triggered automatically by a Web browser, occurs only when an HTML document finishes loading in a Web browser. The load event is often used to execute code that performs some type of visual effect, such as animation, that should not occur until a Web page is completely loaded. In the case of animation, the JavaScript program that executes the animation knows not to begin until it receives a signal in the form of the load event from the Web browser. Figure 2-11 displays a list of JavaScript events and when they occur.

Event	Triggered When
abort	The loading of an image is interrupted
blur	An element, such as a radio button, becomes inactive
click	An element is clicked once
change	The value of an element changes
error	There is an error when loading a document or image
focus	An element becomes active
load	A document or image loads
mouseOut	The mouse moves off an element
mouseOver	The mouse moves over an element
reset	A form resets
select	A user selects a field in a form
submit	A user submits a form
unload	A document unloads

Figure 2-11: JavaScript events

HTML Tags and Events

One of the most commonly used HTML tags that allows users to generate events is the <INPUT> tag. The **<INPUT> tag** creates input fields that interact with users. The <INPUT> tag has a number of attributes, including the TYPE attribute. The basic syntax for the <INPUT> tag is <INPUT TYPE="*input type*">. The TYPE attribute is a required field and determines the type of input field that the <INPUT> tag generates. For example, the statement <INPUT TYPE="radio"> creates a radio button, and the statement <INPUT TYPE="text"> creates a text field. You will use the <INPUT> tag throughout this text. The <INPUT> tag is most often used with forms and is placed within the <FORM>...</FORM> tag pair.

You will learn about forms and how <INPUT> tags are used in forms in Tutorial 6.

The following code shows an example of an <INPUT> tag that includes an onBlur event handler and is placed between a <FORM>...</FORM> tag pair. The blur event occurs when the focus leaves a control. In the example, the onBlur event handler displays the <INPUT> tag's value when it loses focus.

```
<FORM NAME="myForm">
    <INPUT TYPE="text" VALUE="default text"
        NAME="textButton" onBlur="alert(this.value);">
</FORM>
```

Notice that both the <FORM> and <INPUT> tag in the example have NAME attributes. The NAME attribute allows you to assign to an HTML tag a unique name that can be referenced in JavaScript code. In order to reference an HTML tag in a function or from another tag, you append its name to any of its ancestor objects, starting with the Document object. This allows you to retrieve information about a tag or change its properties. The statement `document.myForm.textButton.value = "new value";` could be used in a JavaScript function to change the value of the textButton to *new value*.

....

Unlike most HTML code, the NAME attribute is case-sensitive.

....

Figure 2-12 lists various types of HTML tags and their associated events.

Element	Description	Event
<A>...</A>	Link	click mouseOver mouseOut
<IMG>	Image	abort error load
<AREA>	Area	mouseOver mouseOut
<BODY>...</BODY>	Document body	blur error focus load unload
<FRAMESET>...</FRAMESET>	Frame set	blur error focus load unload

Figure 2-12: HTML elements and associated events

Element	Description	Event
<FRAME>...</FRAME>	Frame	blur focus
<FORM>...</FORM>	Form	submit reset
<INPUT TYPE="text">	Text field	blur focus change select
<TEXTAREA>...</TEXTAREA>	Text area	blur focus change select
<INPUT TYPE="submit">	Submit	click
<INPUT TYPE="reset">	Reset	click
<INPUT TYPE="radio">	Radio button	click
<INPUT TYPE="checkbox">	Check box	click
<SELECT>...</SELECT>	Selection	blur focus change

Figure 2-12: HTML elements and associated events (continued)

Event Handlers

When an event occurs, a program executes JavaScript code that responds to the event. Code that executes in response to a specific event is called an **event handler**. An event itself, such as a click event, only informs JavaScript that it is okay to execute an event handler. You include event handler code as an attribute of the HTML tag that initiates the event. The syntax of an event handler within an HTML tag is:

```
<HTMLtag eventHandler="JavaScript Code">
```

Event handler names are the same as the name of the event itself, but with a prefix of *on*. For example, the event handler for the Click event is onClick, and the event handler for the Load event is onLoad. Recall that HTML tags are not case-sensitive, whereas JavaScript code is. Since event handlers are part of an HTML tag, they are not case-sensitive. Therefore, you could write the name of the onClickEvent event handler as ONCLICK, onclick, or ONclick. However, capitalizing only the first letter of the event name itself is a standard convention.

The JavaScript code for an event handler is contained within the quotation marks following the name of the JavaScript event handler. The following code uses the <INPUT> tag to create a command button, which is similar to an OK or Cancel button. The tag also includes an onClick event handler that executes the built-in JavaScript alert() method, in response to a click event (which occurs when the button is clicked). Notice that the code executed by the onClick event handler (the alert() method) is contained within double quotation marks.

```
<INPUT TYPE="button" onClick="alert('You clicked a
button!')">
```

The built-in JavaScript **alert() method** displays a popup dialog box with an OK button. You pass a single literal string or variable as an argument to the alert() method. Notice in the example that the literal string being passed is contained in single quotation marks, since the alert() method itself is already enclosed in double quotation marks.

The alert() method is the only statement being executed in the example. You can include multiple JavaScript statements if semicolons separate them. For example, to include two statements in the event handler example, a statement that creates a variable and another statement that uses the alert() method to display the variable, you would type the following:

```
<INPUT TYPE="button" onClick="var message='You clicked a
button'; alert(message)">
```

Another built-in JavaScript function that responds to events is prompt(), which is similar to alert(). The **prompt() method** displays a dialog box with a message, a text box, an OK button, and a Cancel button. Any text that is entered into a prompt() method's text box by a user can be assigned to a variable. The syntax for the prompt() method is `variable_name = prompt(message, default_text);`.

The following code shows an example of a prompt() function that displays the text *How old are you?*. The second argument in the prompt() method is the default text *Your Age* that appears in the prompt dialog box's text box. If the user presses the OK button, any text entered into the text box is assigned to the yourAge variable, which then appears in an alert dialog box. If the user presses the OK button without changing the default text, then the default text, *Your Age*, is assigned to the yourAge variable. No value is assigned to the yourAge variable if the user presses the Cancel button.

```
yourAge = prompt("How old are you?", "Your Age");
alert("Your age is " + yourAge);
```

Next you will create an HTML document that demonstrates JavaScript onLoad, onUnload, onClick, and onChange events and uses both the alert() and the prompt() functions.

To create an HTML document that demonstrates JavaScript events:

1 Start your text editor or HTML editor and create a new document.

2 Type the opening <HTML> and <HEAD> tags along with the title, opening <SCRIPT> tag, and HTML comments to hide the code from incompatible browsers:

```
<HTML>
<HEAD>
<TITLE>JavaScript Events</TITLE>
<SCRIPT LANGUAGE="JavaScript1.2">
<!-- HIDE FROM INCOMPATIBLE BROWSERS
```

3 Type **var visitor_name = ""** on the next line to create a variable that will store the name of a visitor to the Web page.

4 Type **function greet_visitor(){** on the next line to begin the greet_visitor() function. You will call the greet_visitor() function with the onLoad event in the <BODY> tag.

5 Add the following statement, which prompts the user for his or her name and assigns the name to the visitor_name variable.

```
visitor_name = prompt("Please enter your name",
     "Enter your name here");
```

6 Type an alert() method that displays a personalized greeting to the visitor, followed by a closing brace for the function.

```
alert("Welcome " + visitor_name + "!");
}
```

7 Next add the following farewell_visitor() function, which will be called by the onUnload event in the <BODY> tag. The farewell_visitor() function also uses the visitor_name variable.

```
function farewell_visitor() {
     alert("Thanks " + visitor_name +
          " for visiting this Web page!");
}
```

8 Type the following lines to close the <SCRIPT> and <HEAD> sections.

```
// STOP HIDING FROM INCOMPATIBLE BROWSERS -->
</SCRIPT>
</HEAD>
```

9 Type the following <BODY> tag that uses the onLoad and onUnload events to call the greet_visitor() and farewell_visitor() functions.

```
<BODY onLoad="greet_visitor();"
onUnload="farewell_visitor();">
```

10 Type <FORM> to start a form section.

11 Create the following two <INPUT> tags. The first <INPUT> tag creates a text field that includes an onChange event handler. The onChange event handler displays an alert() dialog box whenever a user leaves the text field after changing its contents. The second <INPUT> tag creates a button that displays the contents of the text field using its NAME attribute.

```
<INPUT TYPE="text" NAME="text_field" SIZE="25"
   onChange="alert(
        'The value of the text_field has changed.');"><BR>
<INPUT TYPE="button" VALUE="Display Text Field Contents"
   onClick="alert(text_field.value);">
```

12 Add </FORM> to close the form.

13 Add the following tags to close the <BODY> and <HTML> tags:

```
</BODY>
</HTML>
```

14 Save the file as **GreetVisitor.html** in the **Tutorial.02** folder on your Student Disk, then open it in your Web browser. The onLoad event handler is called, and the greet_visitor() function is executed, displaying the prompt dialog box. Figure 2-13 displays an example of the prompt.

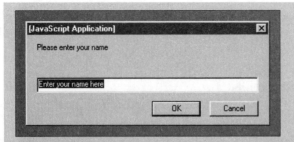

Figure 2-13: The prompt() method

15 Enter your name into the dialog box and click the **OK** button. An alert dialog box displays the personalized greeting. Click the **OK** button on the alert dialog box. Click in the text field and type **Sample Text**, then press the **Tab** key to exit the field. Since you made a change in the text field, the onChange event handler is called, and another alert dialog box appears. Click the **OK** button on the alert dialog box. Now click the Display Textfield contents button to call the onClick event handler, which displays an alert dialog box with the contents of the text field (*Sample Text*). Click the **OK** button on the alert dialog box.

16 To demonstrate the onUnload event handler, open the **CompanyObjects.html** file you created in Section A. Before your Web browser displays the CompanyObjects.html file, the onUnload event handler executes and the farewell_visitor() function executes, displaying the last alert dialog box, which thanks the visitor. Click **OK** to close the alert dialog box.

17 Close the Web browser window.

Links

Recall that HTML documents contain hypertext links, which are used to open files or to navigate to other documents on the Web. You activate a hypertext link by clicking it with your mouse button. A hypertext link in an HTML document is underlined and often a vivid color. Blue is the default color for unvisited links, while red is the default color of previously visited links. The hypertext link can display the actual name and location of a file or HTML document or some sort of descriptive text. Other types of elements, such as images, can also be hypertext links to other HTML documents, images, or files. The text or image used to represent a link in an HTML document is called an **anchor**. Figure 2-14 displays an HTML document containing several anchors.

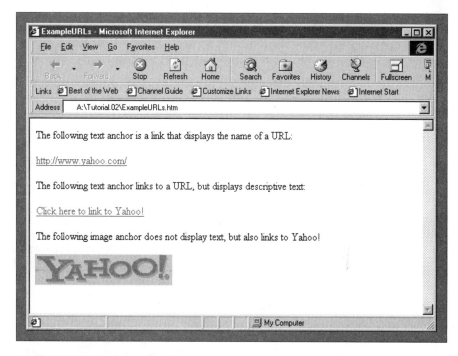

Figure 2-14: HTML document with anchors

You use the <A>...</A> tag pair (the A stands for *anchor*) to create a link in an HTML document. The syntax for the <A> tag is <A *attributes*>anchor text or image</A>. Figure 2-15 displays some of the attributes for the <A> tag.

Attribute	Description
NAME	The name of the anchor
HREF	The URL of the file, HTML document, or image to be loaded
TITLE	The title of the file, HTML document, or image to be loaded

Figure 2-15: Common <A> tag attributes

An anchor uses the Uniform Resource Locator (URL) to specify the name and location of an HTML document. There are two types of URLs in an HTML document: absolute and relative. An **absolute URL** refers to a specific drive and directory or to the full Web address of an HTML document. The following tag displays an anchor of *My Web Site* and contains an absolute reference to an HTML document named index.htm located at a Web site named www.MyWebSite.com.

```
<A HREF="http://www.MyWebSite.com/index.html">My Web Site</A>
```

An absolute URL can also refer to a file on a local computer, as in the following code.

```
<A HREF="c:\MyWebPages\HomePage.html">My Web Site</A>
```

A **relative URL** specifies the location of a file according to the location of the currently loaded HTML document. Relative URLs are used to load HTML documents located on the same computer as the currently displayed HTML document. If the currently displayed HTML document is located at `http://www.MyWebSite.com/WebPages`, then the following relative URL looks in the WebPages folder for the AnotherWebPage.html file:

```
<A HREF="AnotherWebPage.html">Another Web Page</A>
```

You can also use a URL that locates subfolders that are *relative* to the location of the current Web page's folder, as follows:

```
<A HREF="/MoreWebPages/YetAnotherWebPage.html">Yet Another
Web Page</A>
```

When all of your HTML documents reside within the same folder, relative URLs are convenient, since you do not have to type out the entire location of each file. In addition, you do not have to update the location of relative URLs if you rename the folder containing the primary HTML document and linked documents, or move it to a different computer. For example, if you have a primary HTML document that contains 10 links to HTML documents located within the same directory, then you do not have to update the relative links if you move the primary document and the 10 linked documents to a new location. However, if you created each of the 10 links as absolute URLs, then you would need to update each URL before the links would function properly.

tip

If you specify a URL in an HTML document using the <BASE> tag (which establishes a universal URL for the document), then relative URLs are relative to the URL in the <BASE> tag, not to the URL of the HTML document itself. The <BASE> tag is used most often with frames.

Link Events

The primary event used with links is the click event. Clicking a link automatically executes the click event, and the link's associated URL opens. When a user clicks a link, execution of the click event is handled automatically by the Web browser—you do not need to add an onClick event handler to the <A> tag.

There may be cases, however, when you want to override the automatic click event with your own code. For instance, you may want to warn the user about the content of the HTML document that a particular link will open. When you want to override the automatic click event with your own code, you add to the <A> tag an onClick event handler that executes custom code. When you override an internal event handler with your own code, you must return a value of `true` or `false`, using the return statement. A value of `true` indicates that you want the Web browser to continue and open the URL referenced by the link. A value of `false` indicates that you do not want the Web browser to open the link. For example, the <A> tag in Figure 2-16 includes a custom onClick event handler. The warn_user() function that is called by the onClick event handler returns a value generated by the confirm() method. The **confirm() method** displays a dialog box that contains a Cancel button as well as an OK button. When a user clicks the OK button in the confirm dialog box, a value of `true` is returned. When a user clicks the Cancel button, a value of `false` is returned.

```
<HTML>

<HEAD>

<TITLE>Custom onClick Event Example</TITLE>

<SCRIPT LANGUAGE="JavaScript1.2">

<!-- HIDE FROM INCOMPATIBLE BROWSERS

function warnUser() {

     return confirm(
"This link is only for people who love golden retrievers!");

}

// STOP HIDING FROM INCOMPATIBLE BROWSERS -->

</SCRIPT>

</HEAD>

<BODY>

<A HREF="GoldenRetrievers.html" onClick="return
warnUser();">Golden Retriever Club Home Page</A>

</BODY>

</HTML>
```

Figure 2-16: Link with a custom onClick event handler

Notice that there are two return statements in Figure 2-16. The return statement in the warnUser() function returns a value to the onClick event handler. The return statement in the onClick event handler returns the same value to the Web browser.

Two other events that are used with links are the MouseOver and MouseOut events. The **MouseOver event** occurs when the mouse is moved over a link. The MouseOut event occurs when the mouse is moved off a link. One of the most common uses of the MouseOver and MouseOut events is to change the text that appears in a Web browser's status bar. By default, a link's URL appears in the status bar when the mouse passes over a link. Instead, you can use the onMouseOver event handler to display your own custom message for a link in the status bar. To make your custom message appear in the status bar, use the JavaScript **status** property.

The onMouseOut event handler is used to reset the text displayed in the status bar after the mouse is moved off a link. Most often, any text that is displayed in the status bar is cleared using the statement `onMouseOut="status = ' ';"` to set the status property to an empty string. The two single quotation marks specify an empty string. You use single quotation marks instead of double quotation marks since the statement is already contained within a pair of double quotation marks. (Remember that you cannot use double quotation marks inside another set of double quotation marks.) The semicolon marks the end of the JavaScript statement. Instead of an empty string, you can also display another custom message in the status bar.

The following code uses the onMouseOver event handler to display the text *Golden Retriever Club Home Page* in the status bar instead of the link's URL, *GoldenRetrievers.html*. The onMouseOut event handler displays the text *You almost visited the Golden Retriever Home Page!* after the mouse moves off the link:

```
<A HREF="GoldenRetrievers.html" onMouseOver="status =
'Golden Retriever Club Home Page'; return true;"
onMouseOut="status = 'You almost visited the Golden
Retriever Home Page!';">Golden Retriever Club Home Page</A>
```

You can also use the defaultStatus property within a <SCRIPT>...</SCRIPT> tag pair to specify the default text that appears in the status bar whenever the mouse is not positioned over a link. The syntax for the defaultStatus property is `defaultStatus = "Enter default status text here.";`. Note that the defaultStatus property overrides any text specified by an onMouseOut event handler.

Notice that the immediately preceding onMouseOver event handler includes a return statement that returns a value of `true`. Unlike the return value for the onClick event handler, a return value of `true` from the onMouseOver event handler tells the Web browser *not* to perform its own event handling routine of displaying the name of the link's URL in the status bar. It is important to remember that there is no consistency in the return values for event handlers; some event handlers require a value of `true` and others require a value of `false`.

Next you will create two HTML documents that demonstrate the Click, MouseOver, and MouseOut events of a link.

To create an HTML document that demonstrates the Click, MouseOver, and MouseOut events of a link:

1 Start your text editor or HTML editor and create a new document.

2 Type the opening <HTML> and <HEAD> tags along with the title, opening <SCRIPT> tag, and HTML comments to hide the code from incompatible browsers:

```
<HTML>
<HEAD>
<TITLE>Red Page</TITLE>
<SCRIPT LANGUAGE="JavaScript1.2">
<!-- HIDE FROM INCOMPATIBLE BROWSERS
```

3 Add the following function, which will be called from the onClick event handler of a link. The function confirms that a user wants to open the URL specified by a link.

```
function confirmPageChange() {
    return confirm(
"Are you sure you want to display the green page?");
}
```

4 Type the following lines to close the <SCRIPT> and <HEAD> sections:

```
// STOP HIDING FROM INCOMPATIBLE BROWSERS -->
</SCRIPT>
</HEAD>
```

5 Type the opening <BODY> tag, which also includes the BGCOLOR attribute, which determines the document's background color:

```
<BODY BGCOLOR="red">
```

6 Create the following link that contains onClick, onMouseOver, and onMouseOut event handlers:

```
<A HREF="GreenPage.html"
onClick="return confirmPageChange();"
onMouseOver=
"status = 'This link opens the green page'; return true;"
 onMouseOut=
"status ='You did not open the green page!!';">
Click here to open the green page</A>
```

7 Add the following tags to close the <BODY> and <HTML> tags:

```
</BODY>
</HTML>
```

8 Save the file as **RedPage.html** in the **Tutorial.02** folder on your Student Disk, then immediately save it as **GreenPage.html**.

9   Within the new GreenPage.html file, change the text in the <TITLE> tag to **Green Page**.

10   In the confirmPageChange() function, change the word green to **red** within the text string.

11   Change the BGCOLOR attribute in the <BODY> tag to **green**.

12   Within the <A> tag, change the HREF from GreenPage.html to **RedPage.html**. Also change the word green to **red** within the two event handlers in which it appears. Notice that you are using relative URLs since the GreenPage.html and RedPage.html files are located within the same directory.

13   Save the file, then open either RedPage.html or GreenPage.html in your Web browser. Clicking the link in either file should display the confirm dialog box, which in turn should open the other file when you click OK. Also check to see that the status bar text is being updated during the MouseOver and MouseOut events for each file. An example of RedPage.html and the confirm dialog box is displayed in Figure 2-17.

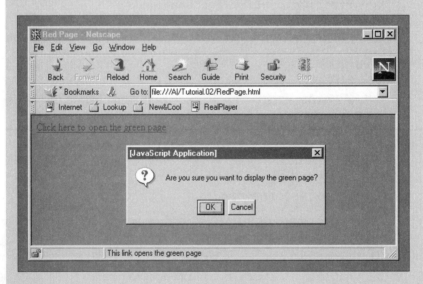

Figure 2-17: RedPage.html and the confirm dialog box

14   Close the Web browser window.

Creating an Image Map

An image map consists of an image that is divided into regions. Each region is then associated with a URL by means of the <A> tag; these regions are called hot zones. You can open each region's associated URL by clicking the hot zone with your mouse. You use the <IMG>, <MAP>, and <AREA> tags to create an image map on a Web page. To create an image map, you must include the following tags on your Web page:

- An <IMG> tag that contains an SRC attribute specifying the name of the image file and a NAME attribute specifying the name of the <MAP>...</MAP> tag pair that contains the mapping coordinates.
- A <MAP>...</MAP> tag pair that includes the NAME attribute used by the <IMG> tag.
- <AREA> tags within the <MAP>...</MAP> tag pair that identify the coordinates within the image that will be recognized as hot zones.

There are two types of image maps: server-side image maps and client-side image maps. With server-side image maps, the code that *maps* each region of an image is located on a server. A client-side image map is part of an HTML document. This tutorial covers client-side image maps.

When an image specified by the <IMG> tag is rendered in an HTML document, the Web browser creates the image within a rectangle corresponding to the height and width of the image. The size of an image's rectangle is measured in pixels. A **pixel** (short for **pic**ture **el**ement) represents a single point on a computer screen. You can think of pixels as thousands or millions of tiny dots arranged in columns and rows on your monitor. The number of pixels available depends on a computer monitor's resolution. For example, a VGA monitor contains 640 columns by 480 rows of pixels, or about 300,000 pixels; a Super VGA monitor contains 1024 columns by 768 rows of pixels, for a total of approximately 800,000 pixels.

You reference an image's pixels with x-axis and y-axis coordinates, starting at the upper-left corner of the image's rectangle and ending at the lower-right corner. Figure 2-18 shows how pixels are referenced in an image that is 200 pixels wide by 200 pixels high.

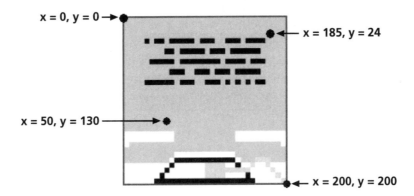

Figure 2-18: Pixel references

The <MAP> tag has only one attribute, NAME, which is used to specify the name of the map. To create a <MAP> tag with a name of imageMap, you use the statement <MAP NAME="imageMap">.

The <AREA> tag is placed between <MAP>...</MAP> tag pairs and contains several attributes, as shown in Figure 2-19.

Attribute	Description
COORDS	The coordinates of the shape in pixels. The coordinates you enter depend on the shape you specify with the SHAPE attribute.
HREF	The URL associated with the area.
NAME	The name of the area.
NOHREF	A placeholder for areas that are not to be associated with a URL.
SHAPE	The shape of the defined region.

Figure 2-19: Common <AREA> tag attributes

When you use the <AREA> tag to define a region as a hot zone on an image map, you use the SHAPE attribute to specify the shape of the region and the COORDS attribute to specify the coordinates of the shape's pixels. The SHAPE attribute can be set to circle, rect (for rectangle), or poly (for polygon). The syntax for each type of shape is as follows:

```
SHAPE=RECT COORDS="upper-left x, upper-left y,
     lower-right x, lower-right y"
SHAPE=CIRCLE COORDS="center-x, center-y, radius"
SHAPE=POLY COORDS="x1,y1, x2,y2, x3,y3,..."
```

To use an image map with an image rendered by the <IMG> tag, you include the USEMAP attribute. The name of the image map must be preceded by the number sign (#) and must be placed within double quotes. The syntax for an <IMG> tag that loads an image named sports.gif and that uses an image map named sports_map is as follows:

```
<IMG SRC="sports.gif" usemap="#sports_map">
```

As with the <A> tag, <AREA> tags can include onMouseOver and onMouseOut event handlers. Figure 2-20 shows an example of an HTML document that creates an image map with four hot zones, one for each quadrant of a rectangle. The total size of the rectangle is 250 pixels in height and 300 pixels in width. Clicking on a hot zone opens the URL corresponding to the HREF attribute in the region's <AREA> tag. The onMouseOver event handler for each region displays custom text in the status bar, and the onMouseOut event handler resets the status bar text to an empty string. Figure 2-21 shows the output.

```
<HTML>
<HEAD>
<TITLE>Sports Map</TITLE>
</HEAD>
<BODY>
<IMG SRC="sports.gif" usemap="#sports_map">
<MAP NAME="sports_map">
<AREA HREF="baseball.html" SHAPE=rect coords="0,0,150,125"
    onMouseOver="status='Baseball Web Page.';
    return true;" onMouseOut="status=''; return true;">
<AREA HREF="football.html" SHAPE=rect coords="150,0,300,125"
    onMouseOver="status='Football Web Page.'; return true"
    onMouseOut="status=''; return true;">
<AREA HREF="soccer.html" SHAPE=rect coords="0,125,150,250"
    onMouseOver="status='Soccer Web Page.'; return true"
    onMouseOut="status=''; return true;">
<AREA HREF="tennis.html" SHAPE=rect    coords="150,125,300,250"
    onMouseOver="status='Tennis Web Page.'; return true"
    onMouseOut="status=''; return true;">
</MAP>
</BODY>
</HTML>
```

Figure 2-20: HTML document with an image map

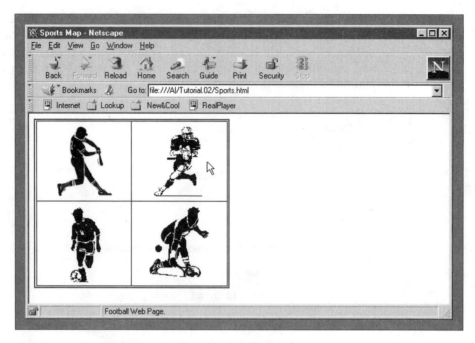

Figure 2-21: Output of an HTML document with an image map

Next you will create the image map of North America that you first previewed at the beginning of this tutorial. The image that is loaded when the Web page is first rendered is a map of North America without any highlighted countries. Passing your mouse over the image highlights each country and displays its name. This is accomplished using a series of maps, one for each North American country. When the mouse passes over a country, a JavaScript function temporarily changes the image being displayed. The maps you will need are in the Tutorial.02 folder on your Student Disk.

To create the image map of North America:

1 First, in the Tutorial.02 folder on your Student Disk create a new folder named **ImageMap**. Copy the six image files **alaska.gif, canada.gif, greenland.gif, continential_us.gif, mexico.gif,** and **north_america.gif** from the Tutorial.02 folder to the new ImageMap folder.

2 Start your text editor or HTML editor and create a new document.

3 Type the opening <HTML> and <HEAD> tags along with the title, opening <SCRIPT> tag, and HTML comments to hide the code from incompatible browsers:

```
<HTML>
<HEAD>
<TITLE>North America</TITLE>
<SCRIPT LANGUAGE="JavaScript1.2">
<!-- HIDE FROM INCOMPATIBLE BROWSERS
```

4 Type the following change_image() function. Each of the onMouseOver event handlers will call this function to display the image associated with each North American country. Each onMouseOver event handler passes the name of the required image file to the argument named image_name. The statement document.north_america.src = image_name; is used to change the image displayed by the <IMG> tag named north_america. You will create the north_america <IMG> tag in the next few steps.

```
function change_image(image_name) {
     document.north_america.src = image_name;
}
```

5 Add the following function that is called by the onMouseOver event handlers to reset the image to north_america.gif once the mouse is moved off a specific country:

```
function reset_image() {
     document.north_america.src = "north_america.gif";
}
```

6 Type the following lines to close the <SCRIPT> and <HEAD> sections:

```
// STOP HIDING FROM INCOMPATIBLE BROWSERS -->
</SCRIPT>
</HEAD>
```

7 Type the opening **<BODY>** tag.

8 Type the following code that creates the image and builds the image map. You should recognize how the onMouseOver and onMouseOut event handlers are passing the names of the necessary image files to the functions. Notice how the onClick event handler returns a value of `false`. This prevents users from directly opening each region's associated image file. Also notice that the <AREA> tags use circle and poly shapes rather than rect.

```
<img src="north_America.gif"
     usemap="#north_America_map" NAME="north_America">
<MAP NAME="north_America_map">
<area shape=circle coords="44,46,20" HREF="alaska.gif"
onMouseOver="change_image('alaska.gif')"
onMouseOut="reset_image()" onClick="return false">
<area shape=poly coords="110,10,144,22,152,60,107,31"
HREF="greenland.gif"
onMouseOver="change_image('greenland.gif')"
onMouseOut="reset_image()" onClick="return false">
<area shape=poly coords=
     "62,45,107,23,162,86,125,111,106,100,55,96,49,64"
HREF="canada.gif"
onMouseOver="change_image('canada.gif')" onMouseOut =
"reset_image()"onClick="return false">
<area shape=poly
coords="60,96,125,105,142,98,134,153,97,155,50,123"
HREF="continental_us.gif"
onMouseOver="change_image('continental_us.gif')"
onMouseOut="reset_image()" onClick="return false">
<area shape=poly
coords="61,135,122,165,109,181,65,159,60,136"
HREF="mexico.gif"
onMouseOver="change_image('mexico.gif')" onMouseOut =
"reset_image()" onClick="return false">
```

help

The HREF attributes in the <AREA> tags do not actually do anything, since the onClick event prevents the hyperlink from functioning by returning a value of false. However, the onMouseOver and onMouseOut events will not function in Navigator if you do not include the HREF attribute.

9   Add the following tags to close the <BODY> and <HTML> tags:

```
</MAP>
</BODY>
</HTML>
```

10   Save the file as **ShowCountry.html** in the ImageMap folder in the **Tutorial.02 folder** on your Student Disk, then open it in your Web browser. Test the program and be sure each image file is being loaded correctly. If you receive errors or the program does not function correctly, check whether you have included all the necessary opening and closing tags. Also make sure you have used the correct case for JavaScript code.

11   Close the browser window.

SUMMARY

- An event or trigger is a specific circumstance that is monitored by JavaScript.

- The <INPUT> tag, which is used for creating input fields that users interact with, generates events. Different types of <INPUT> tag elements generate different events.

- Code that executes in response to a specific event is called an event handler.

- Event handler code is included as an attribute of the HTML tag from which the event is initiated.

- An event handler name is the same as the name of the event itself, but with a prefix of on. The event handler for the Click event is onClick, and the event handler for the Load event is onLoad.

- The built-in JavaScript alert() method displays a popup dialog box with an OK button. The prompt() method displays a dialog box with a message, a text box, a Cancel button, and an OK button.

- There are two types of URLs in an HTML document: absolute and relative. An absolute URL refers to a specific drive and directory or to the full Web address and location of an HTML document. A relative URL specifies the location of a file according to the location of the currently loaded HTML document.

- The confirm() method displays a dialog box with a message, a Cancel button, and an OK button.

- The MouseOver event occurs when the mouse is moved over a link. The MouseOut event occurs when the mouse is moved off a link.

- You can use the JavaScript status property to display custom messages in the status bar.

- An image map consists of an image that is divided into regions. You use the <A> tag to associate each region with a URL.

- An image's pixels are referenced using x-axis and y-axis coordinates, starting at the upper-left corner of the image's rectangle and ending at the lower-right corner.

- You include the USEMAP attribute to use an image map with an image rendered by the <IMG> tag.

- The <AREA> tag can include onMouseOver and onMouseOut event handlers.

QUESTIONS

1. A(n) _____, or trigger, is a specific circumstance that is monitored by JavaScript.
   a. notification
   b. event
   c. alert
   d. prompt

2. The _____ event occurs when an HTML document finishes loading in a Web browser.
   a. load
   b. complete
   c. display
   d. click

3. The _____ tag is used for creating input fields that interact with users.
   a. <INTERFACE>
   b. <USERRESPONSE>
   c. <BUTTON>
   d. <INPUT>

4. What is the correct case of the Click event handler?
   a. OnClick
   b. onCLICK
   c. onClick
   d. event handlers are not case-sensitive

5. Which of the following is the correct syntax?
   a. onClick="alert('You clicked a button!');"
   b. onClick="alert("You clicked a button!");"
   c. onClick="alert(You clicked a button!);"
   d. onClick=alert('You clicked a button!');

6. Multiple JavaScript statements in an event handler
   a. are contained within separate sets of parentheses.
   b. must be separated with the <BR> tag.
   c. must be separated by semicolons.
   d. You cannot include multiple JavaScript statements in an event handler.

7. Which of the following is not a valid JavaScript built-in dialog box function?
   a. confirm()
   b. alert()
   c. prompt()
   d. message()

8. The text or image used to represent a link in an HTML document is known as a(n) _____.
   a. placeholder
   b. anchor
   c. hookup
   d. chain

9. There are two types of URLs: absolute and _____.
   a. static
   b. nonabsolute
   c. permanent
   d. relative

10. You have multiple HTML documents within the same folder that are linked to each other with absolute URLs. If you move the documents to a different Web site,

    a. you must manually update each of the URLs.

    b. it is unnecessary to update the URLs.

    c. the URLs will function correctly provided that they are placed in a folder with the same name as the original.

    d. the URLs will automatically update themselves to reflect the new Web site location.

11. Which of the following is the correct syntax for canceling a link's Click event?

    a. `<A HREF="HomePage.html" onClick="return true;">`

    b. `<A HREF="HomePage.html" onClick="return false;">`

    c. `<A HREF="HomePage.html" onClick="return cancel;">`

    d. `<A HREF="HomePage.html" onClick="return override;">`

12. Which of the following is the correct syntax for printing *Welcome to My Home Page* in the status bar, using the MouseOver event?

    a. `<A HREF="HomePage.html" onMouseOver="status = 'Welcome to My Home Page; return true;">Welcome to My Home Page</A>`

    b. `<A HREF="HomePage.html" onMouseOver="status = true;">Welcome to My Home Page</A>`

    c. `<A HREF="HomePage.html" onMouseOver="status = 'Welcome to My Home Page'; return true;">My Home Page</A>`

    d. `<A HREF="HomePage.html" onMouseOver=status = 'Welcome to My Home Page'; return true;>My Home Page</A>`

13. The default text that appears in the status bar whenever the mouse is not positioned over a link is set using the _____ property.

    a. originalStatus

    b. onMouseOutDefault

    c. defaultText

    d. defaultStatus

14. Which of the following tags is not required for an image map?

    a. `<IMG>`

    b. `<MAP>`

    c. `<AREA>`

    d. `<IMAGEMAP>`

15. A(n) _____ represents a single point on a computer screen.

    a. pixel

    b. bit

    c. cell

    d. element

16. Which of the following shapes is not a valid option of the SHAPE attribute of the `<AREA>` tag?

    a. circle

    b. rectangle

    c. triangle

    d. polygon

E X E R C I S E S

1. Create an HTML document containing a list of links to your favorite Web sites. Create a unique function for each link. Call the functions using each link's onClick event handler. Each function should display a confirm dialog box asking if the user really wants to visit the associated Web page. Save the file as ConfirmLinks.html in the Tutorial.02 folder on your Student Disk.

2. Create a political survey as an HTML document. Create the survey using text fields in a form. Use fields that ask users for their political party affiliation, what state they live in, and the politicians for whom they voted for president, governor, senator, and so on. Include an onLoad event handler that writes *This is an online political survey* to the status bar. As the user enters each field, use an onFocus event handler to display helpful information in the status bar. As the user leaves a text field, use an onBlur event handler to display an alert dialog box containing the information they typed in that text field. Also include an onUnload event handler that displays an alert dialog box containing the text *Thank you for filling out the survey.* Save the file as PoliticalSurvey.html in the Tutorial.02 folder on your Student Disk.

3. Create an "angry" link using the text *Don't Touch Me!*. When your mouse passes over the link, write the text *Whatever You Do, Do NOT Click Me!* to the status bar. Use the onMouseOut event handler to write the text *Thanks for Leaving Me Alone* to the status bar. Use the document ReallyMadLink.html as the link's HREF attribute. Save the file as MadLink.html in the Tutorial.02 folder on your Student Disk. Also create the ReallyMadLink.html file in the Tuorial.02 folder on your Student Disk. The ReallyMadLink.html file should use an onLoad event handler to change the document's background color to black. The onLoad event handler should also display an alert dialog box containing the text *Now You Have Really Made Me Mad!* The ReallyMadLink.html file should include the same "angry" link using the text *Don't Touch Me!*. The onMouseOver event handler for the ReallyMadLink.html file's *Don't Touch Me!* link should write *I will not calm down until you click me again!* to the status bar. Clicking the link redisplays the MadLink.html document.

4. Use a graphics program, such as Paint, to create an image of a stick figure (or a more developed figure, if you have artistic skills). Create an HTML file named BodyParts.html that includes an image map of the stick figure. Create hot spots over each of the figure's body parts. When a mouse passes over each body part, display the part's name in the status bar. Also create alert dialog boxes that display each body part's name when you click it.

5. Create an image map using a scanned photograph of your family and name it FamilyImageMap.html. (If you do not have access to a scanner or digital camera, search the Internet for any public domain family photograph that you can use for practice.) Include an onLoad event handler that writes your family name to the status bar using the defaultStatus property. Create a hotspot over each individual in the photo that writes his or her name and relationship to you in the status bar. Create a personal Web page for each family member that opens when you click on his or her image. Include information about each family member on his or her personal Web page. Also include a link back to the FamilyImageMap Web page.

6. Use a graphics program, such as Paint, to create an image containing the names of animals, then search the Internet for public domain clipart images that represent each animal. Create an HTML document named ShowAnimal.html. In the ShowAnimal.html file, create an image map for the graphic you created that contains the names of the animals. Use each animal's name as a hot spot that displays a picture of the animal when your mouse passes over its name. Create a temporary image that displays the text *Click an animal's name to display its picture here.* when your mouse is not positioned over an animal's name.

Data Types and Operators

case ▶ One of WebAdventure's long-term clients is a large bank, GlobalBank, with an elaborate Web site. The bank likes to add interactive features to its Web site on a regular basis to entice customers to use its online banking services. So far, WebAdventure has added a mortgage calculator and a car loan calculator to GlobalBank's Web site. Recently GlobalBank's marketing department requested that a simple calculator, which customers can use when conducting online transactions or balancing their accounts, be added to the Web site. Your boss, impressed by how quickly you are picking up JavaScript, has put you in charge of developing this calculator program.

Previewing the Calculator Program

In this tutorial, you will create a JavaScript calculator program that displays an online calculator. To create the calculator, you must learn how to work with variables, data types, and operators.

To preview the calculator program:

1   In your Web browser, open the **Tutorial3Calculator.html** file from the Tutorial.03 folder on your Student Disk. An online calculator appears, as shown in Figure 3-1.

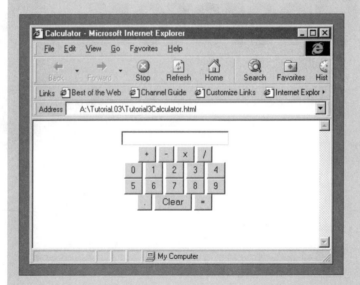

Figure 3-1: Tutorial3Calculator.html

2   Use your mouse to perform various types of calculations with the calculator to see how it works.

3   Next, open the **Tutorial3Calculator.html file** in your text editor or HTML editor and examine the code. In the head of the document, notice the <INPUT> tags and the updateString() function, which work together to perform calculations.

4   Close your text editor or HTML editor when you are finished examining the code.

In this section you will learn:
■ How to use data types
■ About numeric data types
■ About Boolean values
■ How to use strings
■ How to use arrays

Using Data Types and Arrays

Data Types

Variables can contain many different kinds of values—for examples the time, a dollar amount, or a person's name. The values or data contained in JavaScript variables can be classified by categories known as data types. A **data type** is the specific category of information that a variable contains. Data types that can be assigned only a single value are called **primitive types**. JavaScript supports five primitive data types: integer numbers, floating-point numbers, Boolean values, strings, and the null value, all of which are described in Figure 3-2.

Data Type	Description
Integer numbers	Positive or negative numbers with no decimal places
Floating-point numbers	Positive or negative numbers with decimal places or numbers written using exponential notation
Boolean	A logical value of true or false
String	Text such as "Hello World"
Null	An empty value

Figure 3-2: Primitive types

The null value is a data type as well as a value that can be assigned to a variable. Assigning the value null to a variable indicates the variable does not contain a value. A variable with a value of null has a value assigned to it—null is really the value "no value." In contrast, an undefined variable (which you learned about in Tutorial 2) has never had a value assigned to it, has not been declared, or does not exist.

Many programming languages require that you declare the type of data that a variable contains. Programming languages that require you to declare the data types of variables are called **strongly-typed programming languages.** Strong typing is also known as **static typing,** since data types do not change after they have been declared. Programming languages that do not require you to declare the data types of variables are called **loosely-typed programming languages.** Loose typing is also known as **dynamic typing** since data types can change after they have been declared. JavaScript is a loosely-typed programming language. Not only are you not required to declare the data type of variables in JavaScript, you are not allowed to do so. Instead, the JavaScript interpreter automatically determines what type of data is stored in a variable and assigns the variable's data type accordingly. The following code demonstrates how a variable's data type changes automatically each time the variable is assigned a new literal value.

```
changingVariable = "Hello World";  // String
changingVariable = 8;              // Integer number
changingVariable = 5.367;          // Floating-point number
changingVariable = true;           // Boolean
changingVariable = null;           // null
```

The data type of variables can change during the course of program execution. This can cause problems if you attempt to perform an arithmetic operation and one of the variables is a string or the null value. JavaScript includes a typeof() operator that you can use to determine the data type of a variable. An operator is used for manipulating different parts of a statement. (You will learn about operators in Section B.) The syntax for the typeof() operator is `typeof(variablename);`. The values that can be returned by the typeof() operator are listed in Figure 3-3.

Return Value	Returned For
Number	Integers and floating-point numbers
String	Text strings
Boolean	True or false
Object	Objects, arrays, and null variables
Function	Functions
Undefined	Undefined variables

Figure 3-3: Values returned by typeof() operator

Next you will create a program that assigns different data types to a variable and prints the variable's data type. You will use the typeof() operator to determine the data type of each variable.

To create a program that assigns different data types to a variable and prints the variable's data type:

1 Start your text editor or HTML editor and create a new document.

2 Type the <HTML> and <HEAD> sections of the document:

```
<HTML>
<HEAD>
<TITLE>Print Data Types</TITLE>
</HEAD>
```

 tip

As you recall from Tutorial 1, JavaScript code can be placed in either the <HEAD> or <BODY> section. Where you place your JavaScript code will vary, depending on the program you are writing.

3 Add the following code to begin the body of the HTML document and create a preformatted text container:

```
<BODY>
<PRE>
```

4 Add the opening statements for a JavaScript section:

```
<SCRIPT LANGUAGE="JavaScript1.2">
<!-- HIDE FROM INCOMPATIBLE BROWSERS
```

5 Declare a variable named differentType by typing the statement **var differentType;**.

6 Type the following line, which prints the data type contained in the differentType variable. The data type is currently undefined, since it has not yet been assigned a value.

```
document.writeln("The differentType variable is "
    + typeof(differentType));
```

7 Add the following two lines, which assign a string to the differentType variable and repeat the statement that prints the data type.

```
differentType = "This is a text string.";
document.writeln("The differentType variable is "
    + typeof(differentType));
```

8 Now add the following lines, which change the differentType variable to the integer, floating-point, Boolean, and null data types. The statement that prints each data type repeats each time the variable's data type changes.

```
differentType = 100;
document.writeln("The differentType variable is "
     + typeof(differentType));
differentType = 3.679;
document.writeln("The differentType variable is "
     + typeof(differentType));
differentType = false;
document.writeln("The differentType variable is "
     + typeof(differentType));
differentType = null;
document.writeln("The differentType variable is "
     + typeof(differentType));
```

9 Add the following code to close the <SCRIPT>, <PRE>, <BODY>, and <HTML> tags:

```
// STOP HIDING FROM INCOMPATIBLE BROWSERS -->
</SCRIPT>
</PRE>
</BODY>
</HTML>
```

10 Save the file as **PrintDataTypes.html** in the Tutorial.03 folder on your Student Disk. Open the **PrintDataTypes.html** file in your Web browser. You should see the same lines as displayed in Figure 3-4.

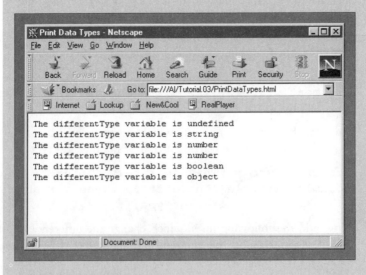

Figure 3-4: PrintDataTypes.html

11 Close the Web browser window.

Numeric Data Types

Numeric data types are an important part of any programming language, and are particularly useful when doing arithmetic calculations. JavaScript supports two numeric data types: integers and floating-point numbers. An **integer** is a positive or negative number with no decimal places. Integer values in JavaScript can range from −9007199254740992 (-2^{53}) to 9007199254740992 (2^{53}). The numbers -250, -13, 0, 2, 6, 10, 100, and 10000 are examples of integers. The numbers -6.16, -4.4, 3.17, .52, 10.5, and 2.7541 are not integers; they are floating-point numbers, since they contain decimal places. A **floating-point number** contains decimal places or is written using exponential notation. **Exponential notation**, or **scientific notation**, is a way of writing very large numbers or numbers with many decimal places, using a shortened format. Numbers written in exponential notation are represented by a value between 1 and 10 multiplied by 10 raised to some power. The value of 10 is written with an uppercase or lowercase *E*. For example, the number 200,000,000,000 can be written in exponential notation as 2.0e11, which means "two times ten to the eleventh power." Floating-point values in JavaScript range from approximately $\pm 1.7976931348623157 \times 10^{308}$ to $\pm 5 \times 10^{-324}$.

▶ **tip**

•••

Floating-point values that exceed the largest positive value of $\pm 1.7976931348623157 \times 10^{308}$ result in a special value of `Infinity`. Floating-point values that exceed the smallest negative value of $\pm 5 \times 10^{-324}$ result in a value of `−Infinity`.

•••

Next you will create a program that assigns integers and exponential numbers to variables and prints the values.

To create a program that assigns integers and exponential numbers to variables and prints the values:

1 Start your text editor or HTML editor and create a new document.

2 Type the <HTML> and <HEAD> sections of the document:

```
<HTML>
<HEAD>
<TITLE>Print Numbers</TITLE>
</HEAD>
```

3 Add the following code to begin the body of the HTML document and to create a preformatted text container:

```
<BODY>
<PRE>
```

4   Add the opening statements for a JavaScript section.

```
<SCRIPT LANGUAGE="JavaScript1.2">
<!-- HIDE FROM INCOMPATIBLE BROWSERS
```

5   Add the following lines that declare an integer variable and a floating-point variable:

```
var integerVar = 150;
var floatingPointVar = 3.0e7;
// floating-point number 30000000
```

6   Now add the following statements to print the variables:

```
document.writeln(integerVar);
document.writeln(floatingPointVar);
```

7   Add the following code to close the <SCRIPT>, <PRE>, <BODY>, and <HTML> tags:

```
// STOP HIDING FROM INCOMPATIBLE BROWSERS -->
</SCRIPT>
</PRE>
</BODY>
</HTML>
```

8   Save the file as **PrintNumbers.html** in the Tutorial.03 folder on your Student Disk. Open the **PrintNumbers.html** file in your Web browser. The integer 150 and the exponential expression 3.0e7 or the number 30,000,000 should appear in your Web browser window.

9   Close the Web browser window.

Boolean Values

A **Boolean value** is a logical value of true or false. You can also think of a Boolean value as being *yes* or *no*, or *on* or *off*. Boolean values are most often used for decision making and comparing data. You used Boolean values in Tutorial 2 when you overrode an internal event handler with your own code. When you override an internal event handler with your own code, you are required to return a value of true or false, using the return statement. You also used the confirm dialog box to return a value of true or false to an event handler. When a user clicks the OK button in the confirm dialog box, a value of true is returned, while clicking the Cancel button returns a value of false. Figure 3-5 displays the program you first saw in Tutorial 2 that demonstrates how a Boolean value is returned to an event handler.

```
<HTML>

<HEAD>

<TITLE>Custom onClick Event Example</TITLE>

<SCRIPT LANGUAGE="JavaScript1.2">

<!-- HIDE FROM INCOMPATIBLE BROWSERS

function warnUser() {

    // The following line generates a Boolean value of true or

    // false and returns it to the event handler

    return confirm(
"This link is only for people who love golden retrievers!");

}

// STOP HIDING FROM INCOMPATIBLE BROWSERS -->

</SCRIPT>

</HEAD>

<BODY>

<A HREF = "GoldenRetrievers.html" onClick = "return
warnUser();">Golden Retriever Club Home Page</A>

</BODY>

</HTML>
```

Figure 3-5: Program that returns a Boolean value to an event handler

In JavaScript programming, you can only use the words true and false to indicate Boolean values. In other programming languages, you can use the integer values of 1 and 0 to indicate Boolean values of true and false—1 indicates true and 0 indicates false. JavaScript converts the values true and false to the integers 1 and 0 when necessary. For example, when you attempt to use a Boolean variable of true in a mathematical operation, JavaScript converts the variable to an integer value of 1.

Boolean values get their name from the nineteenth-century mathematician George Boole, who is credited with developing the theories of mathematical logic.

Strings

A text string contains zero or more characters surrounded by double or single quotation marks. Examples of strings you may use in a program are company names, user names, comments, and other types of text. You can use text strings as literal values or assign them to a variable. You first used literal strings with the document.write() and document.writeln() functions in Tutorial 1. Variables can be assigned a zero-length string value called an empty string. For example, `emptyVariable = ""`; assigns an empty string to the variable emptyVariable. Empty strings are valid values for string literals and are not considered to be null or undefined.

When you want to include a quoted string within a literal string surrounded by double quotation marks, you surround the quoted string with single quotation marks. When you want to include a quoted string within a literal string surrounded by single quotation marks, you surround the quoted string with double quotation marks. Whichever method you use, a string must begin and end with the same type of quotation marks. For example, `document.write("This is a text string.")`; is valid, since it starts and ends with double quotation marks. The statement `document.write("This is a text string.')`; is invalid, since it starts with a double quotation mark and ends with a single quotation mark. In this case you would receive an error message, since the Web browser cannot tell where the literal strings begin and end. Figure 3-6 shows an example of a program that prints literal strings. Figure 3-7 displays the output.

```
<HTML>
<HEAD>
<TITLE>Literal Strings</TITLE>
</HEAD>
<BODY>
<PRE>
<SCRIPT LANGUAGE="JavaScript1.2">
document.writeln("This is a literal string");
document.writeln("This string contains a 'quoted' string");
document.writeln('This is another example of a "quoted" string');
var firstString = "This literal string was assigned to a variable.";
```

Figure 3-6: LiteralStrings program

```
var secondString = 'This literal string was also assigned to a variable.';

document.writeln(firstString);

document.writeln(secondString);

</SCRIPT>

</PRE>

</BODY>

</HTML>
```

Figure 3-6: LiteralStrings program (continued)

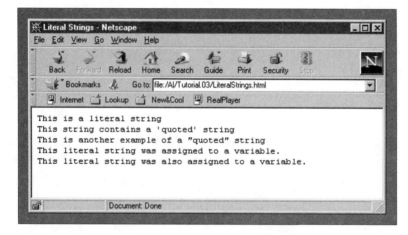

Figure 3-7: Output of LiteralStrings program in a Web browser

Unlike other programming languages, there is no special data type in JavaScript for a single character, such as the *char* data type in the C, C++, and Java programming languages.

You need to use extra care when using single quotations with possessives and contractions in strings, since the JavaScript interpreter always looks for the first closing single or double quotation mark to match an opening single or double quotation mark. For example, consider the following statement:

```
document.writeln('My city's zip code is 01562.');
```

This statement causes an error. The JavaScript interpreter assumes that the literal string ends with the apostrophe following *city* and looks for the closing parentheses for the document.writeln() function immediately following *city's*. To get around this problem, you include an escape character before the apostrophe in *city's*. An **escape character** tells the compiler or interpreter that the character that follows it has a special purpose. In JavaScript, the escape character is the backslash (\). Placing a backslash in front of an apostrophe tells the JavaScript interpreter that the apostrophe is to be treated as a regular keyboard character, such as a, b, 1, or 2, and not as part of a single quotation mark pair that encloses a text string. The backslash in the following statement tells the JavaScript interpreter to print the apostrophe following the word *city* as an apostrophe.

```
document.writeln('My city\'s zip code is 01562.');
```

You can also use the escape character in combination with other characters to insert a special character into a string. When you combine the escape character with other characters, the combination is called an **escape sequence**. The backslash followed by an apostrophe (\') and the backslash followed by a double quotation mark (\") are both examples of escape sequences. Most escape sequences carry out special functions. For example, the escape sequence \t inserts a tab into a string. Figure 3-8 describes some of the escape sequences that can be added to a string in JavaScript.

Escape Sequence	Character
\b	Backspace
\f	Form feed
\n	New line
\r	Carriage return
\t	Horizontal tab
\'	Single quotation mark
\"	Double quotation mark
\\	Backslash

Figure 3-8: JavaScript escape sequences

Notice that one of the characters generated by an escape sequence is the backslash. Since the escape character itself is a backslash, you must use the escape sequence "\\" to include a backslash as a character in a string. For example, to include the path "C:\WebPages\JavaScript_Files\" in a string, you must include two backslashes for every single backslash you want to appear in the string, as in the following statement:

```
document.writeln("My JavaScript files are located in
C:\\WebPages\\JavaScript_Files\\");
```

Figure 3-9 shows an example of a program containing strings with several escape sequences. Figure 3-10 shows the output.

```
<HTML>

<HEAD>

<TITLE>Escape Sequences</TITLE>

</HEAD>

<BODY>

<PRE>

<SCRIPT LANGUAGE="JavaScript1.2">

document.writeln("This line is printed \non two lines.");
    // New line

document.writeln("\tThis line includes a horizontal tab.");
    // Horizontal tab

document.writeln("My personal files are in c:\\personal.");
    // Backslash

document.writeln("My dog's name is \"Noah.\"");
    // Double quotation mark

document.writeln('Massachusetts\' capital is Boston.');
    // Single quotation mark

</SCRIPT>

</PRE>

</BODY>

</HTML>
```

Figure 3-9: Program containing strings with escape sequences

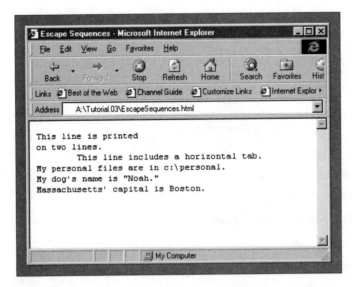

Figure 3-10: Output of program containing strings with escape sequences

In addition to including escape sequences in strings, you can include HTML tags. If you include HTML tags within JavaScript strings, they must be located within a string's opening and closing quotation marks. For example, to include the line break tag <BR> in a string printed with the document.write() function, the statement should read `document.write("There is a line break following this sentence.<BR>");`. HTML tags cannot be used directly within JavaScript code. Therefore, the statement `document.write("There is a line break following this sentence."<BR>);` causes an error, since the <BR> tag is located outside of the literal string. Figure 3-11 shows an example of a program containing strings with HTML tags. Figure 3-12 shows the output.

```
<HTML>

<HEAD>

<TITLE>Strings with HTML Tags</TITLE>

</HEAD>

<BODY>

<PRE>

<SCRIPT LANGUAGE="JavaScript1.2">

heading1_string = "<H1>Hello World (this is the H1 tag)</H1>";

document.writeln(heading1_string);
```

Figure 3-11: Program containing strings with HTML tags

```
heading2_string = "<H2>This line is formatted with the H2 tag</H2>";
document.writeln(heading2_string);
italic_string = "<I>This line is italicized.</I>";
document.writeln(italic_string);
bold_string = "<B>This line is bolded.</B>";
document.writeln(bold_string);
underlined_string = "<U>This line is underlined.</U>";
document.writeln(underlined_string);
formatted_string = "This line includes <I>italicized</I>,
    <B>bolded</B>, and <U>underlined</U> text.";
document.writeln(formatted_string);
hr_string = "Following this line is a horizontal rule.<HR>";
document.writeln(hr_string);
</SCRIPT>
</PRE>
</BODY>
</HTML>
```

Figure 3-11: Program containing strings with HTML tags (continued)

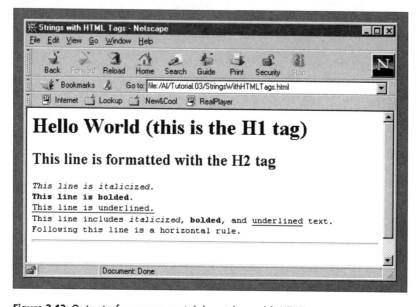

Figure 3-12: Output of program containing strings with HTML tags

Next you will create a file that displays a restaurant's daily menu, by combining strings with escape characters and HTML tags. Note that you can create the same document more easily using only HTML tags. The purpose of this exercise is to demonstrate how text strings can be combined with HTML tags and escape characters.

To create a file that combines strings with escape characters and HTML tags:

1 Start your text editor or HTML editor and create a new document.

2 Type the <HTML> and <HEAD> sections of the document, along with the opening <BODY> tag:

```
<HTML>
<HEAD>
<TITLE>Daily Specials</TITLE>
</HEAD>
<BODY>
```

3 Add the opening statements for a JavaScript section:

```
<SCRIPT LANGUAGE="JavaScript1.2">
<!-- HIDE FROM INCOMPATIBLE BROWSERS
```

4 Declare the following variables and assign strings containing combinations of text, HTML tags, and escape characters.

```
var restaurant = "<H1>Small Town Restaurant</H1><BR>";
var specials = "<H2>Daily Specials for Wednesday</H2>";
var prixfixe = "<I>Prix fixe price:</I> <B>$9.95</B><HR>";
var appetizer = "<H3>Caesar Salad</H3>";
var entree = "<H3>Chef\'s \"Surprise\"</H3>";
var dessert = "<H3>Chocolate Cheesecake</H3><HR>";
```

5 Next, add the following statements to print the variables:

```
document.write(restaurant);
document.write(specials);
document.write(prixfixe);
document.write(appetizer);
document.write(entree);
document.write(dessert);
```

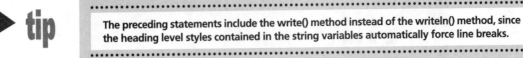

The preceding statements include the write() method instead of the writeln() method, since the heading level styles contained in the string variables automatically force line breaks.

6 Add the following code to close the <SCRIPT>, <PRE>, <BODY>, and <HTML> tags:

```
// STOP HIDING FROM INCOMPATIBLE BROWSERS -->
</SCRIPT>
</BODY>
</HTML>
```

7 Save the file as **DailySpecials.html** in the **Tutorial.03** folder on your Student Disk. Open the **DailySpecials.html** file in your Web browser. Figure 3-13 shows the output.

Figure 3-13: Output of DailySpecials.html

8 Close the Web browser window.

Arrays

An **array** contains a set of data represented by a single variable name. You can think of an array as a collection of variables contained within a single variable. An array is a JavaScript object. In Tutorial 2, you learned how to create objects with the constructor function and the new keyword. Since arrays are objects, you create them using the new keyword and JavaScript's Array() constructor object. The Array() object is comparable to a constructor function and is created using similar syntax, as follows:

```
variable_name = new Array(number of elements);
```

Notice that the Array() constructor object receives a single argument representing the number of elements to be contained in the array. Each piece of data contained in an array is called an **element**. The following code creates an array named animals_list with five elements:

```
animals_list = new Array(5);
```

The numbering of elements within an array starts with an index number of zero (0). You refer to a specific element by enclosing its index number in brackets at the end of the array name. For example, the first element in the animals_list array is animals_list[0], the second element is animals_list[1], the third element is animals_list[2], and so on. You assign values to individual array elements in the same fashion as you assign values to a standard variable, except that you include the index for an individual element of the array. The following code assigns values to the five elements within the animals_list array:

```
animals_list[0] = "dog";       // first element
animals_list[1] = "cat";       // second element
animals_list[2] = "horse";     // third element
animals_list[3] = "elephant";  // fourth element
animals_list[4] = "llama";     // fifth element
```

You use an element in an array in the same manner you use other types of variables. For example, the following code prints the values contained in the five elements of the animals_list array:

```
document.writeln(animals_list[0]); // prints "dog"
document.writeln(animals_list[1]); // prints "cat"
document.writeln(animals_list[2]); // prints "horse"
document.writeln(animals_list[3]); // prints "elephant"
document.writeln(animals_list[4]); // prints "llama"
```

Once you have assigned a value to an array element, you can change it later just as you can change other variables in a program. To change the first array element in the animals_list array from *dog* to *moose*, you include the statement `animals_list[0] = "moose";` in your code. There are no limits placed on the data types that can be stored in the elements of an array. For example, the following code creates an array and stores multiple data types in the array's elements:

```
multiple_types = new Array(5);
multiple_types[0] = "Hello World"; // string
multiple_types[1] = 10;            // integer
multiple_types[2] = 3.156;         // floating-point
multiple_types[3] = true;          // Boolean
multiple_types[4] = null;          // null
```

When you create a new array with the Array() constructor object, declaring the number of array elements is optional. You can create the array without any elements and add new elements to the array as necessary. The size of an array can change dynamically. If you assign a value to an uncreated elements in an array, the element is created automatically, along with any uncreated elements that precede it. For example, the first statement in the following code creates the animal_list array without any elements. The second statement then assigns *aardvark* to the third element, which creates the first two elements (animal_list[0] and animal_list[1]) in the process.

```
animal_list = new Array();
animal_list[2] = "aardvark";
```

Array elements that are created but not assigned values have an initial value of null.

You can assign values to an array's elements when you first create the array. The following code assigns values to the animal_list array when it is created, then prints each of the values, using the array's element numbers:

```
animals_list = new Array("dog", "cat", "horse");
document.writeln(animals_list[0]); // prints "dog"
document.writeln(animals_list[1]); // prints "cat"
document.writeln(animals_list[2]); // prints "horse"
```

Next you will create an array containing the months of the year.

To create an array containing the months of the year:

1 Start your text editor or HTML editor and create a new document.

2 Type the <HTML> and <HEAD> sections of the document:

```
<HTML>
<HEAD>
<TITLE>Months of the Year</TITLE>
</HEAD>
```

3 Add the following code to begin the body of the HTML document and create a preformatted text container:

```
<BODY>
<PRE>
```

4 Add the opening statements for a JavaScript section:

```
<SCRIPT LANGUAGE="JavaScript1.2">
<!-- HIDE FROM INCOMPATIBLE BROWSERS
```

5 Type this statement to declare a new array containing 12 elements:
`var monthsOfYear = new Array(12);`.

6 Assign the 12 months of the year to the 12 elements of the array. Remember that the first element in an array starts with 0. Therefore, the element in the array that will hold January is monthsOfYear[0].

```
monthsOfYear[0] = "January";
monthsOfYear[1] = "February";
monthsOfYear[2] = "March";
monthsOfYear[3] = "April";
monthsOfYear[4] = "May";
monthsOfYear[5] = "June";
monthsOfYear[6] = "July";
monthsOfYear[7] = "August";
monthsOfYear[8] = "September";
monthsOfYear[9] = "October";
monthsOfYear[10] = "November";
monthsOfYear[11] = "December";
```

7 Next, add the following statements to print each element of the array:

```
document.writeln(monthsOfYear[0]);
document.writeln(monthsOfYear[1]);
document.writeln(monthsOfYear[2]);
document.writeln(monthsOfYear[3]);
document.writeln(monthsOfYear[4]);
document.writeln(monthsOfYear[5]);
document.writeln(monthsOfYear[6]);
document.writeln(monthsOfYear[7]);
document.writeln(monthsOfYear[8]);
document.writeln(monthsOfYear[9]);
document.writeln(monthsOfYear[10]);
document.writeln(monthsOfYear[11]);
```

 tip

A looping statement provides a more efficient method for printing all the elements of an array. You will learn about looping statements in Tutorial 4.

8 Add the following code to close the <SCRIPT>, <PRE>, <BODY>, and <HTML> tags:

```
// STOP HIDING FROM INCOMPATIBLE BROWSERS -->
</SCRIPT>
</PRE>
</BODY>
</HTML>
```

9 Save the file as **MonthsOfYear.html** in the **Tutorial.03** folder on your Student Disk. Then open the **MonthsOfYear.html** file in your Web browser. Figure 3-14 shows the output.

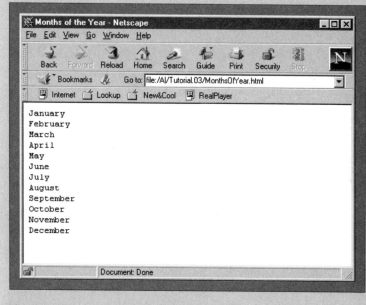

Figure 3-14: Output of MonthsOfYear.html

10 Close the Web browser window.

SUMMARY

- A data type is the specific category of information that a variable contains.

- Data types that can only be assigned a single value are called primitive types.

- The null value is a data type as well as a value that can be assigned to a variable. Assigning the value `null` to a variable indicates the variable does not contain a value.

- JavaScript uses loose typing or dynamic typing and does not require data types of variables to be declared. In JavaScript, data types can change after they have been declared.

- An integer is a positive or negative number with no decimal point.

- A floating-point number contains decimal places or is written using exponential notation. Exponential notation, or scientific notation, is a way of writing very large numbers or numbers with many decimal places, using a shortened format.

■ A Boolean value is a logical value of true or false.

■ Literal strings and string variables contain zero or more characters. A string consisting of zero characters is called an empty string.

■ An escape character is used to tell the compiler or interpreter that the character that follows it has a special purpose. When the escape character is combined with other characters, it is called an escape sequence.

■ An array contains a set of data represented by a single variable name. Each piece of data contained in an array is called an element.

■ You create an array with the Array() constructor object. The Array() constructor object receives a single argument representing the number of elements to be contained in the array. Specifying the number of array elements is optional.

■ The numbering of elements within an array starts with an index number of zero (0).

■ You can create an array without any elements and then add new elements to the array as needed.

■ The size of an array can change dynamically.

■ You can assign values to an array's elements when you first create the array.

QUESTIONS

1. Data types that can be assigned only a single value are called _____ types.
    a. simple
    b. rudimentary
    c. primitive
    d. single-value

2. Which of the following is not a primitive data type?
    a. string
    b. number
    c. Boolean
    d. object

3. Text that is enclosed within quotation marks is _____
    a. a literal string
    b. quoted text
    c. a comment
    d. an element

4. A loosely-typed programming language _____.
    a. does not require data types of variables to be declared
    b. requires data types of variables to be declared
    c. does not have different data types
    d. does not have variables

5. You can determine the data type of a variable using the _____.
    a. returnValue function
    b. typeof() operator
    c. parseFloat() function
    d. toString operator

6. Which of the following is not an integer?
    a. 7.6
    b. 12
    c. 010
    d. 0x1A

7. Which of the following is not a floating-point number?
    a. -439.35
    b. 3.17
    c. 10
    d. -7e11

8. Boolean values in JavaScript are the logical values _____.
    a. minimum and maximum
    b. positive and negative
    c. 0 and 1
    d. true and false

9. Which of the following is the correct syntax for including double quotation marks within a string that is already surrounded by double quotation marks?
    a. `"Some computers have \"artificial\" intelligence."`
    b. `"Some computers have "artificial" intelligence."`
    c. `"Some computers have /"artificial/" intelligence."`
    d. `"Some computers have ""artificial"" intelligence."`

10. The numbering of elements within an array starts with an index number of _____.
    a. -1
    b. 0
    c. 1
    d. 2

11. What is the correct syntax for creating an array?
    a. `variable_name = new Array;`
    b. `variable_name = Array(number of elements);`
    c. `variable_name = new Array(number of elements);`
    d. `new Array(number of elements);`

12. Which of the following refers to the first element in an array named employees[]?
    a. employees[0]
    b. employees[1]
    c. employees[first]
    d. employees[a]

EXERCISES

Save the following exercises in the Tutorial.03 folder on your Student Disk.

1. Create an HTML document that displays a simplified version of your work history, including the names of your former employers, position within each company, and dates of employment. When you create the document, include all HTML commands inside string variables. Also, use the document.write() method instead of the document.writeln() method. To create line breaks, use either an escape character or an HTML tag within the string variables. Save the document as WorkHistory.html.

2. Create an HTML document containing personal information, including your name, age, the type of car you have, the mortgage interest on your house or loan interest on your car, and whether you have a dog. Print each piece of information using the write() or writeln() methods. Next to each item, use the typeof operator to print a message with the item's data type. Be sure to create items for the string, number, and Boolean data types. For example, your name will be the string data type, your age will be the number data type, and an answer of true or false to whether you have a dog will be the Boolean data type. Save the document as PersonalInfo.html.

3. Create an HTML document containing your resume. Use the write() method to build heading sections such as your name, address, former employer names, and dates of employment. Format the heading sections using HTML tags and escape sequences within the text strings that build each line. Create the main paragraphs of the resume in the body section of the document. You will need to use multiple script sections. Save the document as Resume.html in the Tutorial.03 folder on your Student Disk.

4. Create an HTML document that creates and prints an array of all the family members you can think of. The array should be contained in a <SCRIPT> section in the document's <BODY>. Save the document as FamilyArray.html.

5. Create an HTML document that uses arrays to print your favorite songs from the 1990s, along with the year each song was released. Use two arrays in the document, and place them in a <SCRIPT> section in the document's <BODY>. Name the first array songs[] and fill it with a list of your favorite songs from the 1990s. Create another array containing 10 elements for each year in the 90s decade (1990, 1991, 1992, etc.). Name this second array nineties[ ]. Using the arrays, print each song, along with the year it was released. Save the document as SongYears.html.

SECTION B

objectives

In this section you will learn:

- How to use expressions
- How to use arithmetic, assignment, comparison, logical, and string operators
- How to create the calculator program

Expressions and Operators

Expressions

Variables and data become most useful when you use them in an expression. An **expression** is a combination of literal values, variables, operators, and other expressions that can be evaluated by the JavaScript interpreter to produce a result. The JavaScript interpreter recognizes the literal values and variables in Figure 3-15 as expressions.

```
"this is a string variable"    // string literal expression
10                             // integer literal expression
3.156                          // floating-point literal expression
true                           // Boolean literal expression
null                           // null literal expression
employee_number                // variable expression
```

Figure 3-15: Literal and variable expressions

You can use operands and operators to create more complex expressions. **Operands** are variables and literals contained in an expression. **Operators** are symbols used in expressions to manipulate operands. You have worked with several simple expressions so far that combine operators and operands. Consider the following statement:

```
myNumber = 100;
```

This statement is an expression that results in the value 100 being assigned to myNumber. The operands in the expression are the *myNumber* variable name and the integer value *100*. The operator is the equal sign (=) assignment operator. The equal sign operator is an assignment operator, because it *assigns* the value (100) on the right side of the expression to the variable (myNumber) on the left side of the expression. Figure 3-16 lists the main types of JavaScript operators.

Operator Type	Description
Arithmetic	Used for performing mathematical calculations
Assignment	Assigns values to variables
Comparison	Compares operands and returns a Boolean value
Logical	Used for performing Boolean operations on Boolean operands
String	Performs operations on strings

Figure 3-16: JavaScript operator types

Other types of JavaScript operators include bitwise operators, which operate on integer values and are a complex topic.

JavaScript operators are binary or unary. A **binary operator** requires an operand before the operator and an operand after the operator. The equal sign in the statement `myNumber = 100;` is an example of a binary operator. A **unary operator** requires a single operand either before or after the operator. For example, the increment operator (++), an arithmetic operator, is used for increasing an operand by a value of one. The statement `myNumber++` changes the value of the myNumber variable to 101.

The operand to the left of an operator is known as the left operand, and the operand to the right of an operator is known as the right operand.

Next you will learn about the different types of JavaScript operators.

Arithmetic Operators

Arithmetic operators are used to perform mathematical calculations, such as addition, subtraction, multiplication, and division, in JavaScript. You can also return the modulus of a calculation, which is the remainder left when you divide one number by another number. JavaScript's binary arithmetic operators and their descriptions are listed in Figure 3-17. Code examples using the arithmetic binary operators are shown in Figure 3-18.

Operator	Description
+ (addition)	Adds two operands
- (subtraction)	Subtracts one operand from another operand
* (multiplication)	Multiplies one operand by another operand
/ (division)	Divides one operand by another operand
% (modulus)	Divides two operands and returns the remainder

Figure 3-17: Arithmetic binary operators

```
var x, y, returnValue;


// ADDITION

x = 100;

y = 200;

returnValue = x + y;            // returnValue changes to 300


// SUBTRACTION

x = 10;

y = 7;

returnValue = x - y;            // returnValue changes to 3


// MULTIPLICATION

x = 2;

y = 6;

returnValue = x * y;            // returnValue changes 12


// DIVISION

x = 24;

y = 3;
```

Figure 3-18: Examples of arithmetic binary operators

```
returnValue = x / y;            // returnValue changes to 8


// MODULUS

x = 3;

y = 2;

returnValue = x % y;            // returnValue changes to 1
```

Figure 3-18: Examples of arithmetic binary operators (continued)

Notice in Figure 3-18 that when JavaScript performs an arithmetic calculation, it performs the operation on the right side of the assignment operator, then assigns the value to a variable on the left side of the assignment operator. For example, in the statement `returnValue = x + y;`, the operands x and y are added, then the result is assigned to the returnValue variable on the left side of the assignment operator.

You can include a combination of variables and literal values on the right side of an assignment statement. For example, the addition statement could be written `returnValue = 100 + y;`, `returnValue = x + 200;`, or `returnValue = 100 + 200;`. However, you cannot include a literal value as the left operand, since the JavaScript interpreter must have a variable to which to assign the returned value. Therefore, the statement `100 = x + y;` will cause an error.

When performing arithmetic operations on string values, the JavaScript interpreter will attempt to convert the string values to numbers. The variables in the following example are assigned as string values instead of as numbers, since they are contained within quotation marks. Nevertheless, the JavaScript interpreter will correctly perform the multiplication operation and return a value of 6.

```
x = "2";
y = "3";
returnValue = x * y;     // the value returned is 6
```

The JavaScript interpreter will not convert strings to numbers when you use the addition operator. When you use the addition operator with strings, the strings are combined instead of being added together. In the following example, the operation returns a value of 23 since the x and y variables contain strings instead of numbers:

```
x = "2";
y = "3";
returnValue = x + y;     // a string value of 23 is returned
```

Arithmetic operations can also be performed on a single variable using unary operators. Figure 3-19 lists the unary arithmetic operators available in JavaScript.

Operator	Description
++ (increment)	Increases an operand by a value of one
-- (decrement)	Decreases an operand by a value of one
- (negation)	Returns the opposite value (negative or positive) of an operand

Figure 3-19: Arithmetic unary operators

The increment (++) and decrement (--) unary operators can be used as prefix or postfix operators. A **prefix operator** is placed before a variable. A **postfix operator** is placed after a variable. The statements ++myVariable; and myVariable++; both increase myVariable by one. However, the two statements return different values. When you use the increment operator as a prefix operator, the value of the operand is returned *after* it is increased by a value of one. When you use the increment operator as a postfix operator, the value of the operand is returned *before* it is increased by a value of one. Similarly, when you use the decrement operator as a prefix operator, the value of the operand is returned *after* it is decreased by a value of one, and when you use the decrement operator as a postfix operator, the value of the operand is returned *before* it is decreased by a value of one. If you intend to assign the incremented or decremented value to another variable, then whether you use the prefix or postfix operator makes a difference. For example, in the following code the count variable is increased by a value of one, using the prefix increment operator, then assigned to the newValue variable:

```
var count = 10;
var newValue = ++count;  // newValue is assigned '11'
```

In this example, the prefix operator returns a value after adding one to the operand, the count variable is increased to 11, and the newValue variable is assigned a value of 11. In contrast, in the next example, the count variable is increased by a value of one, using the postfix increment operator, then assigned to the newValue variable. The postfix increment operator returns a value before adding one to the operand, and the newValue variable is assigned a value of 10.

```
var count = 10;
var newValue = count++;  // newValue is assigned '10'
```

Unlike the increment and decrement unary operators, the negation (-) unary operator cannot be used as a postfix operator. The negation (-) unary operator must be placed as a prefix in front of the operand that will be changed to a negative value. In the following code, the variable x is initially assigned a value of positive 10; then x is changed to −10 using the negation unary operator.

```
var x = 10;
x = -x;        // x is changed to -10
```

Next you will create a program that performs arithmetic calculations.

To create a program that performs arithmetic calculations:

1 Start your text editor or HTML editor and create a new document.

2 Type the <HTML> and <HEAD> sections of the document:

```
<HTML>
<HEAD>
<TITLE>Arithmetic Examples</TITLE>
</HEAD>
```

3 Add the following code to begin the body of the HTML document and to create a preformatted text container:

```
<BODY>
<PRE>
```

4 Add the opening statements for a JavaScript section:

```
<SCRIPT LANGUAGE="JavaScript1.2">
<!-- HIDE FROM INCOMPATIBLE BROWSERS
```

5 Type the following statements to declare two variables: a number variable to contain a number, which you will use in several arithmetic operations, and a result variable to contain the value of each arithmetic operation.

```
var number = 100;
var result;
```

6 Now add the following statements that perform addition, subtraction, multiplication, and division operations on the number variable and assign each value to the result variable. The result variable is printed each time it changes.

```
result = number + 50;
document.writeln("Result after addition = " + result);
result = number / 4;
document.writeln("Result after division = " + result);
result = number - 25;
document.writeln("Result after subtraction = " + result);
result = number * 2;
document.writeln("Result after multiplication = " + result);
```

7 Next, add the following two statements. The first statement uses the increment operator to increase the value of the number variable by one and assigns the new value to the result variable. The second statement prints the result variable.

Notice that the increment operator is used as a prefix, so the new value is assigned to the result variable. If you used the postfix increment operator, the old value of the number variable would be assigned to the result variable, before the number variable is incremented by one.

```
result = ++number;
document.writeln("Result after increment = " + result);
```

8 Add the following code to close the <SCRIPT>, <PRE>, <BODY>, and <HTML> tags:

```
// STOP HIDING FROM INCOMPATIBLE BROWSERS -->
</SCRIPT>
</PRE>
</BODY>
</HTML>
```

9 Save the file as **ArithmeticExamples.html** in the **Tutorial.03** folder on your Student Disk. Open the **ArithmeticExamples.html** file in your Web browser. Figure 3-20 shows the output.

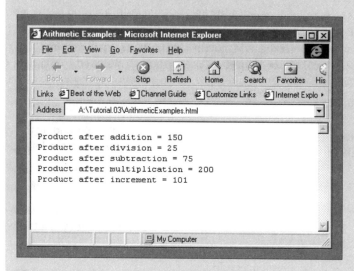

Figure 3-20: Output of ArithmeticExamples.html

10 Close the Web browser window.

Assignment Operators

Assignment operators are used for assigning a value to a variable. You have already used the most common assignment operator, the equal sign (=), to assign values to variables you declared using the var statement. The equal sign assigns an initial value to a new variable or assigns a new value to an existing variable. For example, the following code creates a variable named myCar, uses the equal sign to assign it an initial value, then uses the equal sign again to assign it a new value.

```
var myCar = "Ford";
myCar = "Corvette";
```

JavaScript includes other assignment operators in addition to the equal sign. These additional assignment operators perform mathematical calculations on variables and literal values in an expression, then assign a new value to the left operand. Figure 3-21 displays a list of the common JavaScript assignment operators.

Operator	Description
=	Assigns the value of the right operand to the left operand
+=	Combines the value of the right operand with the value of the left operand or adds the value of the right operand to the value of the left operand and assigns the new value to the left operand
-=	Subtracts the value of the right operand from the value of the left operand and assigns the new value to the left operand
*=	Multiplies the value of the right operand by the value of the left operand and assigns the new value to the left operand
/=	Divides the value of the left operand by the value of the right operand and assigns the new value to the left operand
%=	Divides the value of the left operand by the value of the right operand and assigns the remainder to the left operand (modulus).

Figure 3-21: Assignment operators

You can use the += assignment operator to combine two strings as well as to add numbers. In the case of strings, the string on the left side of the operator is combined with the string on the right side of the operator, and the new value is assigned to the left operator. Before combining operands, the JavaScript interpreter will attempt to convert a non-numeric operand, such as a string, to a number. If a non-numeric operand cannot be converted to a number, you will receive a value of NaN. Figure 3-22 shows code examples of the different assignment operators.

```
var x, y;


x = "Hello ";
x += "World";    // x changes to "Hello World"


x = 100;
y = 200;
x += y;          // x changes to 300


x = 10;
y = 7;
x -= y;          // x changes to 3


x = 2;
y = 6;
x *= y;          // x changes 12


x = 24;
y = 3;
x /= y;          // x changes to 8


x = 3;
y = 2;
x %= y;          // x changes to 1
```

Figure 3-22: Examples of assignment operators

Next you will create an HTML document that uses assignment operators.

To create an HTML document that uses assignment operators:

1 Start your text editor or HTML editor and create a new document.

2 Type the <HTML> and <HEAD> sections of the document:

```
<HTML>
<HEAD>
<TITLE>Assignment Examples</TITLE>
</HEAD>
```

3 Add the following code to begin the body of the HTML document and to create a preformatted text container:

```
<BODY>
<PRE>
```

4 Add the opening statements for a JavaScript section:

```
<SCRIPT LANGUAGE="JavaScript1.2">
<!-- HIDE FROM INCOMPATIBLE BROWSERS
```

5 Type the following statements that perform several assignment operations on a variable named changingVar. After each assignment operation, the result is printed.

```
var changingVar = "text string 1";
changingVar += " & text string 2";
document.writeln("Variable after addition assignment = "
    + changingVar);
changingVar = 100;
changingVar += 50;
document.writeln("Variable after addition assignment = "
    + changingVar);
changingVar -= 30;
document.writeln("Variable after subtraction assignment = "
    + changingVar);
changingVar /= 3;
document.writeln("Variable after division assignment = "
    + changingVar);
changingVar *= 8;
document.writeln("Variable after multiplication assignment = "
    + changingVar);
changingVar %= 300;
document.writeln("Variable after modulus assignment = "
    + changingVar);
```

6   Add the following code to close the <SCRIPT>, <PRE>, <BODY>, and <HTML> tags:

```
// STOP HIDING FROM INCOMPATIBLE BROWSERS -->
</SCRIPT>
</PRE>
</BODY>
</HTML>
```

7   Save the file as **AssignmentExamples.html** in the **Tutorial.03** folder on your Student Disk. Open the **AssignmentExamples.html** file in your Web browser. Figure 3-23 shows the output.

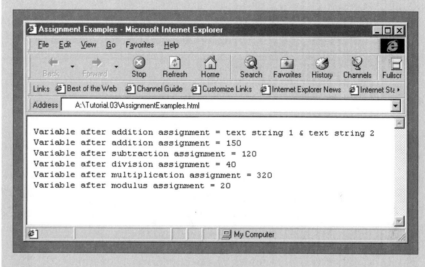

Figure 3-23: Output of AssignmentExamples.html

8   Close the Web browser window.

Comparison Operators

Comparison operators are used to compare two operands for equality and to determine if one numeric value is greater than another. A Boolean value of true or false is returned after two operands are compared. Figure 3-24 lists the JavaScript comparison operators.

Operator	Description
== (equal)	Returns true if the operands are equal
!= (not equal)	Returns true if the operands are not equal
> (greater than)	Returns true if the left operand is greater than the right operand
< (less than)	Returns true if the left operand is less than the right operand
>= (greater than or equal)	Returns true if the left operand is greater than or equal to the right operand
<= (less than or equal)	Returns true if the left operand is less than or equal to the right operand

Figure 3-24: Comparison operators

tip

The comparison operator (==) consists of two equal signs and performs a function different from the assignment operator consisting of a single equal sign (=). The comparison operator *compares* values, while the assignment operator *assigns* values.

You can use number or string values as operands with comparison operators. When two numeric values are used as operands, the JavaScript interpreter compares them numerically. For example, the statement `returnValue = 5 > 4;` results in true, since the number 5 is numerically greater than the number 4. When two non-numeric values are used as operands, the JavaScript interpreter compares them in alphabetical order. The statement `returnValue = "b" > "a";` returns true, since the letter b is alphabetically greater than the letter a. When one operand is a number and the other is a string, the JavaScript interpreter attempts to convert the string value to a number. If the string value cannot be converted to a number, a value of false is returned. For example, the statement `returnValue = 10 == "ten";` returns a value of false, since the JavaScript interpreter cannot convert the string "ten" to a number. Figure 3-25 shows additional code examples using comparison operators.

```
var x = 5, y = 6;

x == y;                             // false

x != y;                             // true

x > y;                              // false

x < y;                              // true

x >= y;                             // false

x <= y;                             // true

x = "text string";

y = "different string";

x != y;                             // true

"abc" == "abc";                     // true

"abc" == "xyz";                     // false
```

Figure 3-25: Examples of comparison operators

Next you will create an HTML document that uses comparison operators.

To create an HTML document that uses comparison operators:

1 Start your text editor or HTML editor and create a new document.

2 Type the <HTML> and <HEAD> sections of the document:

```
<HTML>
<HEAD>
<TITLE>Comparison Examples</TITLE>
</HEAD>
```

3 Add the following code to begin the body of the HTML document and to create a preformatted text container:

```
<BODY>
<PRE>
```

4   Add the opening statements for a JavaScript section:

```
<SCRIPT LANGUAGE="JavaScript1.2">
<!-- HIDE FROM INCOMPATIBLE BROWSERS
```

5   Type the following statements that perform various comparison operations on two variables. The result is assigned to the returnValue variable and printed.

```
var returnValue;
var Value1 = "first text string";
var Value2 = "second text string";
returnValue = Value1 == Value2;
document.writeln("Value1 equal to Value2: "
        + returnValue);
Value1 = 50;
Value2 = 75;
returnValue = Value1 == Value2;
document.writeln("Value1 equal to Value2: "
        + returnValue);
returnValue = Value1 != Value2;
document.writeln("Value1 not equal to Value2: "
        + returnValue);
returnValue = Value1 > Value2;
document.writeln("Value1 greater than Value2: "
        + returnValue);
returnValue = Value1 < Value2;
document.writeln("Value1 less than Value2: "
        + returnValue);
returnValue = Value1 >= Value2;
document.writeln(
        "Value1 greater than or equal to Value2: "
                + returnValue);
returnValue = Value1 <= Value2;
document.writeln(
        "Value1 less than or equal to Value2: "
                + returnValue);
```

6   Add the following code to close the <SCRIPT>, <PRE>, <BODY>, and <HTML> tags:

```
// STOP HIDING FROM INCOMPATIBLE BROWSERS -->
</SCRIPT>
</PRE>
</BODY>
</HTML>
```

7   Save the file as **Comparison Examples.html** in the **Tutorial.03** folder on your Student Disk. Open the **ComparisonExamples.html** file in your Web browser. Figure 3-26 shows the output.

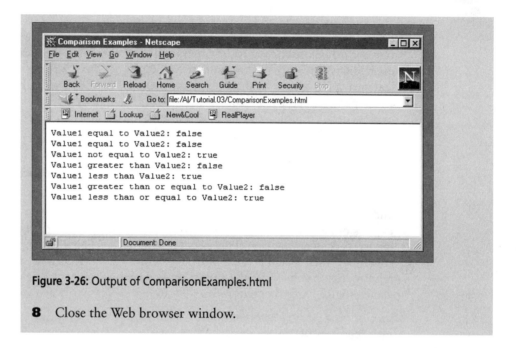

Figure 3-26: Output of ComparisonExamples.html

8 Close the Web browser window.

Logical Operators

Logical operators are used for comparing two Boolean operands for equality. Like comparison operators, a Boolean value of true or false is returned after two operands are compared. Figure 3-27 lists the JavaScript logical operators.

Operator	Description
&& (and)	Returns true if both the left operand and right operand return a value of true, otherwise it returns a value of false.
‖ (or)	Returns true if either the left operand or right operand returns a value of true. If neither operand returns a value of true, then the expression containing the ‖ (or) operator returns a value of false.
! (not)	Returns true if an expression is false and returns false if an expression is true.

Figure 3-27: Logical operators

The && (and) and || (or) operators are binary operators (requiring two operands), while the ! (not) operator is a unary operator (requiring a single operand). Logical operators are often used with comparison operators to evaluate expressions, allowing you to combine the results of several expressions into a single statement. For example, the && (and) operator is used for determining whether two operands return an equivalent value. The operands themselves are often expressions. The following code uses the && operator to compare two separate expressions:

```
var a = 2; var b = 3;
var returnValue = a==2 && b==3;    // returns true
```

In the above example, the left operand evaluates to true since "a" is equal to 2, and the right operand also evaluates to true since "b" is equal to 3. Because both expressions are true, returnValue is assigned a value of true. The statement containing the && operator essentially says "if variable a is equal to 2 AND variable b is equal to 3, then assign a value of true to returnValue. Otherwise, assign a value of false to returnValue." In the following code, however, returnValue is assigned a value of false, since the right operand does not evaluate to true:

```
var a = 2; var b = 3;
var returnValue = a==2 && b==4;    // returns false
```

The logical || (or) statement checks to see if either expression evaluates to true. For example, the statement in the following code says "if a is equal to 2 OR b is equal to 3, assign a value of true to returnValue. Otherwise, assign a value of false."

```
var a = 2; var b = 3;
var returnValue = a==2 ||  b==4;    // returns true
```

The returnValue variable in the above example is assigned a value of true, since the left operand evaluates to true, even though the right operand evaluates to false. This result occurs because the || (or) statement returns true if *either* the left *or* right operand evaluates to true.

The following code is an example of the ! (not) operator, which returns true if an operand evaluates to false and returns false if an operand evaluates to true. Notice that since the ! (not) operator is unary, it requires only a single operand.

```
var x = true;
var returnValue = !x;    // returns false
```

 tip

Logical operators are often used within conditional and looping statements such as the `if else`, `for`, and `while` **statements. You will learn about conditional and looping statements in Tutorial 4.**

Next you will create an HTML document that uses logical operators.

To create an HTML document that uses logical operators:

1 Start your text editor or HTML editor and create a new document.

2 Type the <HTML> and <HEAD> sections of the document:

```
<HTML>
<HEAD>
<TITLE>Logical Examples</TITLE>
</HEAD>
```

3 Add the following code to begin the body of the HTML document and to create a preformatted text container:

```
<BODY>
<PRE>
```

4 Add the opening statements for a JavaScript section:

```
<SCRIPT LANGUAGE="JavaScript1.2">
<!-- HIDE FROM INCOMPATIBLE BROWSERS
```

5 Type the following statements that use logical operators on two variables:

```
var trueValue = true;
var falseValue = false;
var returnValue;
document.writeln(!trueValue);
document.writeln(!falseValue);
document.writeln(trueValue || falseValue);
document.writeln(trueValue && falseValue);
```

6 Add the following code to close the <SCRIPT>, <PRE>, <BODY>, and <HTML> tags:

```
// STOP HIDING FROM INCOMPATIBLE BROWSERS -->
</SCRIPT>
</PRE>
</BODY>
</HTML>
```

7 Save the file as **LogicalExamples.html** in the **Tutorial.03** folder on your Student Disk. Open the **LogicalExamples.html** file in your Web browser. Figure 3-28 shows the output.

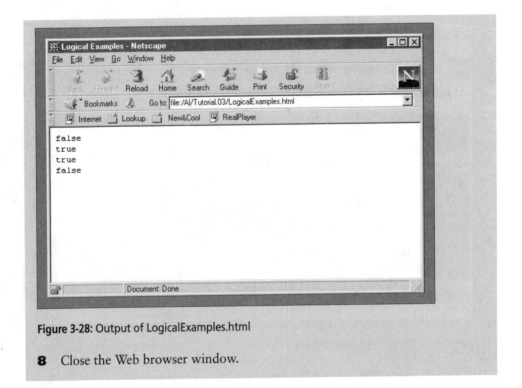

Figure 3-28: Output of LogicalExamples.html

8   Close the Web browser window.

String Operators

JavaScript has two operators that can be used with strings: + and +=. When used with strings, the plus sign is known as the concatenation operator. The **concatenation operator** (+) is used to combine two strings. The following code combines a string variable and a literal string, and assigns the new value to another variable:

```
var firstString = "Ernest Hemingway wrote ";
var newString;
newString = firstString + "<I>For Whom the Bell Tolls</I>";
```

The combined value of the firstString variable and the string literal that is assigned to the newString variable is Ernest Hemingway wrote *For Whom the Bell Tolls.*

You can also use the += assignment operator to combine two strings. The following code combines the two text strings, but without using the newString variable:

```
var firstString = "Ernest Hemingway wrote ";
firstString += "<I>For Whom the Bell Tolls</I>";
```

Note that the same symbol—a plus sign—serves as the concatenation operator and the addition operator. When used with numbers or variables containing numbers, expressions using the concatenation operator will return the sum of the two numbers. However, if you use the concatenation operator with a string value and a number value, the string value and the number value will be combined into a new string value, as in the following example:

```
var textString = "The legal voting age is ";
var votingAge = 18;
newString = textString + votingAge;
```

Next you will create an HTML document that uses string operators.

To create an HTML document that uses string operators:

1 Start your text editor or HTML editor and create a new document.

2 Type the <HTML> and <HEAD> sections of the document:

```
<HTML>
<HEAD>
<TITLE>String Examples</TITLE>
</HEAD>
```

3 Add the following code to begin the body of the HTML document and to create a preformatted text container:

```
<BODY>
<PRE>
```

4 Add the opening statements for a JavaScript section:

```
<SCRIPT LANGUAGE="JavaScript1.2">
<!-- HIDE FROM INCOMPATIBLE BROWSERS
```

5 Type the following statements containing examples of string operators. Use your own name and place of birth where indicated.

```
var name;
firstName = "your first name";
lastName = "your last name";
var placeOfBirth;
name = firstName + " ";
name += lastName;
placeOfBirth = "city where you were born";
placeOfBirth += ", state where you were born";
document.writeln("My name is " + name);
document.writeln("I was born in " + placeOfBirth);
```

6 Add the following code to close the <SCRIPT>, <PRE>, <BODY>, and <HTML> tags:

```
// STOP HIDING FROM INCOMPATIBLE BROWSERS -->
</SCRIPT>
</PRE>
</BODY>
</HTML>
```

7 Save the file as **StringExamples.html** in the **Tutorial.03** folder on your Student Disk. Open the **StringExamples.html** file in your Web browser. The output should contain your name and place of birth.

8 Close the Web browser window.

Operator Precedence

When creating expressions in JavaScript, you need to be aware of the precedence of an operator. **Operator precedence** is the order of priority in which operations in an expression are evaluated. Expressions are evaluated on a left-to-right basis with the highest priority precedence evaluated first. The order of precedence for JavaScript operators is as follows:

- Parentheses/brackets/dot (() [] .) — *highest precedence*
- Negation/increment (! - ++ -- typeof void)
- Multiplication/division/modulus (* / %)
- Addition/subtraction (+ -)
- Comparison (< <= > >=)
- Equality (== !=)
- Logical and (&&)
- Logical or (||)
- Assignment operators (= += -= *= /= %=) — *lowest precedence*

The preceding list does not include all the operators that JavaScript evaluates in the order of precedence. Only operators discussed in this text are listed.

The statement 5 + 2 * 8 evaluates to 21 because the multiplication operator (*) has a higher precedence than the addition operator (+). The numbers 2 and 8 are multiplied first, for a total of 16, then the number 5 is added. If the addition operator had a higher precedence than the multiplication operator, then the statement would evaluate to 56, since 5 would added to 2, for a total of 7, which would then be multiplied by 8.

As you can see from the list, parentheses are the operators with the highest precedence. Parentheses are used with expressions to change the order in which individual operations in an expression are evaluated. For example, the statement 5 + 2 * 8, which evaluates to 21, can be rewritten to (5 + 2) * 8, which evaluates to 56. The parentheses tell the JavaScript interpreter to add the numbers 5 and 2 before multiplying by the number 8. Using parentheses forces the statement to evaluate to 56 instead of 21.

Creating the Calculator Program

The calculator program performs calculations using a special type of conversion function, the eval() function. The **eval()** function evaluates expressions contained within strings. You can include a string literal or string variable as the argument for the eval() function. If the string literal or string variable you pass to the eval() function does not contain an expression that can be evaluated, you will receive an error. The statement `var returnValue = eval("5 + 3");` returns the value 8 and assigns it to the returnValue variable. The statement `var returnValue = eval("10");` also evaluates correctly and returns a value of 10, even though the string within the eval() function did not contain operators. The eval() function has one restriction: You cannot send it a text string that does not contain operators or numbers. For example, the statement `var returnValue = eval("this is a text string");` generates an error, since it does not contain numbers or operators. However, the statement `var returnValue = eval("'this is a text string' + ' and this is another text string'");` evaluates correctly, since the string sent to the eval() function contains the concatenation operator.

Next you will create the Calculator.html program. You will use the inputString variable to contain the operands and operators of a calculation. After a calculation is added to the inputString, the calculation is performed using the eval() function. The updateString function accepts a single value representing a number or operator. The value is then added to the inputString function using the += assignment operator. After the inputString is updated, it is assigned as the value of a text box named Input that will be created with the <INPUT> tag. The Input text box is part of a form named Calculator. The Calculator form and Input text box are called as part of the Document object.

You will learn more about forms in Tutorial 6.

To create the calculator program:

1 Start your text editor or HTML editor and create a new document.

2 Type the <HTML> and <HEAD> sections of the document:

```
<HTML>
<HEAD>
<TITLE>Calculator</TITLE>
```

3   Add the opening statements for a JavaScript section:

```
<SCRIPT LANGUAGE="JavaScript1.2">
<!-- HIDE FROM INCOMPATIBLE BROWSERS
```

4   Type the statement **var inputString = "";** to declare a variable named inputString with an initial value of an empty string.

5   Next, type the following updateString() function, which will be used to update the inputString variable.

```
function updateString(value) {
    inputString += value;
    document.Calculator.Input.value = inputString;
}
```

6   Type the closing </SCRIPT> and </HEAD> tags as follows:

```
// STOP HIDING FROM INCOMPATIBLE BROWSERS -->
</SCRIPT>
</HEAD>
```

7   Add the opening **<BODY>** tag to begin the body of the HTML document.

8   Add the **<CENTER>** tag to align the calculator in the middle of the page.

9   Type **<FORM NAME="Calculator">** to start the Calculator form.

10 Create the Input text box by typing **<INPUT TYPE="text" NAME="Input" Size="22">**.

11 Type the following Input tags that create buttons representing the calculator's operators. Each tag, along with the other tags that you will create, sends a value to the updateString() function, using an onClick method:

```
<BR>
<INPUT TYPE="button" NAME="plus"   VALUE=" + "
    onClick="updateString(' + ')">
<INPUT TYPE="button" NAME="minus"  VALUE=" - "
    onClick="updateString(' - ')">
<INPUT TYPE="button" NAME="times"  VALUE=" x "
    onClick="updateString(' * ')">
<INPUT TYPE="button" NAME="div"    VALUE=" / "
    onClick="updateString(' / ')"><BR>
```

▶ **help**

When you create an <INPUT> tag with a button type of "button," you adjust the width of the button using spaces and characters within the label defined by the VALUE attribute. To adjust each button's spacing, the labels for each of the buttons you create for the calculator program with the VALUE attribute contain additional spaces.

12 Type the following <INPUT> tags for the calculator's numbers:

```
<BR>
<INPUT TYPE="button" NAME="zero"    VALUE=" 0 "
    onClick="updateString('0')">
<INPUT TYPE="button" NAME="one"     VALUE=" 1 "
    onClick="updateString('1')">
<INPUT TYPE="button" NAME="two"     VALUE=" 2 "
    onClick="updateString('2')">
<INPUT TYPE="button" NAME="three"   VALUE=" 3 "
    onClick="updateString('3')">
<INPUT TYPE="button" NAME="four"    VALUE=" 4 "
    onClick="updateString('4')">
<BR>
<INPUT TYPE="button" NAME="five"    VALUE=" 5 "
    onClick="updateString('5')">
<INPUT TYPE="button" NAME="six"     VALUE=" 6 "
    onClick="updateString('6')">
<INPUT TYPE="button" NAME="seven"   VALUE=" 7 "
    onClick="updateString('7')">
<INPUT TYPE="button" NAME="eight"   VALUE=" 8 "
    onClick="updateString('8')">
<INPUT TYPE="button" NAME="nine"    VALUE=" 9 "
    onClick="updateString('9')">
```

13 Add the following <INPUT> tags for the decimal point, clear, and Calc buttons. Notice that the onClick event for the Calc button performs the calculation by using the eval() function with the inputString variable. The calculated value is then assigned as the value of the Input text box.

```
<BR>
<INPUT TYPE="button" NAME="point"   VALUE=" . "
    onClick="updateString('.')">
<INPUT TYPE="button" NAME="clear"   VALUE=" Clear "
    onClick="Input.value=''; inputString=''">
<INPUT TYPE="button" NAME="Calc"    VALUE=" = "
    onClick="Input.value=eval(inputString);">
```

14 Add the following code to close the <FORM>, <CENTER>, <BODY>, and <HTML> tags:

```
</FORM>
</CENTER>
</BODY>
</HTML>
```

15 Save the file as **Calculator.html** in the **Tutorial.03** folder on your Student Disk. Open the **Calculator.html** file in your Web browser. Figure 3-29 shows the output. Test the program to make sure all the functions work properly.

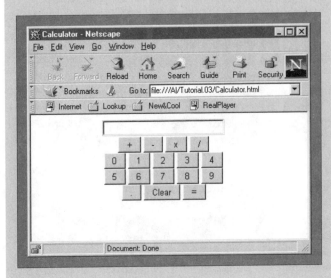

Figure 3-29: Output of Calculator.html

16 Close the Web browser window.

SUMMARY

- An expression is a single literal or variable or a combination of literal values, variables, operators, and other expressions that can be evaluated by the JavaScript interpreter to produce a result.

- Operands are variables and literals contained in an expression.

- Operators are symbols used in expressions to manipulate operands.

- A binary operator requires an operand before the operator and an operand after the operator.

- A unary operator requires a single operand either before or after the operator.

- Arithmetic operators are used for performing addition, subtraction, multiplication, and division in JavaScript.

- When performing arithmetic operations on string values, the JavaScript interpreter attempts to convert the string values to numbers. The JavaScript interpreter will not convert strings to numbers when you use the addition operator.

- The increment (++) and decrement (--) unary operators can be used as prefix or postfix operators. A prefix operator is placed before a variable, and a postfix operator is placed after a variable.

- You use assignment operators to assign a value to a variable.

- You use comparison operators to compare two operands for equality and to determine if one numeric value is greater than another.

- You use logical operators to compare two Boolean operands for equality.

- Logical operators are often used with comparison operators to evaluate expressions, allowing you to combine the results of several expressions into a single statement.

- When used with strings, the plus sign, or addition operator, is known as the concatenation operator.

- Operator precedence is the order of priority in which operations in an expression are evaluated.

- Parentheses are used with expressions to change the order in which individual operations in an expression are evaluated.

- You use the eval() function to evaluate expressions contained within strings.

QUESTIONS

1. Operators that require an operand before the operator and an operand after the operator are called _____ operators.
   a. unary
   b. binary
   c. double
   d. multiplicity

2. The modulus operator (%) _____
   a. converts an operand to base 16 (hexadecimal) format.
   b. returns the absolute value of an operand.
   c. calculates the percentage of one operand compared to another.
   d. divides two operands and returns the remainder.

3. What value is assigned to the returnValue variable in the statement `returnValue = count++;`, assuming that the count variable contains the value 10?
   a. 10
   b. 11
   c. 12
   d. 20

4. What value is assigned to the returnValue variable in the statement `returnValue += "100";`, assuming that the returnValue variable contains the string value "50 Main Street"?
    a. 150
    b. 50 Main Street 100
    c. 100
    d. 100 Main Street 50

5. What value is assigned to the returnValue variable in the statement `returnValue = "First String" == "Second String";`?
    a. First String
    b. Second String
    c. true
    d. false

6. What value is assigned to the returnValue variable in the statement `returnValue = 100!= 200;`?
    a. First String
    b. Second String
    c. true
    d. false

7. What value is assigned to the returnValue variable in the statement `returnValue = 50 == "fifty";`?
    a. true
    b. false
    c. 50
    d. "fifty"

8. The && (and) operator returns true if _____
    a. the left operand returns a value of true.
    b. the right operand returns a value of true.
    c. the left operand and right operand both return a value of true.
    d. the left operand and right operand both return a value of false.

9. The operator that returns true if either its left or right operand returns a value of true is the _____ operand.
    a. ||
    b. ==
    c. %%
    d. &&

10. What value is assigned to the returnValue variable in the statement `returnValue = !x;`, assuming that x has a value of true?
    a. true
    b. false
    c. null
    d. undefined

11. The _____ operator is used for combining two strings.
    a. association
    b. junction
    c. combination
    d. concatenation

12. The order of priority in which operations in an expression are evaluated is known as _____.
    a. prerogative precedence
    b. operator precedence
    c. expression evaluation
    d. priority evaluation

13. The operators with the highest order of precedence in JavaScript are _____.
    a. assignment operators
    b. addition/subtraction operators
    c. comparison operators
    d. parentheses ()

14. What is the value of the expression 4 * (2 + 3)?
    a. 11
    b. -11
    c. 20
    d. 14

15. What value is assigned to the returnValue variable in the statement `returnValue = eval(x + "2 * 2");`, assuming that x has a value of 1?
    a. "1 + 2 * 2"
    b. "12 * 2"
    c. 6
    d. 24

EXERCISES

1. Create an HTML document that calculates the square feet of carpet required to carpet a room. Include three text boxes. Create one text box for the width of the room and another for the length of the room in linear feet. Also create a text box for the cost per square foot of carpeting. When you calculate the cost, add 25% to the total number of square feet to account for closets and other features of the room. Display the total cost in an alert dialog box. Save the document as CarpetCost.html in the Tutorial.03 folder on your Student Disk.

2. What value is assigned to returnValue for each of the following expressions?
    a. `returnValue = 2 == 3;`
    b. `returnValue = "2" + "3";`
    c. `returnValue = 2 >= 3;`
    d. `returnValue = 2 <= 3;`
    e. `returnValue = 2 + 3;`
    f. `returnValue = (2 >= 3) && (2 > 3);`
    g. `returnValue = (2 >= 3) || (2 > 3);`

3. Create an HTML document that declares these five global variables in a <SCRIPT> section contained in the document's <HEAD> section: name, age, monthOfBirth, dateOfBirth, and yearOfBirth. In another <SCRIPT> section, contained in the document's <BODY> section, declare another variable, named birthInfo. Combine all five global variables into the birthInfo variable using the += assignment operator, then print the birthInfo variable, using the document.write() method. Save the document as BirthInfo.html in the Tutorial.03 folder on your Student Disk. Next, open the HTML document and see how it looks. Are you satisfied with the output? How can you improve the formatting and the way the strings were concatenated?

4. Create a temperature conversion calculator that converts Fahrenheit to Celsius and Celsius to Fahrenheit. To convert Fahrenheit to Celsius, subtract 32 from the Fahrenheit temperature, then multiply the remainder by .55. To convert Celsius to Fahrenheit, multiply the Celsius temperature by 1.8, then add 32. Save the document as ConvertTemperature.html in the Tutorial.03 folder on your Student Disk.

5. Use parentheses to modify the order of precedence of the following code so that the final result of x is 581.25. (The result of x using the current syntax is 637.5.) Save the document as ImprovedProgram.html in the Tutorial.03 folder on your Student Disk.

    ```
    var  x  =   75;
    x =    x + 30 * x / 4;
    ```

6. Use the search terms *JavaScript calculat* in an Internet search engine such as Yahoo!, HotBot, Lycos, or AltaVista to search for examples of JavaScript calculations. (Searching for *calculat* returns instances of the words **calculat**or, **calculat**ion, and similar terms.) Visit several of the Web sites containing JavaScript calculation tools and view the HTML and JavaScript code. Write a one-page paper describing the techniques used for creating calculators and other types of JavaScript tools that perform mathematical functions.

Decision Making with Control Structures and Statements

case▶ Cartoon and Animation Warehouse sells cartoon and animated film videos through their Web site. The company came to WebAdventure looking for a way to attract new business to their Web site. The creative staff at WebAdventure suggested running a promotional contest. Visitors to the Web site would take a simple quiz testing their knowledge of cartoons and animated films. People who got all the questions right would get a free T-shirt displaying their favorite cartoon character. Your boss at WebAdventure has asked you to create a quiz prototype to show to the client.

Previewing the CartoonQuiz.html File

In this tutorial, you will create a JavaScript quiz that tests a user's knowledge of cartoons and animated films. You will create several versions of the CartoonQuiz program, using different control structures and statements.

To preview the CartoonQuiz.html file:

1   Open the **CartoonQuiz.html** file from the **Tutorial.04** folder on your Student Disk in your browser. Figure 4-1 displays an example of the program in a Web browser.

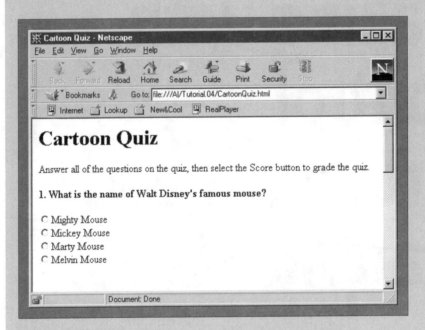

Figure 4-1: Cartoon Quiz

2   Answer the questions on the quiz, then click the Score button at the bottom of the page to see how you did.

3   When you are finished, close your browser window.

4   Next, open the **CartoonQuiz.html** file in your text editor or HTML editor and examine the code. Notice the statements that begin with `for` and `if`. These statements are examples of some of the control structures you will create in this tutorial. The multiple choice alternatives for each question are created using <INPUT> tags within a <FORM>...</FORM> tag pair.

5   Close your text editor or HTML editor when you are finished examining the code.

SECTION A

`o b j e c t i v e s`

In this section you will learn how to use:
- if statements
- if...else statements
- nested if statements
- switch statements

Decision Making

if Statements

When you write a computer program, regardless of the programming language, you often need to execute different sets of statements, depending on some predetermined criteria. For example, you may need to execute different sets of code, depending on the time of day or what type of Web browser is running your program. Additionally, you may need to execute different sets of code, depending on user input. For instance, you may have a Web page where users place online orders. If a user clicks an Add to Shopping Cart button, a set of statements that builds a list of items to be purchased must execute. However, if the user clicks a Checkout button, an entirely different set of statements, which complete the transaction, must execute. The process of determining the order in which statements execute in a program is called **decision making** or **flow control**. The special types of JavaScript statements used for making decisions are called decision-making structures.

One of the more common ways to control program flow is a technique that uses the if statement. The **if statement** is used to execute specific programming code if the evaluation of a conditional expression returns a value of true. The syntax for the if statement is as follows:

```
if (conditional expression) {
     statement(s);
}
```

The if statement contains three parts: the key word if, a conditional expression enclosed within parentheses, and executable statements. Note that the conditional expression must be enclosed within parentheses.

If the condition being evaluated in an if statement returns a value of true, then the statement (or statements) immediately following the if keyword and its condition executes. After the if statement executes, any subsequent code executes normally. Consider the example in Figure 4-2. The if statement uses the equal (==) comparison operator to determine whether exampleVar is equal to 5. Since the condition returns a value of true, two alert dialog boxes appear. The first alert dialog box is generated by the `if` statement when the condition returns a value of `true`, and the second alert dialog box executes after the `if` statement is complete.

```
var exampleVar = 5;

if (exampleVar == 5)       // CONDITION EVALUATES TO 'TRUE'

    alert("The variable is equal to '5'.");

alert("This dialog box is generated after the if statement.");
```

Figure 4-2: An `if` statement that evaluates `true`

 tip

The statement immediately following the `if` statement in **Figure 4-2** can be written on the same line as the `if` statement itself. However, using a line break and indentation makes the code easier to read.

In contrast, the code in Figure 4-3 displays only the second alert dialog box. The condition evaluates to `false`, since exampleVar is assigned the value 4 instead of 5.

```
var exampleVar = 4;

if (exampleVar == 5)       // CONDITION EVALUATES TO 'FALSE'

    alert("This dialog box will not be displayed.");

alert("This is the only dialog box displayed.");
```

Figure 4-3: An `if` statement that evaluates `false`

You can use a command block to construct a decision-making structure using multiple `if` statements. A **command block** refers to multiple statements contained within a set of braces, similar to the way a function's statements are contained within a set of braces. Each command block must have an opening brace ({) and a closing brace (}). If a command block is missing either the opening or closing brace, an error will occur. Figure 4-4 shows a program that runs a command block if the conditional expression within the `if` statement evaluates to true.

When an `if` statement contains a command block, the statements in the command block execute when the `if` statement's condition evaluates to true. After the command block executes, the code that follows executes normally. When an `if` statement's condition evaluates to false, the command block is skipped, and the statements that follow execute. If the conditional expression within the `if` statement in Figure 4-4 evaluates to false, then only the document.writeln() statement following the command block executes.

```
var exampleVar = 5;

if (exampleVar == 5) {      // CONDITION EVALUATES TO 'TRUE'

       document.writeln("The condition evaluates to true.");

       document.writeln("exampleVar is equal to 5.");

       document.writeln("Each of these lines will be printed.");

}

document.writeln(
       "This statement always executes after the if statement.");
```

Figure 4-4: An `if` statement with a command block

When you build an `if` statement, remember that after the `if` statement's condition evaluates, either the first statement following the condition executes or the command block following the condition executes. Any statements following the `if` statement's command or command block execute whether or not the `if` statement's condition evaluates to `true` or `false`.

It is easy to forget to include inside a command block all the statements that are to execute when an `if` statement evaluates to `true`. For example, consider the following code:

```
if (exampleVar == true)
    var conditionTrue = "condition is true";
    alert(conditionTrue);
```

At first glance, the code looks correct. In fact, when the condition evaluates to `true`, the code runs correctly. However, when the condition evaluates to `false`, the alert dialog box displays *undefined,* since the declaration for the conditionTrue variable is skipped. To fix this problem, enclose the two statements within a command block, as follows:

```
if (exampleVar == true) {
    var conditionTrue = "condition is true";
    alert(conditionTrue);
}
```

Now, if the condition evaluates to `false`, both statements will be bypassed, since they are contained within a command block.

The equal operator is only one of several comparison operators that you can use with an `if` statement. You can perform Boolean comparisons using any of the comparison operators you learned about in Tutorial 3. You can also use logical operators in combination with comparison operators. Figure 4-5 displays examples of comparison and logical operators with the `if` statement.

```
var exampleVar1 = 5;

if (exampleVar1 != 3)      // not equal

     document.writeln("This line prints.");

if (exampleVar1 > 3)       // greater than

     document.writeln("This line prints.");

if (exampleVar1 < 3)       // less than

     document.writeln("This line does not print.");

if (exampleVar1 >= 3)      // greater than or equal

     document.writeln("This line prints.");

if (exampleVar1 <= 3)      // less than or equal

     document.writeln("This line does not print.");

var exampleVar2 = false;

if (exampleVar1 > 3 && exampleVar2 == true)   // logical 'and'

     document.writeln("This line does not print.");

if (exampleVar1 == 5 || exampleVar2 == true) // logical 'or'

     document.writeln("This line prints.");

if (!exampleVar2)  // logical 'not'

     document.writeln("This line prints.");
```

Figure 4-5: Comparison and logical operators with the `if` statement

Next you will start creating the CartoonQuiz.html file you saw at the beginning of this tutorial. The program is set up so that users select answer alternatives by means of radio buttons created with the <INPUT> tag. When unselected, a radio button appears as a small empty circle; when selected, it appears to be filled with a black dot. A radio button is usually contained within a group of other radio buttons, and you can select only one of the grouped radio buttons at a time. The term "radio button" comes from car radios that have a group of push buttons, each of which is set to a radio station. In the same manner that you can select only one car radio button at a time, you can select only one radio <INPUT> button contained within a group of other radio buttons. All radio buttons in a group must have the same NAME attribute.

In this version of the quiz, each question is scored immediately. You will create the form containing the radio buttons, then use a series of `if` statements to score each question. First you will create the HTML document and the form section, then you will add the JavaScript code to score each of the questions.

To create the CartoonQuiz.html document and its form section:

1 Start your text editor or HTML editor and create a new document.

2 Type the <HTML> and <HEAD> sections of the document. This section also includes a <SCRIPT>...</SCRIPT> tag pair. You will use the <SCRIPT>...</SCRIPT> tag pair later to create code that scores the quiz:

```
<HTML>
<HEAD>
<TITLE>Cartoon Quiz</TITLE>
<SCRIPT LANGUAGE="JavaScript1.2">
<!-- HIDE FROM INCOMPATIBLE BROWSERS
// ADD CODE HERE
// STOP HIDING FROM INCOMPATIBLE BROWSERS-->
</SCRIPT>
</HEAD>
```

3 Add the following lines, which contain the opening <BODY> tag, the text that will appear at the top of the quiz, and the opening <FORM> tag for the radio buttons:

```
<BODY>
<H1>Cartoon Quiz</H1><P>
Answer all of the questions on the quiz, then select the
Score button to grade the quiz.
```

4 Next, add the following lines for the first question. The four radio buttons represent the answers. Since each button within a radio button group requires the same NAME attribute, these four radio buttons have the same name of "question1." Each radio button is also assigned a value corresponding to its answer number: *a*, *b*, *c*, or *d*. For each radio button group, the onClick event sends the button's value to an individual function that scores the answer. Notice that the value for each button is sent to the function by using the `this` reference in the form of `this.value`. The `this.value` statement essentially says "send *this* button's *value* to the function."

```
<B>1. What is the name of Walt Disney's famous mouse?</B><P>
<INPUT TYPE=radio NAME=question1 VALUE="a"
    onClick="scoreQuestion1(this.value)">Mighty Mouse<BR>
<INPUT TYPE=radio NAME=question1 VALUE="b"
    onClick="scoreQuestion1(this.value)">Mickey Mouse<BR>
<INPUT TYPE=radio NAME=question1 VALUE="c"
    onClick="scoreQuestion1(this.value)">Marty Mouse<BR>
<INPUT TYPE=radio NAME=question1 VALUE="d"
    onClick="scoreQuestion1(this.value)">Melvin Mouse<P>
```

help

You can build the program quickly by copying the input button code for the first question and pasting it for questions two through five. If you use copy and paste to create the input buttons, make sure you change the question number for each input button's name and the function it calls.

5 Add the lines for the second question:

```
<B>2. The character Buzz Lightyear was featured in which
animated film?</B><P>
<INPUT TYPE=radio NAME=question2 VALUE="a"
    onClick="scoreQuestion2(this.value)">Fantasia<BR>
<INPUT TYPE=radio NAME=question2 VALUE="b"
    onClick="scoreQuestion2(this.value)">Hercules<BR>
<INPUT TYPE=radio NAME=question2 VALUE="c"
    onClick="scoreQuestion2(this.value)">Toy Story<BR>
<INPUT TYPE=radio NAME=question2 VALUE="d"
    onClick="scoreQuestion2(this.value)">Mulan<P>
```

6 Add the lines for the third question:

```
<B>3. Pluto is a dog. What is Goofey?</B><P>
<INPUT TYPE=radio NAME=question3 VALUE="a"
    onClick="scoreQuestion3(this.value)">A bear<BR>
<INPUT TYPE=radio NAME=question3 VALUE="b"
    onClick="scoreQuestion3(this.value)">A mule<BR>
<INPUT TYPE=radio NAME=question3 VALUE="c"
    onClick="scoreQuestion3(this.value)">A horse<BR>
<INPUT TYPE=radio NAME=question3 VALUE="d"
    onClick="scoreQuestion3(this.value)">Also a dog<P>
```

7 Add the lines for the fourth question:

```
<B>4. Who was always trying to eat Tweety Bird?</B><P>
<INPUT TYPE=radio NAME=question4 VALUE="a"
    onClick="scoreQuestion4(this.value)">Porky Pig<BR>
<INPUT TYPE=radio NAME=question4 VALUE="b"
    onClick="scoreQuestion4(this.value)">Yosemite Sam<BR>
<INPUT TYPE=radio NAME=question4 VALUE="c"
    onClick="scoreQuestion4(this.value)">Sylvester<BR>
<INPUT TYPE=radio NAME=question4 VALUE="d"
    onClick="scoreQuestion4(this.value)">
    Foghorn Leghorn<P>
```

8 Add the lines for the fifth question:

```
<B>5. What is Winnie the Pooh's favorite food?</B><P>
<INPUT TYPE=radio NAME=question5 VALUE="a"
   onClick="scoreQuestion5(this.value)">Honey<BR>
<INPUT TYPE=radio NAME=question5 VALUE="b"
   onClick="scoreQuestion5(this.value)">Molasses<BR>
<INPUT TYPE=radio NAME=question5 VALUE="c"
   onClick="scoreQuestion5(this.value)">Peanut Butter<BR>
<INPUT TYPE=radio NAME=question5 VALUE="d"
   onClick="scoreQuestion5(this.value)">Yogurt<P>
```

9 Add the following code to close the <FORM>, <BODY>, and <HTML> tags:

```
</FORM>
</BODY>
</HTML>
```

Next you will add the functions to score each of the questions. The functions contain if statements that evaluate each answer.

To add JavaScript code to score each of the questions:

1 Replace the line // ADD CODE HERE with the following function that scores the first question. A response of *Correct Answer* appears if the user provides the correct answer. A response of *Incorrect Answer* appears if the user provides an incorrect answer.

```
function scoreQuestion1(answer) {
    if (answer == "a")
        alert("Incorrect Answer");
    if (answer == "b")
        alert("Correct Answer");
    if (answer == "c")
        alert("Incorrect Answer");
    if (answer == "d")
        alert("Incorrect Answer");
}
```

2 Add the scoreQuestion2() function:

```
function scoreQuestion2(answer) {
    if (answer == "a")
        alert("Incorrect Answer");
    if (answer == "b")
```

```
            alert("Incorrect Answer");
      if (answer == "c")
            alert("Correct Answer");
      if (answer == "d")
            alert("Incorrect Answer");
}
```

3 Add the scoreQuestion3() function:

```
function scoreQuestion3(answer) {
      if (answer == "a")
            alert("Incorrect Answer");
      if (answer == "b")
            alert("Incorrect Answer");
      if (answer == "c")
            alert("Incorrect Answer");
      if (answer == "d")
            alert("Correct Answer");
}
```

4 Add the scoreQuestion4() function:

```
function scoreQuestion4(answer) {
      if (answer == "a")
            alert("Incorrect Answer");
      if (answer == "b")
            alert("Incorrect Answer");
      if (answer == "c")
            alert("Correct Answer");
      if (answer == "d")
            alert("Incorrect Answer");
}
```

5 Add the scoreQuestion5() function:

```
function scoreQuestion5(answer) {
      if (answer == "a")
            alert("Correct Answer");
      if (answer == "b")
            alert("Inorrect Answer");
      if (answer == "c")
            alert("Incorrect Answer");
      if (answer == "d")
            alert("Incorrect Answer");
}
```

6 Save the file as **CartoonQuiz1.html** in the **Tutorial.04** folder on your Student Disk. Open the **CartoonQuiz1.html** file in your Web browser. As you select a response for each question, you will immediately learn whether the answer is correct. Figure 4-6 shows the output, if you select a wrong answer for question 1.

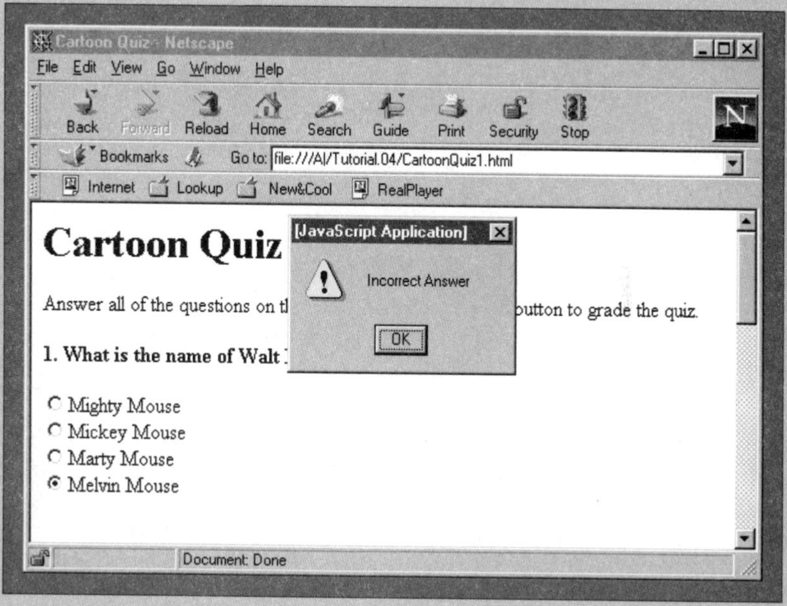

Figure 4-6: Output of CartoonQuiz1.html

7 Close the Web browser window.

if...else **Statements**

When using an `if` statement, you can include an `else` clause to run an alternate set of code if the conditional expression evaluated by the `if` statement returns a value of `false`. For instance, you may have a program that uses an `if` statement whose conditional expression evaluates the value returned from a confirm dialog box that asks users if they invest in the stock market. If the condition evaluates to `true` (the user pressed the OK button), then the `if` statement displays a Web page on recommended stocks. If the condition evaluates to `false` (the user pressed Cancel), then the statements in an `else` clause display a Web page on other types of investment opportunities. An `if` statement that includes an `else` clause is called an `if...else` statement. You can think of an `else` clause as being a backup plan for when the `if` statement's condition returns a value of `false`. The syntax for an `if...else` statement is as follows:

```
if (conditional expression) {
    statement(s);
}
else {
    statement(s);
}
```

You can use command blocks to construct an `if...else` statement as follows:

```
if (condition) {
    statements;
}
else {
    statements;
}
```

An `if` statement can be constructed without the `else` clause. However, the `else` clause can only be used with an `if` statement.

Figure 4-7 shows an example of an `if...else` statement.

```
var today = "Tuesday"

if (today == "Monday")

    document.writeln("Today is Monday");

else

    document.writeln("Today is not Monday");
```

Figure 4-7: Example of an `if...else` statement

In Figure 4-7, the today variable is assigned a value of *Tuesday*. Since `if (today == "Monday")` evaluates to `false`, control of the program passes to the `else` clause, the statement `document.writeln("Today is not Monday");` executes, and the string *Today is not Monday* prints. If the today variable had been assigned a value of *Monday*, the statement `if (today == "Monday")` would have evaluated to `true`, and the statement `document.writeln("Today is Monday");` would have executed. Only one set of statements executes: either the statements following the `if` statement or the statements following the `else` clause. Once either set of statements executes, any code following the `if...else` statements execute normally.

The JavaScript code for the CartoonQuiz1.html file you created earlier uses multiple `if` statements to evaluate the results of the quiz. Although the multiple `if` statements function properly, they can be simplified using an `if...else` statement. Next you will simplify the CartoonQuiz1.html program so that it contains an `if...else` statement instead of multiple `if` statements.

To add `if...else` statements to CartoonQuiz1.html:

1 Return to the **CartoonQuiz1.html** file and immediately save it as **CartoonQuiz2.html**.

2 Since you only need the `if` statement to test for the correct answer, you can group all the incorrect answers in the `else` clause. Modify each of the functions that scores a question so that the multiple `if` statements are replaced with an `if...else` statement. The following code shows how the statements for the scoreQuestion1() function should appear:

```
if (answer == 'b')
        alert("Correct Answer");
else
        alert("Incorrect Answer");
```

3 Save the **CartoonQuiz2.html** document and open it in your Web browser. The program should function the same as when it contained only `if` statements.

4 Close the Web browser window.

Nested `if` and `if...else` Statements

When you make a decision with a control structure such as an `if` or `if...else` statement, you may want the statements executed by the control structure to make other decisions. For instance, you may have a program that uses an `if` statement to ask users if they like sports. If users answer yes, you may want to run another `if` statement that asks users whether they like team sports or individual sports. Since you can include any code you like within the `if` statement or the `else` clause, you can include other `if` or `if...else` statements. An `if` statement contained within an `if` or `if...else` statement is called a **nested `if` statement**. Similarly, an `if...else` statement contained within an `if` or `if...else` statement is called a **nested `if...else` statement**. You use nested `if` and `if...else` statements to perform conditional evaluations in addition to the original conditional evaluation. For example, the following code performs two conditional evaluations before the `document.writeln()` statement executes:

```
var number = 7;
if (number > 5)
    if (number < 10)
        document.writeln(
            "The number is between 5 and 10.");
```

If either of the conditions in this example evaluates to `false`, then the JavaScript interpreter skips the rest of the `if` statement.

You can also nest `if...else` statements. When you use `else` clauses with nested `if` statements, you need to be aware of which `if` statement an `else` clause is associated with. An `else` clause is part of the nearest `if` statement. Consider the following code:

```
var number = 7;
var numberRange;
if (number > 5)
    if (number > 10)
        numberRange = "The number is greater than 10.";
else
    numberRange = "The number is less than 5.";
document.writeln(numberRange);
```

Since an `else` clause is part of the nearest `if` statement, the `else` clause in the above example is part of the second `if` statement. In this case, since the number variable is not greater than 10, the statement in the `else` clause, which assigns *The number is less than 5* to the numberRange variable, executes. This result is incorrect, since the first `if` statement already determined that the number variable was greater than 5. It is easy to mistakenly think that the `else` clause is part of the first `if` statement, since that is how the indentation is aligned. Remember, however, that the JavaScript interpreter does not recognize indentations or white space; you use them only to make code easier to read. The following code shows a modified version of the program with an additional `else` clause that makes the program run correctly:

```
var number = 7;
var numberRange;
if (number > 5)
    if (number > 10)
        numberRange = "The number is greater than 10.";
    else
        numberRange = "The number is less than 10.";
else
    numberRange = "The number is less than 5.";
document.writeln(numberRange);
```

You can nest `if` statements as deeply as you like. However, `if` statements can become difficult to understand if they are nested too deeply. In Figure 4-8, each `if` statement evaluates the country variable, then program control moves to the next `if` statement, which is contained in an `else` clause.

```
var country = "France";
if (country == "Spain")
    document.writeln("Buenos Dias");
else
    if (country == "Germany")
        document.writeln("Guten Tag");
    else
        if (country == "Italy")
            document.writeln("Buon Giorno");
        else
            if (country == "France")
                document.writeln("Bonjour");
            else
                document.writeln(
                    "I don't speak your language!");
```

Figure 4-8: Greeting program with nested `if` statements

Notice that the final `else` clause does not contain an `if` statement. A final `else` clause without an `if` statement, within a set of nested `if` statements, is used to perform a task when none of the preceding `if` statements matches the conditional expression.

A more efficient way to design the program in Figure 4-8 is to include each `if` statement on the same line as the previous `else` clause. Remember that the JavaScript interpreter does not recognize white space. Therefore the statement `else if (country == "Germany")` will function the same, as if it were broken into two separate lines. Figure 4-9 shows a modified version of the program shown in Figure 4-8.

The JavaScript code in the CartoonQuiz2.html file is somewhat inefficient, since it contains multiple functions that perform essentially the same task of scoring the quiz. A more efficient method of scoring the quiz is to include nested decision-making structures within a single function. Next you will modify the JavaScript code in the CartoonQuiz.html file so that it contains a single function that checks the correct answer for all the questions, using nested `if...else` statements.

```
var country = "France";

if (country == "Spain")

    document.writeln("Buenos Dias");

else if (country == "Germany")

    document.writeln("Guten Tag");

else if (country == "Italy")

    document.writeln("Buon Giorno");

else if (country == "France")

    document.writeln("Bonjour");

else

    document.writeln("I don't speak your language!");
```

Figure 4-9: Modified Greeting program with nested `if` statements

To add nested `if...else` statements to the CartoonQuiz program:

1 Return to the **CartoonQuiz2.html** file and immediately save it as **CartoonQuiz3.html**.

2 Delete the five functions within the <SCRIPT>...</SCRIPT> tag pair.

3 Add the first line for the single function that will check all the answers: **function scoreQuestions(number, answer) {**. You will send an answer argument to the scoreQuestions() function, just as you did with the functions that scored each individual question. You will also send a new argument, *number*, which represents the question number, to the scoreQuestions() function.

4 Press **Enter** and add the opening `if` statement that checks to see if the question is equal to 1. If it is, a nested `if...else` statement evaluates the response.

```
if (number == 1) {
    if (answer == 'b')
        alert("Correct Answer");
    else
        alert("Incorrect Answer");
}
```

5   Add an `if...else` statement for question number 2:

```
else if (number == 2) {
    if (answer == 'c')
        alert("Correct Answer");
    else
        alert("Incorrect Answer");
}
```

6   Add an `if...else` statement for question number 3:

```
else if (number == 3) {
    if (answer == 'd')
        alert("Correct Answer");
    else
        alert("Incorrect Answer");
}
```

7   Add an `if...else` statement for question number 4:

```
else if (number == 4) {
    if (answer == 'c')
        alert("Correct Answer");
    else
        alert("Incorrect Answer");
}
```

8   Add an `if...else` statement for question number 5:

```
else if (number == 5) {
    if (answer == 'a')
        alert("Correct Answer");
    else
        alert("Incorrect Answer");
}
```

9   Add a closing brace (}) for the scoreQuestions() function.

10 Within each of the five <INPUT> tags, change the function called within the onClick() event handler to **scoreQuestions(*number*, this.value)**, changing the *number* argument to the appropriate question number. For example, the event handler for question 1 should read: **scoreQuestions(1, this.value)**.

11 Save the HTML document and open it in your Web browser. The program should still function the same way it did with the multiple `if` statements and the multiple functions.

12 Close the Web browser window.

`switch` Statements

Another JavaScript statement that is used for controlling program flow is the `switch` statement. The **switch statement** controls program flow by executing a specific set of statements, depending on the value of an expression. The `switch` statement compares the value of an expression to a label contained within a `switch` statement. If the value matches a particular label, then the statements associated with the label execute. For example, you may have a variable in your program named favoriteMusic. A `switch` statement can evaluate the variable (which is an expression) and compare it to a label within the `switch` construct. The `switch` statement may contain several labels, such as Jazz, Rock, or Gospel. If the favoriteMusic variable is equal to Rock, then the statements that are part of the Rock label execute. Although you could accomplish the same functionality using `if` or `if...else` statements, a `switch` statement makes it easier to organize different "branches" of code that can be executed.

A `switch` construct consists of the following components: the keyword `switch`, an expression, an opening brace, a case label, the keyword `break`, a default label, executable statements, and a closing brace. The syntax for the switch statement is as follows:

```
switch (expression) {
    case label:
        statement(s);
        break;
    case label:
        statement(s);
        break;
    ...
    default:
        statement(s);
}
```

The labels within a `switch` statement are called **case labels** and they mark specific code segments. A `case` label consists of the keyword `case`, followed by a literal value or variable name, followed by a colon. JavaScript compares the value returned from the `switch` statement's expression to the literal value or variable name following the `case` keyword. If a match is found, the `case` label's statements execute. For example, thecase label `case 3.17:` represents a floating-point integer value of 3.17. If the value of a `switch` statement's expression equals 3.17, then the `case 3.17:` label's statements execute. You can use a variety of data types as `case` labels within the same `switch` statement. Figure 4-10 shows examples of different `case` labels.

tip

A `case` label can be followed by a single statement or multiple statements. However, unlike `if` statements, multiple statements for a `case` label do not need to be enclosed within a command block.

```
case exampleVar:                        // variable name

    statement(s)

case "text string":                     // string literal

    statement(s)

case 75:                                // integer literal

    statement(s)

case -273.4:                            // floating-point literal

    statement(s)
```

Figure 4-10: Examples of case labels

Other **programming languages, such as Java and C++, require all** case **labels within a** switch **statement to be of the same data type.**

Another type of label used within switch statements is the default label. The **default label** contains statements that execute when the value returned by the switch statement's conditional expression does not match a case label. A default label consists of the keyword default followed by a colon.

When a switch statement executes, the value returned by the conditional expression is compared to each case label in the order in which it is encountered. Once a matching label is found, its statements execute. Unlike the if...else statement, program execution does not automatically exit the switch construct after a particular case label's statements execute. Instead, the switch statement continues evaluating the rest of the case labels in the list. Once a matching case label is found, evaluation of additional case labels is unnecessary. If you are working with a large switch statement with many case labels, evaluation of additional case labels can potentially slow down your program.

It is good programming design to end a switch statement once it performs its required task. A switch statement ends automatically after the JavaScript interpreter encounters its closing brace (}) or when a break statement is found. A **break statement** is used to exit switch statements and other program control statements such as while, do...while, for, and for...in looping statements. To end a switch statement once it performs its required task, you should include a break statement within each case label.

You will learn more about looping statements in Section B.

Figure 4-11 displays an example of a switch statement contained within a function. When the function is called, it is passed an argument named americanCity. The switch statement compares the contents of the americanCity argument to the case labels. If a match is found, the city's state is returned and a break statement ends the switch statement. If a match is not found, the value *United States* is returned from the default label.

```
function city_location(americanCity) {
    switch (americanCity) {
        case "Boston":
            return "Massachusetts";
            break;
        case "Chicago":
            return "Illinois";
            break;
        case "Los Angeles":
            return "California";
            break;
        case "Miami":
            return "Florida";
            break;
        case "New York":
            return "New York";
            break;
        default:
            return "United States";
    }
}
document.writeln(city_location("Boston"));
```

Figure 4-11: Function containing a switch statement

You can use either the if statement or the switch statement to handle the same flow control procedures. It is more efficient, however, to use the switch statement if you need to evaluate only a single expression. For example, review the

Greeting program in Figure 4-9, which was created using a series of `if...else` statements. The program works, but it is not the most efficient program, because the conditional evaluation that compares the country variable to a specific country name repeats several times. You can write a more efficient version of the same program using a `switch` statement, as shown in Figure 4-12.

```
var country = "Germany";
switch (country) {
    case "Spain":
        document.writeln("Buenos Dias");
        break;
    case "Germany":
        document.writeln("Guten Tag");
        break;
    case "Italy":
        document.writeln("Buon Giorno");
        break;
    case "France":
        document.writeln("Bonjour");
        break;
    default:
        document.writeln("I don't speak your language");
}
```

Figure 4-12: Greeting program using a `switch` statement

Next you will modify the CartoonQuiz program so that the scoreAnswers() function contains a `switch` statement instead of nested `if...else` statements. Each **case** statement in the modified program checks for the question number from the function's number argument. The **switch** statement makes better programming sense, because it eliminates the need to check the question number multiple times, as is necessary with an `if...else` structure.

To add a switch statement to the CartoonQuiz program:

1 Return to the **CartoonQuiz3.html** file and immediately save it as **CartoonQuiz4.html**.

2 Change the if...else statements within the scoreQuestions() function to the following switch statement.

```
switch (number) {
  case 1:
      if (answer == 'b')
              alert("Correct Answer");
      else
              alert("Incorrect Answer");
      break;
  case 2:
      if (answer == 'c')
              alert("Correct Answer");
      else
              alert("Incorrect Answer");
      break;
  case 3:
      if (answer == 'd')
              alert("Correct Answer");
      else
              alert("Incorrect Answer");
      break;
  case 4:
      if (answer == 'c')
              alert("Correct Answer");
      else
              alert("Incorrect Answer");
      break;
  case 5:
      if (answer == 'a')
              alert("Correct Answer");
      else
              alert("Incorrect Answer");
      break;
}
```

3 Save the HTML document and open it in your Web browser. The program should still function the same as it did with the nested if...else statements.

4 Close the Web browser window.

S U M M A R Y

■ Flow control is the process of determining the order in which statements are executed in a program.

■ The `if` statement is used to execute specific programming code if the evaluation of a conditional expression returns `true`.

■ A command block refers to multiple statements contained within a set of braces, similar to the way a function's statements are contained within a set of braces.

■ After an `if` statement's condition evaluates as true, either the first statement following the condition executes or the command block following the condition executes.

■ Statements following an `if` statement's command or command block execute regardless of whether the `if` statement's conditional expression evaluates to `true` or `false`.

■ The `else` clause runs an alternate set of code if the conditional expression evaluated by an `if` statement returns a value of `false`.

■ In an `if...else` construct, only one set of statements executes: either the statements following the `if` statement or the statements following the `else` clause. Once either set of statements executes, any code following the `if...else` construct executes normally.

■ An `if` statement contained within another `if` statement is called a nested `if` statement. Similarly, an `if...else` statement contained within an `if` or `if...else` statement is called a nested `if...else` statement.

■ The `switch` statement controls program flow by executing a specific set of statements, depending on the value returned by an expression.

■ Case labels within a `switch` statement mark specific code segments.

■ The `default` label contains statements that execute when the value returned by the `switch` statement's conditional expression does not match a `case` label. A `default` label consists of only the keyword `default` followed by a colon.

■ When a `switch` statement executes, the value returned by the conditional expression is compared to each `case` label in the order in which it is encountered. Once a matching label is found, its statements execute.

■ A `break` statement is used to exit a `switch` statement.

Q U E S T I O N S

1. The process of determining the order in which statements execute in a program is called _____ .
   a. process manipulation
   b. flow control
   c. programmatic configuration
   d. architectural structuring

2. Which of the following is the correct syntax for an `if` statement?
   a. `if (myVariable == 10);`
      `alert("Your variable is equal to 10.");`
   b. `if myVariable == 10`
      `alert("Your variable is equal to 10.");`
   c. `if (myVariable == 10)`
      `alert("Your variable is equal to 10.");`
   d. `if (myVariable == 10),`
      `alert("Your variable is equal to 10.");`

3. An `if` statement can include multiple statements provided that they _____
   a. execute after the `if` statement's closing semicolon.
   b. are not contained within a command block.
   c. do not include other `if` statements.
   d. are contained within a command block.

4. What happens after you execute an `if` statement?
   a. The statement immediately following the `if` statement executes.
   b. The program ends.
   c. The `if` statement continues looping.
   d. The first matching `case` label in the `if` statement repeats.

5. Which operators can you use with an `if` statement?
   a. only comparison operators
   b. only logical operators
   c. both comparison and logical operators
   d. You cannot use operators with an `if` statement.

6. Which is the correct syntax for an `else` clause?
   a. `else(document.write("Printed from an else clause.");`
   b. `else document.write("Printed from an else clause.");`
   c. `else "document.write('Printed from an else clause.')";`
   d. `else; document.write("Printed from an else clause.");`

7. Which of the following statements is true?
   a. An `if` statement must be constructed with an `else` clause.
   b. An `else` clause can be constructed without an `if` statement.
   c. An `if` statement can be constructed without an `else` clause.
   d. An `else` clause cannot be constructed with an `if` statement.

8. How many `if` statements can be nested in another `if` statement?
   a. 0
   b. 1
   c. 5
   d. as many as necessary

9. The `switch` statement controls program flow by executing a specific set of statements, depending on _____
   a. the result of an `if...else` statement.
   b. the version of JavaScript being executed.
   c. whether an `if` statement executes from within a function.
   d. the value returned by a conditional expression.

10. The `case` labels within a `switch` statement are used to _____
    a. mark specific code segments.
    b. evaluate a conditional expression.
    c. designate code that is to be ignored by the JavaScript interpreter.
    d. leave comments for other programmers.

11. Which of the following is an incorrect syntax for a `case` label within a `switch` statement?
    a. `case "text string":`
    b. `case 5.48 :`
    c. `case myVariable`
    d. `case 10 :`

12. When the value returned by a `switch` statement's conditional expression does not match a `case` label, then the statements within the _____ label execute.
    a. `exception`
    b. `else`
    c. `error`
    d. `default`

13 You can exit a `switch` statement using a(n) _____ statement.
    a. `break`
    b. `end`
    c. `quit`
    d. `complete`

EXERCISES

1. Create a Web page with an `if...else` statement that prompts users as to whether they want to see a personalized greeting. If they select yes, display a prompt dialog box asking for their name, then display the name in an alert dialog box. If they select no, display a generic greeting in an alert dialog box. Save the HTML document as PersonalGreeting.html.

2. Rewrite the following statement using a `switch` statement:

```
if (sport == "golf")
    alert("Golf is played on a golf course.");
else if (sport == "tennis")
    alert("Tennis is played on a tennis court.");
else if (sport == "baseball")
    alert("Baseball is played on a baseball diamond.");
else if (sport == "basketball")
    alert("Basketball is played on a basketball court.");
```

3. Rewrite the following statement using an `if...else` statement:

```
switch (writer) {
    case "Ernest Hemingway":
        alert(writer + " wrote Islands in the Stream");
        break;
    case "William Faulkner":
        alert(writer + " wrote The Sound and the Fury");
        break;
    case "Toni Morrison":
        alert(writer + " wrote Song of Solomon");
        break;
    case "F. Scott Fitzgerald":
        alert(writer + " wrote Tender is the Night");
        break;
    case "Henry Miller":
        alert(writer + " wrote Tropic of Capricorn");
        break;
}
```

4. Create a program that prompts users for the name of the state where they live. Create a decision-making structure that evaluates the name of the state and displays an alert dialog box containing the name of the region where the state is located: North, South, East, West, Midwest, Southwest, and so on. Name the HTML document Regions.html. What is the best decision structure to use for this type of a program?

SECTION B

objectives

In this section you will learn how to use:

- while statements
- do...while statements
- for statements
- for...in statements
- with statements
- continue statements

Repetition

while **Statements**

The statements you have worked with so far execute one after the other in a linear fashion. If, if...else, and switch statements select only a single branch of code to execute, then continue on to the statement that follows. But what if you want to repeat the same statement, function, or code section 5 times, 10 times, or 100 times? For example, you might want to perform the same calculation until a specific number is found. A **loop statement** repeatedly executes a statement or a series of statements while a specific condition is true or until a specific condition becomes true.

One of the simplest types of loop statements is the while statement. The **while statement** is used for repeating a statement or series of statements as long as a given conditional expression evaluates to true. The syntax for the while statement is as follows:

```
while (conditional expression) {
    statement(s);
}
```

Like the if...else and switch statements, the conditional expression that the while statement tests for is enclosed within parentheses following the keyword while. As long as the conditional expression evaluates to true, the statement or command block that follows will execute repeatedly. Each repetition of a looping statement is called an **iteration**. Once the conditional expression evaluates to false, the loop ends and the next statement following the while statement executes.

A while statement will keep repeating until its conditional expression evaluates to false. To end the while statement once the desired tasks have been performed, you must include code that tracks the progress of the loop and changes the value produced by the conditional expression. You track the progress of a while statement, or any other loop, with a counter. A **counter** is a variable that increments or decrements with each iteration of a loop statement.

▶ tip

• •

Many programmers often name counter variables *count*, *counter*, or something similar. The letters *i*, *j*, *k*, and *l* are also commonly used as counter names. Using a name such as *count*, or the letter *i* (for *increment*) or a higher letter, helps you remember (and lets other programmers know) that the variable is being used as a counter.

• •

The following code shows an example of a simple program that uses a `while` statement. The program declares a variable named count and assigns it an initial value of one. The count variable is then used in the `while` statement's conditional expression (`count <= 5`). As long as the count variable is less than or equal to five, the `while` statement will loop. Within the body of the `while` statement, the `document.writeln()` statement prints the value of the count variable, then the count variable increments by a value of one. The `while` statement loops until the count variable increments to a value of six.

```
var count = 1;
while (count <= 5) {
    document.writeln(count);
    ++count;
}
document.writeln("You have printed 5 numbers.");
```

The preceding code prints the numbers 1 to 5, which represent each iteration of the loop. Once the counter reaches 6, the message *You have printed 5 numbers.* is printed to demonstrate when the loop ends. Figure 4-13 shows the output.

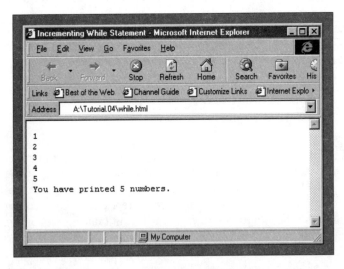

Figure 4-13: Output of a `while` statement using an increment operator

You can also control the repetitions in a `while` loop by decrementing counter variables. Consider the following program code:

```
var count = 10;
while (count > 0) {
    document.writeln(count);
    --count;
}
document.writeln("We have liftoff.");
```

In this example, the initial value of the count variable is 10, and count is decreased by one, using the decrement operator (--). While the count variable is greater than zero, the statement within the `while` loop prints the value of the count variable. When the value of count is equal to zero, the `while` loop ends, and the statement immediately following it prints. Figure 4-14 shows the program's output.

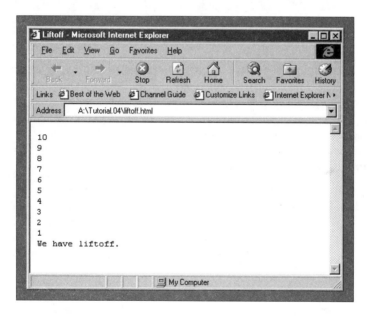

Figure 4-14: Output of a `while` statement using a decrement operator

There are many ways to change the value of a count variable and use count to control the repetitions of a `while` loop. The following example uses the `*=` assignment operator to multiply the value of the count variable by two. Once the count variable reaches a value of 128, the `while` statement ends. Figure 4-15 shows the program's output.

```
var count = 1;
while (count <= 100) {
    document.writeln (count);
    count *= 2;
}
```

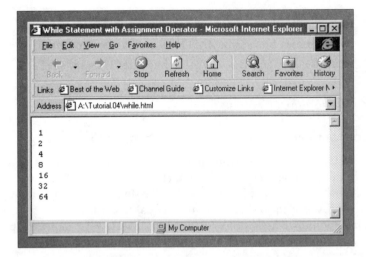

Figure 4-15: Output of a while statement using the *= assignment operator

It is important to include code that monitors a while statement's conditional expression. You also need to include code within the body of the while statement that changes *some* part of the conditional expression. If you do not include code that changes the value used by the conditional expression, your program will be caught in an infinite loop. An **infinite loop** is a situation in which a loop statement never ends because its conditional expression is never updated or is never false. Consider the following while statement:

```
var count = 1;
while (count <= 10) {
    alert("The number is " + count);
}
```

Although the while statement in the above example includes a conditional expression that checks the value of a count variable, there is no code within the while statement's body that changes the count variable's value. The count variable will continue to have a value of 1 through each iteration of the loop. In this case, an alert dialog box containing the text string *The number is 1* appears over and over again, no matter how many times you press the OK button.

tip

In most cases, you must force a Web browser that is caught in an infinite loop to close. The method for forcing the close of an application varies with the computer system. For Windows NT/95/98 operating systems, you can force an application to close by pressing Ctrl+Alt+Delete to access Task List or Task Manager. When the Close Program dialog box appears, click the End Task button.

Next you will create a program that demonstrates the use of the while statement. The program uses a while statement to check the "speed" you enter into a prompt dialog box. The speed is then used as a counter by a while statement. As long as you enter a speed that is under 65 mph, you continue receiving prompt dialog boxes asking for new speeds. If you enter a speed over 65, or less than or equal to 0, then the `while` loop ends.

To create the speed limit program:

1 Start your text editor or HTML editor and create a new document.

2 Type the opening <HTML> tag, the opening lines of a <HEAD> section, and a new <SCRIPT> section:

```
<HTML>
<HEAD>
<TITLE>Speed Limit</TITLE>
<SCRIPT LANGUAGE="JavaScript1.2">
<!-- HIDE FROM INCOMPATIBLE BROWSERS
```

3 Type the opening constructor for a function that accepts a single *speed* argument: `function speedLimit(speed) {`, then press **Enter**.

4 Add the opening constructor for a `while` statement that keeps looping as long as the speed variable is less than or equal to 65: `while(speed <= 65) {`, then press **Enter**.

5 Add the following line within the `while` statement that assigns the input from a prompt dialog box to a variable named newSpeed:

```
var newSpeed = prompt("Your speed is " + speed
    + ". Please enter a new speed", "");
```

6 Press **Enter** and add an `if...else` statement to check to see if the speed is over 65. If the speed is greater than 65, an alert dialog box appears, and the break statement is called.

```
if (newSpeed > 65) {
    alert("You are speeding!");
    break;
}
```

7 Press **Enter** again and add an `if...else` statement to check to see if the speed is less than or equal to 0. If the speed is less than or equal to 0, an alert dialog box appears, and the `break` statement is called.

```
else if (newSpeed <= 0) {
    alert("You are stopped!");
    break;
}
```

8 Next, add a final `else` clause that continues the `while` statement:

```
else {
    speed = newSpeed;
}
```

9 Add the following code to close the `while` statement, function, <SCRIPT> section, and <HEAD> section.

```
    }
}
// STOP HIDING FROM INCOMPATIBLE BROWSERS -->
</SCRIPT>
</HEAD>
```

10 Type the following lines for the opening <BODY> tag, text, and a small <SCRIPT> section, which calls the speedLimit() function in the <HEAD>. The speedLimit() function is sent a starting speed of 55.

```
<BODY>
<H1>Select Reload or Refresh to restart the
SpeedLimit program.</H1><P>
<SCRIPT LANGUAGE="JavaScript1.2">
<!-- HIDE FROM INCOMPATIBLE BROWSERS
speedLimit(55);
// STOP HIDING FROM INCOMPATIBLE BROWSERS -->
</SCRIPT>
```

11 Add the following code to close the <BODY> and <HTML> tags:

```
</BODY>
</HTML>
```

12 Save the file as **SpeedLimit.html** in the **Tutorial.04** folder on your Student Disk. Open the **SpeedLimit.html** file in your Web browser and test the program. Figure 4-16 shows an example.

13 Close the Web browser window.

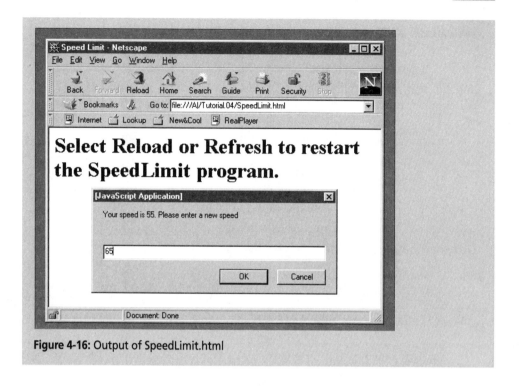

Figure 4-16: Output of SpeedLimit.html

do...while **Statements**

Another JavaScript looping statement that is similar to the `while` statement is the `do...while` statement. The **do...while statement** executes a statement or statements once, then repeats the execution as long as a given conditional expression evaluates to `true`. The syntax for the `do...while` statement is as follows:

```
do {
     statement(s);
} while (conditional expression);
```

As you can see in the syntax description, the statements execute *before* a conditional expression is evaluated. Unlike the simpler `while` statement, the statements in a `do...while` statement always execute once, before a conditional expression is evaluated.

The following `do...while` statement executes once before the conditional expression evaluates the count variable. Therefore, a single line that reads *The count is equal to 2* prints. Once the conditional expression (count < 2) executes, the `do...while` statement ends, since the count variable is equal to 2 and causes the conditional expression to return a value `false`.

```
var count = 2;
do {
     document.writeln("The count is equal to " + count);
     ++count;
} while (count < 2);
```

Note that this do...while example includes a counter within the body of the do...while statement. As with the while statement, you need to include code that changes some part of the conditional expression in order to prevent an infinite loop from occurring.

In the following example, the while statement never executes, since the count variable does not fall within the range of the conditional expression:

```
var count = 2;
while (count > 2) {
     document.writeln("The count is equal to " + count);
     ++count;
}
```

Figure 4-17 shows an example of a do...while statement that prints the days of the week, using an array.

```
<PRE>
<SCRIPT>
var daysOfWeek = new Array();
daysOfWeek[0] = "Monday";
daysOfWeek[1] = "Tuesday";
daysOfWeek[2] = "Wednesday";
daysOfWeek[3] = "Thursday";
daysOfWeek[4] = "Friday";
daysOfWeek[5] = "Saturday";
daysOfWeek[6] = "Sunday";
var count = 0;
do {
     document.writeln(daysOfWeek[count]);
     ++count;
} while (count < 7);
</SCRIPT>
</PRE>
```

Figure 4-17: Example of a do...while statement

In the example in Figure 4-17, an array is created containing the days of the week. A count variable is declared and initialized to zero. Remember, the first subscript or index in an array is zero. Therefore, in the example, the statement `daysOfWeek[0];` refers to Monday. The first iteration of the `do...while` statement prints *Monday*, then increments the count variable by one. The conditional expression in the `while` statement then checks to see if the count variable is less than seven. As long as the count is less than seven (which is one number higher than the largest element in the daysOfWeek[] array), the loop continues. Figure 4-18 shows the output of the Days of Week program in a Web browser:

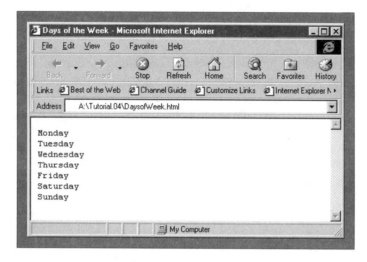

Figure 4-18: Days of Week program in a Web browser

Next you will modify the SpeedLimit program so that it uses a `do...while` statement instead of a `while` statement. Using a `do...while` statement eliminates the need to send an initial speed argument to the speedLimit() function. Instead the speed variable is initialized during the first pass of the `do` statement, then the `while` statement checks it to see if the loop should continue.

To add a do...while statement to the SpeedLimit program:

1 Return to the **SpeedLimit.html** file and immediately save it as **SpeedLimit2.html**.

2 Delete the speed argument in the speedLimit() function constructor.

3 Modify the `while` statement to create a `do...while` statement as follows. Notice that you no longer need the newSpeed variable. Also notice that you no longer need the final `else` clause to assign the value of the newSpeed variable to the speed variable.

```
do {
    var speed = prompt("Your speed is " + speed
        + ". Please enter a new speed", "");
    if (speed > 65) {
        alert("You are speeding!");
        break;
    }
    else if (speed <= 0) {
        alert("You are stopped!");
        break;
    }
} while(speed <= 65)
```

4 Delete the **55** in the statement that calls the speedLimit() function.

5 Save the file, then open it in your Web browser. When you first open it, the message in the dialog box reads *Your speed is undefined*. Remember that when a variable is declared, it contains an initial value of *undefined* until you explicitly assign it a value. Since you removed the speed parameter from the speedLimit() function, the speed variable contains a value of *undefined* until you enter a speed limit into the dialog box and press Enter.

6 Close the Web browser window.

for **Statements**

You can also use the for statement to loop through code. The for statement is used for repeating a statement or series of statements as long as a given conditional expression evaluates to true. The for statement performs essentially the same function as the while statement: if a conditional expression within the for statement constructor evaluates to true, then the for statement executes and will continue to execute repeatedly until the conditional expression evaluates to false. One of the primary differences between the while statement and the for statement is that in addition to a conditional expression, you can also include code in the for statement's constructor to initialize a counter and change its value with each iteration. The syntax of the for statement is as follows:

```
for (initialization expression; condition; update statement) {
    statement(s);
}
```

When the JavaScript interpreter encounters a `for` loop, the following steps occur:

1. The initialization expression is started. For example, if the initialization expression in a `for` loop is `var count = 1;`, then a variable named count is declared and assigned an initial value of 1. The initialization expression is only started once when the `for` loop is first encountered.
2. The `for` loop's condition is evaluated.
3. If the condition evaluation in Step 2 returns a value of `true`, then the `for` loop's statements execute, Step 4 occurs, then the process starts over again with Step 2. If the condition evaluation in Step 2 returns a value of `false`, then the `for` statement ends and the next statement following the `for` statement executes.
4. The update statement in the `for` statement's constructor is executed. For example, the count variable may increment by one.

You can omit any of the three parts of the `for` statement constructor, but you must include the semicolons that separate each section. If you omit a section of the constructor, be sure you include code within the body that will end the `for` statement or your program may get caught in an infinite loop.

Figure 4-19 displays an example of a `for` statement that prints the contents of an array.

```
var fastFoods = new Array();

fastFoods[0] = "pizza";

fastFoods[1] = "burgers";

fastFoods[2] = "french fries";

fastFoods[3] = "tacos";

fastFoods[4] = "fried chicken";

for (var count = 0; count < 5; ++count) {

    document.writeln(fastFoods[count]);

}
```

Figure 4-19: A `for` statement that displays the contents of an array

As you can see in the example, the counter is initialized, evaluated, and incremented within the constructor. You do not need to include a declaration for the count variable before the `for` statement, nor do you need to increment the count variable within the body of the `for` statement. Figure 4-20 shows the output of the Fast Foods program.

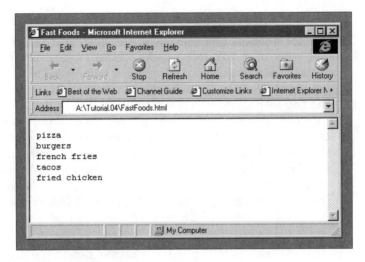

Figure 4-20: Output of Fast Foods program

You can create looping statements that are controlled by counters more efficiently using `for` statements than using `while` statements. Using a `for` statement is more efficient because you do not need as many lines of code. Consider the following `while` statement:

```
var count = 1;
while (count <= 5) {
     document.writeln(count);
     ++count;
}
```

The preceding `while` statement can be created more efficiently using a `for` statement as follows:

```
for (var count = 1; count <= 5; ++count) {
     document.writeln(count);
}
```

There are times, however, when using a `while` statement is preferable to using a `for` statement. If you do not use a counter to update the conditional expression or if the counter must be updated from the body of the loop statement, a `while` construction works better than a `for` construction. The following code relies on a Boolean value returned from a confirm dialog box, rather than a counter, for program control.

```
var i = true;
while (i == true)
  i = confirm(
        "Do you want to redisplay this dialog box?");
```

You could accomplish the same task using a `for` statement, but in this case, the third part of the `for` statement's constructor, which updates the counter, is unnecessary. Therefore, this code is better written using a `while` statement. If you use a `for` statement instead of a `while` statement in the above example, you must leave the update section out of the `for` statement's constructor. You must also remember to leave in the semicolon that separates the conditional section from the update section. If you leave the update section in the constructor, you could create an infinite loop. The following code performs essentially the same task as the above `while` example, but causes an infinite loop, since the constructor always changes the i variable to `true` with each iteration. No matter how many times you press the confirm dialog box's cancel button, which assigns a value of `false` to the i variable, the `for` constructor reassigns the variable to `true` each time the code repeats, causing an infinite loop.

```
for (var i = true; i == true; i = true) {
  i = confirm(
        "Do you want to redisplay this dialog box?");
}
```

To make the above `for` loop function correctly without causing an infinite loop, you must remove the update section from the constructor, as follows:

```
for (var i = true; i == true;) {
  i = confirm(
        "Do you want to redisplay this dialog box?");
}
```

Figure 4-21 shows an example of the same Days of Week program you saw in Figure 4-18 that prints the contents of an array, but this time using a `for` statement instead of a `do...while` statement. Notice that the declaration of the count variable, the conditional expression, and the statement that increments the count variable are now all contained within the `for` statement's constructor. Using a `for` statement instead of a `do...while` statement simplifies the program somewhat, since you do not need as many lines of code.

```
<PRE>
<SCRIPT>
var daysOfWeek = new Array();
daysOfWeek[0] = "Monday";
daysOfWeek[1] = "Tuesday";
daysOfWeek[2] = "Wednesday";
daysOfWeek[3] = "Thursday";
daysOfWeek[4] = "Friday";
daysOfWeek[5] = "Saturday";
daysOfWeek[6] = "Sunday";
for (var count = 0; count < 7; ++count) {
     document.writeln(daysOfWeek[count]);
}
</SCRIPT>
</PRE>
```

Figure 4-21: Example of a for statement

Next you will create a final version of the Cartoon Quiz program that uses a single for statement containing a nested if statement to score the quiz. While the for statement you create is somewhat more complicated than the if, if...else, and switch statements, it takes up considerably fewer lines of code. You will also include a Score button that grades the entire quiz after a user is finished, instead of grading the quiz answer by answer.

To create the final version of the Cartoon Quiz program:

1 Open the **CartoonQuiz4.html** file from the **Tutorial.04** folder on your Student Disk and immediately save it as **CartoonQuizFinal.html**.

2 Delete the entire scoreQuestions() function from the <HEAD> section, then add the following lines to create two arrays: answers[] and correctAnswers[]. The answers[] array holds the answers selected each time the quiz runs, and the correctAnswers[] array holds the correct response for each of the questions. The code assigns the correct responses to each element of the correctAnswers[] array.

```
var answers = new Array(5);
var correctAnswers = new Array(5);
correctAnswers[0] = "b";
correctAnswers[1] = "c";
correctAnswers[2] = "d";
correctAnswers[3] = "c";
correctAnswers[4] = "a";
```

3 Press **Enter** and type the following function, which assigns the response from each question to the appropriate element in the answers[] array. The program sends the actual question number (1–5) to the function using the onClick event of each radio button. To assign question responses to the correct element, 1 must be subtracted from the question variable, because the elements in an array start with 0.

```
function recordAnswer(question, answer) {
    answers[question-1] = answer;
}
```

4 Type the opening constructor for the function that scores the quiz: `function scoreQuiz() {`. You call this function from a new Score button.

5 Press **Enter** and type `var totalCorrect = 0;` to declare a new variable and assign it an initial value of 0. The totalCorrect variable holds the number of correct answers.

6 Press **Enter** and type the opening constructor for a `for` loop that scores the quiz: `for(var count = 0; count < 5; ++count) {`. A counter named count initializes to a value of 0, since 0 is the starting index of an array. The conditional expression checks to see if count is less than or equal to the number of elements in the answers[] array. Finally, the count variable increments by one with each iteration of the loop.

7 Press **Enter** and add the following `if` statement within the `for` loop. The `if` statement compares each element within the answers[] array to each corresponding element within the correctAnswers[] array. If the elements match, the totalCorrect variable increments by one.

```
if (answers[count] == correctAnswers[count])
    ++totalCorrect;
```

8 Add the closing brace for the `for` loop. Then add the code for an alert dialog box that shows how many questions were answered correctly:

```
}
alert("You scored " + totalCorrect
    + " out of 5 answers correctly!");
```

9 Add a closing brace (`}`) for the scoreQuiz() function.

10 Change the name of the function called from the onClick event handlers in the radio buttons from scoreQuestions() to **recordAnswer()**.

11 Finally, add the following <INPUT> tag immediately after the last radio button for question 5. The <INPUT> tag creates a command button whose onClick event handler calls the scoreQuiz() function.

```
<INPUT TYPE=button VALUE="Score" onClick =
"scoreQuiz();"><P>
```

12 Save the file, then open it in your Web browser window. Test the program by answering all five questions and pressing the Score button. The result in your Web browser should appear similar to Figure 4-22, depending on how many questions you answered correctly.

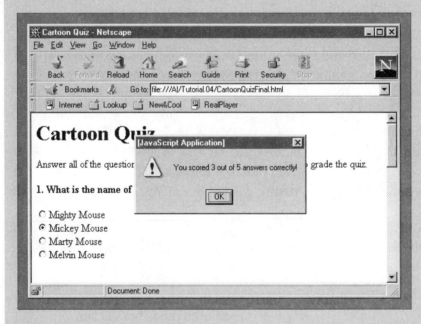

Figure 4-22: Output of CartoonQuizFinal.html

13 Close the Web browser window.

for...in Statements

In Tutorial 2 you worked with objects and properties. As you recall, you use special types of functions called constructor functions to create objects. The variables within a constructor function are the data of any objects created from the constructor function and are referred to as properties. The **for...in statement** is a looping statement that executes the same statement or command block for all the properties within an object. This is useful, for instance, if you want to print the names of all the properties in an object. The syntax for the `for...in` statement is as follows:

```
for (variable in object) {
    statement(s);
}
```

The variable name in the `for...in` statement constructor holds an individual object property. The object name in the constructor represents the name of an object that has been instantiated in a program. Unlike the other loop statements, the `for...in` statement does not require a counter or any other type of code to control how the loop functions. Instead, the `for...in` statement automatically assigns each property in an object to the variable name, performs the necessary statements on the property, then moves to the next property and starts over. The `for...in` statement ends automatically once it reaches the last property in an object. A typical use of the `for...in` statement is to retrieve the names of properties within an object, as shown in Figure 4-23.

```
function Animal(type, sound, transport_mode) {

    this.animal_type = type; // object property

    this.animal_sound = sound; // object property

    this.animal_transport_mode = transport_mode;
        // object property

}
livestock = new Animal("cow", "moo", "walk");
        // instantiate object
for (prop in livestock) {    // this for loop prints

    document.writeln(prop); // the names of the properties

}
```

Figure 4-23: A `for...in` statement printing the names of properties within an object

In the `for...in` statement in Figure 4-23, the variable name prop holds the names of each property in the livestock object, which was instantiated from the Animal constructor function. The document.writeln() statement then writes the name of each property to the Web browser window as follows:

```
animal_type
animal_sound
animal_transport_mode
```

....

There is no set order or way to control how the properties in an object are assigned to a for...in statement's variable.

....

One of the benefits of the for...in statement is that it **enumerates,** or assigns an index to, each property in an object, which is similar to the way elements in an array are indexed. You can use an enumerated object property to access the values contained within an object's properties. The code in Figure 4-24 is similar to the code in Figure 4-23, except that the document.writeln() statement within the body of the for...in statement has been changed to document.writeln(livestock[prop]);.

```
function Animal(type, sound, transport_mode) {

    this.animal_type = type;

    this.animal_sound = sound;

    this.animal_transport_mode = transport_mode;

}

livestock = new Animal("cow", "moo", "walk");

for (prop in livestock) {

    document.writeln(livestock[prop]);

}
```

Figure 4-24: A for...in statement printing the properties within an object

Each iteration of the for...in statement in Figure 4-24 now prints the contents of each property ("cow," "moo," and "walk") rather than just the property names. The code passes the livestock object to the document.writeln() method, along with the prop variable enclosed in brackets (livestock[prop]. You would use this same technique to print the contents of an array. Unlike the elements in an array, however, you cannot refer to an object's enumerated properties outside of a for...in loop; doing so generates an error. The statement document.writeln(livestock[prop]); causes an error outside of a for...in loop.

Next you will create a program that uses the for...in statement to print the properties in an object.

To create a program that uses the `for...in` statement to print the properties in an object:

1 Start your text editor or HTML editor and create a new document.

2 Type the opening <HTML> and <HEAD> sections of the document:

```
<HTML>
<HEAD>
<TITLE>Car Properties</TITLE>
```

3 Type the opening lines for a <SCRIPT> section:

```
<SCRIPT LANGUAGE="JavaScript1.2">
<!-- HIDE FROM INCOMPATIBLE BROWSERS
```

4 Type the following class constructor that creates a Car constructor function:

```
function Car(make, model, color, doors) {
    this.car_make = make;
    this.car_model = model;
    this.car_color = color;
    this.car_doors = doors;
}
```

5 Type the following code to close the <SCRIPT> and <HEAD> sections.

```
// STOP HIDING FROM INCOMPATIBLE BROWSERS -->
</SCRIPT>
</HEAD>
```

6 Add the following code to begin the body of the HTML document and to create a preformatted text container:

```
<BODY>
<PRE>
```

7 Add the opening statements for the JavaScript section, which calls the function in the <HEAD> section:

```
<SCRIPT LANGUAGE="JavaScript1.2">
<!-- HIDE FROM INCOMPATIBLE BROWSERS
```

8 Type `sports_car = new Car();` to instantiate a new sports_car object based on the Car constructor function.

9 Add the following lines to assign values to each of the sports_car properties:

```
sports_car.car_make = "Triumph";
sports_car.car_model = "Spitfire";
sports_car.car_color = "Yellow";
sports_car.car_doors = 2;
```

10 Press **Enter** and create the following `for...in` statement to print the properties of the sports_car object:

```
for (prop in sports_car) {
  document.writeln(sports_car[prop]);
}
```

11 Add the following code to close the <SCRIPT>, <PRE>, <BODY>, and <HTML> tags:

```
// STOP HIDING FROM INCOMPATIBLE BROWSERS -->
</SCRIPT>
</PRE>
</BODY>
</HTML>
```

12 Save the file as **SportsCar.html** in the **Tutorial.04** folder on your Student Disk. Open the **SportsCar.html** file in your Web browser. Figure 4-25 shows the output.

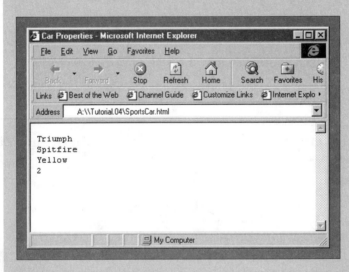

Figure 4-25: Output of SportsCar.html

13 Close the Web browser window.

with **Statements**

Another statement that is used for working with object properties is the `with` statement. The `with` **statement** eliminates the need to retype the name of an object when properties of the same object are being referenced in a series. Placing the statements within a `with` statement removes the need to retype the name of the object for each property; you can simply use the name of the property within a statement without referencing the property's source object. The syntax for the with statement is as follows:

```
with (object) {
    statement(s);
}
```

In a with statement, the name of the object you want to reference is placed within the parentheses following the with keyword. The statements that will use properties of the object are then placed within braces. The following code repeats the document.writeln() method three times:

```
document.writeln("Mark Twain wrote: ");
document.writeln("Everybody talks about the weather, ");
document.writeln("but nobody does anything about it.");
```

You can eliminate the multiple references to the document object in the above code by placing the statements within a with statement, as follows:

```
with (document) {
    writeln("Mark Twain wrote: ");
    writeln("Everybody talks about the weather, ");
    writeln("but nobody does anything about it.");
}
```

The with statement is often used to eliminate the need to retype long object names. Figure 4-26 shows an example of a with statement that assigns values to properties of an unusually long object name.

```
function Animal(type, sound, transport_mode) {

    this.animal_type = type;

    this.animal_sound = sound;

    this.animal_transport_mode = transport_mode;

}

animal_that_lives_in_the_forest = new Animal();

with (animal_that_lives_in_the_forest) {

    animal_type = "wolf";

    animal_sound = "growl";

    animal_transport_mode = "run";

}
```

Figure 4-26: Example of a with statement assigning values to object properties

Without the with statement in Figure 4-26, the lines that assign values to the object properties would need to be written as follows:

```
animal_that_lives_in_the_forest.animal_type = "wolf";
animal_that_lives_in_the_forest.animal_sound = "growl";
animal_that_lives_in_the_forest.animal_transport_mode = "run";
```

Next you will add a with statement to the SportsCar.html file.

To add a with statement to the SportsCar.html file:

1 Return to the **SportsCar.html** file and immediately save it as **SportsCar2.html**.

2 Locate the following lines that assign values to the sports_car object's properties:

```
sports_car.car_make = "Triumph";
sports_car.car_model = "Spitfire";
sports_car.car_color = "Yellow";
sports_car.car_doors = 2;
```

3 Add a with statement to simplify the four lines as follows:

```
with (sports_car) {
   car_make = "Triumph";
   car_model = "Spitfire";
   car_color = "Yellow";
   car_doors = 2;
}
```

4 Save the file and reopen it in your Web browser. The output should be the same as in Figure 4-25.

5 Close the Web browser window.

continue Statements

You learned in Section A that break statements are used for exiting switch, while, do...while, for, and for...in statements. The break-statement halts the switch or looping statement and executes the next statement that follows the switch or loop construct. A similar statement, used only with looping statements, is the continue statement. The **continue statement** halts a looping statement and restarts the loop with a new iteration. You use the continue statement when you want to stop the loop for the current iteration, but want the loop to continue with a new iteration. For example, you may have a program that uses a for statement to loop through the elements of an array containing a list of stocks. For stocks worth more than $10, you print information to the screen such as purchase price, number of shares, and so on. However, for stocks worth less than $10, you use the `continue` statement to skip that stock and move on to a new iteration. Figure 4-27 displays a `for` loop containing a `break` statement. Figure 4-28 displays the same `for` loop, but with a `continue` statement.

```
for(var count = 1; count <=5; ++count) {

    if(count == 3)

        break;

    document.writeln(count);

}
```

Figure 4-27: A for loop with a break statement

```
for(var count = 1; count <=5; ++count) {

    if(count == 3)

        continue;

    document.writeln(count);

}
```

Figure 4-28: A for loop with a continue statement

The `for` loop in Figures 4-27 and 4-28 contains an `if` statement that checks if the current value of count equals 3. In Figure 4-27, when count equals 3, the `break` statement immediately ends the `for` loop. The output of Figure 4-27 is:

```
1
2
```

In Figure 4-28, when count equals 3, the `continue` statement also stops the current iteration of the `for` loop, and the program skips printing the number 3. However, the loop continues to iterate until the conditional expression `count <= 5` is `false`. The output of Figure 4-28 is:

```
1
2
4
5
```

Next you will add a `continue` statement to the SportsCar.html file so that the car_model property does not print.

To add a `continue` statement to the SportsCar.html file so that the car_model property is not printed:

1 Save the SportsCar.html file as **SportsCar3.html**.

2 Add the following lines just before `document.writeln` `(sports_car[prop]);`:

```
if (prop == "car_model")
    continue;
```

When the `for` statement encounters the car_model property, the `if` statement executes the `continue` statement, which immediately starts a new iteration of the `for` loop, preventing the car_model property from printing.

3 Save the **SportsCar3.html file** and open it in your Web browser. The output should appear similar to Figure 4-29.

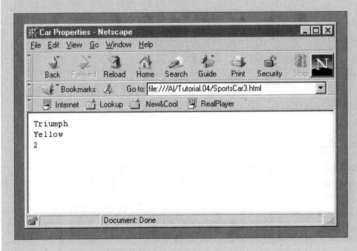

Figure 4-29: Output of SportsCar3.html

4 Close the Web browser window.

 # S U M M A R Y

- A loop statement repeatedly executes a statement or a series of statements as long as a specific condition is `true` or until a specific condition becomes `true`.

- The `while` statement is used for repeating a statement or series of statements as long as a given conditional expression evaluates to `true`.

- Each repetition of a looping statement is called an iteration.

- You must include code that tracks the progress of the `while` statement and changes the value produced by the conditional expression once the desired tasks have been performed.

- A counter is a variable that increments with each iteration of a loop statement.

- If a counter variable is beyond the range of a `while` statement's conditional expression, then the `while` statement will be bypassed completely.

- In an infinite loop, a loop statement never ends because its conditional expression is never updated.

- The `do...while` statement executes a statement or statements once, then repeats the execution as long as a given conditional expression evaluates to `true`.

- The `for` statement is used for repeating a statement or series of statements as long as a given conditional expression evaluates to `true`.

- You can omit any of the three parts of the `for` statement constructor, but you must include the semicolons that separate each section. If you omit a section of the constructor, be sure you include code within the body that will end the `for` statement, or your program may get caught in an infinite loop.

- The `for...in` statement executes the same statement or command block for all the properties within an object.

- The variable name in the `for...in` statement constructor holds an individual object property. The object name in the constructor represents the name of an object that has been instantiated in a program. Unlike the other loop statements, the `for...in` statement does not require a counter or any other type of code to control how the loop functions.

- The `for...in` statement enumerates, or assigns an index to, each property in an object.

- The `with` statement eliminates the need to retype the name of an object when properties of the same object are being referenced in a series.

- The `continue` statement halts a looping statement and restarts the loop with a new iteration.

 # QUESTIONS

1. Each repetition of a looping statement is called a(n) _____.
   a. recurrence
   b. iteration
   c. duplication
   d. re-execution

2. Counter variables _____
   a. are used to count the number of times that a looping statement has repeated.
   b. count the number of times that the Web browser has been opened and closed.
   c. are used to count how many times a JavaScript program has been executed.
   d. are only used within `if` or `if...else` statements.

3. Which of the following is the correct syntax for a `while` statement?

```
a. while (i <= 5, ++i) {
        document.writeln(i);
   }
b. while (i <= 5) {
        document.writeln(i);
        ++i;
   }
c. while (i <= 5);
        document.writeln(i);
        ++i;
d. while (i <= 5; document.writeln(i)) {
        ++i;
   }
```

4. Counter variables _____.
   a. can only be incremented
   b. can only be decremented
   c. can be changed using any conditional expression
   d. do not change

5. An infinite loop is caused _____
   a. when you omit the closing brace for a decision-making structure.
   b. when a conditional expression never evaluates to `false`.
   c. when a conditional expression never evaluates to `true`.
   d. whenever you execute a `while` statement.

6. In most cases, what must you do if you are caught in an infinite loop in JavaScript?
   a. add a break statement to the JavaScript code
   b. reload the HTML document in a Web browser window
   c. nothing—the program will end normally
   d. force the close of the Web browser window

7. If a `do...while` statement's conditional expression evaluates to `false`, how many times will the `do...while` statement execute?
   a. never
   b. once
   c. twice
   d. Repeatedly—this conditional expression causes an infinite loop.

8. Which of the following is the correct syntax for a `do...while` statement?

a. ```
do while (i < 10) {
        alert("Printed from a do...while loop.");
}
```

b. ```
do { while (i < 10)
        alert("Printed from a do...while loop.");
}
```

c. ```
do {
        alert("Printed from a do...while loop.");
        while (i < 10)
}
```

d. ```
do {
        alert("Printed from a do...while loop.");
} while (i < 10);
```

9. Which of the following is the correct syntax for a `for` statement?

a. ```
for (var i = 0; i < 10; ++i)
        alert("Printed from a for statement.");
```

b. ```
for (var i = 0, i < 10, ++i)
        alert("Printed from a for statement.");
```

c. ```
for {
        alert("Printed from a for statement.");
} while (var i = 0; i < 10; ++i)
```

d. ```
for (var i = 0; i < 10);
        alert("Printed from a for statement.");
        ++i;
```

10. When is a `for` statement's initialization expression executed?

a. when the `for` statement begins executing

b. with each repetition of the `for` statement

c. when the counter variable is incremented

d. when the `for` statement ends

11. What type of counter should you use with a `for...in` statement?

a. a Boolean variable

b. an incremental or decremental variable

c. an array's length property

d. You do not need to use a counter with the `for...in` statement.

12. What does a `for...in` statement's property variable hold?

a. an object name

b. the name of an object's property

c. a counter variable

d. the name of a class constructor

13. When does a `for...in` loop end?

a. after you close the JavaScript program

b. when you press Ctrl+Break

c. when its conditional expression evaluates to false

d. when the last property has been read

14. The _____ statement eliminates the need to retype the name of an object when properties of the same object are being referenced in a series.
a. `having`
b. `include`
c. `with`
d. `contains`

15. The_____ statement halts a looping statement, but instead of exiting the loop construct entirely, it restarts the loop with a new iteration.
a. `proceed`
b. `reiterate`
c. `restart`
d. `continue`

E X E R C I S E S

1. Rewrite the following `while` statement, using a `for` loop.

```
var count = 25;
while (count >= 0) {
      document.writeln("The current number is " + count);
      --count;

}
```

2. Rewrite the following statement using a `while` loop:

```
for(var i=1; i <= 15; ++i) {
      if (i == 10)
            break;
      else
            document.writeln("The current number is " + i);
}
```

3. Simplify the following program using `with` statements:

```
function Employee(name, number, position, department) {
      this.employee_name = name;
      this.employee_social_security = number;
      this.employee_position = position;
      this.employee_department = department;
}
new_entry_level_employee = new Employee();
new_entry_level_employee.employee_name = "John Doe";
new_entry_level_employee.employee_social_security = "000-12-3456";
new_entry_level_employee.employee_position = "Intern";
new_entry_level_employee.employee_department = "Accounting";
document.writeln(new_entry_level_employee.employee_name);
document.writeln(new_entry_level_employee.employee_social_security);
document.writeln(new_entry_level_employee.employee_position);
document.writeln(new_entry_level_employee.employee_department);
```

4. Change the program you created in Exercise 3 so that each of the Employee properties are printed with a `for...in` statement.

5. Create a questionnaire that prompts visitors to your Web site for personal information such as name, address, occupation, and so on. Assign each piece of information to an array, then use a `for` loop that prints the information to the screen. Name the HTML document Questionnaire.html.

Windows and Frames

5

case ▶ WebAdventure is creating a Web site for a large popular zoo. The zoo hopes the Web site will help attract new visitors and help in its fundraising efforts. Part of the Web site will be a virtual zoo for children that includes pictures of animals, educational information, and games. You have been asked to create an HTML document that displays the picture of an animal when a user clicks a hyperlink of the animal's name. In simple Web pages, when users click a hyperlink, a new Web page replaces the original page. However, you do not want the animal's picture to completely replace the original virtual zoo page. Your solution is to create an HTML document using frames, which are independent, scrollable portions of a Web browser window, with each frame capable of containing its own unique HTML document or image file.

Previewing the VirtualZoo Program

In this tutorial you will create a "Virtual Zoo" Web page that displays a picture of an animal after a user clicks an animal's name. The list of animals is in one frame of the HTML document and each animal's picture appears in another frame.

To preview the Tutorial5_VirtualZoo.html program:

1 Open the **Tutorial5_VirtualZoo.html** file from the **Tutorial.05** folder on your Student Disk in your Web browser. Figure 5-1 displays an example of the program in a Web browser.

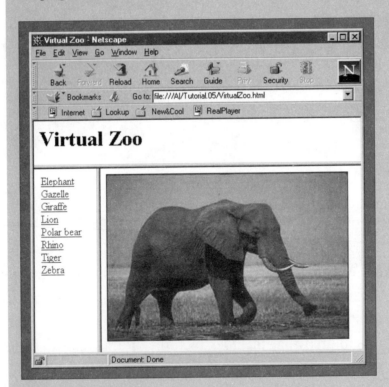

Figure 5-1: Tutorial5_VirtualZoo.html in a Web browser

2 Click the different animal names in the left frame to display each animal's picture in the right frame.

3 When you finish, close the Web browser window.

4 Next, open the **Tutorial5_VirtualZoo.html** file in your text editor or HTML editor and examine the code. Notice the <FRAMESET> and <FRAME> tags. These tags create the three panels that compose the Tutorial5_VirtualZoo program. Each panel has a unique URL, as specified by the SRC attribute of each <FRAME> tag.

5 Close your text editor or HTML editor when you are finished examining the code.

SECTION A
objectives

In this section you will learn:
- About the JavaScript object model
- About the Window object
- How to open and close windows
- How to work with timeouts and intervals

Working with Windows

The JavaScript Object Model

There may be situations in which you want to control the Web browser using JavaScript. For example, you may want to change the Web page being displayed or write information to the Web browser's status bar. Or, you may want to control elements of the HTML document itself. To control the Web browser window or the HTML document, you use the JavaScript object model. The **JavaScript object model** is a hierarchy of JavaScript objects, each of which provides programmatic access to a different aspect of an HTML page or the Web browser window. You can use methods and properties of objects in the JavaScript object model to manipulate the window, frames, and HTML elements displayed in a Web browser. You do not have to explicitly create any of the objects or arrays in the JavaScript object model; they are created automatically when a Web browser opens an HTML document. The JavaScript object model is displayed in Figure 5-2.

The JavaScript object model is also called the **browser object model, client-side object model**, and **Navigator object model**.

You will learn about frames in Section B.

As you can see from Figure 5-2, the Window object is the top-level object in the JavaScript object model. The **Window object** represents a Web browser window or an individual frame within a window. The Web browser automatically creates the Window object, and you use its properties and methods to control the Web browser window.

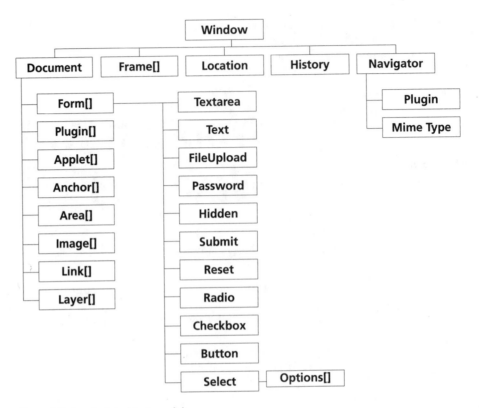

Figure 5-2: JavaScript object model

Another important object in the JavaScript object model is the Document object that represents the HTML document displayed in a window. The Document object descends from a Window object. The write() and writeln() methods, with which you are familiar, refer to the Document object. The statement `document.write("This is an example");` adds the text *This is an example* to an HTML document when it is rendered by a Web browser. All HTML elements exist within an HTML document represented by the Document object, and each element is represented in JavaScript by its own object. Therefore, the Document object is the parent or ancestor object for all the elements you create on an HTML page. The Form object, which is used by JavaScript to represent forms created with the <FORM>...</FORM> tag pair, descends from the Document object, which descends from the Window object. The Radio object, which is used by JavaScript to represent a radio button created with an <INPUT> tag, descends from the Form object, which descends from the Document object, which descends from the Window object.

You will learn more about the Document object in Tutorial 7.

In this text, objects in the JavaScript object model are referred to with an upper-case letter (*Document* object). However, when using the object name in code, you must always use a lowercase letter because you are actually referring to a *property* of the object. For example, in the statement `document.writeln("text string");`, the word *document* (with a lowercase d) represents the `document` property of the Document object.

Some of the JavaScript objects listed in Figure 5-2 represent arrays that contain other objects. In the figure, those objects that are arrays are followed by brackets, such as Form[] or Image[]. The contents of these array objects are created from the elements in an HTML document. For example, the Image object contains an images[] array that lists all the <IMG> tags in an HTML document.

To refer to a JavaScript object in code, you must refer to all of its ancestors as a series of properties separated by periods. Consider an <IMG> tag named myImage. To refer to the SRC property of the myImage object, you must include the myImage object's ancestor, the Document object. The syntax is `document.myImage.src`. Consider the following code that creates a simple form containing a single text field created with the <INPUT> tag:

```
<FORM NAME="myForm">
<INPUT TYPE="text" NAME="myTextBox">
</FORM>
```

To display the value of the text box in an alert dialog box, you must use the statement `alert(document.myForm.myTextBox.value);`. The myForm object (which is part of the Form object array) is appended to the document object as a property while the myTextBox object (which is part of the Text object array) is appended to the myForm object as a property. Finally, the value property of the Text object returns the text contained in the text box. Using statements such as `alert(myForm.myTextBox.value);` or `alert(myTextBox.value);` will generate errors, since they do not refer to all the text box's ancestor objects.

When listing an object's ancestors, it is not necessary to include the Window object. The Web browser automatically assumes that you are always referring to the currently displayed window, which is the top-level object in the JavaScript object model. You *could* list the Window object as part of an object's ancestors. For example, the statement `alert(window.document.myForm.myTextBox.value);` will work just as well as the statement `alert(document.myForm.myTextBox.value);`. However, since Web browsers automatically assume you are referring to the current window, listing the Window object is usually unnecessary.

tip

In Internet Explorer, you do not always need to use all of an object's ancestors. For example, you could eliminate the Document object in the above example using the statement `alert(myForm.myTextBox.value);` and the code would function correctly. However, for an HTML document containing JavaScript code to be compatible with both Internet Explorer and Navigator, you should always refer to all of an object's ancestors.

In some cases, it is necessary to include the Window object when you need to clearly distinguish between the Window object and the Document object. For example, event-handling code automatically assumes you are referring to the Document object instead of the Window object. Therefore, in event-handling code you should include the Window object when explicitly referring to the Web browser window.

Since a Web browser assumes you are referring to the current Window object, you also do not need to explicitly refer to the Window object when using one of its properties or methods. For example, the alert() dialog box is a method of the Window object. The full syntax for the alert() method is `window.alert(text);`, although, as you have seen throughout this text, the syntax `alert(text);` (without the Window object) works equally well. If you were required to include the Window object, your code could become quite lengthy. For example, if you needed to use the Window object to refer to the value of the myTextBox element on myForm, you would need to write:

```
window.alert(window.document.myForm.myTextBox.value);
```

Removing the references to the Window object shortens the statement somewhat, as in the following example:

```
alert(document.myForm.myTextBox.value);
```

Another way of referring to the Window object is by using the self property. The **self property** refers to the current Window object. Using the self property is identical to using the window property to refer to the Window object. For example, the following lines are identical:

```
window.alert("text string");
self.alert("text string");
```

Some JavaScript programmers prefer to use the window property, while other JavaScript programmers prefer to use the self property. Whichever property you choose is up to you. However, if you attempt to decipher JavaScript code created by other programmers, it is important to be aware that both of these properties refer to the current Window object.

The Window Object

The Window object includes several properties that contain information about the Web browser window. For instance, the `status` property contains information displayed in a Web browser's status bar. Also contained in the Window object are various methods that allow you to manipulate the Web browser window itself. Methods of the Window object you have already used include the alert(), confirm(), and prompt() methods used for displaying dialog boxes. Figure 5-3 lists common Window object properties, and Figure 5-4 lists common Window object methods.

Property	Description
defaultStatus	Default text that is written to the status bar
document	A reference to the Document object
frames[]	An array listing the frame objects in a window
history	A reference to the History object
location	A reference to the Location object
opener	The Window object that opens another window
parent	The parent frame that contains the current frame
self	A self-reference to the Window object—identical to the window property
status	Temporary text that is written to the status bar
top	The topmost Window object that contains the current frame
window	A self-reference to the Window object—identical to the self property
name	The name of a window

Figure 5-3: Window object properties

Method	Description
alert()	Displays a simple message dialog box with an OK button
blur()	Removes focus from a window
clearTimeout()	Cancels a set timeout
close()	Closes a window
confirm()	Displays a confirmation dialog box with OK and Cancel buttons
focus()	Makes a Window object the active window
open()	Opens a new window
prompt()	Displays a dialog box prompting a user to enter information
setTimeout()	Executes a function after a specified number of milliseconds have elapsed

Figure 5-4: Window object methods

Opening and Closing Windows

Navigator and Internet Explorer both allow you to open new Web browser windows in addition to the Web browser window or windows that may already be open. There are several reasons why you may need to open a new Web browser window. You may want to launch a new Web page in a separate window, allowing users to continue viewing the current page in the current window. Or, you may want to use an additional window to display information such as a picture or an order form.

Whenever a new Web browser window is opened, a new Window object is created to represent the new window. You can have as many Web browser windows open as your system will support, each displaying a different Web page. For example, you can have one Web browser window display Microsoft's Web site, another Web browser window display Netscape's Web site, and so on. You can manually open a new Web browser window in Navigator by selecting New Window from the File menu. In Internet Explorer, you select Window from the New submenu on the File menu. When you manually open a new Web browser window, the new window opens the same URL or file that is displayed in the first Web browser window. If a Web browser window is opened to the Course Technology Web site (http://www.course.com) and you open a new window, the new window also displays the Course Technology Web site.

With JavaScript you can open a new Web browser window using the open() method of the Window object. The syntax for the open() method is `window.open("URL", "name", options);`. The *URL* argument represents the Web address or filename to be opened. The *name* argument is used to assign a value to the name property of the new Window object. Note that quotation marks enclose both the URL and name arguments. The *options* argument represents a string that controls how the new Web browser window will appear. You can include all or none of the open() method arguments. The statement `window.open("http://www.course.com");` opens the Course Technology Web site in a new Web browser window, as shown in Figure 5-5. If you exclude the URL argument, then a blank Web page opens. For example, the statement `window.open();` opens the Web browser window displayed in Figure 5-6.

Figure 5-5: Web browser window opened with a URL argument of the open() method

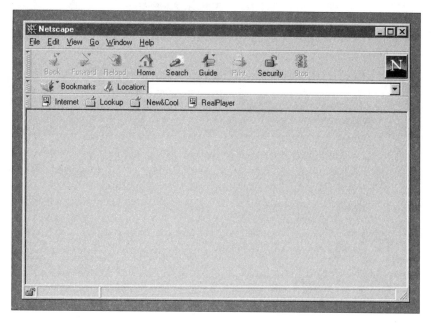

Figure 5-6: Web browser window opened with the `window.open();` statement

You can use the name property of a Window object to specify a window as the target in which a hypertext link's URL opens or the results of a form submission appear. The program in Figure 5-7 creates a new, empty Web browser window named *targetWindow*. The original window includes a hypertext link that opens the Course Technology home page in the new targetWindow Web browser window. Notice that the URL for the open() method is a blank string (""), since we want to open the new Web browser window to a blank page. After the open() method executes, the statement `self.focus` returns focus to the original Web browser window.

```
<HEAD>

<SCRIPT LANGUAGE="JavaScript1.2">

<!-- HIDE FROM INCOMPATIBLE BROWSERS

window.open("", "targetWindow");

self.focus();

// STOP HIDING FROM INCOMPATIBLE BROWSERS -->

</SCRIPT>

</HEAD>

<A HREF="http://www.course.com" TARGET="targetWindow">

Visit the Course Technology home page.</A>
```

Figure 5-7: A JavaScript program that includes name and target arguments

If the name argument of the open() method is already in use by another Web browser window, then JavaScript changes focus to the existing Web browser window instead of creating a new window.

When you open a new Web browser window, you can customize its appearance using the options argument of the open() method. Figure 5-8 lists some common options that can be used with the open() method.

All the options listed in Figure 5-8, with the exception of the width and height options, are set using values of *yes* or *no*, or *1* for yes and *0* for no. To include the status bar, the options string should read "status=yes". The width and height options are set using integers representing pixels. For example, to create a new window that is 200 pixels high by 300 pixels wide, the string should read "height=200,width=300". When including multiple items in the options string, you must separate the items by commas.

Name	Description
directories	Includes directory buttons
height	Sets the window's height
location	Includes the URL Location text box
menubar	Includes the menu bar
resizable	Determines if the new window can be resized
scrollbars	Includes scroll bars
status	Includes the status bar
toolbar	Includes the Standard toolbar
width	Sets the window's width

Figure 5-8: Common open() method options

If you exclude the options string of the open() method, then all the normal options will be included in the new Web browser window. However, if you include the options string, you must include all the components you want to create for the new window; that is, the new window is created with only the components you explicitly specify. The following open() method creates the Web browser window displayed in Figure 5-9. The new Web browser window contains no interface elements, since the only items included in the options string were height and width properties. Interface elements include the menu bar, toolbars, scroll bars, and other items with which users interact.

```
window.open("http://www.course.com", "Course",
    "height=300,width=600 ");
```

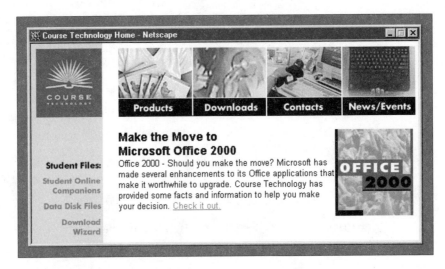

Figure 5-9: Web browser window with no interface elements

In comparison, the options string in the following open() method includes the toolbar and scroll bars. Figure 5-10 displays the window that is generated.

```
window.open("http://www.course.com", "Course",
    "height=300,width=600,toolbar=yes,scrollbars=yes");
```

Figure 5-10: Web browser window with toolbar and scroll bars

tip

If you include spaces in the options string of an open() method, the options may not display properly in Netscape Navigator. For an open() method to work properly with both Netscape Navigator and Internet Explorer, do not include any spaces in an options string.

A Window object's name property can be used only to specify a target window with hypertext links or forms, and cannot be used in JavaScript code. If you want to control the new window using JavaScript code located within the Web browser in which it was *created*, then you must assign the new Window object created with the open() method to a variable. The statement `var newWindow = open("http://www.course.com");` assigns an object representing the new Web browser window to a variable named newWindow. You can then use any of the properties and methods of the Window object with the newWindow variable. For example, if you want to set the focus to the newWindow variable using the focus method of the Window object, use the statement `newWindow.focus();`. The close() method is the Window object method you will probably use the most with variables representing other Window objects. For example, to close the Web browser window represented by the newWindow variable, use the statement `newWindow.close();`.

tip

It is not necessary to include the Window object when listing an object's ancestors. However, the Document object also contains methods named open() and close(), which are used for opening and closing HTML documents. Therefore, the Window object is usually included with the open() and close() methods, in order to distinguish between the Window object and the Document object.

Next you will create a program that displays an HTML document containing a picture of a polar bear in a separate window. First you will create a source document from which you will be able to open a new window.

To create the source document:

1 Start your text editor or HTML editor and create a new document.

2 Type the opening <HTML>, <HEAD>, and <SCRIPT> sections of the document:

```
<HTML>
<HEAD>
<TITLE>See the Polar Bear</TITLE>
<SCRIPT LANGUAGE="JavaScript1.2">
<!-- HIDE FROM INCOMPATIBLE BROWSERS
```

3 Create the following function that opens the PolarBear.html file. The new window containing the PolarBear.html file is created without any interface elements so that it appears as a simple "image window." The only items included in the options string in the window.open() method are height and width parameters.

```
function openPolarBear() {
window.open("PolarBear.html", "PolarBear",
        "height=350,width=320");
}
```

4 Add the following to close the <HEAD> and <SCRIPT> sections:

```
// STOP HIDING FROM INCOMPATIBLE BROWSERS -->
</SCRIPT>
</HEAD>
```

5 Add **<BODY>** to begin the body of the HTML document and press **Enter**.

6 Type **<H1>See the Polar Bear</H1>** to create a heading 1 tag for the HTML document and press **Enter**.

7 Next add the following lines to create a hyperlink to the PolarBear.html document. The link to the PolarBear.html file is formatted with the <H2> tag. Note that instead of allowing the hyperlink to open the PolarBear.html document in the current window, an onClick event calls the openPolarBear() function, which uses the window.open() method to open the document in a new window. The onClick event then returns a value of false. If the onClick() event did not return a value of false, the PolarBear.html document would be opened in the current window as well as the new window.

```
<H2><A HREF="PolarBear.html"
onClick="openPolarBear(); return false;">
Click here to see the polar bear.</A></H2>
```

8 Add the following lines to close the <BODY> and <HTML> tags:

```
</BODY>
</HTML>
```

9 Save the file as **PolarBearMain.html** in the **Tutorial.05** folder on your Student Disk.

Next you will create the PolarBear.html document.

To create the PolarBear.html document:

1 Create a new document in your text editor or HTML editor.

2 Type the <HTML> and <HEAD> sections of the document:

```
<HTML>
<HEAD>
<TITLE>Polar Bear</TITLE>
</HEAD>
```

3 Add **<BODY>** to begin the body of the HTML document and press **Enter**.

4 Add the following heading tag and press **Enter**.

```
<H1>This is a Polar Bear</H1>
```

5 Add an <IMG> tag that displays an image named PolarBear.jpg. A copy of the PolarBear.jpg file is located in the Tutorial.05 folder on your Student Disk.

```
<IMG SRC="PolarBear.jpg">
```

6 Next add the following <FORM> and <INPUT> tags to create a button. When you click the button, the self.close() method is called to close the PolarBear.html document. Note that you can also use window.close() to perform the same task.

```
<FORM>
<INPUT TYPE=button NAME="quit"
VALUE=" Click here to close this window "
onClick="self.close();">
</FORM>
```

7 Add the following lines to close the <BODY> and <HTML> tags:

```
</BODY>
</HTML>
```

8 Save the file as **PolarBear.html** in the **Tutorial.05** folder on your Student Disk.

9 Open the **PolarBearMain.html** file in your Web browser, then click the *Click here to see the polar bear* link. Your screen should appear similar to Figure 5-11.

10 Close the **PolarBear.html** file by clicking the *Click here to close this window* button, then close the Web browser window containing the PolarBearMain.html file.

 tip

Some monitor settings may cause the *Click here to close this window* button in the window containing PolarBear.html to be cut off. If you do not see the *Click here to close this window* button, try changing the height and width parameters of the window.open() method in PolarBearMain.html.

Figure 5-11: PolarBearMain.html and PolarBear.html windows

Working with Timeouts and Intervals

As you develop Web pages, you may need to have some JavaScript code execute repeatedly, without user intervention. Alternately, you may want to create animation or some other type of repetitive task that needs to execute automatically. You use the timeout and interval methods of the Window object to create code that performs functions that execute automatically. The **setTimeout() method** of the Window object is used in JavaScript to execute code after a specific amount of time has elapsed. Code executed with the setTimeout() method executes only once. The syntax for the setTimeout() method is `var variable = setTimeout("code", milliseconds);`. This variable declaration assigns a reference to the setTimeout() method to a variable. The code argument must be enclosed in double or single quotes and can be a single JavaScript statement, a series of JavaScript statements, or a function call. The amount of time the Web browser should wait before executing the code argument of the setTimeout() method is expressed in milliseconds. A millisecond is one thousandth of a second; there are 1000 milliseconds in a second. For example, five seconds is equal to 5000 milliseconds. The **clearTimeout() method** of the Window object is used to cancel a setTimeout() method before its code executes. The clearTimeout() method receives a single argument, which is the variable that represents a setTimeout() method call.

Figure 5-12 shows a program that contains a setTimeout() method call and a clearTimeout() method call. The setTimeout() method is contained in the <HEAD> section of the HTML document and is set to execute after 10000 milliseconds (10 seconds) have elapsed. If a user clicks the OK button, a buttonPressed() function calls the clearTimeout() method.

```
<HTML>

<HEAD>

<TITLE>Timeouts</TITLE>

<SCRIPT LANGUAGE="JavaScript1.2">

<!-- HIDE FROM INCOMPATIBLE BROWSERS

var buttonNotPressed = setTimeout(
     "alert('You must press the OK button to continue!')",
     10000);

function buttonPressed() {

     clearTimeout(buttonNotPressed);

     alert("The setTimeout() method was canceled!");

}

// STOP HIDING FROM INCOMPATIBLE BROWSERS -->

</SCRIPT>

</HEAD>

<BODY>

<FORM>

<INPUT TYPE=button NAME="OK" VALUE=" OK "
     onClick="buttonPressed();">

</FORM>

</BODY>

</HTML>
```

Figure 5-12: Program using setTimeout() and clearTimeout() methods

Two other methods of the Window object are the setInterval() method and the clearInterval() method. The **setInterval() method** is similar to the setTimeout() method, except that it repeatedly executes the same code after being called only once. The **clearInterval() method** is used to clear a setInterval() method call in the same fashion that the clearTimeout() method clears a setTimeout() method. The setInterval() and clearInterval() methods are most often used for starting animation code that executes repeatedly. The syntax for the setInterval() method is the same as the syntax for the setTimeout() method: var *variable* = setInterval("*code*", *milliseconds*);. As with the clearTimeout() method, the clearInterval() method receives a single argument, which is the variable that represents a setInterval() method call. You will use the setInterval() method and the clearInterval() method extensively when creating animation in Tutorial 7.

Next you will add a setTimeout() method to the PolarBearMain.html file. The setTimeout() method automatically calls the confirmPolarBear() method if a user does not click the polar bear link within 10 seconds.

To add a setTimeout() method to the PolarBearMain.html file:

1 Return to the **PolarBearMain.html** file in your text editor or HTML editor.

2 Declare a global variable that reads **var polarBearOpened;** before the openPolarBear() function. A setTimeout() method will be assigned to the polarBearOpened variable. As you learned in Tutorial 2, global variables are available to all parts of a JavaScript program, not just to an individual function, as are local variables.

3 Add the following confirmPolarBear() function after the openPolarBear() function. The confirmPolarBear() function will be called when the timeout expires. The confirm() statement prompts the user to open the PolarBear.html file.

```
function confirmPolarBear() {
  var confirmation =
      confirm("Do you want to see the polar bear or not?");
  if (confirmation == true)
      window.open('PolarBear.html', 'PolarBear',
      'height=350,width=320');
}
```

4 Position your cursor just before the closing bracket of the <BODY> tag, add a space, and add a timeout statement that reads **onLoad="var polarBearOpened = setTimeout('confirmPolarBear()', 10000);"**. If the timeout is not cleared within 10 seconds, the statement calls the confirmPolarBear message.

5 Finally, to cancel the timeout if the user clicks the polar bear link, add the statement **clearTimeout(polarBearOpened);** just before the window.open() statement in the openPolarBear() function.

6 Save the file, then open it in your Web browser. Wait 10 seconds and see if the confirm dialog box appears, prompting you to open the PolarBear.html file. When you see the confirm dialog box, click **OK** to make sure the code works properly.

7 Close both Web browser windows.

S U M M A R Y

- The Window object represents a Web browser window or an individual frame within a window.

- The hierarchy of JavaScript objects is called the JavaScript object model. It is important to understand the hierarchy of the JavaScript object model because an object's descendants are properties of the object.

- You can use methods and properties of objects in the JavaScript object model to manipulate the window, frames, and HTML elements displayed in a Web browser.

- An important object in the JavaScript object model is the Document object, which represents the HTML document displayed in a window.

- Although objects in the JavaScript object model are referred to in this text with an uppercase letter (Document object), you must always use a lowercase letter when using the object name in code, since you are actually referring to a property of the object.

- It is usually not necessary to include the Window object when listing an object's ancestors in a statement, because the Web browser automatically assumes that you are always referring to the currently displayed window, which is the top-level object in the JavaScript object model. In some cases, it is necessary to include the Window object when you need to clearly distinguish between the Window object and the Document object.

- You can use the open() method of the Window object to open a new Web browser window.

- You can use the name property of a Window object to specify a target window in which a hypertext link's URL opens the location where the results of a form submission appear.

- In the open() method, the URL argument represents the Web address or filename to be opened. The name argument assigns a value to the name property of the new Window object. The options argument represents a string that controls how the new Web browser window will appear.

- If you exclude the options string of the open() method, then all the normal options will be created in the new Web browser window. If you include the options string, then you must include all the components you want to be created with the new window—the new window is created with only the components you explicitly specify.

■ A Window object's name property can only be used to specify a target window with hypertext links or forms, and cannot be used in JavaScript code. If you want to use JavaScript code to control the new window located within the Web browser where it was created, then you must assign the new Window object that was created with the open() method to a variable.

■ The Window object is usually included with the open() and close() methods to clearly distinguish between the Window object and the Document object.

■ The setTimeout() method of the Window object is used in JavaScript to execute code after a specific amount of time has elapsed.

■ The clearTimeout() method of the Window object is used to cancel a setTimeout() method call before its code executes.

■ The setInterval() method of the Window object repeatedly executes the same code after being called only once.

■ The clearInterval() method of the Window object is used to cancel a setInterval() method call.

QUESTIONS

1. The Window object represents a(n) _____.
   a. <SCRIPT>...</SCRIPT> tag pair
   b. HTML document
   c. Web browser window
   d. <HEAD>...</HEAD> tag pair

2. Which of the following terms does *not* refer to the JavaScript object model?
   a. browser object
   b. client-side object
   c. Navigator object
   d. Internet Explorer object

3. The Document object represents _____
   a. the objects in a form.
   b. the HTML document displayed in a window.
   c. all JavaScript functions and methods within an HTML document.
   d. the Web browser window.

4. Which is the proper syntax for referring to the Document object in JavaScript code?
   a. `document.writeln("text string");`
   b. `Document.writeln("text string");`
   c. `DOCUMENT.writeln("text string");`
   d. `doc.writeln("text string");`

5. What is the correct syntax for referring to the value of a text box named inputField located on a form named application?
   a. `inputField.value`
   b. `application.inputField.value`
   c. `document.application.inputField.value`
   d. `application.value.inputField`

6. The self property refers to _____.
   a. a control that has the focus
   b. the currently executing function
   c. the current Document object
   d. the current Window object

7. What happens when you include an empty string as the first argument in the window.open() method?
   a. An empty window is opened.
   b. You receive an error message.
   c. A duplicate copy of the current window is opened.
   d. Nothing. The JavaScript interpreter ignores the statement.

8. Which of the following arguments are used for including both horizontal and vertical scroll bars in a new Web browser window created with the window.open() method?
   a. `verticalscroll=1,horizontalscroll=1`
   b. `showScrollbars=on`
   c. `scrollbars=true`
   d. `scrollbars=yes`

9. If you exclude the options string in the window.open() method, _____
   a. the new Web browser window will be created with just a menu bar and a toolbar.
   b. a blank Web browser window opens without any user interface items.
   c. all the normal options will be included in the new Web browser window.
   d. you will receive an error message.

10. The amount of time in the setTimeout() method is expressed in _____.
    a. milliseconds
    b. seconds
    c. minutes
    d. 10-second intervals

11. A setTimeout() method is canceled using the _____ method.
    a. cancelTimeout()
    b. clearTimeout()
    c. endTimeout()
    d. You cannot cancel the setTimeout() method.

12. How many times does code executed with a setInterval() method automatically repeat?
    a. once
    b. twice
    c. continuously
    d. never

13. A setInterval() method is canceled using the _____ method.
   a. cancelInterval()
   b. clearInterval()
   c. endInterval()
   d. You cannot cancel the setInterval() method.

 # E X E R C I S E S

1. Create an HTML document that contains a list of hyperlinks to your favorite recipes. Clicking each hyperlink opens a document in a separate window to display the selected recipe. Include a close button within each recipe's window. Name the main HTML document Recipes.html, and name each recipe document according to the recipe name. For example, if you have a recipe for apple pie, name its associated HTML document ApplePie.html. Save each file in the Tutorial.05 folder on your Student Disk.

2. Create an online "application" that prompts users for personal information such as their name, address, city, state, zip code, date of birth, and so on. Use a prompt dialog box to gather each piece of information, then save the data in unique variable names. Use a confirm dialog box to prompt users as to whether or not they would like to display the information they entered. If users select yes, display all the variables in a single alert dialog box. Separate each value with a line break. Before you display a variable, check to see if its value is empty, using a decision structure. If the variable is empty, exclude it from the alert dialog box. Save the file as VitalInfo.html in the Tutorial.05 folder on your Student Disk.

3. Create an HTML document that repeatedly turns a defaultStatus message on and off in the status bar, similar to a blinking neon sign. You will need to use a decision structure such as an `if...then` statement to create the document. Save the document as FlashGreeting.html in the Tutorial.05 folder on your Student Disk.

4. Create an html document that allows users to play a guessing game. Think of a number and assign it to a variable. Use the <INPUT> tag in a form to create a text box that a user can use to guess the number. Use another <INPUT> tag to create a button named Guess. Write a timeout that asks users if they want to continue the game if they do not press the Guess button within 10 seconds. If the user selects Cancel, close the Web browser window. If the user decides to continue, then restart the game and the timeout. Save the file as GuessNumber.html in the Tutorial.05 folder on your Student Disk.

In this section you will learn:
- How to create frames
- How to use the TARGET attribute
- How to create nested frames
- How to format frames
- About the NOFRAMES tag
- About the Location object
- About the History object
- About the Navigator Object
- How to reference frames and windows

Working with Frames and Other Objects

Creating Frames

The HTML documents you have created so far have consisted of a single Window object that can hold only one URL at a time. Using frames, you can split a single Web browser window into multiple windows, each of which can open a different URL. **Frames** are independent, scrollable portions of a Web browser window, with each frame capable of containing its own URL. JavaScript treats each frame in an HTML document as an individual window. Each individual frame has its own Window object, separate from other frames in the document. In addition, each frame is part of a top-level HTML document that defines the frames in a window. The top-level HTML document contains a Window object from which each frame's Window object is descended. Although frames are HTML elements and are not actually created using JavaScript, JavaScript is frequently used to programmatically access and control individual frames.

An HTML document is divided into frames using the **<FRAMESET>...</FRAMESET> tag pair**. <FRAME> tags and other <FRAMESET>...</FRAMESET> tag pairs are the only items that can be placed inside a <FRAMESET>...</FRAMESET> tag pair. The Web browser ignores any other text or tags. The <FRAMESET>...</FRAMESET> tag pair replaces the <BODY>...</BODY> tag pair that is used in nonframe HTML documents. Be sure not to include <BODY> tags within an HTML document containing <FRAMESET> tags. If you do, the <FRAMESET> tag is ignored and only the information contained in the <BODY> tags is displayed.

Frames in an HTML document can be created in horizontal rows, vertical columns, or both. Two attributes of the <FRAMESET> tag, ROWS, and COLS, determine whether frames are created as rows or columns. The **ROWS attribute** determines the number of horizontal frames to create. The **COLS attribute** determines the number of vertical frames to create. To set the dimensions of the frame, you assign a string to the ROWS or COLS attribute containing the percentage of space or number of pixels each row or column should take up on the screen, separated by commas. For example, `<FRAMESET ROWS="50%, 50%" COLS="50%, 50%">` creates two rows, which each take up 50 percent of the height of the screen, and two columns, which each take up 50 percent of the width of the screen. Figure 5-13 shows an example of the frames created using `<FRAMESET ROWS="50%, 50%" COLS="50%, 50%">`.

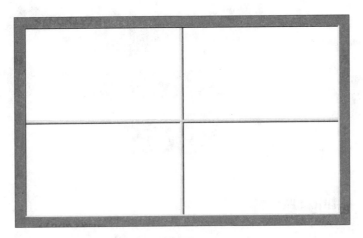

Figure 5-13: Frames created with `<FRAMESET ROWS="50%, 50%" COLS="50%, 50%">`

tip

You must define more than one row or more than one column or your frames will be completely ignored by the Web browser.

You can create frames using just rows or just columns. For example, Figure 5-14 shows the frames created with `<FRAMESET ROWS="50%, 50%">`, and Figure 5-15 shows the frames created with `<FRAMESET COLS="50%, 50%">`.

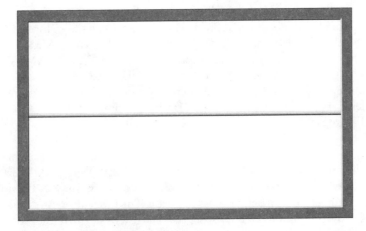

Figure 5-14: Frames created with `<FRAMESET ROWS="50%, 50%">`

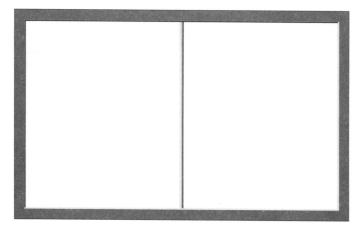

Figure 5-15: Frames created with `<FRAMESET COLS="50%, 50%">`

When you use percentages to specify the dimensions of a frame, the percentages are relative to the size of the window; that is, percentages adjust for the size of the window. In contrast, pixels represent exact or absolute sizes. They do not adjust for the size of the window. Users can set different default dimensions for their Web browser windows or resize their Web browser windows. Relative percentages can take these variations into account, whereas exact pixels cannot. For example, if you create two frames, each 100 pixels wide, they will not adjust for the actual dimensions of users' Web browser windows. If a user's screen is too small, your frames may be cut off. If a user's screen is a larger size, your frames might look strangely small. These size problems do not occur when you use percentages, because with percentages, the dimensions of the frame are calculated on the basis of the visible window.

It is helpful to use an asterisk (*) to represent the size of frames in your document that do not require an exact number of pixels or exact window percentage. The asterisk allocates any remaining screen space to an individual frame. If more than one frame is sized using an asterisk, then the remaining screen space is divided evenly. For example, `<FRAMESET COLS="100, *">` creates two frames in a column, using pixels to represent one column and an asterisk to represent the other column. The left column will always remain 100 pixels wide, but the right column will resize according to the visible screen space.

You can use combinations of pixels, percentages, and the asterisk to create frames. For example, the tag `<FRAMESET ROWS="100, 50%, *"` creates three rows: the first row is 100 pixels high, the second row takes up 50% of the visible window, and the asterisk allocates the remainder of the visible window to the third row.

The `<FRAMESET>` tag creates the initial frames within an HTML document. The **`<FRAME>` tag** is used to specify options for individual frames, including a frame's URL. The SRC attribute of the `<FRAME>` tag specifies the URL to be opened in an individual frame. Frame tags are placed within the `<FRAMESET>`...`</FRAMESET>` tag pair. Frames can be assigned a name using the NAME attribute; this name can then be used as a target for a hyperlink. You need a separate frame tag for each frame in your window.

The URLs of frames are opened in the order in which each <FRAME> tag is encountered, on a left-to-right, top-to-bottom basis. For example, the following code creates four frames, in two columns and two rows. Figure 5-16 shows the order in which the URL specified by a <FRAME> tag loads into each frame. The text displayed in each frame is contained within each file specified by the SRC attribute of each frame.

```
<FRAMESET ROWS="50%, 50%" COLS="50%, 50%">
     <FRAME SRC="FirstURL.html">
     <FRAME SRC="SecondURL.html">
     <FRAME SRC="ThirdURL.html">
     <FRAME SRC="FourthURL.html">
</FRAMESET>
```

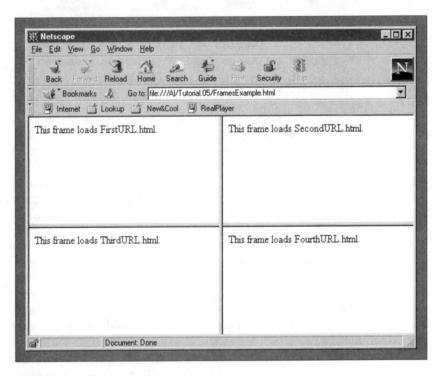

Figure 5-16: URL load order

Next you will start creating the Virtual Zoo program that you saw in the Tutorial preview. First you will create the main HTML document containing the program's <FRAMESET> and <FRAME> tags. This program creates a narrow column, the left frame that contains the list of animal names. The right frame is a larger column, taking up the remainder of the screen width, that displays an animal's picture.

To create the main HTML document for the Virtual Zoo program:

1 Start your text editor or HTML editor and create a new document.

2 Type the <HTML> and <HEAD> sections of the document:

```
<HTML>
<HEAD>
<TITLE>Virtual Zoo</TITLE>
</HEAD>
```

3 Add **<FRAMESET COLS="20%, *">** to start the frame set. The 20% in the code creates the narrow column on the left; the asterisk creates the wide column on the right.

4 Add the following two <FRAME> tags. The first <FRAME> tag opens an HTML file named list.html, which contains a list of animal names. The second frame opens an HTML file named welcome.html, which contains an opening message to display in the right frame. The window containing list.html is named *list*, and the window containing welcome.html is named *display*.

```
<FRAME SRC="list.html" NAME="list">
<FRAME SRC="welcome.html" NAME="display">
```

5 Type the following lines to close the <FRAMESET> and <HTML> tags::

```
</FRAMESET>
</HTML>
```

6 Save the file as **VirtualZoo.html** in the **Tutorial.05** folder on your Student Disk. Before you can open the VirtualZoo.html file, you need to create the welcome.html and list.html files.

Next you will create the welcome.html file. You will create the list.html file later.

To create welcome.html file:

1 Create a new document in your text editor or HTML editor.

2 Type the opening <HTML> and <BODY> tags:

```
<HTML>
<BODY>
```

3 Add the following line to instruct the user to click an animal name in the list, and press **Enter**:

```
Click an animal in the list to display its picture.
```

4 Type the closing <HTML> and <BODY> tags:

```
</BODY>
</HTML>
```

5 Save the file as **welcome.html** in the **Tutorial.05** folder on your Student Disk.

Using the TARGET Attribute

One popular use of frames creates a "table of contents" frame on the left side of a Web browser window with a "display" frame on the right side of the window to show the contents of a URL selected from a link in the table of contents frame. This type of design eliminates the need to open a separate Web browser window when you want to display the contents of another URL, as you did with the PolarBear.html file in Section A. Figure 5-17 shows an HTML document that is split into two frames. Each frame displays a different HTML document associated with a different URL. The left frame contains an HTML document that lists musical instruments, and the right frame contains an HTML document instructing the user to select an instrument. When you click the name of a musical instrument, a new document containing its picture and description opens in the right frame, as shown in Figure 5-18.

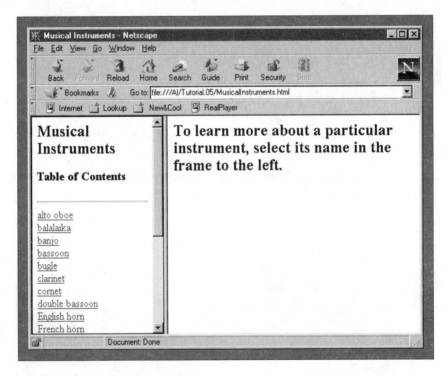

Figure 5-17: Musical Instruments document

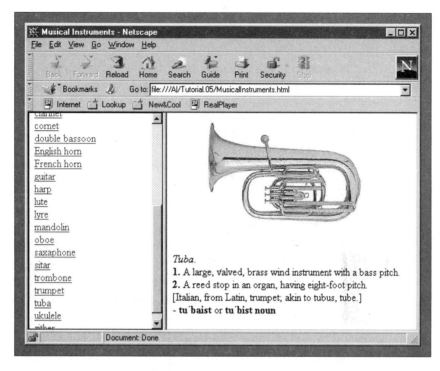

Figure 5-18: Musical Instruments document after selecting an instrument

Figure 5-19 shows the <FRAMESET> and <FRAME> tags used to create the Musical Instruments document.

```
<HTML>

<HEAD>

<TITLE>Musical Instruments</TITLE>

</HEAD>

<FRAMESET COLS="200,*">

     <FRAME SRC="InstrumentsList.html" NAME="list">

     <FRAME SRC="Welcome.html" NAME="display">

</FRAMESET>

</HTML>
```

Figure 5-19: Musical Instruments program

In the Musical Instruments program, two column frames are created. The first column is 200 pixels wide, and the second column takes up the remainder of the window. Two <FRAME> tags open HTML documents in each individual frame. The left frame of the Musical Instruments document contains hyperlinks for each instrument name. You can cause the HTML document for each hyperlink to open in the right frame, using the TARGET attribute of the <A> tag. The **TARGET attribute** determines in which frame or Web browser window a URL opens. For example, the name assigned to the right frame in the Musical Instruments document is *display*. When you click the tuba hyperlink in the left frame (named *list*), the tuba.html file opens in the display frame. The syntax for the <A> tag to open the tuba.html file in the display frame is <A HREF="tuba.html" TARGET="display">.

When you are using the same target window or frame for a long list of hyperlinks, it is easier to use the <BASE> tag instead of repeating the TARGET attribute within each hyperlink. The **<BASE> tag** is used to specify a default target for all links in an HTML document, using the assigned name of a window or frame. The following code uses the TARGET attribute repeatedly:

```
<A HREF="altooboe.html" TARGET="display">alto oboe</A><BR>
<A HREF="balalaika.html" TARGET="display">balalaika</A><BR>
<A HREF="banjo.html" TARGET="display">banjo</A><BR>
<A HREF="bassoon.html" TARGET="display">bassoon</A><BR>
<A HREF="bugle.html" TARGET="display">bugle</A><BR>
...additional instruments
```

You can write these statements more efficiently using the <BASE> tag, as follows:

```
<BASE TARGET="display">
<A HREF="altooboe.html">alto oboe</A><BR>
<A HREF="balalaika.html">balalaika</A><BR>
<A HREF="banjo.html">banjo</A><BR>
<A HREF="bassoon.html">bassoon</A><BR>
<A HREF="bugle.html">bugle</A><BR>
...additional instruments
```

Next you will create the list.html file, which contains a list of the animals in the Virtual Zoo program.

To create the list.html file:

1 Start your text editor or HTML editor and create a new document.

2 Type the opening <HTML> and <BODY> sections:

```
<HTML>
<BODY>
```

3 Since each animal's picture will always open in the right frame, add **<BASE TARGET="display">** to specify the right frame (named display) as the default target.

4 Press **Enter**, then add the following list of links for each animal. Note that instead of opening an HTML file in the display window, you are opening each .jpg graphic file instead. (The .jpg files for the animals are located in the Tutorial.05 folder on your Student Disk.)

```
<A HREF="Elephant.jpg">Elephant</A><BR>
<A HREF="Gazelle.jpg">Gazelle</A><BR>
<A HREF="Giraffe.jpg">Giraffe</A><BR>
<A HREF="Lion.jpg">Lion</A><BR>
<A HREF="PolarBear.jpg">Polar bear</A><BR>
<A HREF="Rhino.jpg">Rhino</A><BR>
<A HREF="Tiger.jpg">Tiger</A><BR>
<A HREF="Zebra.jpg">Zebra</A><BR>
```

5 Type the closing <HTML> and <BODY> tags:

```
</BODY>
</HTML>
```

6 Save the file as **list.html** in the **Tutorial.05** folder on your Student Disk.

7 Now that you have created the list.html file and the welcome.html file, you can open the **VirtualZoo.html** file in your Web browser. Click on each animal's name to see if the program works correctly. Figure 5-20 shows an example of the file displaying the giraffe in a Web browser.

Figure 5-20: VirtualZoo.html in a Web browser

8 Close the Web browser window.

Nesting Frames

JavaScript treats each frame in an HTML document as an individual window. Therefore, each individual frame (which is also a window) within a window can contain its own set of frames. You accomplish this nesting by including a <FRAME-SET>...</FRAMESET> tag pair *inside* another <FRAMESET>...</FRAMESET> tag pair. Frames that are contained within other frames are called **nested frames**.

As a Web browser starts creating frames, the URLs of frames are loaded in the order in which each <FRAME> tag is encountered. The following code creates a parent frame set consisting of two rows and two columns. A nested frame set that also consists of two rows and two columns is created within the second frame. The text displayed in each frame is contained within each file specified by the SRC attribute of each frame. Figure 5-21 displays how the frames would appear.

```
// The following line creates the main frame set
<FRAMESET ROWS="50%, 50%" COLS="50%, 50%">
     // The following line assigns frame1.html as the
     // URL of the first frame in the main frame set
     <FRAME SRC="frame1.html">
     // The following line creates a nested frame set
     // inside the second frame in the main frame set
     <FRAMESET ROWS="50%, 50%" COLS="50%, 50%">
          // The following lines assign URLs
     // to the nested frames
          <FRAME SRC="frame1.html">
          <FRAME SRC="frame2.html">
          <FRAME SRC="frame3.html">
          <FRAME SRC="frame4.html">
     </FRAMESET>
     // The following lines assign URLs to the
     // third and fourth frames in the main frame set
     <FRAME SRC="frame3.html">
     <FRAME SRC="frame4.html">
</FRAMESET>
```

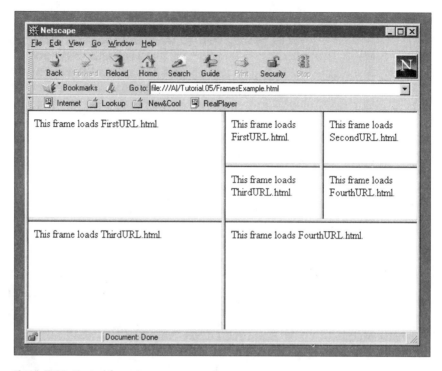

Figure 5-21: Nested frames

In the above example, the first <FRAMESET> tag creates the four parent frames in the window. The first <FRAME> tag assigns the URL frame1.html to the first frame in the parent frame set. The second <FRAMESET> tag is nested inside the second frame in the parent frame set. Each nested frame is then assigned a URL. The nested frames displayed in Figure 5-21 are more complicated than are normally found.

The following code shows a more typical example, using the Musical Instrument program. The right column of the parent frame contains a nested frame set consisting of two rows. The first row displays a picture of the musical instrument and the second row displays the description. Figure 5-22 shows how the Musical Instrument program with a nested frame appears in a Web browser.

```
<HTML>
<HEAD>
<TITLE>Musical Instruments</TITLE>
</HEAD>
<FRAMESET COLS="200,*">
    <FRAME SRC="left.html" NAME="list">
    <FRAMESET ROWS="75%,*">
        <FRAME SRC="instruments.jpg" NAME="picture">
        <FRAME SRC="welcome.html" NAME="description">
    </FRAMESET>
</FRAMESET>
</HTML>
```

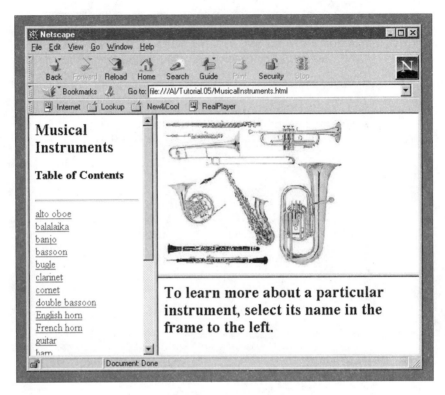

Figure 5-22: Musical Instruments program with nested frames

Next you will modify the Virtual Zoo program so that it includes a nested frame. The parent frame set will consist of two rows: the first row will display a title for the Virtual Zoo, and the second row will contain a nested frame set, consisting of the animal list and the frame that displays the animal's picture.

To add a nested frame to the Virtual Zoo program:

1   Open the **VirtualZoo.html** file in your text editor or HTML editor.

2   Add **<FRAMESET ROWS="20%,*">** above the existing <FRAMESET> tag. The existing frame set will be nested inside a new frame set.

3   After the opening tag for the new frame set, add **<FRAME SRC="title.html" NAME="title">** to specify that a document named title.html will be opened in the first frame.

4   Create a closing **</FRAMESET>** tag before the document's closing </HTML> tag to end the new frame set.

5   Save and close the file.

Next you need to create the title.html file that will be opened in the first frame of the Virtual Zoo program.

To create the title.html file:

1 Create a new document in your text editor or HTML editor.

2 Type the opening <HTML> and <BODY> tags:

```
<HTML>
<BODY>
```

3 Add **<H1>Virtual Zoo</H1>** to create a title line formatted with the <H1> tag.

4 Type the closing <HTML> and <BODY> tags:

```
</BODY>
</HTML>
```

5 Save the file as **title.html** in the **Tutorial.05** folder on your Student Disk, and then reopen the **VirtualZoo.html** file in your Web browser. Figure 5-23 shows an example of the file with the gazelle selected.

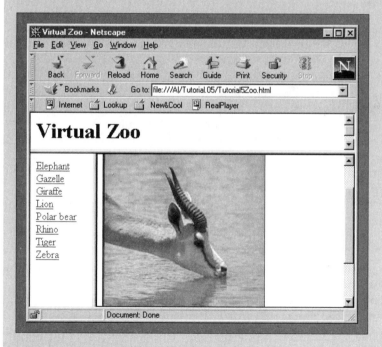

Figure 5-23: VirtualZoo.html with nested frames

6 Close the Web browser window.

Frame Formatting

The <FRAME> tag contains several attributes that change a frame's appearance and behavior. Figure 5-24 lists the attributes of the <FRAME> tag.

Attribute	Description
SRC	Specifies the URL to be opened in a frame
NAME	Assigns a name to an individual frame
NORESIZE	Disables the user's ability to resize an individual frame
SCROLLING	Determines whether a frame should include scroll bars
MARGINHEIGHT	Specifies the top and bottom margins of the frame in pixels
MARGINWIDTH	Specifies the left and right margins of the frame in pixels

Figure 5-24: <FRAME> tag attributes

You have already used the SRC attribute to specify a URL for a frame. You have also used the NAME attribute to specify a frame as a target for a hypertext link. The **NORESIZE attribute** disables the user's ability to resize an individual frame. You use the NORESIZE attribute when, for example, you want to add a title that should always be visible in a frame or on a Web page. Or, you may want to create a list of hyperlinks at the bottom of a Web page to help users navigate through your site. Normally, users can adjust the size of frames to suit their own purposes. To disable resizing of a frame, add the NORESIZE attribute to the <FRAME> tag.

By default, a Web browser will automatically add scroll bars to a frame when the contents of the frame are larger than the visible area. You can disable a frame's scroll bars using the **SCROLLING attribute**. Three values can be assigned to the SCROLLING attribute: yes, no, and auto. A value of *yes* always turns on the scroll bars, even when the contents of a frame fit within the visible area. A value of *no* completely disables a frame's scroll bars, even when the contents of a frame do not fit within the visible area. *Auto* turns the scroll bars on and off, depending on the visibility of the contents within a frame. Selecting a value of *auto* is equivalent to not including the SCROLLING attribute in the <FRAME> tag.

The following code shows an example of a program that includes both the NORESIZE and SCROLLING attributes. Figure 5-25 shows the output. The program contains three frames. The top frame provides a title for the Web page, and the bottom frame contains navigation buttons and hyperlinks. The middle frame contains the main content of the Web page. Since we do not want the user to resize the top and bottom frames, the NORESIZE attribute is included in the <FRAME> tags for the top and bottom frames. The SCROLLING attribute has also been set to no for the top and bottom frames, since the user does not need to scroll through them.

```
<FRAMESET ROWS="20%, *, 20%">
    <FRAME SRC="header.html" NORESIZE SCROLLING=no>
    <FRAME SRC="body.html">
    <FRAME SRC="navigationbar.html" NORESIZE SCROLLING=no>
</FRAMESET>
```

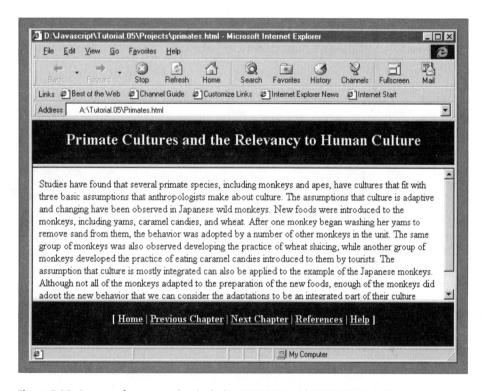

Figure 5-25: Output of program that includes NORESIZE and SCROLLING attributes

In the program output in Figure 5-25, the NORESIZE attribute in the top and bottom frame essentially eliminates resizing in the middle frame as well.

The **MARGINHEIGHT** and **MARGINWIDTH** attributes determine the margins of the frame in pixels. Figure 5-26 shows the output of the program in Figure 5-24 after the attributes MARGINHEIGHT=50 and MARGINWIDTH=50 have been added to the <FRAME> tag for the middle frame. The new tag for the middle frame reads <FRAME SRC="body.html" MARGINHEIGHT=50 MARGINWIDTH=50>.

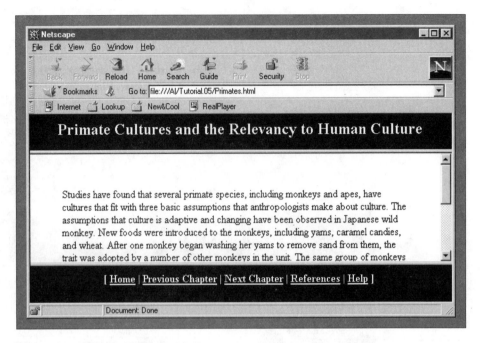

Figure 5-26: Middle frame changed to `<FRAME SRC="body.html" MARGINHEIGHT=50 MARGINWIDTH=50>`

Next you will add NORESIZE and SCROLLING attributes to the title frame of the Virtual Zoo program.

To add NORESIZE and SCROLLING attributes to the title frame of the Virtual Zoo program:

1 Open the **VirtualZoo.html** file in your text editor or HTML editor.

2 Add **NORESIZE** and **SCROLLING=no** just before the closing bracket for the `<FRAME SRC="title.html" NAME="title">` line.

3 Save and close the file, then open the **VirtualZoo.html** file in your Web browser. You should no longer see a scroll bar in the title frame. You should also be unable to resize the title frame.

The NOFRAMES Tag

Just as some older Web browsers are incompatible with JavaScript, they are also incompatible with frames. In Tutorial 1, you learned how to use the <NOSCRIPT>...</NOSCRIPT> tag pair to display a message to users of Web browsers that are incompatible with JavaScript. The **<NOFRAMES>...</NOFRAMES>**

tag pair is a similar type of tag; it displays an alternate message to users of Web browsers that are not capable of displaying frames. The <NOFRAMES>...</NOFRAMES> tag pair usually follows the <FRAME-SET>...</FRAMESET> tag pair. The following code shows an example of the <NOFRAMES> tag.

```
<FRAMESET ROWS="20%, *, 20%">
    <FRAME SRC="header.html" NORESIZE SCROLLING=no>
    <FRAME SRC="body.html">
    <FRAME SRC="navigationbar.html"
        NORESIZE SCROLLING=no>
</FRAMESET>
<NOFRAMES>
You cannot view this Web page because your Web browser
does not support frames. To view a no frames version of this
Web page,click <A HREF="no_frames.html">here</A>
</NOFRAMES>
```

tip

Web browsers that are capable of displaying frames ignore the <NOFRAMES> tag.

Next you will add a <NOFRAMES> tag to the Virtual Zoo program.

To add a <NOFRAMES> tag to the Virtual Zoo program:

1 Return to the **VirtualZoo.html** file in your text editor or HTML editor.

2 After the last closing </FRAMESET> tag, add the following <NOFRAMES>...</NOFRAMES> tag pair to warn users of frame-incompatible browsers that they cannot use this Web page.

```
<NOFRAMES>
You cannot view this Web page because your Web browser
does not support frames.
</NOFRAMES>
```

3 Save and close the file. Now, if someone opens the VirtualZoo.html file in a frames-incompatible browser, they will see the NOFRAMES message.

The Location Object

When you want to allow users to open one Web page from within another Web page, you usually create a hypertext link with the <A> tag. You can also use JavaScript code and the Location object to open Web pages. The **Location object** allows you to change to a new Web page from within JavaScript code. One reason you may want to change Web pages with JavaScript code is to redirect visitors to your Web site to a different or updated URL. The Location object contains several properties and methods for working with the URL of the document currently open in a Web browser window. When you use a method or property of the Location object, you must include a reference to the Location object itself. For example, to use the href property, you must write `location.href = URL;`. Figure 5-27 lists the Location object's properties.

Name	Description
hash	A URL's anchor
host	A combination of the URL's hostname and port sections
hostname	A URL's hostname
href	The full URL address
pathname	The URL's path
port	The URL's port
protocol	The URL's protocol
search	A URL's search or query portion

Figure 5-27: Location object properties

The properties of the Location object allow you to modify individual portions of a URL. When you modify any properties of the Location object, you generate a new URL, and the Web browser automatically attempts to open that new URL. Instead of modifying individual portions of a URL, it is usually easier to change the href property, which represents the entire URL. For example, the statement `location.href = "http://www.netscape.com";` opens the Netscape home page.

The Location object includes two methods: reload() and replace(). The **reload() method** of the Location object is equivalent to the Reload button in Netscape Navigator or the Refresh button in Internet Explorer; it causes the page currently displayed in the Web browser to open again. You can use the reload() button without any arguments, as in `location.reload();`, or you can include a Boolean argument of true or false. Including an argument of true forces the current Web page to reload from the server where it is located, even if no changes have been made to it. For example, the statement `location.reload(true);` forces the current page to reload. If you include an argument of false, or do not include any argument at all, then the Web page reloads only if it has changed.

The **replace() method** of the Location object is used to replace the currently loaded URL with a different one. This method works somewhat differently from loading a new document by changing the href property. The replace() method actually *overwrites* one document with another and replaces the old URL entry in the Web browser's history list with the new URL. In contrast, the href property opens a different document and *adds* it to the history list. You will learn about the history list next.

The History Object

The **History object** maintains a history list of all the documents that have been opened during the current Web browser session. Each Web browser window and frame, regardless of how many windows and frames you have open, contains its own internal History object. You can write a JavaScript program that uses the history list to navigate to Web pages that have been opened during a Web browser session. If you create custom navigation controls, such as form buttons, then you can add functionality to the controls using JavaScript code and the History object. The History object includes three methods, listed in Figure 5-28.

Method	Description
back()	The equivalent of clicking a Web browser's Back button
forward()	The equivalent of clicking a Web browser's Forward button
go()	Opens a specific document in the history list

Figure 5-28: Methods of the History object

This text describes only the properties and methods of the History object that are available to both Navigator 4 and Internet Explorer 4.

When you use a method or property of the History object, you must include a reference to the History object itself. For example, to use the back() method, you must write `history.back()`.

The back() and forward() methods allow a program to move backwards or forwards in a Web browser's history list. The code in Figure 5-29 shows how you can use the back() and forward() methods to control the page displayed in a Window object named samplePages. The page displayed in the samplePages window has been changed several times (using the href property of the Location object) to create a history list. The source page contains two buttons that simulate a Web browser's forward and back buttons. Clicking the back or forward buttons changes the page that is displayed in the samplePages window.

```
<SCRIPT LANGUAGE="JavaScript1.2">

<!-- HIDE FROM INCOMPATIBLE BROWSERS

samplePages = window.open("FirstWebPage.html", "WebPages");

samplePages.location.href = "SecondWebPage.html";

samplePages.location.href = "ThirdWebPage.html";

// STOP HIDING FROM INCOMPATIBLE BROWSERS -->

</SCRIPT>

<BODY>

<FORM>

<INPUT TYPE=button NAME="Back" VALUE=" Back "
    onClick="samplePages.history.back();">

<INPUT TYPE=button NAME="Forward" VALUE=" Forward "
    onClick="samplePages.history.forward();">

</FORM>

</BODY>
```

Figure 5-29: Program using the back() and forward() methods of the History object

The go() method is used for navigating to a specific Web page that has been previously visited. The argument of the go() method is an integer that indicates how many pages, forward or backward, you want to navigate. For example, `history.go(-2);` opens the Web page that is two pages back in the history list; the statement `history.go(3);` opens the Web page that is three pages forward in the history list. The statement `history.go(-1);` is equivalent to using the back() method, and the statement `history.go(1);` is equivalent to using the forward() method. The go() method can also be used with a string representing a previously opened Web page's URL. If you use only a portion, or substring, of the URL, the closest match in the history list is opened. For example, in the following code the Course Technology Web site is opened using the URL method of the Location object, then the Netscape home page is opened. The Web browser is then returned to the Course Technology home page, using the statement `history.go("Course");`.

```
location.href = "http://www.course.com";
location.href = "http://www.netscape.com";
history.go("Course");
```

Instead of using the `history.go("Course");` statement to navigate to the Course Technology Web site in the above example, you can use the statement `history.go(-1);` or `history.back();`.

The History object contains a single property, the length property, which contains the specific number of documents that have been opened during the current browser session. To use the length property, you use the syntax `history.length;`. The length property does not contain the URLs of the documents themselves, only an integer representing how many documents have been opened. The following code uses an alert dialog box to display the number of Web pages that have been visited during a Web browser session:

```
location.href = "FirstWebPage.html";
location.href = "SecondWebPage.html";
location.href = "ThirdWebPage.html";
alert("You have visited " + history.length
    + " Web pages.");
```

The Navigator Object

The **Navigator object** is used to obtain information about the current Web browser. The Navigator object gets its name from Netscape Navigator, but is also supported by Internet Explorer. The Navigator object does not contain any methods, only the properties listed in Figure 5-30.

Property	Returns
appCodeName	The Web browser code name
appName	The Web browser name
appVersion	The Web browser version
language	The language, such as English or French, used by the Web browser
platform	The operating system in use
userAgent	The user agent

Figure 5-30: Navigator object properties

Internet Explorer does not support the language property listed in Figure 5-30. Instead, it uses two other properties: userLanguage and systemLanguage.

Netscape Navigator and Internet Explorer each contain unique methods and properties that cannot be used with the other browser. The two browsers are incompatible with each other. For example, Netscape Navigator contains a method named home() that opens a Web browser's home page. Internet Explorer does not support the home() method. If you try to run a JavaScript program that contains the home() method in Internet Explorer, you will receive an error. Due to these types of incompatibilities, programmers use the properties of the Navigator object to determine which type of Web browser is running. The statement `browserType = navigator.appName;` returns the name of the Web browser in which the code is running to the browserType variable. You can then use the browserType variable to determine which code to run for the specific browser type.

The following with statement prints the six properties of the Navigator object for Netscape Navigator. Figure 5-31 shows the output.

```
with (navigator) {
    document.writeln("Browser code name: " + appCodeName);
    document.writeln("Web browser name: " + appName);
    document.writeln("Web browser version: " + appVersion);
    document.writeln("Language: " + language);
    document.writeln("Operating platform: " + platform);
    document.writeln("User agent: " + userAgent);
}
```

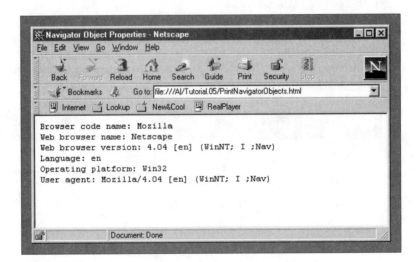

Figure 5-31: Output of Navigator object properties program

Next you will print the properties of the Navigator object for the Web browser you are using. Since Navigator and Internet Explorer contain different property names in their Navigator objects, you will use the `for...in` statement to loop through the properties in your specific type of Web browser.

tip

You learned about the `for...in` statement in Tutorial 4.

To print the properties of the Navigator object for the Web browser you are using:

1 Start your text editor or HTML editor and create a new document.

2 Type the <HTML> and <HEAD> sections of the document:

```
<HTML>
<HEAD>
<TITLE>Navigator Properties</TITLE>
</HEAD>
```

3 Add **<BODY>** to begin the body of the HTML document and press **Enter**.

4 Add an opening <PRE> tag and the opening statements for a JavaScript section:

```
<PRE>
<SCRIPT LANGUAGE="JavaScript1.2">
<!-- HIDE FROM INCOMPATIBLE BROWSERS
```

5 Type the following for...in statement to print the name and value for all the properties in the Navigator object:

```
for (prop in navigator) {
    document.writeln(prop + ": " + navigator[prop]);
}
```

6 Add the following code to close the <SCRIPT>, <PRE>, <BODY>, and <HTML> tags:

```
// STOP HIDING FROM INCOMPATIBLE BROWSERS -->
</SCRIPT>
</PRE>
</BODY>
</HTML>
```

7 Save the file as **NavigatorObjects.html** in the **Tutorial.05** folder on your Student Disk. Open the **NavigatorObjects.html** file in your Web browser. Figure 5-32 shows the output as it appears in Navigator. Figure 5-33 shows the output as it appears in Internet Explorer.

help

Figure 5-32 includes the plugins property, which is unique to Navigator. Figure 5-33 includes properties that are not available in Navigator, such as the systemLanguage and userLanguage properties.

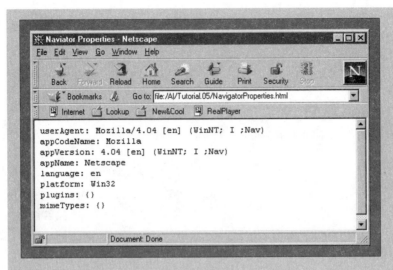

Figure 5-32: Output of NavigatorObjects.html in Navigator

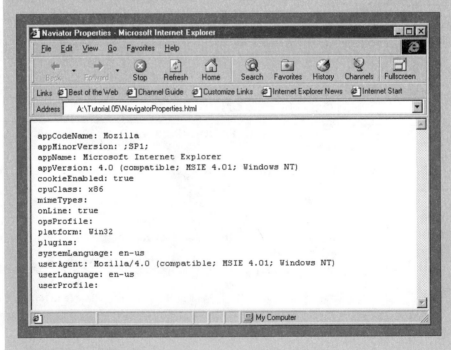

Figure 5-33: Output of NavigatorObjects.html in Internet Explorer

8   Close the Web browser window.

Referring to Frames and Windows

When working with multiple frames and windows, you need to be able to refer to individual frames and windows in JavaScript code. When you create a new window, for instance, you may want to change the content displayed in that window. Or, if you have multiple frames in a window, you may need to change the content displayed in one frame, depending on a link selected in another frame. Recall from Section A that some of the objects in the JavaScript object model, including the Frame object, are arrays of objects. The Frame object includes a frames[] array that contains all the frames in a window. The first frame in a window is referred to as frames[0], the second frame is referred to as frames[1], and so on. If a window contains no frames, then the frames[] array is empty. To refer to a frame within the same frame set, you use the **parent property** of the Window object combined with the frame's index number from the frames[] array. For example, if you have an HTML document that creates four frames, the frames can be referred to as parent.frames[0], parent.frames[1], parent.frames[2], and parent.frames[3], respectively.

To better understand how to use the parent property and frames[] array, consider the HTML document shown in Figure 5-34.

Figure 5-34: Parent property and frames[] array example

The two frames in Figure 5-34 were created using the following code:

```
<FRAMESET ROWS="50%, 50%">
    <FRAME SRC="frame1.html" NAME="FirstFrame">
    <FRAME SRC="frame2.html" NAME="SecondFrame">
</FRAMESET>
```

The first frame refers to the second frame's URL by using an onClick event in an <INPUT> tag, as follows:

```
<INPUT TYPE="button"
    VALUE="Click here to display the 2nd frame's URL "
    onClick="alert(parent.frames[1].location.href);">
```

As you can see in this code, the statement `parent.frames[1].loca-tion.href` returns the URL of the second frame. If the button were returning the first frame's URL, you would use the statement `self.location.href` or `par-ent.frames[0].location.href`, since it is the first frame in the frames[] array. Note that in order to display the href property of the Location object, you must include `location` in the statement, since it is necessary to refer to all of an object's ancestors (with the exception of the Window object).

tip

∙∙

Remember that each frame contains its own Window object, as well as its own Location, History, and Navigator objects.

∙∙

In addition to using the element index number of the frames[] array to refer to a frame, you can use the name you assigned with the <FRAME> tag. The statement `alert(parent.SecondFrame.location.href);` also identifies the second frame's URL.

Referring to single frame sets with the parent property is fairly straightforward. When you are working with nested frame sets, referring to individual frames is more complex. To refer to a frame set that is one level above the current frame set, you use a second parent property. If you are working with a nested frame set and want to refer to the URL of the third frame in the frame set that *contains* the nested frame set, you use the statement `parent.parent.frames[2].location.href`. Figure 5-35 shows a variation of the program in Figure 5-34. In this figure, the two frames on the right are nested within a parent frame set. The column frame on the left is the first frame in the parent frame set. The two frames on the right are nested within the second frame of the parent frame set. For the frame containing the button to obtain the URL of the column frame, you use the statement `parent.parent.frames[0].location.href`.

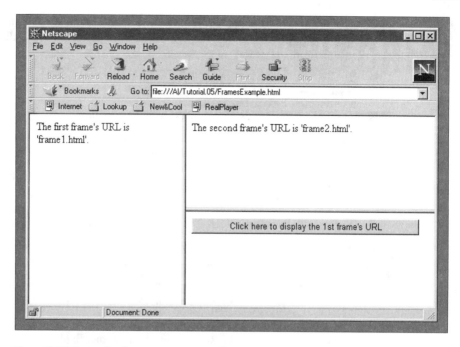

Figure 5-35: Example of a parent.parent reference

Another property that is used to refer to a window is the top property of the Window object. The **top property** refers to the topmost window in an HTML document. When working with frames, the top property refers to the window that constructed the frames. For example, if the code to create a parent frame set is located in a file named FramesExample.html, then the statement `top.location.href` would return the full URL for the FramesExample.html document, no matter which frame it was used in. When the top property is used in an HTML document that does not contain frames, then it refers to the window itself.

S U M M A R Y

- Frames are independent, scrollable portions of a Web browser window, with each frame capable of containing its own URL.

- Each frame has its own Window object, separate from other frames in the document.

- An HTML document is divided into frames using the <FRAMESET>...</FRAMESET> tag pair.

- The ROWS attribute of the <FRAMESET> tag determines the number of rows to create in a frame set. The COLS attribute of the <FRAMESET> tag determines the number of columns to create in a frame set.

■ The <FRAME> tag is used for specifying options for individual frames, including a frame's URL. The SRC attribute of the <FRAME> tag specifies the URL to be opened in an individual frame.

■ The URLs of frames are opened in the order in which each <FRAME> tag is encountered, from left to right and top to bottom.

■ The TARGET attribute determines in which frame or window a URL opens.

■ The <BASE> tag uses an assigned name of a window or frame to specify a default target for all links in an HTML document.

■ Frames that are contained within other frames are called nested frames.

■ The NORESIZE attribute disables the ability to resize an individual frame.

■ You can disable a frame's scroll bars with the SCROLLING attribute.

■ The <NOFRAMES>...</NOFRAMES> tag pair displays an alternate message to users of Web browsers that are unable to display frames.

■ The Location object contains several properties and methods for working with the URL of the document currently open in a Web browser window.

■ The reload() method of the Location object is equivalent to the Reload button in Netscape Navigator or the Refresh button in Internet Explorer.

■ The replace() method of the Location object replaces the currently loaded URL with a different URL.

■ The **History object** maintains a history list of all the documents that have been opened during the current Web browser session.

■ The back() and forward() methods of the History object allow a program to move backwards or forwards in a Web browser's history list.

■ The go() method of the History object is used for navigating to a specific Web page that has been previously visited.

■ The Navigator object is used to obtain information about the current Web browser.

■ The Frame object includes a frames[ ] array that contains all the frames in a window.

■ To refer to a frame within the same frame set, you use the parent property of the Window object combined with the frame's array index number. You can also use the name you assigned with the <FRAME> tag to refer to a frame within the same frame set.

■ When you want to refer to a frame set that is one level above the current frame set, you use a second parent property.

■ The top property refers to the topmost window in an HTML document.

QUESTIONS

1. Which of the following tag pairs is used to create frames?
   a. <BEGIN FRAME>...</END FRAME>
   b. <FRAMESET>...</FRAMESET>
   c. <NEW FRAME>...</NEW FRAME>
   d. <FRAMEBUILD>...</FRAMEBUILD>

2. The size of rows and columns in a frame can be set using a percentage of the screen size or by using _____.
   a. inches
   b. picas
   c. pixels
   d. a Web browser's internal sizing capability

3. Which symbol can be used to allocate any remaining screen space to an individual frame?
   a. *
   b. &
   c. %
   d. #

4. The URLs of frames are loaded in the order in which each <FRAME> tag is encountered _____.
   a. alphabetically
   b. top to bottom and left to right
   c. left to right and top to bottom
   d. according to each <FRAME> tag's ORDER attribute

5. Which is the correct syntax for a <FRAME> tag that loads a URL of MyHomePage.html?
   a. <FRAME HREF="MyHomePage.html">
   b. <FRAME URL="MyHomePage.html">
   c. <FRAME HTML="MyHomePage.html">
   d. <FRAME SRC="MyHomePage.html">

6. The _____ attribute of the <A> tag determines into which frame or window a URL opens.
   a. OPENINWIN
   b. SELECT
   c. GOAL
   d. TARGET

7. The _____ tag is used for specifying a default target for all links in an HTML document using the assigned name of a window or frame.
   a. <BASE>
   b. <SOURCE>
   c. <TARGET>
   d. <DEFAULT>

8. A frame set contained within another frame set is called a(n) _____ frame.
   a. controlling
   b. relative
   c. nested
   d. integral

9. To prevent a user from resizing a frame, you include the _____ attribute within the <FRAME> tag.
   a. NORESIZE
   b. RESIZE=NO
   c. FIXED
   d. LOCKED

10. Which of the following attributes of the <FRAME> tag turns off scroll bars for an individual frame?
   a. verticalscroll=0, horizontalscroll=0
   b. showScrollbars=off
   c. scrolling=no
   d. scrollbars=no

11. Which attribute(s) of the <FRAME> tag is/are used to determine a frame's left and right margins?
   a. SIDEMARGINS
   b. INSIDE and OUTSIDE
   c. MARGINLEFT and MARGINRIGHT
   d. MARGINWIDTH

12. Which tag pair is used to display an alternate message to users of Web browsers that are unable to display frames?
   a. <NOFRAMES>...</NOFRAMES>
   b. <NOSCRIPT>...</NOSCRIPT>
   c. <ALTERNATE>...</ALTERNATE>
   d. <MISSINGFRAMES>...</MISSINGFRAMES>

13. The History object is used for _____.
   a. determining when changes have been made to either an individual HTML document or the Web site where it is contained
   b. tracking which users have accessed a particular Web site
   c. tracking which users have accessed a particular HTML document
   d. maintaining a list of the documents that have been opened for the current session of a Web browser window

14. Which of the following is *not* a method of the History object?
   a. back()
   b. forward()
   c. go()
   d. next()

15. The full URL of a Web page is located in the _____ property of the History object.

    a. src

    b. href

    c. hash

    d. url

16. To overwrite one HTML document with another, and replace the old URL entry in the Web browser's list of previously visited Web sites, you use the _____ method of the History object.

    a. reload()

    b. refresh()

    c. replace()

    d. open()

17. The _____ object is used to obtain information about the current Web browser.

    a. Window

    b. Browser

    c. Explorer

    d. Navigator

E X E R C I S E S

1. Create an HTML document with two frames. One frame takes up 200 pixels on the left side of the screen, and the other frame takes up the remainder of the right portion of the screen. Use hyperlinks to create a list of your favorite Web sites in the left frame. When a user clicks a favorite Web site in the left frame, it should open in the right frame. Format the frames so they cannot be resized. Save the file as Favorites.html in the Tutorial.05 folder on your Student Disk.

2. Create an HTML document with two frames. One frame takes up 75 percent of the upper portion of the screen, and the other frame takes up 25 percent of the bottom portion of the screen. In the bottom frame, use hyperlinks to create your navigation buttons Previous, Next, and Go To. Use onClick events and the methods of the History and Location objects to make each button work. Save the file as PersonalNavigator.html in the Tutorial.05 folder on your Student Disk.

3. Create an HTML document that includes a button that displays all the properties of the Navigator object for your Web browser in an alert dialog box. Insert a line break between each property name. Save the HTML document as BrowserProperties.html in the Tutorial.05 folder on your Student Disk.

TUTORIAL

Forms

6

case ▶ Many of WebAdventure's clients want to include guest books, comment forms, surveys, shopping carts used for placing orders online, and games as part of their Web sites. Web sites use forms to create these applications. One of WebAdventure's clients, a new software company, wants to create an online product registration form to gather information from customers. WebAdventure has asked you to learn how to develop this product registration form.

Previewing the Product Registration Form

The form you will create in this tutorial is a product registration form. In Section A, you will learn how to put the different form tags together to create the product registration form. In Section B, you will learn how to use JavaScript to validate and check the form's data, as well as submit the form's data to a Web server or to an e-mail address.

To preview the Product Registration form:

1 In your Web browser, open the **Tutorial6_ProductRegistration.html** file from the Tutorial.06 folder on your Student Disk. The Tutorial6_ProductRegistration.html file creates two frames. The bottom frame displays the first page of the Product Registration form, Tutorial6_CustomerInfo.html. After a user clicks the Next button at the bottom of Tutorial6_CustomerInfo.html, the second page, Tutorial6_ProductInfo.html, appears. The frame at the top of the page contains hidden form fields that store the values of each field when a user switches from the Tutorial6_CustomerInfo.html file to the Tutorial6_ProductInfo.html file. Figure 6-1 displays an example of the customer information form in Navigator.

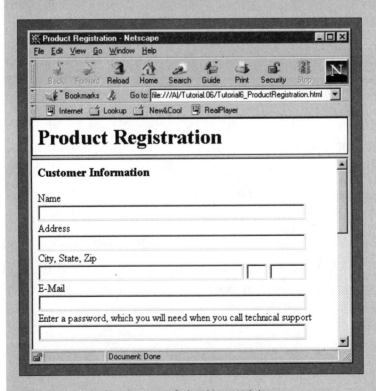

Figure 6-1: Tutorial6_CustomerInfo.html in a Web browser

2 Before entering data into the form's fields, scroll to the bottom of the **Tutorial6_CustomerInfo.html** form and click the **Next** button. You will see an alert dialog box warning you that several fields on the form are required. Fill in the required fields. If you make a mistake, click the **Reset** button to start the form over. When you are finished, click the **Next** button. The second form, shown in Figure 6-2, collects product information.

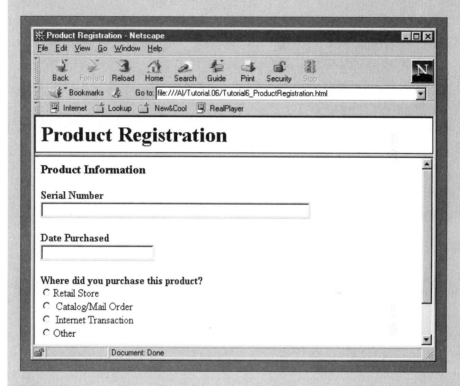

Figure 6-2: Tutorial6_ProductInfo.html

3 Fill in the product information fields and click the **Submit** button. To submit the forms, you must fill in the serial number and date fields, or an alert dialog box will appear. The Submit button on the Tutorial6_ProductInfo.html form is used to send the form's data to a Web server. Since you do not have a server to work with, clicking the Submit button does nothing. At the end of this tutorial, you will learn how to submit the form's data to an e-mail address.

4 When you are finished, close the Web browser window.

5   Next, examine the code for the Tutorial6_CustomerInfo.html and the Tutorial6_ProductInfo.html files in your text editor or HTML editor. The form tags in the <BODY> section of each file create the controls displayed on each form. The <SCRIPT>...</SCRIPT> tag pair in each file's <HEAD> section copies the values from each field to hidden fields in the Tutorial6_TopFrame.html file that appears in the frame at the top of the product registration page. The hidden fields keep track of each field's value when a user navigates between the Tutorial6_CustomerInfo.html and the Tutorial6_ProductInfo.html files. It is the contents of these hidden fields that are sent to a Web server—not the contents of the fields on the Tutorial6_CustomerInfo.html and the Tutorial6_ProductInfo.html files.

6   Close your text editor or HTML editor when you are finished examining the code.

Working with Forms in JavaScript

Overview of Forms

Forms are one of the most common HTML elements used with JavaScript. Many Web sites use forms to collect information from users and transmit that information to a server for processing. Typical forms you may encounter on the Web include order forms, surveys, and applications. Another type of form frequently found on Web pages is a form that gathers search criteria from a user. After the search criteria are entered, the information is sent to a database on a server. The server then queries the database, using the data gathered in the search form, and returns the results to a Web browser. You use JavaScript to make sure a form's fields were entered properly and to perform other types of preprocessing before the data is sent to the server. Without JavaScript, the only action that HTML can take on a form's data is to send it to a server for processing.

To process the data submitted from a Web browser to a server, you use a special protocol named Common Gateway Interface (CGI). Although there are now other ways of dealing with data transmitted to a server, including ASP, ISPI, and NSAPI, CGI is one of the oldest and most popular methods. Although it is not directly related to JavaScript programming, you will learn about CGI in this tutorial, since the processing of data on a server (for example, running a query against a database) is an important aspect of Web programming. You will also learn how to use forms and JavaScript to create programs and Web pages that do not require data to be processed on a server.

Since the focus of this text is on JavaScript programming, this tutorial does not cover the formatting and design aspects of forms. If you would like information on formatting and designing forms, refer to *Creating Web Pages with HTML*, written by Patrick Carey and published by Course Technology in their New Perspectives series.

You can also use HTML forms to create many types of programs that are driven by JavaScript and do not involve transmitting data to a server for processing. For example, the calculator program in Tutorial 2 is created with a form, and its functionality is created with JavaScript commands. In addition, forms provide a way of adding user interface controls, such as buttons and text boxes, to an HTML document. Without forms, few HTML elements other than hyperlinks can be used for interacting with users. A form within an HTML document can consist of a single button or control or can be composed of multiple elements. Figure 6-3 shows an example of a form containing custom navigation buttons.

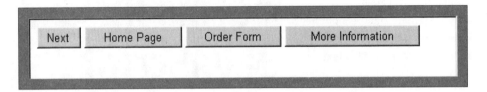

Figure 6-3: Custom navigation buttons created with a form

In earlier tutorials, you have seen a common form element, the <INPUT> tag, in action in several examples and have used it in various exercises. You have also used the <FORM> tag itself in several exercises. In Tutorial 2, you learned about JavaScript events; events associated with the <INPUT> tag are among the most commonly used types of JavaScript events. Although you have used the <FORM> and <INPUT> tags, there are many other important aspects of forms that you should know about.

The Common Gateway Interface

The **Common Gateway Interface**, or **CGI**, is a simple protocol that allows Web pages to communicate with Web-server-based programs. CGI's function is to start a Web-server-based program, then pass and receive environment variables to and from it. An **environment variable** is part of an operating system, not just part of a function or a program, as are JavaScript variables. An example of a CGI environment variable is server_name, which contains the domain name or IP address of a Web server. A Web-server-based application that processes CGI environment variables is called a **CGI script** or **CGI program** and can be designed to perform a multitude of functions. Do not confuse the CGI protocol itself with a CGI script. The CGI protocol's primary purpose is to send the data received from a Web page to a program on a server, then to send any response from the program back to the Web page. The program that runs on the server can be a database program or some type of custom application. You can write server programs in a scripting language such as AppleScript, PERL, and TLC, or in a programming language such as Visual C++, Visual Basic, or others.

CGI scripts are used to process information entered into HTML forms. HTML form elements are used to pass information that is entered into a form to CGI environment variables. These CGI environment variables are then sent to a CGI script on a Web server. The CGI script performs some sort of action, such as a query, and either sends a response back to the requesting Web page or generates a new HTML document. Figure 6-4 shows an example of a CGI script written in PERL that generates a new Web page as a response to the requesting Web page.

```perl
# !/usr/local/bin/perl
#
# formdata.pl— "Form Data Received" program
#
# The following line prints the CGI response header that
# is required for HTML output. Each \n sends
# a blank line (response headers must be followed
# by a blank line).
print "Content-type: text/html\n\n" ;


# The following lines print the HTML response
# page to STDOUT:
print <<EOF ;
<HTML>
<HEAD><TITLE>Form Data Received</TITLE></HEAD>
<BODY>
<H1>Your form data has been received.</H1>
</BODY>
</HTML>
EOF


exit ;
```

Figure 6-4: CGI script written in PERL

Do not worry about understanding how the PERL code in the CGI script functions. The example only demonstrates that CGI allows an HTML page to interact with a Web server application or programming language *other* than JavaScript.

The purpose of this text is to teach JavaScript. It does not explain the structure or syntax of other programming languages used to create CGI scripts. When a CGI script is included in an example, this text explains only the CGI script's functionality and not how the script or program works.

The <FORM> Tag

All forms begin and end with the <FORM>...</FORM> tag pair. The **<FORM>...</FORM> tag pair** designates a form within an HTML document and contains all text and tags that make up a form. You can include as many forms as you like within an HTML document. However, unlike frames, you cannot nest one form inside another form. Be sure to close each form with a closing </FORM> tag. If the JavaScript interpreter encounters a new <FORM> tag before a closing </FORM> tag, then all the form elements following the second form tag will be included as part of the first form. Figure 6-5 shows an HTML document containing two forms. Figure 6-6 shows the document as it appears in a Web browser.

```
<HTML>
<HEAD>
<TITLE>Two Forms</TITLE>
</HEAD>
<BODY>
<H1>This document contains two forms.</H1><P>
<H2>This is the first form.</H2><P>
<FORM>
<INPUT TYPE="text">
<INPUT TYPE="button", VALUE="Click Me">
</FORM>
<HR>
<H2>This is the second form.</H2><P>
<FORM>
```

Figure 6-5: HTML document with two forms

```
<INPUT TYPE="text">

<INPUT TYPE="button", VALUE="Click Me"

</FORM>

</BODY>

</HTML>
```

Figure 6-5: HTML document with two forms (continued)

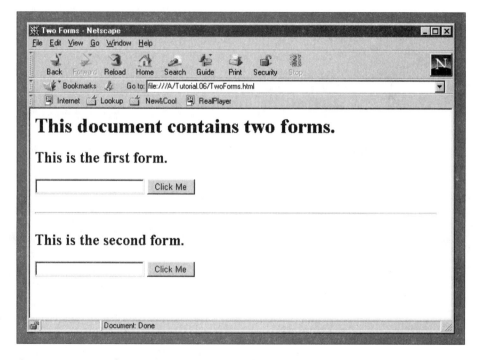

Figure 6-6: Output of HTML document with two forms

You can use a variety of attributes with the <FORM> tag , as shown in Figure 6-7.

Attribute	Description
ACTION	Specifies a URL to which a form's data will be submitted. If this attribute is excluded, the data is sent to the URL that contains the form. Typically you would specify the URL of a program on a server or an e-mail address.
METHOD	Determines how a form's data will be submitted. The two options for this attribute are GET and POST. The default option, GET, appends a form's data as one long string to the URL specified by the ACTION attribute. The POST option sends a form's data as a transmission separate from the URL specified by the ACTION attribute. Although GET is the default, POST is considered the preferred option, since it allows the server to receive the data separately from the URL.
ENCTYPE	Specifies the format of the data being submitted. The default value is *application/x-www-form-urlencoded*.
TARGET	Specifies a window in which any results returned from the server appear.
NAME	Designates a name for the form.

Figure 6-7: Attributes of the <FORM> tag

The ENCTYPE attribute specifies an encoding protocol known as Multipurpose Internet Mail Extension, or MIME. Encoding with MIME ensures that data is not corrupted when transmitted across the Internet. The MIME protocol was originally developed to allow different file types to be transmitted as attachments to e-mail messages. Now MIME has become a standard method of exchanging files over the Internet, although the technology is still evolving. MIME types are specified using two-part codes separated by a forward slash (/). The first part specifies the MIME type, and the second part specifies the MIME subtype. The default MIME type of `application/x-www-form-urlencoded` specifies that a form's data should be encoded as one long string. The only other MIME types allowed with the ENCTYPE attribute are `multipart/form-data`, which encodes each field as a separate section, and `text/plain`, which is used to submit form data to an e-mail address.

tip

If you would like more information on encoding, refer to the *Internet Engineering Task Force's Request for Comments* document number 1867 at http://www.ics.uci.edu/ pub/ietf/html/rfc1867.txt.

Consider the code in Figures 6-8 and 6-9, which shows how to use attributes of the <FORM> tag. The code in Figure 6-8 contains HTML tags that set up a document with three frames; one of the frames includes a form. The code in Figure 6-9 displays the HTML tags for the simple form contained in the frame named *subscription*. Figure 6-10 shows how the program appears in a Web browser.

```
<HTML>

<HEAD>

<TITLE>Emily the Chimp</TITLE>

</HEAD>

<FRAMESET ROWS="85%,*">

     <FRAMESET COLS="52%,*">

             <FRAME SRC="Emily.jpg" NAME="Emily">

             <FRAME SRC="dialog.html" NAME="dialog">

     </FRAMESET>

     <FRAME SRC="subscription.html" NAME="subscription">

</FRAMESET>

</HTML>
```

Figure 6-8: Three frames document

```
<HTML>

<BODY>

<FORM ACTION="http://www.Emily-the-Chimp/cgi-bin/subscribe"
     METHOD="post" NAME="subscriptionForm" TARGET="dialog">

<INPUT TYPE="text" SIZE=50>

<INPUT TYPE="submit" VALUE="Subscribe">

</FORM>

</BODY>

</HTML>
```

Figure 6-9: Subscription frame

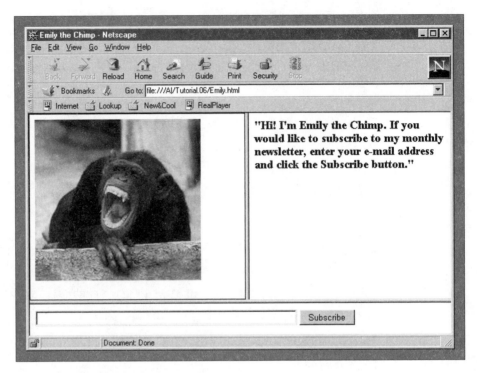

Figure 6-10: Emily the Chimp Web page

The <FORM> tag in Figure 6-9 contains an ACTION attribute that sends the form's data to the URL `http://www.Emily-the-Chimp/cgi-bin/ process_subscription`. The METHOD attribute of the <FORM> tag specifies that the form's data will be sent with the POST method instead of the default GET method. Since the ENCTYPE attribute is omitted, the form's data will be encoded with the default *application/x-www-form-urlencoded* format. The form is also assigned a name of *subscriptionForm*. The last attribute in the <FORM> tag, TARGET, is set to *dialog*. The TARGET attribute specifies the window in which text and HTML tags returned from the server are to be rendered. In this case, TARGET is set to the *dialog* frame created by the code shown in Figure 6-8. Let's assume that the form is submitted using the Subscribe button. After the data is received by the server, the imaginary *process_subscription* CGI script adds the e-mail address to a database, then returns a message to the *dialog* frame, as shown in Figure 6-11.

Next you will start creating the Product Registration document that you saw in the preview of this tutorial. You use frames to create the Product Registration document. First you will create the main HTML document that loads the frame set tags. Then you will create the HTML documents for each frame.

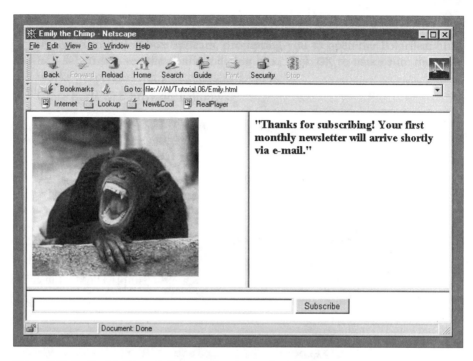

Figure 6-11: Emily the Chimp Web page after form submission

To create the main HTML document that loads the frame set tags for the Product Registration form:

1 Start your text editor or HTML editor and create a new document.

2 Type the <HTML> and <HEAD> sections of the document:

```
<HTML>
<HEAD>
<TITLE>Product Registration</TITLE>
</HEAD>
```

3 Add **<FRAMESET ROWS="60, *">** to start the frame set. The top frame, which is set to 60 pixels, contains the title of the Product Registration form. The bottom frame takes up the remainder of the screen and contains the form itself.

4 Add the following two <FRAME> tags. The first <FRAME> tag opens an HTML file named TopFrame.html, which contains the form title. The second frame opens an HTML file named CustomerInfo.html, which contains the first form. The window containing TopFrame.html is named *topframe,* and the bottom window containing CustomerInfo.html is named *bottomframe.*

```
<FRAME SRC="TopFrame.html" NAME="topframe" SCROLLING=no>
<FRAME SRC="CustomerInfo.html" NAME="bottomframe">
```

5 Type the following lines to close the <FRAMESET> and <HTML> tags:

```
</FRAMESET>
</HTML>
```

6 Save the file as **ProductRegistration.html** in the **Tutorial.06** folder on your Student Disk.

7 Close **ProductRegistration.html**.

Next you will create the TopFrame.html file, which appears in the frame named *topframe*.

To create the TopFrame.html file:

1 Create a new document in your text editor or HTML editor.

2 Add the following tags to create the simple HTML file containing the heading for the form:

```
<HTML>
<BODY>
<H1>Product Registration</H1>
</BODY>
</HTML>
```

3 Save the file as **TopFrame.html** in the **Tutorial.06** folder on your Student Disk.

4 Close **TopFrame.html**.

Finally, you will create the CustomerInfo.html file that contains the form tags for the Product Registration document.

To create the CustomerInfo.html file:

1 Create a new document in your text editor or HTML editor.

2 Type the <HTML>, Head, and <BODY> tags of the document:

```
<HTML>
<HEAD>
<TITLE>Customer Information</TITLE>
</HEAD>
<BODY>
```

3 Type <H3>Customer Information</H3> as a subtitle for the Product Registration document.

4 Add the following two tags to create the form section. Throughout this section, you will add form elements between these tags.

```
<FORM NAME="customerInfo">
</FORM>
```

tip

> Since you will not actually be submitting this form to a CGI script, the <FORM> tag does not include the ACTION, METHOD, and ENCTYPE attributes.

5 Add the following code to close the <BODY> and <HTML> tags:

```
</BODY>
</HTML>
```

6 Save the file as **CustomerInfo.html** in the **Tutorial.06** folder on your Student Disk. Do not open the CustomerInfo.html file, since it does not yet contain any form elements.

7 Close your text editor or html editor.

Form Elements: an Overview

There are three tags used within the <FORM>...</FORM> tag pair to create form elements: <INPUT>, <SELECT>, and <TEXTAREA>. The <INPUT> tag, as you know, is used to create input fields that users interact with. The <SELECT> tag displays choices in a drop-down menu or scrolling list known as a selection list. The <TEXTAREA> tag is used to create a text field in which users can enter multiple lines of information. Any form elements into which a user can enter data, such as a text box, or that a user can select or change, such as a radio button, are called **fields**.

The <INPUT>, <TEXTAREA>, and <SELECT> tags can include NAME and VALUE attributes. The NAME attribute defines a name for a tag, and the VALUE attribute defines a default value. When you submit a form to a CGI script, the form's data is submitted in name=value tag pairs, based on the NAME and VALUE attributes of each tag. For example, if you have a text <INPUT> field created with the statement `<INPUT TYPE="text" NAME="company_info" VALUE="ABC Corp.">`, then a name=value tag pair of *company_info=ABC Corp.* will be sent to a CGI script (unless the default value is changed to something else). If you intend to submit your form to a CGI script, you must include a NAME attribute for each <INPUT>, <TEXTAREA>, and <SELECT> tag. You are not required to include a VALUE attribute or enter a value into a field before the form data is submitted, since a value of null or empty is legal. However, it is a good idea to validate a form's data using JavaScript before the data is submitted to a CGI script. To validate the data using JavaScript, you need to specify a value for the VALUE attribute.

tip

> You will learn how to validate a form's data using JavaScript in Section B.

Input Fields

The <INPUT> tag is used to create **input fields** that use different types of interface elements to gather information. Attributes of the <INPUT> tag include ALIGN, CHECKED, MAXLENGTH, NAME, SIZE, TYPE, VALUE, and SRC. The TYPE attribute determines the type of element to be rendered and is a required attribute. Valid values for the TYPE attribute are text, password, radio, checkbox, reset, button, submit, image, and hidden. Values for each attribute must be surrounded by quotation marks in order to function properly with both Navigator and Internet Explorer. Figure 6-12 lists attributes of the <INPUT> tag, describes their functions, and describes their syntax.

Attribute	Description
ALIGN	Specifies the alignment of an image created with the TYPE attribute. Valid values are ABSBOTTOM, ABSMIDDLE, BASELINE, BOTTOM, LEFT, MIDDLE, RIGHT, TEXTTOP, and TOP
CHECKED	Determines whether or not a radio button or a check box is selected
MAXLENGTH	Sets the maximum number of characters that can be entered into a field
NAME	Designates a name for the element; part of the name=value tag pair that is used to submit data to a CGI script
SIZE	Accepts an integer value that determines how many characters wide a text field is
SRC	Specifies the URL of an image
TYPE	Specifies the type of element to be rendered; TYPE is a required attribute. Valid values are text, password, radio, checkbox, reset, button, submit, image, and hidden
VALUE	Sets an initial value in a field or a label for buttons; part of the name=value tag pair that is used to submit data to a CGI script

Figure 6-12: Common attributes of the <INPUT> tag

Text Boxes

An <INPUT> tag with a type of *text* (<INPUT TYPE="text">) creates a simple text box that accepts a single line of text. You can include the NAME, VALUE, MAXLENGTH, and SIZE attributes with the <INPUT TYPE="text"> tag. The following tags create the text boxes shown in Figure 6-13:

```
<FORM ACTION="http://example_url/cgi-bin/cgi_program"
    METHOD="post" NAME="exampleForm">
```

```
Name<BR>
<INPUT TYPE="text" NAME="name"
    VALUE="The White House" SIZE=50><BR>
Address<BR>
<INPUT TYPE="text" NAME="address"
    VALUE="1600 Pennsylvania Ave." SIZE=50><BR>
City, State, Zip<BR>
<INPUT TYPE="text" NAME="city"
    VALUE="Washington" SIZE=38>
<INPUT TYPE="text" NAME="state"
    VALUE="DC" SIZE=2 MAXLENGTH=2>
<INPUT TYPE="text" NAME="zip"
    VALUE="20500" SIZE=5 MAXLENGTH=5>
</FORM>
```

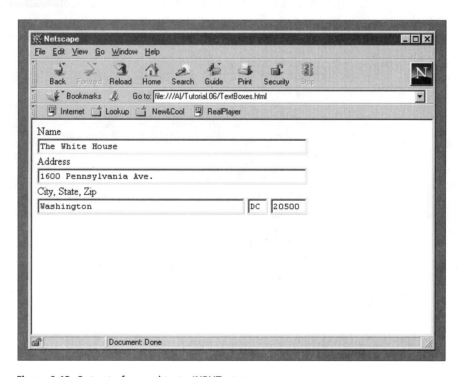

Figure 6-13: Output of several text <INPUT> tags

When you include the VALUE attribute in a text <INPUT> tag, the specified text is used as the default value when the form is first loaded, as shown in Figure 6-13.

Next you will add the first few text <INPUT> tags to the CustomerInfo.html file.

To add text <INPUT> tags to the CustomerInfo.html file:

1 Open the **CustomerInfo.html file** in your text editor or HTML editor.

2 Within the file's <FORM>...</FORM> tag pair, add the following text <INPUT> tags, which gather a customer's name, address, city, state, zip, and e-mail address.

```
Name<BR>
<INPUT TYPE="text" NAME="name" SIZE=50><BR>
Address<BR>
<INPUT TYPE="text" NAME="address" SIZE=50><BR>
City, State, Zip<BR>
<INPUT TYPE="text" NAME="city" SIZE=38>
<INPUT TYPE="text" NAME="state" SIZE=2 MAXLENGTH=2>
<INPUT TYPE="text" NAME="zip" SIZE=5 MAXLENGTH=5><BR>
E-Mail<BR>
<INPUT TYPE="text" NAME="email" SIZE=50><BR>
```

3 Save and close the **CustomerInfo.html** document, then open the **ProductRegistration.html** file in your Web browser. The text <INPUT> fields in your file should appear similar to Figure 6-14.

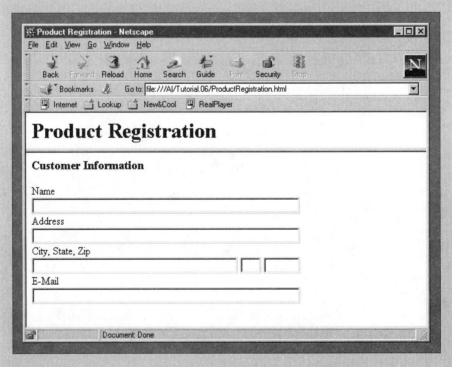

Figure 6-14: Product Registration program after adding text <INPUT> fields

4 Close the Web browser window.

Password Boxes

An <INPUT> tag with a type of *password* (<INPUT TYPE="password">) is similar to an <INPUT> tag with a type of text. However, each character that a user types in a password box appears as an asterisk to hide it from anyone who may be looking over the user's shoulder. You can include the NAME, VALUE, MAXLENGTH, and SIZE attributes with the <INPUT TYPE="password"> tag. The following code creates a password box with a maximum length of eight characters:

```
<FORM ACTION="http://exampleurl/cgi-bin/cgi_program"
     METHOD="post" NAME="exampleForm">
Please enter a password of 8 characters or less:<BR>
<INPUT TYPE="password" NAME="password" MAXLENGTH=8>
</FORM>
```

Next you will add a password <INPUT> tag to the CustomerInfo.html file that prompts users to enter a password that they will use when they call technical support.

To add a password <INPUT> tag to the CustomerInfo.html file:

1 Open the **CustomerInfo.html file** in your text editor or HTML editor.

2 After the last text <INPUT> tag, add the following lines for the password <INPUT> tag, which prompts users for a password that they will use when they call technical support:

```
Enter a password, which you will need when you call
technical support<BR>
<INPUT TYPE="password" NAME="password" SIZE=50><P>
```

3 Save and close the **CustomerInfo.html** document, then open **ProductRegistration.html** in your Web browser. Test the password field to see if the password you enter appears as asterisks. The password <INPUT> field in your file should appear similar to Figure 6-15.

4 Close the Web browser window.

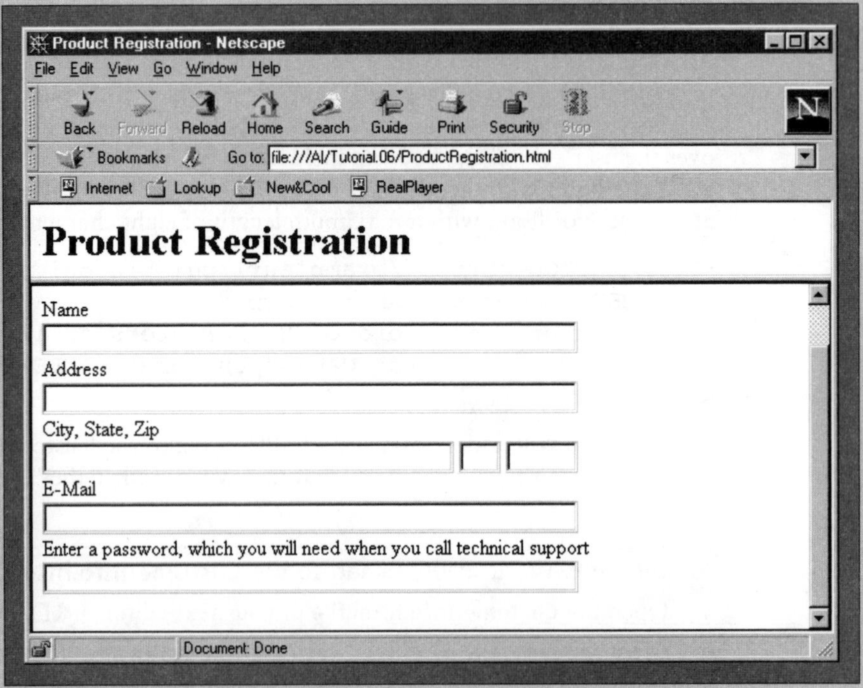

Figure 6-15: Product Registration program after adding a password <INPUT> field

Radio Buttons

An <INPUT> tag with a type of radio (<INPUT TYPE="radio">) is usually used to create a group of radio buttons from which you can select only one value. To create a group of radio buttons, all radio buttons in the group must have the same NAME attribute. Each radio button requires a VALUE attribute. Only one checked radio button in a group creates a name=value pair when a form is submitted to a CGI script. You can also include the CHECKED attribute in a radio <INPUT> tag to select an initial value for a group of radio buttons. If the CHECKED attribute is not included in any of the <INPUT TYPE="radio"> tags in a radio button group, then the first radio button in the group is selected when the form loads. The following code creates a group of five radio buttons.

```
<FORM ACTION="http://exampleurl/cgi-bin/cgi_program"
    METHOD="post" NAME="exampleForm">
```

```
Please select your favorite type of music:<BR>
<INPUT TYPE="radio" NAME="music"
     VALUE="jazz">Jazz<BR>
<INPUT TYPE="radio" NAME="music"
     VALUE="classical">Classical<BR>
<INPUT TYPE="radio" NAME="music"
     VALUE="country">Country<BR>
<INPUT TYPE="radio" NAME="music"
     VALUE="rock" CHECKED>Rock<BR>
<INPUT TYPE="radio" NAME="music"
     VALUE="r&b">Rhythm and Blues<BR>
</FORM>
```

Next you will add to the CustomerInfo.html file radio button <INPUT> tags that prompt the user for the type of computer platform they are using.

To add radio <INPUT> tags to the CustomerInfo.html file:

1 Open the **CustomerInfo.html file** in your text editor or HTML editor.

2 After the password <INPUT> field, add the following radio <INPUT> tags. Users select one radio button to indicate the type of computer platform they use. Notice that each radio button is given the same NAME attribute of *platform*.

```
What platform do you use?<BR>
<INPUT TYPE="radio" NAME="platform"
     VALUE="win95-98">Windows 95/98
<INPUT TYPE="radio" NAME="platform"
     VALUE="winnt">Windows NT
<INPUT TYPE="radio" NAME="platform"
     VALUE="unix">UNIX
<INPUT TYPE="radio" NAME="platform"
     VALUE="mac">Macintosh<P>
```

3 Save and close the **CustomerInfo.html** document, then open the ProductRegistration.html file in your Web browser. The radio button <INPUT> fields in your file should appear similar to Figure 6-16.

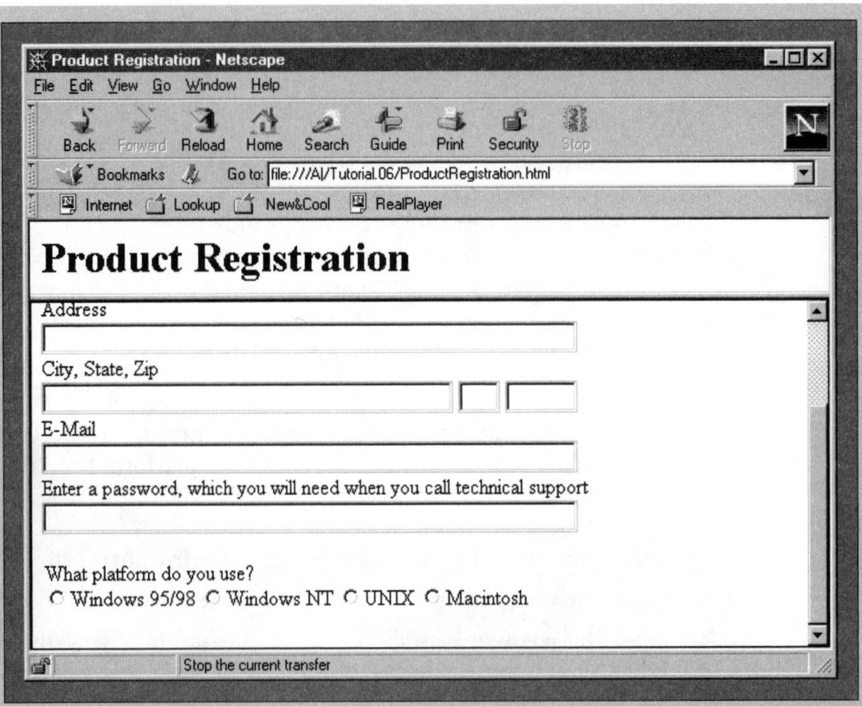

Figure 6-16: Product Registration program after adding radio <INPUT> fields

4   Close the Web browser window.

Check Boxes

An <INPUT> tag with a type of *checkbox* (<INPUT TYPE="checkbox">) creates a box that can be set to yes (checked) or no (unchecked). You use check boxes when you want users to select whether or not to include a certain item or to allow users to select multiple values from a list of items. Include the CHECKED attribute in a checkbox <INPUT> tag to set a check box's initial value to *yes*. You can also include the NAME and VALUE attributes with the checkbox <INPUT> tag. If a check box is selected (checked) when a form is submitted, then the check box's name=value pair is included in the form's data. If a check box is not selected, a name=value pair will not be included in the form's submitted data.

The following code creates several check boxes:

```
<FORM ACTION="http://example_url/cgi-bin/cgi_program"
    METHOD="post" NAME="exampleForm">
<H3>Which programming languages do you know?</H3>
<INPUT TYPE="checkbox" NAME="prog_languages"
    VALUE="JavaScript"
    CHECKED>JavaScript<BR>
<INPUT TYPE="checkbox" NAME="prog_languages"
    VALUE="Java">Java<BR>
<INPUT TYPE="checkbox" NAME="prog_languages"
    VALUE="Visual Basic">
```

```
Visual Basic<BR>
<INPUT TYPE="checkbox" NAME="prog_languages"
    VALUE="Visual C++">
Visual C++<BR>
</FORM>
```

Like radio buttons, you can group check boxes by giving each check box the same NAME value, although each check box can have a different value. Unlike radio buttons, users can select as many check boxes in a group as they like. When multiple check boxes on a form share the same name, then multiple name=value pairs, each using the same name, are submitted to the CGI script. In the preceding example, if the JavaScript and Java check boxes are selected, then two name=value pairs, prog_languages=JavaScript and prog_languages=Java, are submitted. Note that you are not required to group check boxes with the same NAME attribute. While a common group name helps to identify and manage groups of check boxes, it is often easier to keep track of individual values when each check box has a unique NAME attribute.

Next you will add the CustomerInfo.html file checkbox <INPUT> tags that prompt users for the types of software they use. Later in this tutorial, you will copy each check box (and all other form fields) to corresponding hidden fields on another form. In order to make it easier to keep track of individual check box values as they are copied to the hidden form fields, each checkbox will include a unique NAME value.

To add checkbox <INPUT> tags to the CustomerInfo.html file:

1 Open the **CustomerInfo.html file** in your text editor or HTML editor.

2 After the last radio <INPUT> field, add the following checkbox <INPUT> tags that prompt users for the types of software they use.

```
What types of software do you use? (check all
    that apply)<BR>
<INPUT TYPE="checkbox" NAME="wp" VALUE="wp">
    Word Processing<BR>
<INPUT TYPE="checkbox" NAME="ss" VALUE="ss">
    Spreadsheets<BR>
<INPUT TYPE="checkbox" NAME="db" VALUE="db">
    Database<BR>
<INPUT TYPE="checkbox" NAME="gr" VALUE="gr">
    Graphics/CAD<BR>
<INPUT TYPE="checkbox" NAME="pr" VALUE="pr">
    Programming<P>
```

3 Save and close the **CustomerInfo.html** document, then open the ProductRegistration.html file in your Web browser. The checkbox <INPUT> fields in your file should appear similar to those in Figure 6-17.

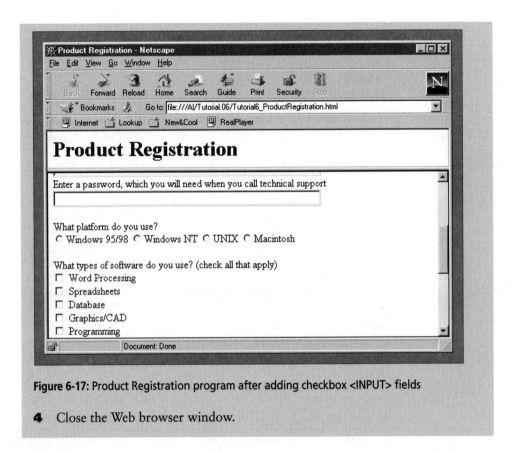

Figure 6-17: Product Registration program after adding checkbox <INPUT> fields

4   Close the Web browser window.

Reset Buttons

An <INPUT> tag with a type of *reset* (<INPUT TYPE="reset">) clears all of a form's entries and resets each form element to its initial value specified by the VALUE attribute. Although you can include the NAME attribute for a reset button if you want to refer to it in JavaScript code, it is not required since reset buttons are never submitted to a CGI script as part of a form's data. If you do not include a VALUE attribute, then the default label of the reset button, *Reset*, appears.

The following code creates a form with a reset button. Figure 6-18 shows the resulting Web page after entering some data.

```
<H3>BillingInformation</H3>
<FORM ACTION="http://exampleurl/cgi-bin/cgi_program"
    METHOD="post" NAME="exampleForm">
<B>Name</B><BR>
<INPUT TYPE="text" NAME="name" SIZE=50><BR>
<B>Address</B><BR>
<INPUT TYPE="text" NAME="address" SIZE=50><BR>
<B>City, State, Zip</B><BR>
<INPUT TYPE="text" NAME="city" SIZE=38>
```

```
<INPUT TYPE="text" NAME="state" SIZE=2>
<INPUT TYPE="text" NAME="zip" SIZE=5 MAXLENGTH=5><BR>
<B>Credit Card</B><BR>
<INPUT TYPE="radio" NAME="creditcard" CHECKED>VISA
<INPUT TYPE="radio" NAME="creditcard">MasterCard
<INPUT TYPE="radio" NAME="creditcard">
     American Express<BR>
<INPUT TYPE="radio" NAME="creditcard">Discover
<INPUT TYPE="radio" NAME="creditcard">
     Diners Club<BR>
<B>Credit Card Number</B><BR>
<INPUT TYPE="text" NAME="cc#"
     VALUE="xxxx xxxxxx xxxxx" SIZE=50><BR>
<B>Expiration Date</B><BR>
<INPUT TYPE="text" NAME="expdate"
     VALUE="1/1/99" SIZE=50><P>
<INPUT TYPE="reset">
</FORM>
```

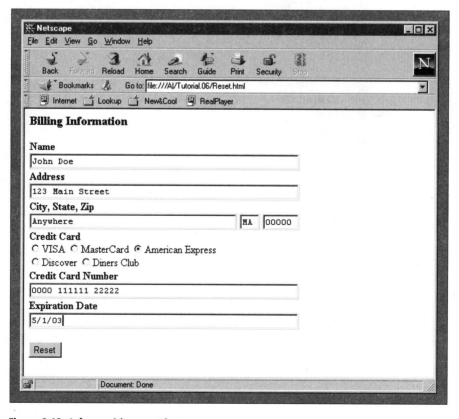

Figure 6-18: A form with a reset button

If you click the reset button in the form shown in Figure 6-18, then the contents of each field clear or reset to their default values, as shown in Figure 6-19.

▶ **tip**

The width of a button created with the reset <INPUT> tag depends on the number of characters in its VALUE attribute.

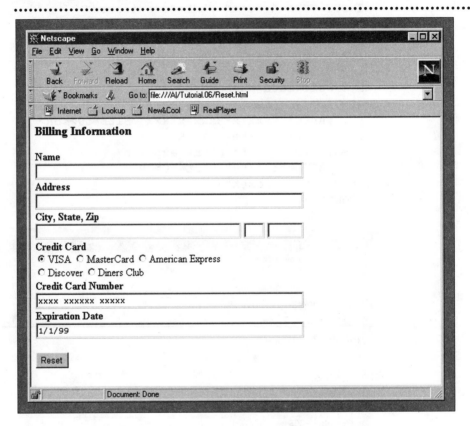

Figure 6-19: Output of a form after clicking the Reset button

Next you will add a reset <INPUT> tag to the CustomerInfo.html file.

To add a reset <INPUT> tag to the CustomerInfo.html file:

1 Open the **CustomerInfo.html file** in your text editor or HTML editor.

2 After the last checkbox <INPUT> field, add **<INPUT TYPE="reset">**.

3 Save and close the **CustomerInfo.html** document, then open the **ProductRegistration.html** file in your Web browser. The reset <INPUT> field in your document should appear similar to that in Figure 6-20.

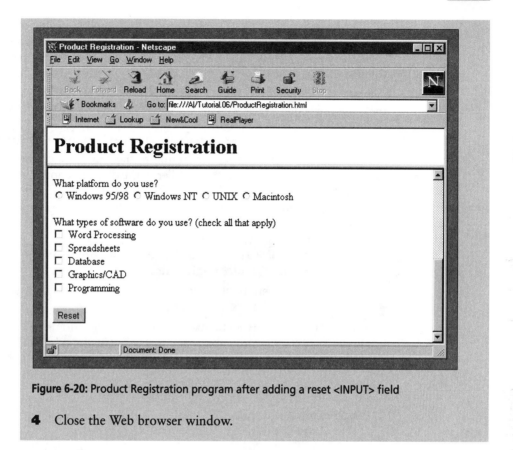

Figure 6-20: Product Registration program after adding a reset <INPUT> field

4 Close the Web browser window.

Command Buttons

An <INPUT> tag with a type of *button* (<INPUT TYPE="command">) creates a command button similar to the OK and Cancel buttons you see in dialog boxes. Command buttons are also similar to submit and reset buttons. However, command buttons do not submit form data to a CGI script as submit buttons do, nor do they clear the data entered into form fields as do reset buttons. Instead, command buttons use an onClick event handler to execute JavaScript code that performs some type of function such as a calculation. Although a command button does not require an event handler, it is essentially useless without one, since its main purpose is to execute JavaScript code. You are not required to include the NAME and VALUE attributes, since a user cannot change the value of a command button. If you include the NAME and VALUE attributes, then the default value set with the VALUE attribute is transmitted to a CGI script along with the rest of the form's data. The following code creates a simple command button:

```
<INPUT TYPE="button" NAME="command_button"
    VALUE="Click Here"
    onClick="alert('You Clicked a Command Button');">
```

The code for the <INPUT> tag creates a button with a value of *Click Here* and a name of *command_button*. The <INPUT> tag's onClick event handler in the preceding example displays an alert dialog box containing the text *You Clicked a Command Button*.

••

The width of a button created with the <INPUT TYPE="button"> tag is based on the number of characters in its VALUE attribute.

••

Next you will add a command button to the CustomerInfo.html file. The button will contain an onClick event handler that calls a function that opens a second page of the Product Registration form. The second page is another HTML document named ProductInfo.html.

To add a button <INPUT> tag to the CustomerInfo.html file that opens a second page of the Product Registration form:

1 Open the **CustomerInfo.html file** in your text editor or HTML editor.

2 Just before the closing </HEAD> tag, create the following <SCRIPT>...</SCRIPT> tag pair, along with a function that uses the HREF property of the Location object to replace the CustomerInfo.html file with an HTML document named ProductInfo.html.

```
<SCRIPT LANGUAGE="JavaScript1.2">
<!-- HIDE FROM INCOMPATIBLE BROWSERS
function nextForm() {
    location.href="ProductInfo.html";
}
// STOP HIDING FROM INCOMPATIBLE BROWSERS -->
</SCRIPT>
```

3 After the reset <INPUT> field in the body of the HTML document, add the following code to create a button <INPUT> tag named *next*. The button's onClick event calls the nextForm() function you added in Step 2.

```
<INPUT TYPE="button" NAME="next" VALUE=" Next "
    onClick="nextForm()"><P>
```

4 Save and close the **CustomerInfo.html** document.

Next, you will create the ProductInfo.html file that opens when a user clicks the next button.

To create the ProductInfo.html file:

1 Create a new document in your text editor or HTML editor.

2 Type the following <HTML>, <HEAD>, and <BODY> tags to start the ProductInfo.html file:

```
<HTML>
<HEAD>
<TITLE>Product Information</TITLE>
</HEAD>
<BODY>
```

3 Create a heading for the document, using an <H3>...</H3> tag pair:

```
<H3>Product Information</H3>
```

4 Type the following form section, which contains a text box for the product's serial number, a text box for the date of purchase, a radio button group to select how the product was purchased, and a reset button.

```
<FORM NAME="productInfo">
<B>Serial Number</B><BR>
<INPUT TYPE="text" NAME="serial" SIZE=50><P>
<B>Date Purchased</B><BR>
<INPUT TYPE="text" NAME="date" SIZE=20><P>
<B>Where did you purchase this product?</B><BR>
<INPUT TYPE="radio" NAME="where" VALUE="retail">Retail
    Store<BR>
<INPUT TYPE="radio" NAME="where" VALUE="catalog_mail">
   Catalog/Mail Order<BR>
<INPUT TYPE="radio" NAME="where" VALUE="internet">
   Internet Transaction<BR>
<INPUT TYPE="radio" NAME="where" VALUE="other">Other<P>
<INPUT TYPE="reset">
```

5 Type the closing </FORM>, </BODY>, and </HTML> tags:

```
</FORM>
</BODY>
</HTML>
```

6 Save the file as **ProductInfo.html** in the **Tutorial.06** folder on your Student Disk. Close the **ProductInfo.html** file. Now open the **ProductRegistration.html** file in your Web browser and click the **Next** button. The bottom frame of the document should open the ProductInfo.html file, as shown in Figure 6-21.

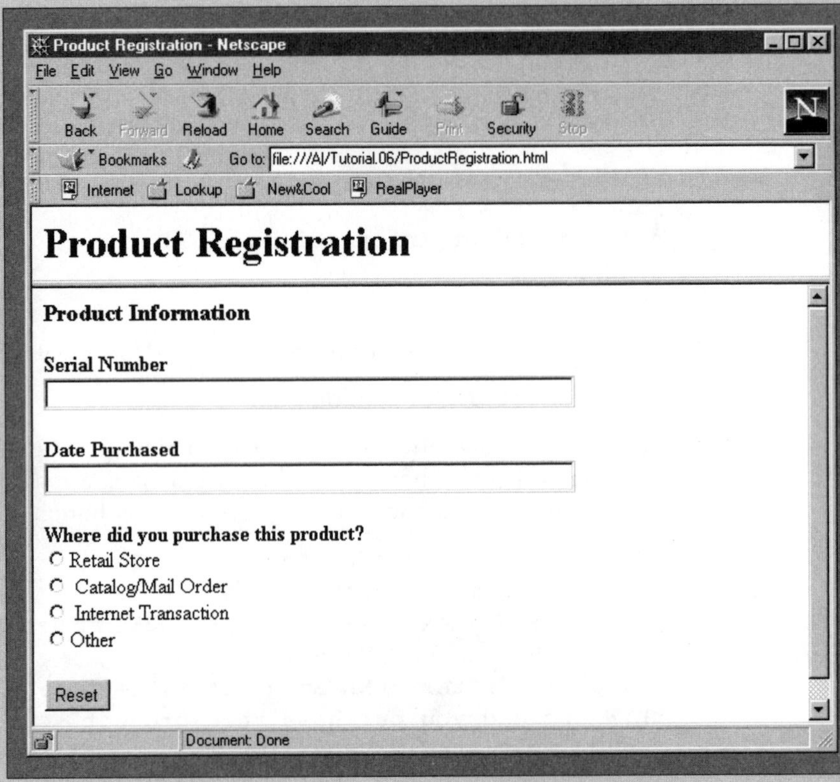

Figure 6-21: ProductInfo.html file in bottom frame of the ProductRegistration.html file

7 Close the Web browser window.

Submit Buttons

An <INPUT> tag with a type of *submit* (<INPUT TYPE="submit">) creates a button that submits the form to a CGI script on a server. The ACTION attribute of the <FORM> tag that creates the form determines to what URL the form is submitted. You can include the NAME and VALUE attributes with the submit <INPUT> tag. If you do not include a VALUE attribute, then the default label of the submit button, *Submit Query*, appears.

The following code creates a Web page with a submit button:

```
<H1>Video of the Month Club</H1>
<H3>Select the types of movies you like to see and
click the videocassette image.<BR>
A new movie will be sent to you every month.<H3>
<FORM ACTION="http://exampleurl/cgi-bin/cgi_program"
    METHOD="post" NAME="exampleForm">
<INPUT TYPE="checkbox" NAME="genre" VALUE="action">
```

```
Action
<INPUT TYPE="checkbox" NAME="genre" VALUE="adventure">
Adventure<BR>
<INPUT TYPE="checkbox" NAME="genre" VALUE="comedy">
Comedy
<INPUT TYPE="checkbox" NAME="genre" VALUE="drama">
Drama<BR>
<INPUT TYPE="checkbox" NAME="genre" VALUE="sci_fi">
Science Fiction
<INPUT TYPE="checkbox" NAME="genre" VALUE="western">
Westerns<P>
<INPUT TYPE="submit" NAME="submit_button" VALUE="Submit Query">
</FORM>
```

tip

The width of a button created with the submit <INPUT> tag is based on the number of characters in its VALUE attribute.

Next you will add a submit <INPUT> tag to the ProductInfo.html file.

To add a submit <INPUT> tag to the ProductInfo.html file:

1 Open the **ProductInfo.html file** in your text editor or HTML editor.

2 After the reset <INPUT> field, add **<INPUT TYPE="submit" VALUE="Submit Query">**.

3 Save and close the **ProductInfo.html** document, then open the **ProductRegistration.html** file in your Web browser. Click the **Next** button to display the ProductInfo.html file in the bottom frame of the Web page. The submit button in your file should appear similar to the submit button shown in Figure 6-22. Nothing will actually happen if you click the submit button, since the <FORM> tag in the ProductInfo.html file does not include an ACTION attribute.

4 Close the Web browser window.

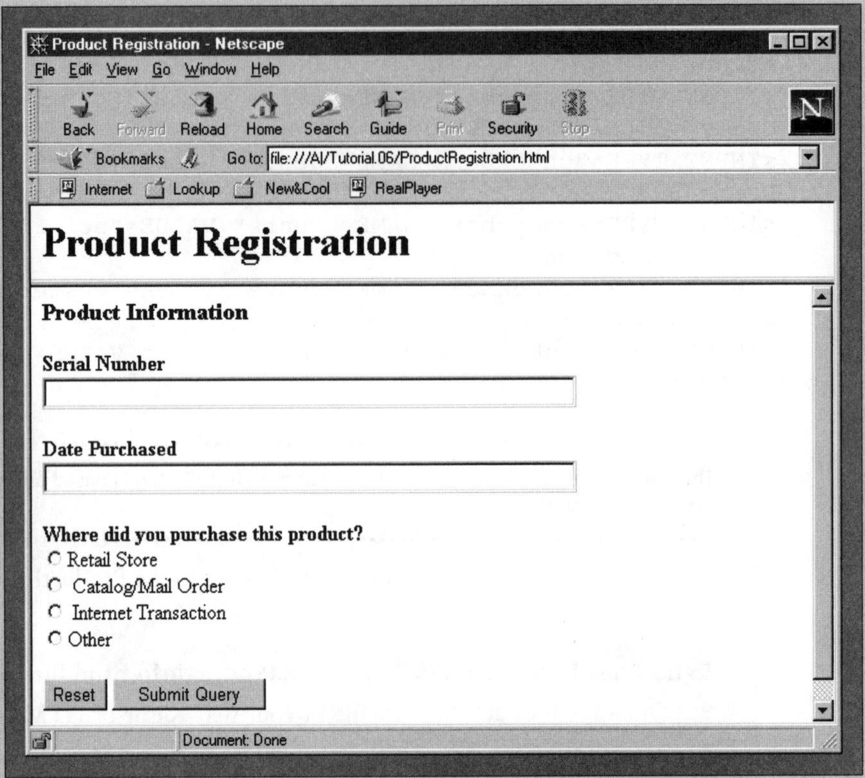

Figure 6-22: Product Registration program after adding a submit <INPUT> field

Image Submit Buttons

An <INPUT> tag with a type of *image* (<INPUT TYPE="image">) creates a button that displays a graphical image and submits a form to a CGI script on a server. The image <INPUT> tag performs exactly the same function as the submit <INPUT> tag. Include the SRC attribute to specify the image to display on the button. You can also include the NAME, VALUE, and ALIGN attributes with the image <INPUT> tag. The following code creates the Web page with an image <INPUT> tag, as shown in Figure 6-23:

```
<H1>Video of the Month Club</H1>
<H3>Select the types of movies you like to see and
click the videocassette image.<BR>
A new movie will be sent to you every month.<H3>
<FORM ACTION="http://exampleurl/cgi-bin/cgi_program"
     METHOD="post" NAME="exampleForm">
<INPUT TYPE="checkbox" NAME="genre" VALUE="action">
Action
```

```
<INPUT TYPE="checkbox" NAME="genre" VALUE="adventure">
Adventure<BR>
<INPUT TYPE="checkbox" NAME="genre" VALUE="comedy">
Comedy
<INPUT TYPE="checkbox" NAME="genre" VALUE="drama">
Drama<BR>
<INPUT TYPE="checkbox" NAME="genre" VALUE="sci_fi">
Science Fiction
<INPUT TYPE="checkbox" NAME="genre" VALUE="western">
Westerns<P>
<INPUT TYPE="image" SRC="videocas.jpg">
</FORM>
```

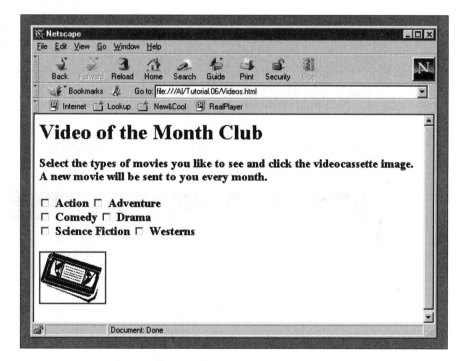

Figure 6-23: Output of a form with an image <INPUT> tag

Image <INPUT> tags are also used to create server-side image maps, which are similar to the client-side North America image map you created in Tutorial 2. The primary difference between server-side and client-side image maps is that with server-side image maps, most of the work is done on the server; for client-side image maps, most of the work is done in a Web browser.

Selection Lists

The **<SELECT>...</SELECT> tag pair** creates a **selection list** that presents users with fixed lists of values from which to choose. The selection list appears as a drop-down menu and can include a scroll bar, depending on the number of items in the list. Figure 6-24 lists the attributes of the <SELECT> tag.

Attribute	Description
MULTIPLE	Specifies whether a user can select more than one item from the list
NAME	Designates a name for the selection list
SIZE	Determines how many lines of the selection list appear. If this attribute is excluded or set to one, then the selection list is a drop-down style menu.

Figure 6-24: Attributes of the <SELECT> tag

<OPTION> tags, placed between the selection list's <SELECT>...</SELECT> tag pair, specify the items that appear in a selection list. Figure 6-25 lists the attributes of the <OPTION> tag.

Attribute	Description
SELECTED	An optional attribute that determines if an item is initially selected in the selection list when the form first loads
VALUE	The value submitted to a CGI script

Figure 6-25: Attributes of the <OPTION> tag

The following code creates two selection lists:

```
<FORM ACTION="http://exampleurl/cgi-bin/cgi_program"
    METHOD="post" NAME="exampleForm">
This selection list displays a drop-down-style menu:<BR>
<SELECT NAME="music">
<OPTION VALUE="jazz">Jazz
<OPTION VALUE="classical">Classical
<OPTION VALUE="country">Country
<OPTION VALUE="rock" SELECTED>Rock
<OPTION VALUE="r&b">Rhythm and Blues
</SELECT><P>
```

```
This selection list displays 3 items:<BR>
<SELECT NAME="music" SIZE=3>
<OPTION VALUE="jazz">Jazz
<OPTION VALUE="classical" SELECTED>Classical
<OPTION VALUE="country">Country
<OPTION VALUE="rock">Rock
<OPTION VALUE="r&b">Rhythm and Blues
</SELECT>
</FORM>
```

Next you will add to the CustomerInfo.html file a selection list that determines if the product is used at work, at school, at home, or in a home office.

To add a selection list to the CustomerInfo.html file:

1 Open the **CustomerInfo.html file** in your text editor or HTML editor.

2 Just above the <INPUT> tag for the reset button, add the following tags to create the selection list that determines if the product is used at work, at school, at home, or in a home office:

```
Where will you use this product?
<SELECT NAME="location">
    <OPTION VALUE="work">Work
    <OPTION VALUE="school">School
    <OPTION VALUE="home">Home
    <OPTION VALUE="home_office">Home Office
</SELECT><P>
```

3 Save and close the **CustomerInfo.html** document, then open the **ProductRegistration.html** file in your Web browser. The selection list in your browser window should appear similar to that in Figure 6-26.

4 Close the Web browser window.

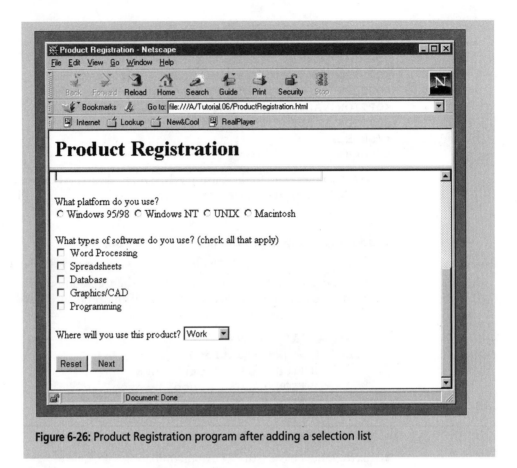

Figure 6-26: Product Registration program after adding a selection list

Multiline Text Fields

The <TEXTAREA> tag is used to create a field in which users can enter multiple lines of information. Fields created with the <TEXTAREA>...</TEXTAREA> tag pair are known as **multiline text fields** or **text areas**. The <TEXTAREA> tag can be created with the three attributes described in Figure 6-27:

Attribute	Description
NAME	Designates a name for the text area
COL	Specifies the number of columns to be displayed in the text area
ROWS	Specifies the number of rows to be displayed in the text area

Figure 6-27: Attributes of the <TEXTAREA> tag

The only items you place between the <TEXTAREA>...</TEXTAREA> tags are default text and characters you want to display in the text area when the form loads. Any characters placed between the <TEXTAREA>...</TEXTAREA> tags, including tab marks and paragraph returns, will be included in a text area. For example, a line of text that is indented with two tabs and placed between the <TEXTAREA>...</TEXTAREA> tags will be indented with two tabs when it appears in the text area.

The following tags create a text area consisting of 50 columns and 10 rows, with default text of *Enter additional information here*.

```
<FORM ACTION="http://exampleurl/cgi-bin/cgi_program"
    METHOD="post" NAME="exampleForm">
Comments<BR>
<TEXTAREA COLS=50 ROWS=10>
Enter additional information here
</TEXTAREA>
</FORM>
```

Next you will add to the CustomerInfo.html file a multiline text area in which users can type additional comments.

To add a multiline text area to the CustomerInfo.html file:

1 Open the **CustomerInfo.html file** in your text editor or HTML editor.

2 Just above the <INPUT> tag for the reset button, press **Enter** to start a new line. Then add the following tags to create the multiline text area for additional comments:

```
Comments<BR>
<TEXTAREA NAME="comments" COLS=40 ROWS=5>
Enter any additional comments here
</TEXTAREA><P>
```

3 Save the **CustomerInfo.html** document, then open the **ProductRegistration.html** file in your Web browser. The multiline text area in your Product Registration document should appear similar to that in Figure 6-28.

4 Close the Web browser window.

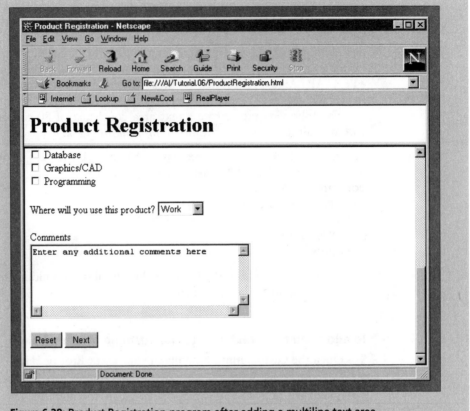

Figure 6-28: Product Registration program after adding a multiline text area

SUMMARY

- The Common Gateway Interface, or CGI, is a simple protocol used to communicate between Web pages and Web-server-based applications.

- An environment variable is part of an operating system, not just part of a function or a program, as are JavaScript variables.

- A Web-server-based application that processes CGI environment variables is called a CGI script (or CGI program) and can be designed to perform many different functions.

- CGI scripts are often placed within a bin or cgi-bin directory on a Web server and have an extension of .cgi.

- The <FORM>...</FORM> tag pair designates a form within an HTML document and contains all text and tags that make up a form.

- Three tags used within the <FORM>...</FORM> tag pair are <INPUT>, <SELECT>, and <TEXTAREA>.

- Any form elements into which a user can enter data, such as a text box, or that a user can select or change, such as a radio button, are called fields.

- When you submit a form to a CGI script, the form's data is submitted in name=value tag pairs, based on the NAME and VALUE attributes of the <INPUT>, <TEXTAREA>, and <SELECT> tags.

- The <INPUT> tag is used to create input fields that gather information, using different types of user interface elements.

- An <INPUT> tag with a type of text creates a simple text box that accepts a single line of text.

- An <INPUT> tag with a type of password displays each character a user types as an asterisk, to hide the password from anyone who may be looking over the user's shoulder.

- An <INPUT> tag with a type of checkbox creates a box that can be set to yes (checked) or no (unchecked).

- An <INPUT> tag with a type of reset clears all of a form's entries and resets each form element to its initial value specified by the VALUE attribute.

- An <INPUT> tag with a type of button creates a command button similar to the OK and Cancel buttons you see in dialog boxes.

- An <INPUT> tag with a type of submit creates a button that displays text, such as Submit Query, and submits the form to a CGI script on the server.

- An <INPUT> tag with a type of image creates a button that displays a graphical image and submits the form to a CGI script on the server.

- The <SELECT>...</SELECT> tag pair creates a selection list that presents users with fixed lists of values from which to choose.

- The <TEXTAREA> tag is used to create a field in which users can enter multiple lines of information. Fields created with the <TEXTAREA>...</TEXTAREA> tag pair are known as multiline text fields or text areas.

Q U E S T I O N S

1. Which of the following items are not created with forms?
   a. guest books
   b. questionnaires
   c. online order systems
   d. They are all created with forms.

2. CGI is _____
   a. a high-level programming language similar to Visual C++.
   b. a low-level programming language similar to JavaScript.
   c. a simple protocol that allows Web pages to communicate with Web-server-based programs.
   d. a machine language.

3. CGI scripts are usually placed _____
   a. within a *bin* or *cgi-bin* directory on a Web server.
   b. in the local operating system's utility folder.
   c. in the folder where Netscape Navigator or Internet Explorer are installed.
   d. within a <SCRIPT>...</SCRIPT> tag pair.

4. How many forms can be created in an HTML document?
   a. 1
   b. 2
   c. as many as necessary
   d. None. Forms are not created in HTML documents.

5. The ACTION attribute of the <FORM> tag _____
   a. designates a function to execute.
   b. creates a button used for starting a program.
   c. closes the Web browser window.
   d. specifies a URL where a form's data will be submitted.

6. What is the default submission option for the METHOD attribute of the <FORM> tag?
   a. GET
   b. POST
   c. SEND
   d. SUBMIT

7. What is the default data format for the ENCTYPE attribute of the <FORM> tag?
   a. application/jpeg/gif
   b. cgi.bin
   c. application/x-www-form-urlencoded
   d. text/plain

8. How is a form's data submitted to a CGI script?
   a. in value,name tag pairs
   b. in name=value tag pairs
   c. as values separated by commas
   d. as values separated by paragraph marks

9. The text <INPUT> tag _____
   a. displays a static label.
   b. creates a simple text box that accepts a single line of text.
   c. creates a text box that accepts multiple lines of text.
   d. is a type of scrolling banner used for displaying messages in a Web browser window.

10. The SIZE attribute is used with the _____ <INPUT> tag.
a. button
b. image
c. text
d. submit

11. Each character entered into a text box created with a password <INPUT> tag appears _____.
a. with the ampersand (&) symbol
b. with the number (#) symbol
c. as a percentage (%)
d. as an asterisk (*)

12. Which attribute is used to designate a single button in a radio group as the default?
a. CHECKED
b. CHECK
c. SELECTED
d. DEFAULT

13. Which of the following statements about check boxes is true?
a. You can only select one check box in group at a time.
b. You can select as many check boxes as necessary.
c. When you select one check box, all other check boxes in the same group are also selected.
d. Check boxes are not used for user input.

14. What is the purpose of the reset <INPUT> tag?
a. to reload the current Web page
b. to reset the contents of a single form element to its default value
c. to reset all form elements to their default values
d. to close and restart the Web browser

15. What type of <INPUT> tag creates a command button similar to the OK and Cancel buttons found in dialog boxes?
a. radio
b. ok_cancel
c. dialog
d. button

16. What is the default value of a submit button's label?
a. Submit
b. Query
c. Submit Query
d. Execute

17. Which type of <INPUT> tag can be used to submit a form's data to a CGI script?
a. image
b. radio
c. checkbox
d. button

18. The contents of a selection list are determined by which HTML tags?
    a. <SELECT>
    b. <CONTENTS>
    c. <ITEMS>
    d. <OPTION>

19. Which is the correct syntax for creating a text area?
    a. <TEXT COLS=50 ROWS=10></TEXT>
    b. <TEXTAREA COLS=50 ROWS=10></TEXTAREA>
    c. <TEXT SIZE=50></TEXT>
    d. <TEXTAREA SIZE=50></TEXTAREA>

 # E X E R C I S E S

1. Create a form to be used as a software development bug report. Include fields such as product name and version, type of hardware, operating system, frequency of occurrence, and proposed solutions. Save the file as BugReport.html in the Tutorial.06 folder on your Student Disk.

2. Create a form to be used for tracking, documenting, and managing the process of interviewing candidates for professional positions. Include fields such as candidate's name, communication abilities, professional appearance, computer skills, business knowledge, and the interviewer's comments. Save the file as Interview.html in the Tutorial.06 folder on your Student Disk.

3. Create a form that collects business development contacts. Include fields such as company, position, and date of last contact. Save the file as BusinessDevelopmentContacts.html in the Tutorial.06 folder on your Student Disk.

4. Create a consent form for a school trip. Include fields such as child's name, parent or guardian's signature, and name, address, and telephone number of child's physician. Save the file as ConsentForm.html in the Tutorial.06 folder on your Student Disk.

5. Create your own online stationery using a form. Use text fields for the recipient's address and use a text area field for the body of the letter. Include a selection list of frequently used names. When a user clicks a name on the list, populate the recipient fields with the selected person's mailing information. Format the title of the stationery and your personal information using standard HTML tags. Save the file as Stationery.html in the Tutorial.06 folder on your Student Disk.

In this section you will learn:
- About hidden form fields
- About the Form object
- How to reference forms and form elements
- About form event handlers, methods, and properties
- How to e-mail a form's data

Validating a User's Input to a Form

Hidden Form Fields

A special type of form element, called a **hidden form field**, allows you to hide information from users. Hidden form fields are created with the <INPUT> tag. A Web browser cannot display hidden form fields, nor can users edit hidden form fields in any way from a Web browser window. Hidden form fields temporarily store information that needs to be sent to a server along with the rest of a form but that a user does not need to see. Examples of information stored in hidden fields include the result of a calculation or some other type of information that your program needs later. You create hidden form fields using the same syntax used for other fields created with the <INPUT> tag: `<INPUT TYPE="hidden">`. NAME and VALUE are the only attributes that you can include with a hidden form field.

Figure 6-29 contains the form section of the Calculator program you created in Tutorial 3. The program has been modified to include functions to store and recall numbers. Figure 6-30 shows the modified calculator in a Web browser. The three new form elements used to add storage functionality to the program are as follows:

```
<INPUT TYPE="button" NAME="mem" VALUE=" M+   "
    onClick="storedValue.value=Input.value";>
<INPUT TYPE="button" NAME="recall" VALUE=" MRC "
    onClick="Input.value=storedValue.value";>
<INPUT TYPE="hidden" NAME="storedValue">
```

The first new button, named mem, stores the value of the Input text box in the hidden form field named storedValue. The second new button, named recall, retrieves the information stored in the hidden storedValue field and places it in the Input text box.

```
<HTML>
<HEAD>
<TITLE>Calculator</TITLE>
<SCRIPT LANGUAGE="JavaScript1.2">
<!-- HIDE FROM INCOMPATIBLE BROWSERS
var inputString = "";
var count = 0;
function updateString(value) {
    inputString += value;
    document.Calculator.Input.value = inputString;
}
// STOP HIDING FROM INCOMPATIBLE BROWSERS -->
</SCRIPT>
</HEAD>
<BODY>
<CENTER>
<FORM NAME="Calculator">
<INPUT TYPE="text" NAME="Input" Size="22"><BR>
<INPUT TYPE="button" NAME="plus" VALUE=" + "
    onClick="updateString(' + ')">
<INPUT TYPE="button" NAME="minus" VALUE=" - "
    onClick="updateString(' - ')">
<INPUT TYPE="button" NAME="times" VALUE=" x "
    onClick="updateString(' * ')">
<INPUT TYPE="button" NAME="div" VALUE=" / "
    onClick="updateString(' / ')">
<INPUT TYPE="button" NAME="mod" VALUE=" MOD "
    onClick="updateString(' % ')"><BR>
<INPUT TYPE="button" NAME="zero" VALUE=" 0 "
    onClick="updateString('0')">
```

Figure 6-29: Calculator.html with memory functions

```
<INPUT TYPE="button" NAME="one" VALUE=" 1 "
     onCLick="updateString('1')">
<INPUT TYPE="button" NAME="two" VALUE=" 2 "
     onCLick="updateString('2')">
<INPUT TYPE="button" NAME="three" VALUE=" 3 "
     onClick="updateString('3')">
<INPUT TYPE="button" NAME="four" VALUE=" 4 "
     onClick="updateString('4')"><BR>
<INPUT TYPE="button" NAME="five" VALUE=" 5 "
     onCLick="updateString('5')">
<INPUT TYPE="button" NAME="six" VALUE=" 6 "
     onClick="updateString('6')">
<INPUT TYPE="button" NAME="seven" VALUE=" 7 "
     onClick="updateinputString('7')">
<INPUT TYPE="button" NAME="eight" VALUE=" 8 "
     onCLick="updateString('8')">
<INPUT TYPE="button" NAME="nine" VALUE=" 9 "
     onClick="updateString('9')"><BR>
<INPUT TYPE="button" NAME="point" VALUE=" . "
     onClick="updateString('.')">
<INPUT TYPE="button" NAME="clear" VALUE=" Clear "
     onClick="Input.value=''; inputString=''">
<INPUT TYPE="button" NAME="Calc" VALUE=" = "
     onClick="Input.value=eval(inputString)"><BR>
<INPUT TYPE="button" NAME="mem" VALUE=" M+ "
     onClick="storedValue.value=Input.value";>
<INPUT TYPE="button" NAME="recall" VALUE=" MRC "
     onClick="Input.value=storedValue.value";>
```

Figure 6-29: Calculator.html with memory functions (continued)

```
<INPUT TYPE="hidden" NAME="storedValue">
</FORM>
</CENTER>
</BODY>
</HTML>
```

Figure 6-29: Calculator.html with memory functions (continued)

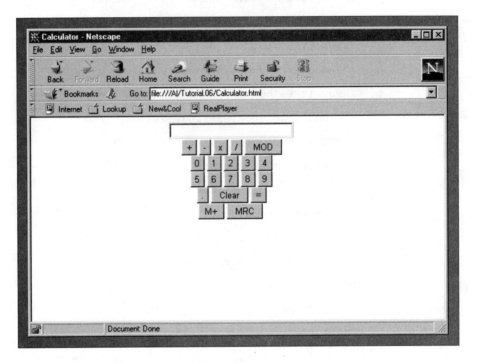

Figure 6-30: Calculator.html in a Web browser

Next you will add hidden form fields to the ProductRegistration.html document you created in Section A. The ProductRegistration.html document has a serious problem: when you click the Next button to move from the Customer Information form to the Product Information form, the information entered into the Customer Information form disappears because the ProductInfo.html document replaces the CustomerInfo.html document. To solve this problem, we are going to add hidden form fields to the TopFrame.html file, which displays in the frame at the top of the window. The fields in the Customer Information form and the Product Information form will be copied to and stored in the hidden form fields in a "master form" in the TopFrame.html file. First you will add the hidden form fields to the TopFrame.html file.

To add hidden form fields to TopFrame.html:

1 Open the **TopFrame.html file** in your text editor or HTML editor.

2 Add the following form and form elements before the </BODY> tag. The name of each form element corresponds to the name of a form element in CustomerInfo.html and ProductInfo.html.

```
<FORM NAME="hiddenElements">
<INPUT TYPE="hidden" NAME="name">
<INPUT TYPE="hidden" NAME="address">
<INPUT TYPE="hidden" NAME="city">
<INPUT TYPE="hidden" NAME="state">
<INPUT TYPE="hidden" NAME="zip">
<INPUT TYPE="hidden" NAME="email">
<INPUT TYPE="hidden" NAME="password">
<INPUT TYPE="hidden" NAME="platform">
<INPUT TYPE="hidden" NAME="wp">
<INPUT TYPE="hidden" NAME="ss">
<INPUT TYPE="hidden" NAME="db">
<INPUT TYPE="hidden" NAME="gr">
<INPUT TYPE="hidden" NAME="pr">
<INPUT TYPE="hidden" NAME="comments">
<INPUT TYPE="hidden" NAME="location">
<INPUT TYPE="hidden" NAME="serial">
<INPUT TYPE="hidden" NAME="date">
</FORM>
```

3 Save and close the **TopFrame.html file**.

Before you can write the code that copies the contents of each field in the CustomerInfo.html and ProductInfo.html files to the corresponding hidden form fields in TopFrame.html, you need to learn how to work with the Form object.

The Form Object

JavaScript is often used with forms to validate or process a form's data before the data is submitted to a CGI script on a server. For example, customers may use an online order form to order merchandise from your Web site. When a customer clicks the form's Submit button, you need to make sure that information, such as the shipping address and credit card information, is entered correctly. Although you cannot use JavaScript to verify certain types of information, such as a valid credit card number, you can use JavaScript to verify that required fields are not left blank. To use JavaScript to verify form information, you use the properties, methods, and events of the **Form object**.

tip

• •

If a form requires advanced or complex validation or processing, it is a good idea to have a CGI script on a server do the work, since servers are usually much more powerful than an end user's desktop computer or workstation.

• •

Referencing Forms and Form Elements

Tutorial 5 introduced the JavaScript object model. Recall that some of the objects in the JavaScript object model are arrays of other objects. For instance, the Window object includes a frames[] array that contains all the frames in a window. Similarly, the Document object includes a **forms[] array** that contains all of an HTML document's forms. If a window does not contain any forms, then the forms[] array is empty. The first form in a document is referred to as document.forms[0], the second form is referred to as document.forms[1], and so on.

Just as the Document object has a forms[] array, the Form object has an elements[] array. You can reference each element on a form, using the Form object's **elements[] array**. Each element on a form is assigned to the elements[] array in the order in which it is encountered by the JavaScript interpreter. To refer to an element on a form, you reference the index number of the form in the forms[] array, followed by the appropriate element index number from the elements[] array. For example, if you want to refer to the first element in the first form of an HTML document, use the statement `document.forms[0].elements[0];`. The third element in the second form is referenced using the statement `document.forms[1].elements[2];`. The following code shows an example of how each element on a form is assigned to the elements[] array:

```
<FORM NAME="exampleForm">
The following element is assigned to elements[0]
<INPUT TYPE="text" NAME="field1">
The following element is assigned to elements[1]
<INPUT TYPE="text" NAME="field2">
The following element is assigned to elements[2]
<INPUT TYPE="text" NAME="field3">
The following element is assigned to elements[3]
<INPUT TYPE="text" NAME="field4">
The following element is assigned to elements[4]
<INPUT TYPE="text" NAME="field5">
</FORM>
```

When a form is created with the <FORM> tag, it can be assigned a name with the NAME attribute. To reference a form by name, you append the form's name to the Document object. For example, you reference a form created with a NAME attribute of orderForm by using the statement `document.orderForm`.

Similarly, you can assign a name to each form element with the NAME attribute. Why is it important to name form elements? If you intend to submit a form to a CGI script, you must include a NAME attribute for each form element. Naming an element also gives you an alternative to referencing the element by its position in the elements[] array. For example, if you have an element named textField1 on a form named orderForm, then you can refer to it using the statement `document.orderForm.textField1;`.

tip

You are not required to include a NAME attribute for a <FORM> tag that will be submitted to a CGI script. The NAME attribute of the <FORM> tag is only used to make it easier to refer to the form in JavaScript.

Next you will add to the CustomerInfo.html and ProductInfo.html files code that copies form field values to the corresponding hidden fields in the TopFrame.html file. First you will add code to the CustomerInfo.html file.

To add to the CustomerInfo.html file code that copies form field values to the corresponding hidden fields in the TopFrame.html file:

1 Open the **CustomerInfo.html** file in your text editor or HTML editor.

2 In the function named nextForm(), above the line that reads `location.href="ProductInfo.html";`, insert a new line and add the following code, which copies the values in the CustomerInfo.html fields to the hidden form fields in TopFrame.html. The statements use the parent property of the Window object to refer to each frame's name. The code appears complicated at first, but remember that you have already learned how each of the statements is constructed. If you break down the parts of each statement, they will begin to make sense. For example, on the left side of the first statement, *parent* refers to the Registration.html document that defined the frame set, *topframe* refers to the frame at the top of the window that contains the TopFrame.html document, and *document* refers to the TopFrame.html file's Document object. The next item in the statement is the form name in the TopFrame.html file, *hiddenElements*, followed by *name*, which refers to the name field on the hiddenElements form. The last portion of the left side of the statement is *value*, which returns the information entered into the *name* field. The right side of the statement is similar to the left side, except that it does not require the parent property or the name of the frame, since you are referring to the current frame.

```
parent.topframe.document.hiddenElements.name.value =
    document.customerInfo.name.value;
parent.topframe.document.hiddenElements.address.value =
    document.customerInfo.address.value;
parent.topframe.document.hiddenElements.city.value =
    document.customerInfo.city.value;
parent.topframe.document.hiddenElements.state.value =
    document.customerInfo.state.value;
parent.topframe.document.hiddenElements.zip.value =
    document.customerInfo.zip.value;
parent.topframe.document.hiddenElements.email.value =
    document.customerInfo.email.value;
```

```
parent.topframe.document.hiddenElements.password.value =
    document.customerInfo.password.value;
parent.topframe.document.hiddenElements.platform.value =
    document.customerInfo.platform.value;
if (document.customerInfo.wp.checked == true)
    parent.topframe.document.hiddenElements.wp.checked =
    true;
if (document.customerInfo.ss.checked == true)
    parent.topframe.document.hiddenElements.ss.checked =
    true;
if (document.customerInfo.db.checked == true)
    parent.topframe.document.hiddenElements.db.checked =
    true;
if (document.customerInfo.gr.checked == true)
    parent.topframe.document.hiddenElements.gr.checked =
    true;
if (document.customerInfo.pr.checked == true)
    parent.topframe.document.hiddenElements.pr.checked =
    true;
parent.topframe.document.hiddenElements.location.value =
    document.customerInfo.location.value;
parent.topframe.document.hiddenElements.comments.value =
    document.customerInfo.comments.value;
```

3 Save and close the **CustomerInfo.html** file.

4 Open the **ProductRegistration.html** file in your Web browser and test the program.

5 Close the Web browser window.

Next you will add code that confirms that users have entered data into several required fields before they pressed the Next button. The required fields are name, address, city, state, zip, and password.

To add code that confirms that users have entered data into several required fields before they pressed the Next button:

1 Open the **CustomerInfo.html** file in your text editor or HTML editor.

2 Add the following statements just above the statement that reads `location.href="ProductInfo.html";`. The if statement uses the logical or operator, ||, to make sure all the required fields are entered. If any one of the fields is equal to an empty string, `""`, then an alert dialog box appears informing users that they must fill in all the fields. If all the fields have been entered, then the else clause executes the `location.href="ProductInfo.html";` statement.

```
   if (parent.topframe.document.hiddenElements
         .name.value == ""
|| parent.topframe.document.hiddenElements
         .address.value == ""
|| parent.topframe.document.hiddenElements
         .city.value == ""
|| parent.topframe.document.hiddenElements
         .state.value == ""
|| parent.topframe.document.hiddenElements
         .zip.value == ""
|| parent.topframe.document.hiddenElements
         .password.value == "")
         alert("You must fill in the name, address, city,
               state, zip, and password fields.");
   else
```

3 Save and close the **CustomerInfo.html** file.

4 Open the **ProductRegistration.html** file in your Web browser. Leave several of the required fields blank and click the Next button to see if you receive the alert dialog box.

5 Click **OK** to close the alert dialog box.

6 Fill in all the required fields and check to see if the ProductInfo.html file loads properly after you press the **Next** button.

7 Close the Web browser window.

You also need to add code that copies the field values from the ProductInfo.html file to the corresponding hidden fields in TopFrame.html and confirms that any required fields are not empty. Since the ProductInfo.html file does not contain a Next button, as does the CustomerInfo.html file, you need to add the code that copies the field values by using an onSubmit event handler, which you will learn about next.

Form Event Handlers

In Tutorial 2, you learned about many of the event handlers that can be used in JavaScript. Two additional event handlers, onSubmit and onReset, are available for use with the <FORM> tag. The **onSubmit event handler** executes when a form is submitted to a CGI script using a submit <INPUT> tag or an image <INPUT> tag. The onSubmit event handler is often used to verify or validate a form's data before it is sent to a server. The **onReset event handler** executes when a reset button is selected on a form. You use the onReset event handler to confirm that a user really wants to reset the contents of a form. Both the onSubmit and onReset event handlers are placed before the closing bracket of a <FORM> tag. The following code shows how a form tag with onSubmit and onReset event handlers is written:

```
<FORM ACTION="http://exampleurl/cgi-bin/cgi_program"
    METHOD="post" NAME="exampleForm"
    onSubmit="JavaScript statements;"
    onReset="JavaScript statements;">
```

When you use the onSubmit and onReset event handlers, you need to return a value of true or false, depending on whether the form should be submitted or reset. For example, the following code returns a value of true or false, depending on whether the user presses the OK button or the Cancel button in the confirm dialog box. If the user presses the OK button, the confirm dialog box returns a value of true, and the onSubmit event executes. If the user presses the Cancel button, the confirm dialog box returns a value of false, and the onSubmit event does not execute.

```
<FORM ACTION="http://exampleurl/cgi-bin/cgi_program"
    METHOD="post" NAME="exampleForm"
    onReset="return confirm(
    'Are you sure you want to reset the form?')">
```

Figure 6-31 shows a program that includes both onSubmit and onReset event handlers. The program uses one function to validate the form's data when the onSubmit event handler executes, and another function to confirm whether the user really wants to reset a form.

```
<SCRIPT LANGUAGE="JavaScript1.2">

<!-- HIDE FROM INCOMPATIBLE BROWSERS

function confirmSubmit() {

    var sendForm = confirm(
        "Are you sure you want to submit the form?");

    if (sendForm == true)

        return true;

    return false;

}

function confirmReset() {

    var resetForm = confirm(
        "Are you sure you want to reset the form?");

    if (resetForm == true)

        return true;

    return false;
```

Figure 6-31: Program with onSubmit and onReset event handlers

```
}
// STOP HIDING FROM INCOMPATIBLE BROWSERS -->
</SCRIPT>
<FORM ACTION="http://exampleurl/cgi-bin/cgi_program"
    METHOD="post" NAME="exampleForm"
    onSubmit="return confirmSubmit();"
    onReset="return confirmReset();">
Name<BR>
<INPUT TYPE="text" NAME="name" SIZE=50><BR>
Address<BR>
<INPUT TYPE="text" NAME="address" SIZE=50><BR>
City, State, Zip<BR>
<INPUT TYPE="text" NAME="city" SIZE=38>
<INPUT TYPE="text" NAME="state" SIZE=2 MAXLENGTH=2>
<INPUT TYPE="text" NAME="zip" SIZE=5 MAXLENGTH=5><BR>
<INPUT TYPE="reset">
<INPUT TYPE="submit">
</FORM>
```

Figure 6-31: Program with onSubmit and onReset event handlers (continued)

Next you will add an onReset event handler to confirm that users really want to reset the CustomerInfo.html and ProductInfo.html forms.

To add an onReset event handler to confirm that users really want to reset the CustomerInfo.html and ProductInfo.html forms:

1 Open the **CustomerInfo.html** file in your text editor or HTML editor.

2 Add the following confirmReset() function above the nextForm() function in the <SCRIPT>...</SCRIPT> tag pair in the file's <HEAD> section:

```
function confirmReset() {
    var resetForm = confirm(
        "Are you sure you want to reset the form?");
    if (resetForm == true)
        return true;
    return false;
}
```

3 Next before the closing bracket of the <FORM> tag, add `onReset="return confirmReset();"`.

4 Save and close the **CustomerInfo.html** file.

5 Open the **ProductInfo.html** file in your text editor or HTML editor and add a **<SCRIPT>...</SCRIPT>** tag pair to the **<HEAD>** section. Between the <SCRIPT>...</SCRIPT> tag pair, add the same confirmReset() function you added to the CustomerInfo.html file.

6 Add the event handler `onReset="return confirmReset();"` before the closing bracket of the <FORM> tag.

7 Save and close the **ProductInfo.html** file.

8 Open the **ProductRegistration.html** file in your Web browser. Enter some data into the fields in the Customer Information form, then click the Reset button to see if you receive the warning. Click **OK** to close the alert dialog box. Fill in the required information on the Customer Information form, and click **Next**. Then test the Reset button in the ProductInfo.html file. Click **OK** to close the alert dialog box.

9 Close the Web browser window.

Next you will add to the ProductInfo.html file an onSubmit event that validates the fields in ProductInfo.html and then copies the data from each field to the corresponding hidden form fields in TopFrame.html.

To add an onSubmit event and code to the ProductInfo.html file:

1 Open the **ProductInfo.html** file in your text editor or HTML editor.

2 Add an onSubmit event `onSubmit="return submitForm();"` to the <FORM> tag just before the tag's closing bracket.

3 In the <SCRIPT>...</SCRIPT> tag pair, add `function submitForm() {` above the confirmReset() function, to create the opening lines of the submitForm() function.

4 Next, add to the submitForm() function the following statements, which copy the ProductInfo.html fields to the corresponding hidden fields in TopFrame.html:

```
parent.topframe.document.hiddenElements.serial.value =
        document.productInfo.serial.value;
parent.topframe.document.hiddenElements.date.value =
        document.productInfo.date.value;
```

5   Following the lines that copy fields from ProductInfo.html to TopFrame.html, add the following if statement to confirm that users have filled in all the required fields. For the ProductInfo.html file, the serial number and date fields must be filled in. If the required fields are filled in, a value of true is returned, and the form is submitted. If a value of false is returned, the onSubmit event is cancelled.

```
if (parent.topframe.document.hiddenElements.serial.
     value == ""
|| parent.topframe.document.hiddenElements.date.
     value == "") {
     alert(
"You must fill in the date and serial number.");
     return false;
}
```

6   Add the closing bracket } for the submitForm() function.

7   Save **ProductInfo.html**. Remember that the TopFrame.html file contains the hidden form fields that we have used to gather data from both the CustomerInfo.html and ProductInfo.html files. Before you can test the submitForm() function, you must add a statement that submits the hidden form fields in TopFrame.html. To submit the contents of a form from JavaScript, you learn about form methods, which are covered next.

Form Methods

The Form object contains only two methods: submit() and reset(). The **submit() method** is used to submit a form without the use of a submit <INPUT> tag. The **reset() method** is used to clear a form without the use of a reset <INPUT> tag. The submit() and reset() methods perform the same functions as the submit and reset buttons. However, the onSubmit and onReset event handlers do not execute when you use the submit() and reset() methods. Any validation that needs to be performed must be included in the code that calls the submit() and reset() methods.

The submit() and reset() methods are used with forms that do not include submit or reset buttons. Figure 6-32 shows a program that uses the submit() and reset() methods. The program consists of a game in which the user must correctly count several groups of items. If a user counts one group of items wrong, the reset() method clears the form, and the user must start over. Once a user enters each item count correctly, the form is automatically submitted. The program uses the onChange event handler to call the confirmAnswers() function. The confirmAnswers() function checks the picture and answer arguments that it is passed, then takes the appropriate action, using if statements. The last if statement in the confirmAnswers() function checks to see if the three global variables for the three items have all been set to true. If all three global variables have been set to true, then the form is submitted. Figure 6-33 shows the program output in a Web browser window.

```
<HTML>
<HEAD>
<TITLE>Counting Contest</TITLE>
<SCRIPT LANGUAGE="JavaScript1.2">
<!-- HIDE FROM INCOMPATIBLE BROWSERS
var apples = 7; var runners = 6; var pushpins = 3;
var applesCorrect; var runnersCorrect; var pushpinsCorrect;
function confirmAnswers(picture, answer) {
     if (picture == "apples") {
          if (answer == "7") applesCorrect = true;
          else {
               alert("Sorry! You must start over.");
               document.contestForm.reset();
          }
     }
     if (picture == "runners") {
          if (answer == "6") runnersCorrect = true;
          else {
               alert("Sorry! You must start over.");
               document.contestForm.reset();
          }
  }
     if (picture == "pushpins") {
          if (answer == "3") pushpinsCorrect = true;
          else {
               alert("Sorry! You must start over.");
               document.contestForm.reset();
          }
     }
     if (applesCorrect == true && runnersCorrect == true &&
```

Figure 6-32: Program with submit() and reset() methods

```
pushpinsCorrect == true) {

        alert("Congratulations! You will be entered in the

contest.");

        document.contestForm.submit();

    }

}

// STOP HIDING FROM INCOMPATIBLE BROWSERS -->

</SCRIPT>

</HEAD>

<BODY>

<H1>How Many Items Can You Count?</H1>

<H2>Count the number of items in each picture.

If you count all the items correctly, you will be entered

into a drawing to win a free trip.</H2>

<H3>Watch out! If you enter the wrong number of items for

any picture, you will need to start over from the

beginning.</H3>

<FORM ACTION="http://exampleurl/cgi-bin/cgi_program"

      METHOD="post" NAME="contestForm">

<IMG SRC="apples.jpg"><IMG SRC="runners.jpg"><IMG

SRC="pushpins.jpg"><P>

Apples: <INPUT TYPE="text" SIZE="15"

onChange="confirmAnswers('apples', this.value);">

Runners: <INPUT TYPE="text" SIZE="15"

onChange="confirmAnswers('runners', this.value);">

Pushpins: <INPUT TYPE="text" SIZE="15"

onChange="confirmAnswers('pushpins', this.value);">

</FORM>

</BODY>

</HTML>
```

Figure 6-32: Program with submit() and reset() methods (continued)

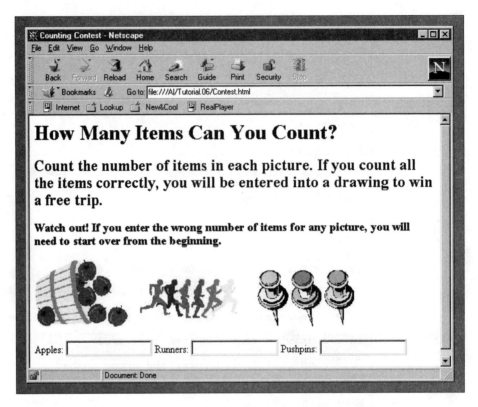

Figure 6-33: Output of program with submit() and reset() methods in a Web browser

Next, you will add to the ProductInfo.html file statements that submit the contents of TopFrame.html using the submit() method.

To add statements to the ProductInfo.html file that submit the contents of TopFrame.html using the submit() method:

1 Return to the **ProductInfo.html** file in your text editor or HTML editor.

2 Before the closing bracket of the submitForm() function, add the following else clause that submits the hidden form fields in TopFrame.html. Note that false is returned to the onSubmit event handler to prevent the ProductInfo.html file from also submitting its own form fields.

```
else {
parent.topframe.document.hiddenElements.submit();
return false;
}
```

3 Save and close **ProductInfo.html**.

4 Open the **ProductRegistration.html** file in your Web browser. Enter data into the required fields in the Customer Information form, then click the **Next** button. Click the **Submit** button without entering any data into the Product Information form. You should receive an alert dialog box.

If you enter data and click the Submit button, nothing will happen since we are not working with a Web server. At the end of this section you will add code that submits the form's data to an e-mail address.

5 Click **OK** to close the alert dialog box, then close the Web browser window.

Form Properties

The Form object includes several properties that correspond to the attributes of the <FORM> tag. It also includes properties containing information about a form's elements. Properties of the Form object are listed in Figure 6-34. You should be familiar with most of these properties from Section A.

Property	Description
action	The URL to which a form's data will be submitted
method	The method by which a form's data will be submitted: GET or POST
enctype	The format of the data being submitted
target	The window in which any results returned from the server are displayed
name	The name of the form
elements[]	An array representing a form's elements
length	The number of elements on a form

Figure 6-34: Properties of the Form object

All the properties of the Form object, with the exception of the name, elements[], and length properties, can be modified in JavaScript code.

The length property is useful for retrieving the number of elements on a form. Figure 6-35 contains a program that uses the length property to determine if a form's fields have been filled out. The program's onSubmit event calls a function named confirmFields(). The confirmFields() function uses a `while` statement to loop through the elements[] array. If an element in the elements[] array is empty, then a variable named missingFields increments by one. When the `while` statement finishes, an `if` statement checks to see if the missingFields variable is greater than zero. If it is, then an alert dialog box appears telling the user how many fields are missing. Notice that one is being subtracted from the length property, since we do not want to count the submit button as one of the fields that needs to be filled out.

```
<SCRIPT LANGUAGE="JavaScript1.2">
<!-- HIDE FROM INCOMPATIBLE BROWSERS
function confirmFields() {
    var count = 0;
    var missingFields = 0;
    while (count < document.exampleForm.length - 1) {
        if (document.exampleForm.elements[count].value == "")
            missingFields = ++missingFields;
            ++count;
    }
    if (missingFields > 0) {
        alert("You are missing " + missingFields + " out of " +
            (document.exampleForm.length - 1) + " fields.");
        return false;
    }
    return true;
}
// STOP HIDING FROM INCOMPATIBLE BROWSERS -->
</SCRIPT>
<FORM ACTION="http://exampleurl/cgi-bin/cgi_program"
    METHOD="post" NAME="exampleForm"
    onSubmit="confirmFields();">
Name<BR>
<INPUT TYPE="text" NAME="name" SIZE=50><BR>
Address<BR>
```

Figure 6-35: Confirm fields program

```
<INPUT TYPE="text" NAME="address" SIZE=50><BR>

City, State, Zip<BR>

<INPUT TYPE="text" NAME="city" SIZE=38>

<INPUT TYPE="text" NAME="state" SIZE=2 MAXLENGTH=2>

<INPUT TYPE="text" NAME="zip" SIZE=5 MAXLENGTH=5><BR>

<INPUT TYPE="submit">

</FORM>
```

Figure 6-35: Confirm fields program (continued)

E-mailing a Form's Data

Most of the forms you have seen so far have contained data that is transmitted to a CGI script on a server. Instead of submitting a form's data to a CGI script, another option is to send the form's data to an e-mail address. Sending a form's data to an e-mail address is a much simpler process than creating and managing a CGI script. Instead of relying on a complex CGI script on a server to process the data, you rely on the recipient of the e-mail message to process the data. For instance, a Web site may contain an online order form for some type of product. After the user clicks the form's Submit button, the data for the order can be sent to the e-mail address of whomever is responsible for filling the order. For large organizations that deal with hundreds or thousands of orders a day, e-mailing each order to a single individual is not the ideal solution. For smaller companies or Web sites that do not have a high volume of orders, e-mailing a form's data is a good solution.

To e-mail a form's data instead of submitting it to a CGI script, you replace the CGI script's URL in the <FORM> tag's ACTION attribute with `mailto:email_address`. Figure 6-36 shows an example of code that generates a form whose data will be e-mailed to a fictitious e-mail address, john_howe@exampledomain.com.

```
<HTML>

<HEAD>

<TITLE>Customer Information</TITLE>

</HEAD>

<BODY>

<H2>Customer Information</H2>

<FORM ACTION="mailto:john_howe@exampledomain.com"

    METHOD="post" ENCTYPE="text/plain" NAME="customer_information">

Name<BR>

<INPUT TYPE="text" NAME="name" SIZE=50><BR>

Address<BR>

<INPUT TYPE="text" NAME="address" SIZE=50><BR>

City, State, Zip<BR>

<INPUT TYPE="text" NAME="city" SIZE=38>

<INPUT TYPE="text" NAME="state" SIZE=2 MAXLENGTH=2>

<INPUT TYPE="text" NAME="zip" SIZE=5 MAXLENGTH=5><BR>

E-Mail<BR>

<INPUT TYPE="text" NAME="email" SIZE=50><P>

<INPUT TYPE="reset">

<INPUT TYPE="submit">
```

Figure 6-36: Form code with an ACTION attribute of `mailto`

When you send a form's data to an e-mail address, use the ENCTYPE type *text/plain*. The ENCTYPE type *text/plain* ensures that the data arrives at the e-mail address in a readable format. Figure 6-37 shows an example of the e-mail message received by john_howe@exampledomain.com after the form generated by the code in Figure 6-36 is submitted. The e-mail message is displayed in Outlook Express.

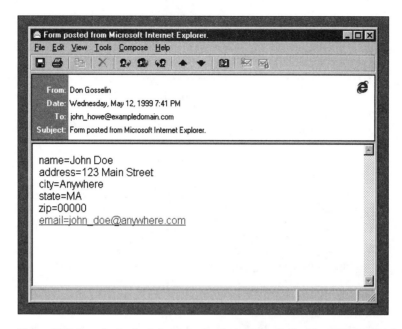

Figure 6-37: Data in Outlook Express after being e-mailed with an ENCTYPE of *text/plain*

If you omit the ENCTYPE of *text/plain*, the form's data is sent using the default type of *application/x-www-form-urlencoded*. When a form's data is sent via e-mail using ENCTYPE *application/x-www-form-urlencoded*, it can be difficult to read and work with. Figure 6-38 shows the data sent from the same program when the form is submitted with an ENCTYPE of *application/x-www-form-urlencoded*.

```
name=John+Doe&address=123+Main+Street&city=Anywhere&state=MA

&zip=00000&email=john_doe@anywhere.com
```

Figure 6-38: Data e-mailed with an ENCTYPE of *application/x-www-form-urlencoded*

tip

You can use the data shown in the e-mail in Figure 6-38. However, you would need to write a special program that converts the data to a readable format.

The drawback to e-mailing form data is that not all Web browsers support the `mailto:email_address` option with the <FORM> tag's ACTION attribute. In addition, the performance of the `mailto:email_address` option is unreliable. Some Web browsers that do support the e-mailing of form data do not properly place the data within the body of an e-mail message. If you write a Web page that e-mails form data, be sure to test it thoroughly before using it.

**tip**

··
When users click the Submit button for a form that is e-mailed, they may receive a security warning or be given a chance to edit the e-mail, depending on how their e-mail application is configured.
··

Next you will change the <FORM> tag of the Product Registration program so that the form's data is e-mailed to your e-mail address whenever it is submitted. In order to be sure this exercise works properly, you must be using Internet Explorer 4.0 or higher or Navigator 4.0 or higher.

To change the <FORM> tag of the Product Registration program so that the form's data is e-mailed to your e-mail address whenever it is submitted:

1 Open the **TopFrame.html** file in your text editor or HTML editor.

2 Add the following attributes just before the closing bracket of the <FORM> tag. Replace *email_address* with your own e-mail address.

```
ACTION="mailto:email_address" METHOD="post"
ENCTYPE="text/plain"
```

3 Save and close **TopFrame.html**, then open the **ProductRegistration.html** file in your Web browser. Fill in the fields for each form, then submit it. Depending on your e-mail configuration, you may receive warning dialog boxes or be given a chance to edit the e-mail message.

4 Wait several minutes before retrieving the new message from your e-mail, since transmission time on the Internet can vary. After you receive the e-mail, examine the message to see how the form data appears.

5 Close your e-mail program and the Web browser window.

SUMMARY

■ Hidden form fields are created with the <INPUT> tag and are used to hide information from users.

■ You use the properties, methods, and events of the Form object to verify form information with JavaScript.

■ The Document object includes a forms[] array that contains all of an HTML document's forms.

■ Each element on a form can be referenced using the elements[] array of the Form object.

■ The onSubmit event handler executes when a form is submitted to a CGI script, using a submit <INPUT> tag or an image <INPUT> tag.

■ The onReset event handler executes when a reset button on a form is clicked.

- The submit() method is used to submit a form in JavaScript without the use of a submit <INPUT> tag.

- The reset() method is used to clear a form in JavaScript without the use of a reset <INPUT> tag.

- The Form object includes several properties that correspond to the attributes of the <FORM> tag, as well as properties containing information about a form's elements.

- The length property is useful for retrieving the number of elements on a form.

- A form's data can be submitted to an e-mail address instead of a CGI script by using an ACTION attribute of `mailto`.

 # QUESTIONS

1. What is the correct syntax for creating a hidden form field?
   a. <HIDDEN VALUE=" *text to be hidden*">
   b. <HIDDEN>*text to be hidden*</HIDDEN>
   c. <INPUT TYPE="hidden" NAME="storedValue">
   d. <INPUT TYPE="hide" NAME="storedValue">

2. Form data can be verified in JavaScript using the properties, methods, and events of the _____ object.
   a. Form
   b. Document
   c. Window
   d. Data

3. If the first form in an HTML document is named myForm, which of the following can be used to refer to the form in JavaScript code?
   a. myForm.document
   b. document.frames[1]
   c. document.forms[0]
   d. document.forms[1]

4. Each element on a form can be referenced using the _____ array.
   a. elements[]
   b. input[]
   c. components[]
   d. forms[]

5. Which of the following statements is true about the NAME attribute of the <FORM> tag?
   a. You cannot include a NAME attribute with the <FORM> tag.
   b. The NAME attribute of the <FORM> tag is required if the form will be submitted to a CGI script.
   c. You cannot refer to a form in JavaScript if it does not include the NAME attribute.
   d. The NAME attribute of the <FORM> tag is only used to make it easier to refer to the form in JavaScript.

6. An HTML document contains two frames. The first frame is named leftFrame, and the second frame is named rightFrame. The right frame contains a form named myForm with a checkbox <INPUT> tag named myCheckbox. The myCheckbox element is the second element on the form. Which statement can be used *from the leftFrame* to change the value of myCheckbox to true?
    a. `parent.rightFrame.elements[0].checked = true;`
    b. `parent.document.rightFrame.elements[1].checked = true;`
    c. `myForm.myCheckbox.value = true;`
    d. `myForm.myCheckbox.checked = true;`

7. What is the onSubmit event handler often used for?
    a. saving a form to a local file before it is submitted to a CGI program
    b. periodically refreshing a Web browser window in order to show a form's most current data
    c. checking for new e-mail messages when a Web browser window opens or closes
    d. verifying or validating a form's data before it is sent to a server

8. Which of the following is the correct syntax for an onReset event handler?
    a. <BUTTON onReset="functionName()";>
    b. <RESET onReset="functionName()";>
    c. <FORM onReset="functionName()";>
    d. <SUBMIT onReset="functionName()";>

9. In order to cancel the onSubmit or onReset event handlers, what does a JavaScript function or code need to do?
    a. return a value of false
    b. return a value of true
    c. execute the stop or quit methods
    d. Nothing. The onSubmit and onReset events are canceled as soon as a corresponding event handler is encountered by the JavaScript interpreter.

10. The Form object contains two methods: the submit() method and the _____ method.
    a. resubmit()
    b. execute()
    c. process()
    d. reset()

11. The _____ property returns the number of form elements.
    a. length
    b. number
    c. elements
    d. fields

12. Which ENCTYPE type should be used to send a form's data to an e-mail address?
    a. application/jpeg/gif
    b. cgi.bin
    c. application/x-www-form-urlencoded
    d. text/plain

EXERCISES

1. Create a purchase order form for a hardware store. Include selection lists for standard items such as hammers, wrenches, and other tools. Use JavaScript to verify that customers fill out required information such as billing and shipping information. Save the file as PurchaseOrder.html in the Tutorial.06 folder on your Student Disk.

2. Create a math quiz for a 6th grade class. Use hidden fields for the answers to the quiz. Name the label of the submit button *Score Quiz*. When students click the submit button, execute the onSubmit event handler and determine if they have answered all the questions. If they have answered all the questions, score the quiz using the answers in the hidden fields. If they have not answered all the questions, cancel the onSubmit event and use an alert dialog box to instruct them to answer all the questions before selecting the Score Quiz button. Save the file as MathQuiz.html in the Tutorial.06 folder on your Student Disk.

3. Create a product order form. Use three separate HTML documents, each containing different forms. The first page should include product information, the second page should include customer billing information, and the third page should include shipping information. Allow the customer to navigate backward and forward among the three pages. Store information entered into a form in hidden fields so that it is saved when a customer changes pages. Also include JavaScript to verify that required fields have been entered or selected. Name your files and save them in the Tutorial.06 folder on your Student Disk.

4. Create a form to allow users to sign up for a professional conference. Have the forms submitted to your e-mail address. Save the file as Conference.html in the Tutorial.06 folder on your Student Disk.

5. Create an RSVP form for a party you are hosting. Your guests should fill out the form and submit it to your e-mail address. Save the file as RSVP.html in the Tutorial.06 folder on your Student Disk.

6. Create a form for processing vacation requests from employees. Use JavaScript to verify that employees fill out required information such as the dates they will be taking their vacations. Name the form's submit button *Submit Request*. Find someone in your class who can act as your manager and submit the form to his or her e-mail address. Save the file as VacationRequest.html in the Tutorial.06 folder on your Student Disk.

Dynamic HTML and Animation

case ▶ More and more of WebAdventure's clients are asking if their Web sites can include formatting and images that can be updated without having to reload an HTML document from the server. They also want to find innovative ways to use animation and interactivity to attract and retain visitors and make their Web sites effective and easy to navigate. Since standard HTML cannot perform these types of effects, your manager has asked that you learn how to use dynamic HTML (DHTML) in order to better serve their clients' needs. One client, Rocking Horse Toys, Inc., wants to include an animated rocking horse on their Web page as a corporate logo. Your manager also wants you to use your DHTML skills to create an animated logo for WebAdventure.

Previewing the Animation Files

Dynamic HTML allows HTML tags to be changed after a Web page is rendered by a browser. The ability to render HTML tags dynamically allows you to add animation, among other things, to Web pages. This tutorial uses animation to study dynamic HTML techniques. You will create two different animations while learning about dynamic HTML: a rocking horse and the Earth revolving around the sun. Both animation sequences are examples that could be used for advertising purposes or as visually appealing effects to draw visitors to a Web page.

To preview the rocking horse animation:

1 In your Web browser, open the **Tutorial7_RockingHorse.html** file from the Tutorial.07 folder on your Student Disk. Figure 7-1 displays an example of the Tutorial7_RockingHorse.html file in Navigator.

Figure 7-1: Tutorial7_RockingHorse.html in Navigator

2 Click the **Start Rocking** button to begin the animation. After you have viewed the animation, click the **Stop Rocking** button.

3 Close the Web browser window.

4 Next, examine the code for the Tutorial7_RockingHorse.html file in your text editor or HTML editor. The <SCRIPT> section contains several global variables used in the animation. The animation itself is executed using the rockHorse() function, which is called by the startRocking() function. The button in the body of the document uses an onClick method to call the startRocking() function.

5 Close your text editor or HTML editor when you are finished examining the code.

Now you will preview the orbit animation.

To preview the orbit animation:

1 In your Web browser, open the **Tutorial7_OrbitMaster.html** file from the Tutorial.07 folder on your Student Disk. Note that the Tutorial7_OrbitMaster.html file opens Tutorial7_OrbitIE.html if you are using Internet Explorer or Tutorial7_OrbitNavigator.html if you are using Navigator. Figure 7-2 displays an example of the orbit animation as it appears in Navigator.

2 Close the Web browser window.

3 Examine the code for the OrbitMaster.html file in your text editor or HTML editor. The onLoad event in the <BODY> tag calls a checkBrowser() function that opens a different version of the animation file, Tutorial7_OrbitIE.html or Tutorial7_OrbitNavigtor.html, depending on whether Internet Explorer or Navigator is running.

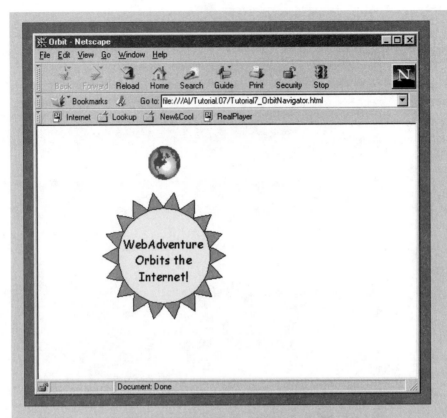

Figure 7-2: Orbit animation in Navigator

4 Next, compare the code for the Tutorial7_OrbitIE.html and the Tutorial7_OrbitNavigator.html files. Both files contain an orbit() function. Notice the differences in the statements for each file. Also notice that each file uses different HTML tags. Section B explains why Internet Explorer and Navigator require different JavaScript syntax and HTML tags for dynamic HTML files.

SECTION A

objectives

In this section you will learn:

■ About dynamic HTML
■ About the Document Object Model
■ About Document object properties
■ About Document object methods
■ About the Image object
■ About animation with the Image object
■ About image caching

Dynamic Object Model

Dynamic HTML

The Web is used for many purposes. Researchers, scientists, and others in academic settings use the Web to display, search for, and locate information. Commercial applications of the Web include publishing, advertising, and entertainment. Many businesses today have Web sites, and in the future most businesses will probably have a presence on the Web. To attract and retain visitors, Web sites must be exciting and visually stimulating. Businesses, in particular, want their Web sites to include advertising, animation, interactivity with users, intuitive navigation controls, and many other types of effects that will help sell their products.

In addition to business sites, the Web has many forms of entertainment, including games, animation, and multimedia presentations. Animations and multimedia presentations need to load quickly in order to keep users interested. Games must be exciting and interactive. For example, visitors to a Web site that features a chess game must be able to move the chess pieces.

HTML would be much more useful if it were dynamic. The term dynamic in Internet terminology means several things. Primarily, "dynamic" refers to Web pages that respond to user requests through buttons or other types of controls. For example, a dynamic Web page may allow a user to change the document's background color, process a query when a user submits a form, or interact with a user in other ways, such as through an online game or quiz. The term dynamic also refers to various types of effects that are displayed automatically in a Web browser, such as animation.

You can simulate limited dynamism and interactivity with hypertext links. Consider the Web page displayed in Figure 7-3, which displays photos of WebAdventure's programmers. This single Web page has links to seven other Web pages that are identical except for the picture that appears. Figure 7-4 shows the tags for the HTML file that displays Erica Miller's page.

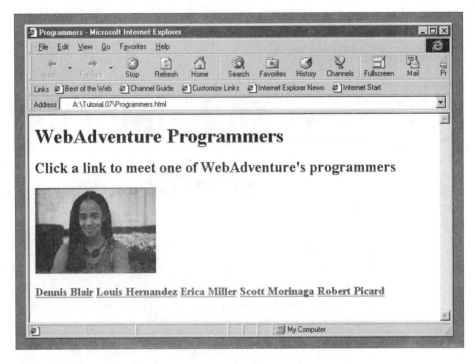

Figure 7-3: Programmers.html

Hypertext links do not change the currently displayed document, but load new ones from the server instead, so they cannot produce true dynamic effects. When a user clicks a link on the Programmers Web page, it appears as if only the graphic changes. In reality, the entire page is replaced. The Web browser has to find the correct Web page on the server, transfer that file to your computer, and then render the new document. While you might not notice the time it takes for these steps to occur in this simple example, the transfer and rendering time for a large, complex Web page could be significant. If this Web page were dynamic, only the file displayed by the <IMG> tag would change, and the work would be performed locally by a Web browser rather than by a server. Changing only the image would be much more effective and efficient.

```
<HTML>

<HEAD>

<TITLE>Programmers</TITLE>

</HEAD>

<BODY>

<H1>WebAdventure Programmers</H1>
```

Figure 7-4: Miller.html

```
<H2>Click a link to meet one of

WebAdventure's programmers</H2>

<IMG NAME="programmer_pic" SRC="Miller.jpg"><P>

<H3>

<A HREF="Blair.html">Dennis Blair</A>

<A HREF="Hernandez.html">Louis Hernandez</A>

<A HREF="Miller.html">Erica Miller</A>

<A HREF="Morinaga.html">Scott Morinaga</A>

<A HREF="Picard.html">Raymond Picard</A>

</H3>

</BODY>

</HTML>
```

Figure 7-4: Miller.html (continued)

Several combined Internet technologies, called dynamic HTML or DHTML, allow HTML tags to change dynamically and allow Web pages to be rendered dynamically. The term DHTML can refer to different combinations of technologies that give a dynamic quality to HTML pages. Technologies used for creating DHTML include JavaScript, VBScript, CGI, Java, Active Server Pages, and others. For our purposes, DHTML includes the following technologies:

- JavaScript
- HTML
- Cascading style sheets

As you work through this tutorial, remember that DHTML does not refer to a single technology, but to several technologies combined.

Cascading style sheets are used to manage the formatting information of HTML documents. You will learn about cascading style sheets in Section B.

Figure 7-5 displays two popular DHTML features: a slider menu that "pops out" when users hold their mouse over it and marquee text that scrolls a message across the screen. The marquee text is displayed at the bottom of the browser window, just beneath the text *WebAdventure's Mission*.

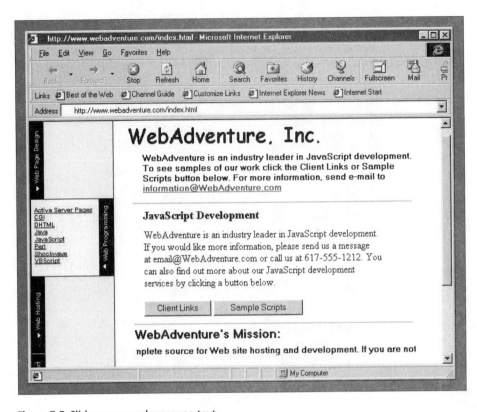

Figure 7-5: Slider menu and marquee text

Figure 7-6 displays a game written in DHTML. The game is a version of the classic Tetris game and combines animation (the movement of game pieces) with interactivity (keys that rotate and move each piece).

The TetriScript game in Figure 7-6 was created by Kazuhiro Moriyama of Tochigi, Japan. You can find many of his other excellent JavaScript games at http://plaza.harmonix.ne.jp/~jimmeans/.

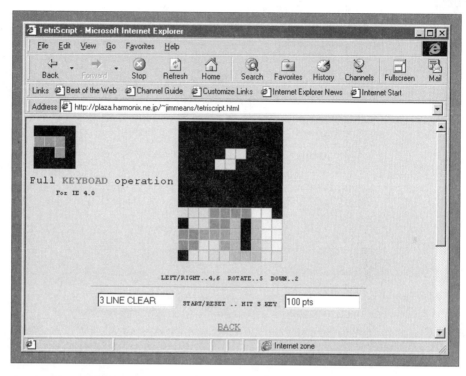

Figure 7-6: TetriScript game

Document Object Model

At the core of DHTML is the Document Object Model, displayed in Figure 7-7. The **Document Object Model**, or **DOM**, represents the HTML document displayed in a window and provides programmatic access to a document's elements. The DOM is actually the Document object branch of the JavaScript object model you learned about in Tutorial 5. Whenever you have used images and forms or have referred to the Document object, you have used the DOM. You have used two methods of the Document object, write() and writeln(), extensively.

The Document object refers not only to HTML documents, but also to other file types that are displayed in a Web browser, such as .jpg, .gif, and .xml. .jpg and .gif are image file formats. .xml is a file format for structured documents that uses tags similar to HTML.

Figure 7-7 lists only the HTML objects that are part of the DOM. The DOM also includes events, properties, and methods. You learned about events in Tutorial 2. The properties and methods of the DOM are discussed in this section.

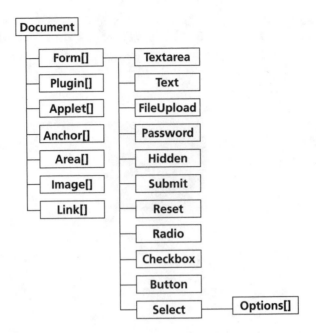

Figure 7-7: Document Object Model

The DOM enables JavaScript to access individual HTML elements by turning each tag in an HTML document into its own programmatic object. This functionality lets you change individual HTML elements dynamically after a page has been rendered, without having to reload the page from the server. You refer to an HTML tag using its NAME attribute or by referring to an element number in an Array object. The following code shows a simple form that dynamically changes the text displayed in a text <INPUT> tag when a user clicks a button. Figure 7-8 shows the output of the program in a Web browser. In the onClick events, the code uses the `this` reference with the Form object along with the elements[] array. Note that the code does not load a new HTML document or reload the original document, but *dynamically* changes only the value of the text box. This type of functionality is not possible without DHTML.

```
<H2>Click to display each New England state capital</H2>
<FORM NAME="states">
<INPUT TYPE="text"><P>
<INPUT TYPE="button" VALUE="Maine"
    onClick="this.form.elements[0].value='Augusta';">
<INPUT TYPE="button" VALUE="Massachusetts"
    onClick="this.form.elements[0].value='Boston';">
<INPUT TYPE="button" VALUE="Connecticut"
    onClick="this.form.elements[0].value='Hartford';"><BR>
<INPUT TYPE="button" VALUE="Rhode Island"
    onClick="this.form.elements[0].value='Providence';">
```

```
<INPUT TYPE="button" VALUE="Vermont"
    onClick="this.form.elements[0].value='Montpelier';">
<INPUT TYPE="button" VALUE="New Hampshire"
    onClick="this.form.elements[0].value='Concord';">
</FORM>
```

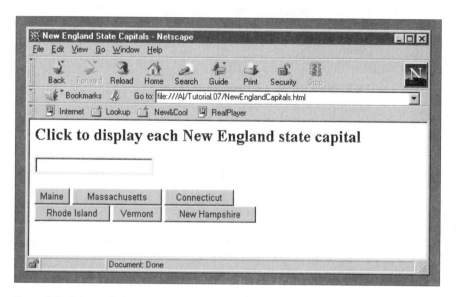

Figure 7-8: State capitals program

Implementation of DHTML is evolving, even though the individual technologies that make up DHTML are accepted standards. Because DHTML is an evolving technology, there is no accepted standard for the DOM. Version 4 of both Navigator and Internet Explorer support a primitive version of the DOM known as Level 0. However, Internet Explorer 4 supports a number of DOM objects that are completely incompatible with Level 0, and therefore are incompatible with Navigator 4. Navigator 4 also contains objects that are incompatible with Level 0, but not as many as are found in Internet Explorer. At the time of this writing, the World Wide Web Consortium (W3C) is drafting a new DOM standard known as Level 1. DOM Level 1 is expected to include many of the objects, properties, and methods that are currently available in Internet Explorer 4. However, DOM Level 1 will not be available until the release of Internet Explorer 5 and Navigator 5. Even after the new Web browser versions are released, it will be some time before they are fully embraced by the market. To develop DHTML Web pages that will work in the majority of browsers in use, you should use only DOM Level 0 objects until Internet Explorer 5 and Navigator 5 are in wide use.

Where possible, this tutorial covers only the objects, properties, and methods that are compatible with both Navigator 4 and Internet Explorer 4.

Document Object Properties

The Document object contains various properties used for manipulating HTML objects. The properties of the Document object are listed in Figure 7-9.

Property	Description
alinkColor	The color of an active link as specified by the ALINK attribute of the <BODY> tag
anchors[]	An array referring to the document's anchors
applets[]	An array referring to the document's applets
bgColor	The background color of the document as specified by the BGCOLOR attribute of the <BODY> tag
cookie	Specifies a cookie for the current document
domain	The domain name of the server where the current document is located
embeds[]	An array referring to the document's plugins and ActiveX controls
fgColor	The foreground text color of the document as specified by the FGCOLOR attribute of the <BODY> tag
forms[]	An array referring to the document's forms
images[]	An array referring to the document's images
lastModified	The date the document was last modified
linkColor	The color of the document's unvisited links as specified by the LINK attribute of the <BODY> tag
links[]	An array referring to the document's links
referrer	The URL of the document that provided a link to the current document
title	The title of the document as specified by the <TITLE>...</TITLE> tag pair in the document's <HEAD> section
URL	The URL of the current document
vlinkColor	The color of the document's visited links as specified by the VLINK attribute of the <BODY> tag

Figure 7-9: Document object properties

In Navigator 4.0, the majority of the Document object properties can be set only *before* the document is rendered. Only the bgColor property can be set dynamically after the document has been rendered. Therefore, in Level 0 DHTML, many Document object properties are of limited use in creating dynamic documents. The properties are more useful for retrieving information about the current document. For example, the following function displays a document's title, URL, and date of last modification in an alert dialog box:

```
function documentStatistics() {
    alert(document.title + "\n" + document.URL + "\n"
        + document.lastModified);
}
```

In contrast to Navigator 4.0, Internet Explorer 4.0 allows you to dynamically change many of the Document object properties after the document is rendered. Keep in mind, though, that Internet-Explorer-compatible documents that dynamically change Document object properties will not function with Navigator. In Navigator, only the bgColor property can be set dynamically after the document has been rendered. Figure 7-10 shows an example of a program designed for Internet Explorer that uses the setInterval() method to dynamically change the bgColor and fgColor of a document every 1000 milliseconds (one second). The changeColor() function is called by using a setInterval() method in the onLoad event of the <BODY> tag. The example creates a sort of "flashing sign" that could be used in an advertisement on a Web site. Figure 7-11 shows the first iteration of the program, which contains black text on a white background, and Figure 7-12 shows the second iteration, which contains white text on a black background.

```
<SCRIPT LANGUAGE="JavaScript1.2">
<!-- HIDE FROM INCOMPATIBLE BROWSERS
var backColor = "black";
var textColor = "white";
function changeColor() {
    if (backColor == "black") {
        backColor = "white";
        textColor = "black";
        document.bgColor = backColor;
        document.fgColor = textColor
    }
    else {
        backColor = "black";
        textColor = "white";
        document.bgColor = backColor;
        document.fgColor = textColor
    }
}
// STOP HIDING FROM INCOMPATIBLE BROWSERS -->
</SCRIPT>
<BODY onLoad="setInterval("changeColor();",1000);">
<H2>Choose WebAdventure for all your Internet needs!</H2>
</BODY>
```

Figure 7-10: Changing bgColor and fgColor properties

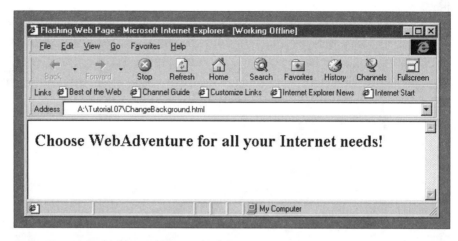

Figure 7-11: Black text on a white background

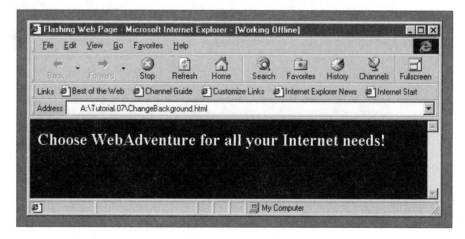

Figure 7-12: White text on a black background

tip

Remember that the changing bgColor and fgColor program only functions in Internet Explorer 4.0 or higher.

Next you will create a Web page whose background color automatically changes every few seconds using the setInterval() method. Our goal is to create programs that are compatible with both Internet Explorer and Navigator. Therefore, you will not include code that automatically changes the foreground color of text, as in the preceding example, since the fgColor property cannot be set dynamically in Navigator.

To create a Web page whose background color automatically changes every few seconds using the setInterval() method:

1 Start your text editor or HTML editor and create a new document.

2 Type the opening <HTML> and <HEAD> sections of the document:

```
<HTML>
<HEAD>
<TITLE>Changing Background</TITLE>
```

3 Add the opening statements for the JavaScript section in the <HEAD> section:

```
<SCRIPT LANGUAGE="JavaScript1.2">
<!-- HIDE FROM INCOMPATIBLE BROWSERS
```

4 Type **var currentColor = "blue";** to create a variable that keeps track of which color is currently displayed.

5 Type the following function, which changes the color of the Web page's background using the bgColor property of the Document object. You will call this function using the onLoad event handler in the <BODY> tag.

```
function changeBackground() {
      if (currentColor == "blue") {
            document.bgColor = "red";
            currentColor = "red";
      }
      else {
            document.bgColor = "blue";
            currentColor = "blue";
      }
}
```

6 Add the following tags to close the <SCRIPT> and <HEAD> sections.

```
// STOP HIDING FROM INCOMPATIBLE BROWSERS -->
</SCRIPT>
</HEAD>
```

7 Create the following <BODY> tag that includes an onLoad event handler that uses the setInterval() method to call the changeBackground() function in the head:

```
<BODY onLoad="setInterval('changeBackground();',2000);">
```

8 Type the following line to explain the purpose of the Web page:

```
<B>The background of this Web page changes from
blue to red every two seconds.</B>
```

9 Add the following lines to close the <BODY> and <HTML> tags:

```
</BODY>
</HTML>
```

10 Save the file as **ChangingBackground.html** in the **Tutorial.07** folder on your Student Disk. Open the **ChangingBackground.html** file in your Web browser. The background should change from blue to red every two seconds.

11 Close the Web browser window.

Document Object Methods

As you create Web pages, you may want to dynamically create a new HTML document. For example, after running a CGI script that processes an online order, you may want to dynamically generate a new HTML document that confirms the order. The document object includes four methods for dynamically generating Web pages: write(), writeln(), open(), and close(). You have used the write() and writeln() methods throughout this text to add content to a new Web page as it is being rendered. The **open() method** opens a window or frame other than the current window or frame, and is used to update its contents with the write() and writeln() methods. You can include an argument with the open() method specifying the MIME type of the document to be displayed. If you do not include an argument, a default MIME type of *text/html* is used. The **close() method** notifies the Web browser that you are finished writing to the window or frame and that the document should be displayed. If you use the write() and writeln() methods without using the open() method, the contents of the current window are overwritten.

You learned about MIME types in Tutorial 6.

A limitation of the write() and writeln() methods is that they cannot be used to change content after a Web page has been rendered. You can execute the write() and writeln() methods in the current document after it is rendered, but doing so will overwrite the existing document's content. Although the write() and writeln() methods are not used for dynamically changing an existing Web page, they are used for dynamically creating new windows or frames.

As you know, the write() and writeln() methods of the Document object require a text string as an argument. The only difference between the write() and writeln() methods is that the writeln() method adds a carriage return after the line. For a Web browser to recognize the line break following the writeln() method, you must enclose the <SCRIPT>...</SCRIPT> tag pair containing the writeln() method within a <PRE>...</PRE> tag pair. You can include line breaks without the <PRE> tag and writeln() method by including the escape character (\n) within the text argument of the write() method. The following code illustrates how the write() method and escape character work:

```
<SCRIPT LANGUAGE="JavaScript1.2">
document.write("Hello World\n")
document.write("This line is printed
     below the 'Hello World' line.")
</SCRIPT>
```

Rather than using separate write() and writeln() line methods, you can generate multiple lines of text with a single write() method by including each text string as an argument, separated by commas. The following code performs the same function as the preceding example, but this time using only a single write() method:

```
<SCRIPT LANGUAGE="JavaScript1.2">
document.write("Hello World\n", "This line is printed
     below the 'Hello World' line.")
</SCRIPT>
```

The following code generates a new window that may be used as a redirection window when a document cannot be found or is unavailable. The code opens a new window, then uses the write() method to generate a message along with a link to the referrer property of the Document object. The referrer property returns the URL of the Web page that opened the current Web page. In this case, the referrer property is used to create a link back to the source URL. Once the write() method is finished, the close() method executes and displays the page in a new window. Since both the Window and Document objects contain open() and close() methods, the code includes each object reference, to differentiate between the two. Figure 7-13 shows how the new window appears.

```
var message = "<H2>The Web page you requested is
     currently unavailable.</H2>"
var link = "Click <A HREF='" + document.referrer
     + "'>here</A> to return to the last Web page."
redirectWindow = window.open("");
redirectWindow.document.open("text/html");
redirectWindow.document.write(message, link);
redirectWindow.document.close();
```

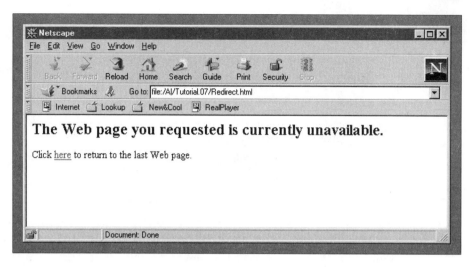

Figure 7-13: Redirection window

The Image Object

One of the most visually pleasing parts of a Web page is its images. Without images, a Web page would be nothing more than a collection of text and hypertext links. Web pages today include images in the form of company logos, photographs of products, drawings, animation, image maps like the one you created in Tutorial 2, and other types of graphics. Commerce-oriented Web pages that did not include images would be hard pressed to attract—and keep—visitors.

The ability to include images in a Web page is not new. You simply include an <IMG> tag with the SRC attribute set to the URL of the image you want to display. Each <IMG> tag in an HTML document is represented in the DOM images[] array by an Image object. An **Image object** represents images created using the <IMG> tag. If you want to change an image on the basis of a user's selection, as part of a timed advertising routine, or for simple animation, you must use JavaScript with an Image object.

Figure 7-14 lists Image object properties, and Figure 7-15 lists Image object events.

Property	Description
border	A read-only property containing the border width, in pixels, as specified by the BORDER attribute of the <IMG> tag
complete	A Boolean value that returns true when an image is completely loaded
height	A read-only property containing the height of the image as specified by the HEIGHT attribute of the <IMG> tag
hspace	A read-only property containing the amount of horizontal space, in pixels, to the left and right of the image, as specified by the HSPACE attribute of the <IMG> tag
lowsrc	The URL of an alternate image to display at low resolution
name	A name assigned to the tag
src	The URL of the displayed image
vspace	A read-only property containing the amount of vertical space, in pixels, above and below the image, as specified by the VSPACE attribute of the <IMG> tag
width	A read-only property containing the width of the image as specified by the WIDTH attribute of the <IMG> tag

Figure 7-14: Image object properties

Event	Description
onLoad	Executes after an image is loaded
onAbort	Executes when the user cancels the loading of an image, usually by clicking the Stop button
onError	Executes when an error occurs while loading an image

Figure 7-15: Image object events

One of the most important elements of the Image object is the src property, which allows JavaScript to change an image dynamically.

tip

The src and lowsrc properties are the only Image properties that can be changed after a document has been rendered in Navigator. Internet Explorer allows you to modify most of the other properties dynamically.

Figure 7-16 shows a modified version of the same program you saw in Figure 7-4 and illustrates the use of the src property. In this case, the hypertext links for each programmer are replaced with form buttons. Most important, the HTML document is not replaced when the user clicks a different programmer. Instead, the picture displayed by the <IMG> tag is replaced dynamically, by means of the src property of the Image object. This new program is much more efficient than loading a new HTML document each time you want to display a new picture, as was the case in the earlier example. The default image in the program is the first programmer in the list, Dennis Blair. Figure 7-17 shows the program in a Web browser.

```
<HTML>

<HEAD>

<TITLE>Programmers</TITLE>

</HEAD>

<BODY>

<H1>WebAdventure Programmers</H1>

<H2>Click a button to meet one of

WebAdventure's programmers</H2>

<IMG NAME="programmer_pic" SRC="blair.jpg"><P>

<FORM NAME="programmer_list">

    <INPUT TYPE="button" VALUE="Dennis Blair"

        onClick="document.programmer_pic.src='blair.jpg'">

    <INPUT TYPE="button" VALUE="Louis Hernandez"

        onClick="document.programmer_pic.src='hernandez.jpg'">

    <INPUT TYPE="button" VALUE="Erica Miller"

        onClick="document.programmer_pic.src='miller.jpg'">

    <INPUT TYPE="button" VALUE="Scott Morinaga"

        onClick="document.programmer_pic.src='morinaga.jpg'">

    <INPUT TYPE="button" VALUE="Raymond Picard"

        onClick="document.programmer_pic.src='picard.jpg'">

</FORM>

</H3>

</BODY>
```

Figure 7-16: Programmers.html

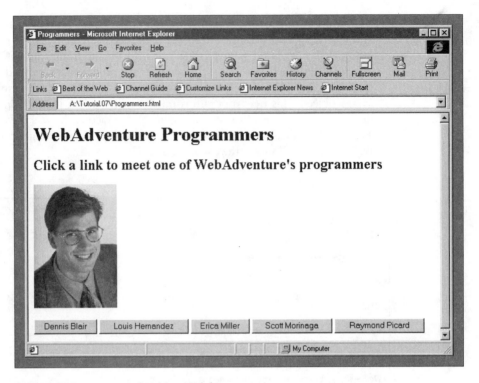

Figure 7-17: Programmers.html in a Web browser

Next, you will create a document that allows users to dynamically change the image displayed with an <IMG> tag. You will create three buttons that allow users to display different sized versions of the same image. The images you will use in the document are located in the Tutorial.07 folder on your Student Disk.

To create a document that allows user to dynamically change the image displayed with an <IMG> tag:

1   Start your text editor or HTML editor and create a new document.

2   Type the <HTML> and <HEAD> sections of the document:

```
<HTML>
<HEAD>
<TITLE>Image Options</TITLE>
</HEAD>
```

3   Add **<BODY>** to start the body section, then type **<FORM>** to start a form.

4   Create the following <INPUT> tags that will change the image of a bird to small, medium, or large. The tags use the onClick event handler to change the height and width properties of the Image object.

```
<INPUT TYPE="button" VALUE=" Small Bird "
     onClick="document.bird.src='smallbird.gif';">
<INPUT TYPE="button" VALUE=" Medium Bird "
     onClick="document.bird.src='mediumbird.gif';">
<INPUT TYPE="button" VALUE=" Big Bird "
     onClick="document.bird.src='largebird.gif';">
```

5 Type the closing **</FORM>** tag.

6 Next add the following line, which adds the <IMG> tag. The image is initially set to smallbird.gif.

```
<IMG SRC="smallbird.gif" NAME="bird">
```

7 Type the closing **</BODY>** and **</HTML>** tags.

8 Save the file as **ChangeImage.html** in the **Tutorial.07** folder on your Student Disk. Open the **ChangeImage.html** file in your Web browser. Figure 7-18 shows how the document appears in a Web browser after the user selects the Medium Bird button.

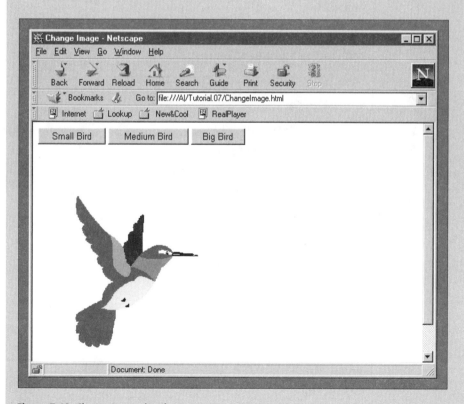

Figure 7-18: ChangeImage.html

9 Close the Web browser window.

Animation with the Image Object

In Tutorial 5, you learned how to use the setTimeout() and setInterval() methods to automatically execute JavaScript code. By combining the src attribute of the Image object with the setTimeout() or setInterval() methods, you can create simple animation in an HTML document. What animation means in this context is not necessarily a complex cartoon character, but any situation in which a sequence of images changes automatically. Web animation can also include traditional animation involving cartoons and movement. Examples of JavaScript programs that use animation include a simple advertisement in which two images change every couple of seconds and the ticking hands of an online clock (each position of a clock's hands requires a separate image). Figure 7-19 contains a program that uses the setInterval() method to automatically swap two advertising images every couple of seconds. Figure 7-20 shows the two images.

```
<HTML>

<HEAD>

<TITLE>Advertisement</TITLE>

<SCRIPT LANGUAGE="JavaScript1.2">

<!-- HIDE FROM INCOMPATIBLE BROWSERS

var qa = "q";

function changeImage() {

    if (qa == "q") {

            document.animation.src = "answer.jpg";

            qa = "a";

    }

    else {

            document.animation.src = "question.jpg";

            qa = "q";

    }

}

// STOP HIDING FROM INCOMPATIBLE BROWSERS -->

</SCRIPT>

</HEAD>
```

Figure 7-19: Changing images program

```
<BODY onLoad="var begin=setInterval('changeImage()',2000);">
<IMG SRC="question.jpg" NAME="animation"><P>
</BODY>
</HTML>
```

Figure 7-19: Changing images program (continued)

question.jpg

answer.jpg

Figure 7-20: Advertising images

If you would like to see how the flashing advertising program functions, a copy of it named Advertisement.html is in the Tutorial.07 folder on your Student Disk.

True animation involving movement requires a different graphic, or frame, for each movement that a character or object makes. This text does not intend to teach the artistic skills necessary for creating frames in an animation sequence. Instead, the goal is to show how to use JavaScript and the Image object to perform simple animation by swapping frames displayed by an <IMG> tag.

Do not confuse animation frames with frames created with the <FRAMESET> and <FRAME> tags.

As an example of frames in an animation sequence, Figure 7-21 shows six frames, each frame containing a motion that a runner goes through.

Figure 7-21: Animation frames

You create an animated sequence with JavaScript by using the setInterval() or setTimeout() methods to cycle through the frames in an animation series. Each iteration of a setInterval() or setTimeout() method changes the frame displayed by an <IMG> tag. The speed of the animation depends on how many milliseconds are passed as an argument to the setInterval() or setTimeout() methods.

When creating animation sequences, it is important to make sure that each frame of the animation is created with the same HEIGHT and WIDTH attributes of the <IMG> tag, in order for all images in the sequence to display in the same size.

Figure 7-22 contains code that animates the frames in Figure 7-21. The code assigns the frames to a runner[] array. Once the Run button is clicked, a setInterval() method executes an `if` statement that changes the displayed frame based on the curRunner variable. Once the curRunner variable reaches five (the highest element in an array with six elements), it resets to zero (the first element in the array), and the animation sequence starts over from the beginning. The name of each graphic for the frames shown in Figure 7-21 corresponds to an element number in the runner[] array. The Stop button uses the clearInterval() method to stop the startInterval() method. Figure 7-23 shows an example of the program in a Web browser.

```
<HTML>

<HEAD>

<TITLE>Runners</TITLE>

<SCRIPT LANGUAGE="JavaScript1.2">

<!-- HIDE FROM INCOMPATIBLE BROWSERS
```

Figure 7-22: Runner animation code

```
var runner = new Array(6);

var curRunner = 0;

var startRunning;

runner[0] = "runner0.jpg";

runner[1] = "runner1.jpg";

runner[2] = "runner2.jpg";

runner[3] = "runner3.jpg";

runner[4] = "runner4.jpg";

runner[5] = "runner5.jpg";

function marathon() {

     if (curRunner == 5)

          curRunner = 0;

     else

          ++curRunner;

     document.animation.src = runner[curRunner];

}
// STOP HIDING FROM INCOMPATIBLE BROWSERS -->

</SCRIPT>

</HEAD>

<BODY>

<IMG SRC="runner0.jpg" NAME="animation"><P>

<FORM>

<INPUT TYPE="button" NAME="run" VALUE=" Run "
onClick="startRunning=setInterval('marathon()',100);">
<INPUT TYPE="button" NAME="stop" VALUE=" Stop "

     onClick="clearInterval(startRunning);">

</FORM>

</BODY>

</HTML>
```

Figure 7-22: Runner animation code (continued)

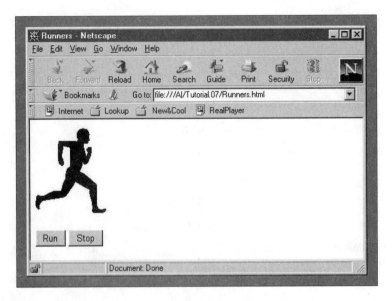

Figure 7-23: Runner animation in a Web browser

If you would like to see how the runner animation functions, a copy of it named Runner.html is in the Tutorial.07 folder on your Student Disk.

Although the runner animation adds a dynamic aspect to images, it does have one shortcoming: the animation does not actually move across the screen, but takes place within the confines of the space taken up by the single <IMG> tag. The runner is animated, but appears as if he is running in place. In the next section, you will learn how to use style sheets to change an image's position on screen, so that animation actually appears to be traveling.

Next you will create an animated rocking horse. The six images required for the animation are located in the Tutorial.07 folder on your Student Disk. Figure 7-24 shows the figures.

The rocking horse animation will be similar to the runner animation. However, unlike the runner animation, the rocking horse animation cannot redisplay the first frame, rockinghorse0.jpg, after displaying the last frame, rockinghorse5.jpg. If it did, the animation would not run smoothly. The rocking horse animation must cycle back down through each frame after the last frame is reached, instead of starting over again at the first frame.

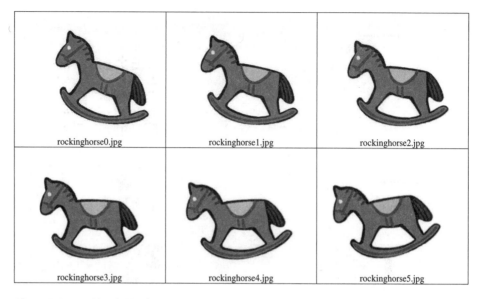

rockinghorse0.jpg   rockinghorse1.jpg   rockinghorse2.jpg

rockinghorse3.jpg   rockinghorse4.jpg   rockinghorse5.jpg

Figure 7-24: Rocking horse frames

To create the rocking horse animation:

1 Start your text editor or HTML editor and create a new document.

2 Type the <HTML> and <HEAD> sections of the document:

```
<HTML>
<HEAD>
<TITLE>Rocking Horse</TITLE>
```

3 Add the opening statements for a JavaScript section:

```
<SCRIPT LANGUAGE="JavaScript1.2">
<!-- HIDE FROM INCOMPATIBLE BROWSERS
```

4 Type the following four variables. The horses variable will contain the names of the six image files. The curHorse variable will be used in an `if` statement as a counter. The direction variable will be used to determine if the horse should "rock" right or left. The begin variable will be assigned to the setInterval() method that starts the animation.

```
var horses = new Array(5);
var curHorse = 0;
var direction;
var begin;
```

5   Assign the image files to the corresponding elements in the horses array:

```
horses[0] = "rockinghorse0.jpg";
horses[1] = "rockinghorse1.jpg";
horses[2] = "rockinghorse2.jpg";
horses[3] = "rockinghorse3.jpg";
horses[4] = "rockinghorse4.jpg";
horses[5] = "rockinghorse5.jpg";
```

6   The following function will actually perform the animation. The first `if` statement checks the curHorse variable to see if it is equal to 0 or 5. If the variable is equal to 0, the direction variable is set to *right*, if it is equal to 5, the direction variable is set to *left*. The next `if` statement then checks the direction variable to determine whether to increment or decrement the curHorse variable. The final statement in the function changes the image displayed by an <IMG> tag named *animation* to the image that corresponds to the element in the horses[] array that matches the curHorse variable. You will create the animation <IMG> tag in Step 9.

```
function rockHorse() {
    if (curHorse == 0)
        direction = "right";
    else if (curHorse == 5)
        direction = "left";
    if (direction == "right")
        ++curHorse;
    else if (direction == "left")
        --curHorse;
    document.animation.src = horses[curHorse];
}
```

7   Next, add the following function, which will be called from a Start Rocking button in the body of the document. The first statement uses the clearInterval() method to cancel the animation if it is already running. If you do not include this statement, then the user could click the Start Rocking button several times, which would cause multiple instances of the setInterval() method to occur. Multiple instances of the same setInterval() method will cause your computer to execute as many animation sequences as there are instances of the setInterval() method, which could make the animation appear to run faster than desired or function erratically. The last statement in the function is the setInterval() method that runs the rockHorse function() you created in Step 6.

```
function startRocking() {
    clearInterval(begin);
    begin = setInterval("rockHorse()",100);
}
```

8 Add the following code to close the <SCRIPT> and <HEAD> tags:

```
// STOP HIDING FROM INCOMPATIBLE BROWSERS -->
</SCRIPT>
</HEAD>
```

9 Add the following body section of the document. The <IMG> tag, named *animation*, opens the first frame in the animation, rockinghorse0.jpg. The Start Rocking button uses the onClick event handler to execute the startRocking() function, and the Stop Rocking button clears the setInterval() method executed by the startRocking() function.

```
<BODY>
<H1>Rocking Horse Toys, Inc.</H1><P>
<IMG SRC="rockinghorse0.jpg" NAME="animation"><P>
<FORM>
<INPUT TYPE="button" NAME="run" VALUE=" Start Rocking "
    onClick="startRocking()">
<INPUT TYPE="button" NAME="stop" VALUE=" Stop Rocking "
    onClick="clearInterval(begin)">
</FORM>
</BODY>
```

10 Type a closing </HTML> tag.

11 Save the file as **RockingHorse.html** in the **Tutorial.07** folder on your Student Disk. Open the **RockingHorse.html** file in your Web browser and see if it functions correctly.

12 Close the Web browser window.

Image Caching

In the rocking horse program, you may have noticed that the loading of each image appears to be jerky, erratic, or slow. This effect happens because JavaScript does not save a copy of the image in memory that can be used whenever necessary. Instead, each time a different image is loaded by an <IMG> tag, JavaScript must physically open or reopen the image from its source. You probably accessed the rocking horse image files directly from the Student Disk on your local computer, and if you have a particularly fast computer, you may not have noticed a loading problem. If you did experience erratic loading of the images, then you can imagine how erratic and slow the animation would appear if you had to download the images from the Web server *each time they are loaded*. A technique for eliminating multiple downloads of the same file is called image caching. **Image caching** temporarily stores image files in memory on a local computer. This technique allows JavaScript to store and retrieve an image from memory rather than download the image each time it is needed.

Images are cached using the Image() constructor of the Image object. The Image() constructor creates a new Image object. There are three steps for caching an image in JavaScript:

- Create a new object using the Image() constructor
- Assign a graphic file to the src property of the new Image object
- Assign the src property of the new Image object to the src property of an <IMG> tag

In the following code, the SRC attribute of the <IMG> tag named myImage is initially set to an empty string "". In the <SCRIPT> section, a new Image object named newImage is created. The newImage object is used to save and access the memory cache containing the image file. A file named graphic.jpg is assigned to the src property of the newImage object. The src property of the newImage object is then assigned to the src property of the <IMG> tag.

```
<SCRIPT LANGUAGE="JavaScript1.2">
<!-- HIDE FROM INCOMPATIBLE BROWSERS
newImage = new Image()
newImage.src = "graphic.jpg"
document.myImage.src = newImage.src
// STOP HIDING FROM INCOMPATIBLE BROWSERS -->
</SCRIPT>
<BODY>
<IMG NAME="myImage" SRC="first_graphic.jpg">
</BODY>
```

Be sure to understand that in the preceding code, the graphic.jpg file is *not* assigned directly to the src property of the <IMG> tag. Instead, the *newImage object* is assigned to the src property of the <IMG> tag. If you assigned the graphic.jpg file directly to the src property of the <IMG> tag using the statement `document.myImage.src = "graphic.jpg";`, then the file would reload from its source each time it was needed. The newImage object opens the file once and saves it to a memory cache.

Figure 7-25 shows a version of the runner animation code modified to use image caching. The lines that add each image file to the runner[] array have been replaced by a `for` loop. As you learned in Tutorial 4, the `for` statement is used to repeat a statement or series of statements as long as a given conditional expression evaluates to true. The `for` loop in Figure 7-25 assigns a new object to each element of the runner[] array until the counter *i* is greater than six, which represents the highest element in the array. Each object in the runner[] array is then assigned an image file using the src property. In the marathon() function, the runner[curRunner] operator in the statement `document.animation.src = runner[curRunner];` now includes the src property so that the statement reads `document.animation.src = runner[curRunner].src;`.

```
<HTML>
<HEAD>
<TITLE>Runners</TITLE>
<SCRIPT LANGUAGE="JavaScript1.2">
<!-- HIDE FROM INCOMPATIBLE BROWSERS
var runner = new Array(6);
var curRunner = 0;
var startRunning;
for(var i = 0; i < 6; ++i) {
    runner[i] = new Image();
    runner[i].src = "runner" + i + ".jpg";
}
function marathon() {
    if (curRunner == 5)
        curRunner = 0;
    else
        ++curRunner;
    document.animation.src = runner[curRunner].src;
}
// STOP HIDING FROM INCOMPATIBLE BROWSERS -->
</SCRIPT>
</HEAD>
<BODY>
<IMG SRC="runner1.jpg" NAME="animation"><P>
<FORM>
```

Figure 7-25: Runner animation code after adding caching

```
<INPUT TYPE="button" NAME="run" VALUE=" Run "
onClick="startRunning=setInterval('marathon()',100);">

<INPUT TYPE="button" NAME="stop" VALUE=" Stop "
        onClick="clearInterval(startRunning);">

</FORM>

</BODY>

</HTML>
```

Figure 7-25: Runner animation code after adding caching (continued)

Next, you will modify the rocking horse program so that it includes image caching.

To add image caching to the RockingHorse.html document:

1 Return to the RockingHorse.html file in your text editor or HTML editor, then save it as a new file named **RockingHorseCache.html** in the **Tutorial.07** folder on your Student Disk.

2 Locate the following six statements that assign each rocking horse frame to the horses[] array:

```
horses[0] = "rockinghorse0.jpg";
horses[1] = "rockinghorse1.jpg";
horses[2] = "rockinghorse2.jpg";
horses[3] = "rockinghorse3.jpg";
horses[4] = "rockinghorse4.jpg";
horses[5] = "rockinghorse5.jpg";
```

3 Replace the preceding statements with the following `for` statement. The `for` statement creates a new Image object within each element of the horses[] array. Each object in the horses[] array is then assigned an image file using the src property.

```
for(var i = 0; i < 6; ++i) {
    horses[i] = new Image();
    horses[i].src = "rockinghorse" + i + ".jpg";
}
```

4 Add the src property to the `document.animation.src = horses[curHorse];` statement in the rockHorse() function so that it reads `document.animation.src = horses[curHorse].src;`

5 Save the document and open it in your Web browser. If you previously experienced erratic animation, the new animation should appear much smoother.

6 Close the Web browser window.

Even when you use image caching, the images must all be loaded into an Image object before the animation will function correctly. Often, you will want animation to start as soon as a page finishes loading. The rocking horse program is designed to start as soon as a page finishes loading. However, although a page has finished loading, all the images may not have finished downloading and may not be stored in image caches. If you run the rocking horse program across an Internet connection, the onLoad event handler of the <BODY> tag may execute the animation sequence before all the frames are transferred and assigned to Image objects (depending on Internet connection speed). The animation will still function, but will be erratic until all the images have been successfully stored in Image objects. To be certain that all images are downloaded into a cache before commencing an animation sequence, you use the onLoad event handler of the Image object.

Figure 7-26 shows another modified version of the runner program. This time, the program does not include a Run or Stop button. Instead, a `for` loop in the <SCRIPT> section executes each Image object's onLoad event. First, each element in the runner[] array is assigned a new Image object. Next, each Image object in the runner[] array is assigned a corresponding frame of runner animation images. The statement `runner[i].onload = runMarathon();` assigns the runMarathon() function to each Image object's onLoad event. After the image assigned to each Image object in the runner[] array finishes loading, its onLoad event executes the runMarathon() function, which increments the imagesLoaded variable by one each time an image loads into the runner[] array. Once the imagesLoaded variable equals six (which indicates that all the images have been downloaded), the marathon() function executes using the same setInterval() statement that was originally located in the onClick event for the Run button.

```
<HTML>

<HEAD>

<TITLE>Runner</TITLE>

<SCRIPT LANGUAGE="JavaScript1.2">

<!-- HIDE FROM INCOMPATIBLE BROWSERS

var runner = new Array(6);

var curRunner = 0;

var startRunning;

var imagesLoaded = 0;

for(var i = 0; i < 6; ++i) {

     runner[i] = new Image();

     runner[i].src = "runner" + i + ".jpg";

     runner[i].onload = runMarathon;
```

Figure 7-26: Runner animation code after adding an onLoad event

```
}
function runMarathon() {
    ++imagesLoaded;
    if (imagesLoaded == 6)
        startRunning=setInterval("marathon()",100);
}
function marathon() {
    if (curRunner == 5)
        curRunner = 0;
    else
        ++curRunner;
    document.animation.src = runner[curRunner].src;
}
// STOP HIDING FROM INCOMPATIBLE BROWSERS -->
</SCRIPT>
</HEAD>
<BODY>
<IMG SRC="runner1.jpg" NAME="animation"><P>
</BODY>
</HTML>
```

Figure 7-26: Runner animation code after adding an onLoad event (continued)

Next you will add to the rocking horse program an image onLoad event that executes the animation after all the images load. You will also modify the program so that the animation executes as soon as all the images load.

To add an image onLoad event to the rocking horse program and to modify it so that the animation executes as soon as all the images load:

1 Return to the RockingHorseCache.html file in your text editor or HTML editor, then save it as a new file named **RockingHorseImageLoad.html** in the **Tutorial.07** folder on your Student Disk.

2 Add **var imagesLoaded = 0;** after the **var begin;** statement. The imagesLoaded variable will keep count of the number of images loaded.

3 Add the statement `horses[i].onload = loadImages;` just before the closing brace in the `for` loop that assigns each rocking horse image file to the horses[] array. As each image is loaded, its onLoad event calls the loadImages() function.

4 After the `for` loop, create the following loadImages() function, which is called from the `horses[i].onload = loadImages;` statement you added in Step 3. The function increments the imagesLoaded variable each time it is called. After the imagesLoaded variable equals six, a setInterval() method executes the rockHorse() function.

```
function loadImages() {
    ++imagesLoaded;
    if (imagesLoaded == 6)
        begin=setInterval("rockHorse()",100);
}
```

5 Delete the startRocking() function from the <SCRIPT> section, and delete the form from the body of the document.

6 Save the document and open it in your Web browser. The animation should begin as soon as all the images load.

7 Close the Web browser window.

In the next section, you will learn how to use cascading style sheets to create more complex types of animation.

SUMMARY

- Dynamic HTML (DHTML) combines several Internet technologies, including JavaScript, HTML, and cascading style sheets, to allow HTML tags to change dynamically, Web pages to be rendered dynamically, and users to interact with Web pages.

- The Document Object Model (DOM) represents the HTML document displayed in a window and provides programmatic access to a document's elements.

- Navigator and Internet Explorer support a primitive version of the DOM known as Level 0. There is currently no accepted standard for the DOM.

- The open() method opens a window or frame other than the current window or frame, to update its contents with the write() and writeln() methods.

- The close() method notifies the Web browser that you are finished writing to the window or frame and that the document should be displayed.

- The images[] array contains all of an HTML document's images in the same manner that the forms[] array contains all of an HTML document's forms. If an HTML document does not contain any images, then the images[] array is empty.
- An Image object represents images created using the <IMG> tag.
- One of the most important elements of the Image object is the src property, which allows JavaScript to change an image dynamically.
- By combining the src attribute of the Image object with the setTimeout() or setInterval() methods, you can create simple animation in an HTML document.
- You create an animated sequence with JavaScript by using the setInterval() or setTimeout() methods to cycle through the frames in an animation series.
- Image caching, which temporarily stores image files in memory, is a technique for eliminating multiple downloads of the same file. This technique allows JavaScript to store and retrieve an image from memory rather than download the image each time it is needed.
- You use the onLoad event handler of the Image object to be certain that all images are downloaded into a cache before commencing an animation sequence.

QUESTIONS

1. Which of the following programming languages cannot be used to interact with users?
   a. Java
   b. CGI
   c. Perl
   d. HTML

2. DHTML is created using _____
   a. JavaScript.
   b. HTML.
   c. cascading style sheets.
   d. all of the above

3. Which version of the DOM is supported by both Navigator 4 and Internet Explorer 4?
   a. Level 0
   b. Level 1
   c. Level 2
   d. none of the above

4. _____ represents the HTML document displayed in a window and provides programmatic access to a document's elements.
   a. The Window object
   b. JavaScript
   c. The DOM
   d. The Frame object

5. In Navigator, the majority of the Document object properties can be set _____

a. only before the document is rendered.
b. only after the document is rendered.
c. both before and after the document is rendered.
d. Document object properties cannot be set in Navigator.

6. In Internet Explorer, the majority of the Document object properties can be set _____

a. only before the document is rendered.
b. only after the document is rendered.
c. both before and after the document is rendered.
d. Document object properties cannot be set in Internet Explorer.

7. The _____ method opens a window or frame other than the current window or frame, in order to update its contents with the write() and writeln() methods.
a. draw()
b. get()
c. update()
d. open()

8. The _____ method notifies the Web browser that you are finished writing to the window or frame and that the document should be displayed.
a. complete()
b. close()
c. update()
d. refresh()

9. The _____ array contains all of an HTML document's images.
a. images[]
b. pictures[]
c. graphics[]
d. figures[]

10. Each image in an HTML page is represented in JavaScript by the _____ object.
a. Picture
b. Graphic
c. Image
d. Figure

11. Simple animation can be created with JavaScript using the setInterval() or setTimeout() methods and the _____ property of an image.
a. GIF
b. JPG
c. BMP
d. SRC

12. The speed of animation in JavaScript depends on _____

    a. the animation speed option, which is set in the Options dialog box in Internet Explorer or the Preferences dialog box in Navigator.

    b. the speed of a computer's microprocessor.

    c. how many frames are used in the animation sequence.

    d. how many milliseconds are passed as an argument to the setInterval() or setTimeout() methods.

13. Which of the following is not a necessary step in image caching?

    a. Create a new object using the Image() constructor.

    b. Assign a graphic file to the src property of the new Image object.

    c. Assign the src property of the new Image object to the src property of an <IMG> tag.

    d. Download a copy of an image file to a local hard drive.

14. To be certain that all images are downloaded into a cache before commencing an animation sequence, you use the _____ of the Image object.

    a. onLoad event handler

    b. animation property

    c. loadImages() method

    d. images[] array

EXERCISES

1. Create a document with two vertical frames. Create a series of buttons in the left frame. Each button should represent the name of a state in your area. Use a dictionary or encyclopedia to look up statistical information on each state, such as the name of the capital, the name of the governor, population, and so on. Use the open(), close(), and writeln() methods to write the information to the right frame when a user clicks a state button. Save the document as StateStatistics.html in the Tutorial.07 folder on your Student Disk.

2. Use Paint or another graphics program to create a series of frames in which a stick figure performs jumping jacks. In each frame, position the stick figure in one step or stage of performing a jumping jack. Use JavaScript to animate the frames. Save the document as JumpingJacks.html in the Tutorial.07 folder on your Student Disk.

3. The Tutorial.07 folder on your Student Disk contains six images of a windmill: windmill1.gif through windmill6.gif. Use JavaScript to animate the images. Save the document as Windmill.html in the Tutorial.07 folder on your Student Disk.

4. Use Paint or another graphics program to create three pictures of a traffic light. One image should have the green light illuminated, one image should have the yellow light illuminated, and one image should have the red light illuminated. Use JavaScript to cycle through the images. Save the document as TrafficLight.html in the Tutorial.07 folder on your Student Disk.

5. The Tutorial.07 folder on your Student Disk contains two images of a pennant: pennant1.gif and pennant2.gif. Use JavaScript to animate the images so that they appear to be blowing in the wind. Save the document as Pennant.html in the Tutorial.07 folder on your Student Disk.

6. Using an Internet search engine, such as Yahoo!, or a graphics program to which you have access, locate an animal image for each letter of the alphabet, such as aardvark for A, beaver for B, and so on. (To search for images, use key words such as clip art, images, pictures, .jpg, or .gif. Make sure the images you find are in the public domain.) Use Paint or another graphics program to add a corresponding letter of the alphabet to each image. Use JavaScript to write a program that cycles through the letters of the alphabet. Save the document as AnimalAlphabet.html in the Tutorial.07 folder on your Student Disk.

In this section you will learn:

■ About cascading style sheets

■ How to use JavaScript with styles in Navigator and Internet Explorer

■ About cascading style sheet positioning

■ How to use positioning in Navigator and Internet Explorer

■ About cross-browser compatibility

Animation and Cascading Style Sheets

Cascading Style Sheets

Cascading style sheets are one of the three technologies used for creating DHTML. **Cascading style sheets** (**CSS**, also called style sheets) are a standard set by the World Wide Web Consortium for managing the formatting information of HTML documents. Formatting information includes fonts, backgrounds, colors, layout, and other aspects of the appearance of an HTML document, as opposed to its content. A single piece of formatting information is called a style. Prior to styles, Web page designers applied formatting to individual HTML tags to control the appearance of a Web page. With CSS, Web page designers can centrally manage styles for a single HTML page and create a consistent look across different Web pages. In essence, CSS separates a document's content from its appearance.

DHTML uses JavaScript to manipulate CSS to dynamically change the appearance of tags and the position of elements in an HTML document. For example, your Web page may have a series of buttons that users can click to change the appearance of the page according to their personal tastes. Later in this section, you will see how CSS is used to create traveling animation by allowing HTML elements to be dynamically repositioned on a page.

CSS is of most interest to Web page designers, since it allows much greater control and management of the visual aspects of a Web page than is possible with HTML. Our purpose for looking at CSS is to see how to make Web pages more dynamic using JavaScript and DHTML. Therefore, this section only includes a cursory overview of CSS styles and syntax. If you would like more information on CSS, visit the World Wide Web Consortium's Web site at http://www.w3.org.

CSS styles are created using name/value pairs separated by a colon. The name portion of the name/value pair refers to a specific CSS style attribute known as a **property**. Each CSS property can be formatted with different values, depending on the property. Figure 7-27 contains examples and descriptions of common CSS properties.

CSS Property	Description	Code Example
border-color	Specifies an element's border color	`border-color: blue;`
font-family	Specifies the font name	`font-family: arial;`
font-style	Specifies the font style: normal, italic, or oblique	`font-style: italic;`
font-weight	Specifies font weight: normal, bold, bolder, lighter, or a number between 100 and 900; 400 is the equivalent of normal, and 700 is the equivalent of bold	`font-weight: bold;`
margin-left	Adjusts the left margin	`margin-left: 1in;`
margin-right	Adjusts the right margin	`margin-right: 1in;`
text-align	Determines the alignment of text: center, justify, left, or right	`text-align: center;`

Figure 7-27: Common CSS properties

There are two types of CSS styles: inline styles and document-level style sheets. **Inline styles** determine the appearance of individual tags in an HTML document. You define inline styles using the STYLE attribute along with a string containing the name/value pairs for each style you want to include. Multiple properties are separated by semicolons. The following code shows an <H1> tag with an inline style that changes the font-family to *serif*, the font-weight to *bold*, and the font-style to *italic*:

```
<H1 STYLE="font-family: serif; font-weight: bold;
    font-style: italic>
```

Document-level style sheets determine global formatting for HTML tags. You create document-level style sheets within a set of <STYLE>...</STYLE> tag pairs placed in the <HEAD> section of a document. Any style instructions for a specific tag are applied to all associated tags contained in the body of the document. The tag to which specific style rules in a style sheet apply is called a **selector**. You can include multiple selectors within a style sheet if the rules for each selector are enclosed in a pair of braces {}. As with inline styles, multiple properties for a selector are separated by semicolons. The following code shows an example of a style sheet for the <H1>, <H2>, and <BODY> tags. Each tag is followed by a pair of braces containing style instructions. All instances of the tags in the body of the document are formatted using these style instructions.

```
<STYLE>
H1 {color: red; font-family: "ms sans serif";
    font-size: 24pt; font-weight: bold;}
H2  {color: black; font-family: "ms sans serif";
```

```
        font-size: 18pt; margin-top: 0.25in; margin-left: 1in;}
BODY {color: blue; font-family: "arial";
        font-size: 12pt; font-weight: medium;}
</STYLE>
```

Another method of applying styles to tags in an HTML document is by using the CLASS attribute. The **CLASS attribute** can be applied to any HTML tag and identifies various elements as part of the same group. The syntax for the CLASS attribute is *<TAG CLASS="class name">*. You replace the TAG portion of the syntax with an HTML tag you want to include as part of the class. To include an <H1> tag and a <P> tag as part of a class named myClass, you use the syntax <H1 CLASS="myClass"> and <P CLASS="myClass">. You can create two types of CSS classes in an HTML document: a regular class and a generic class. A **regular class** is used to define different style instructions for the same tag. For example, you may need two or more different versions of the <H1> tag in a document. You create a regular class within the <STYLE>...</STYLE> tag pair by appending a class name to a style with a period. You then include the appropriate class name within the necessary tags in the document's body section. The following code contains two regular classes, level1 and level2, that define the formatting instructions for different instances of the <P> tag.

```
<STYLE>
P.level1 {color: black; font-family: "serif";
        font-size: 10pt;font-weight: medium; text-indent: 1in}
P.level2 {color: green; font-family: "serif";
        font-size: 8pt;font-style: italic; text-indent: 2in}
</STYLE>
<BODY>
<P CLASS="level1">This is the level1 class</P>
<P CLASS="level2">This is the level2 class</P>
</BODY>
```

A **generic class** is similar to a regular class, except that it is not associated with any particular tag. You create a generic class within the <STYLE>...</STYLE> tag pair using a class name preceded by a period, but without appending it to a tag. The following code shows an example of a generic class named *highlight* that formats text in yellow, Arial, and with a blue background. Notice that in the body section, the generic class is applied to two different styles: bold <B> and strong <STRONG>.

```
<STYLE>
.highlight {color: yellow; font-family: arial;
        background: blue}
</STYLE>
<BODY>
<P>This <B CLASS="highlight">line</B> contains two
<STRONGCLASS="highlight">examples</STRONG>
of the generic class.</P>
</BODY>
```

The ID attribute is also used to apply styles. The value of an **ID attribute** uniquely identifies individual tags in an HTML document. The syntax for the ID attribute is `<TAG ID="unique name">`. An ID is similar to a class, except that it is applied only to a single occurrence of a specific ID attribute in the body of an HTML document. You create ID attributes within <STYLE>...</STYLE> tag pairs, and the name of an ID is preceded by the number sign #, as in the following example:

```
<STYLE>
#biggreenline {color: green; font-family: arial;
     font-size: 24pt}
</STYLE>
<BODY>
<P ID="biggreenline">The formatting for this
     ID class applies only to this line.</P>
</BODY>
```

To give you an idea of how much easier it is to manage an HTML document's appearance using styles, Figure 7-28 shows an example of an HTML document created without a style sheet. Notice that the formatting for the <H1> and <H2> tags repeats with each recurrence of the tag.

```
<HTML>

<HEAD>

<TITLE>Example of Individually Formatted Tags</TITLE>

</HEAD>

<BODY>

<H1><FONT SIZE=6 COLOR="red" FACE="arial">

First instance of Heading 1</FONT></H1>

<H2><FONT SIZE=5 COLOR="black" FACE="arial"><I>

First instance of Heading 2</FONT></I></H2>

<H1><FONT SIZE=6 COLOR="red" FACE="arial">
```

Figure 7-28: Individually formatted tags

```
Second instance of Heading 1</FONT></H1>

<H2><FONT SIZE=5 COLOR="black" FACE="arial"><I>

Second instance of Heading 2</FONT></I></H2>

</BODY>

</HTML>
```

Figure 7-28: Individually formatted tags (continued)

Now examine the same document with CSS styles in Figure 7-29. Notice how the style sheet separates the document's content from its appearance. If you want to change the appearance of an element, such as the color of the <H1> tag, you need to change it only once in the style sheet, instead of changing it whenever the tag occurs in the document. The output for both versions of the document is shown in a Web browser in Figure 7-30.

```
<HTML>

<HEAD>

<TITLE>Example of Style Sheet Heading Tags</TITLE>

</HEAD>

<STYLE>

H1 {color: red; font-family: "ms sans serif";
     font-size: 24pt;}

H2  {color: black; font-family: "ms sans serif";
      font-size: 18pt; font-style: italic}

</STYLE>

<BODY>

<H1>First instance of Heading 1</H1>

<H2>First instance of Heading 2</H2>

<H1>Second instance of Heading 1</H1>

<H2>Second instance of Heading 2</H2>

</BODY>

</HTML>
```

Figure 7-29: Style sheet heading tags

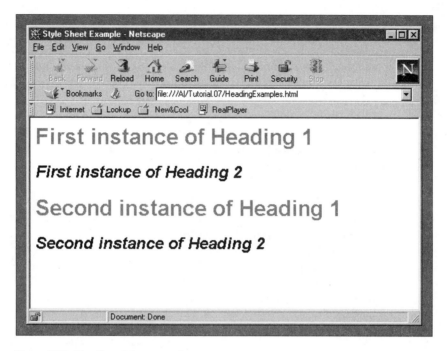

Figure 7-30: Heading styles example

Using JavaScript with CSS Styles

CSS styles determine the formatting of HTML document elements. To modify CSS styles after a Web browser renders a document, you use JavaScript. As mentioned in Section A, there are no compatible DHTML standards that work with both Internet Explorer and Navigator. This incompatibility is particularly evident when using JavaScript to manipulate CSS styles. Internet Explorer and Navigator support incompatible Document object properties and methods. Because JavaScript uses Document object properties and methods to access CSS styles, if you want to use JavaScript code to manipulate CSS, you have three options:

- Write code that functions only in Navigator.
- Write code that functions only in Internet Explorer.
- Write both sets of code and execute the correct set depending on which Web browser is in use.

This section briefly explains, for each browser, how to use JavaScript to refer to CSS styles and presents some techniques for writing DHTML code that functions in both browsers. Since DHTML is evolving quickly, we will not spend much time on either Microsoft- or Netscape-specific methods for using JavaScript with CSS. Remember that when both browsers completely support Level 1 of the DHTML standard, the ways in which Microsoft and Netscape currently allow JavaScript to interact with CSS will likely change drastically or become obsolete.

Using JavaScript and CSS Styles in Navigator

The Navigator Document Object Model accesses the styles for selectors using the tags, classes, and ID properties of the Document object. The **tags** property provides access to the styles of tags in an HTML document. The **classes** property provides access to the styles of classes in an HTML document. The **ids** property provides access to the styles of **ID** attributes in an HTML document.

The tags, classes, and ID properties are available only in Navigator.

To refer to a CSS style in Navigator, you append the tags, classes, or ids property to the Document object with a period, followed by a period and the name of a CSS selector, followed by another period and a CSS property. The general syntax for referring to CSS styles in Navigator is `document.tags, classes, or ids property.selector.property`. When you refer to a CSS property containing a hyphen in JavaScript code, you remove the hyphen and convert the first word to lowercase and the first letter of subsequent words to uppercase. CSS properties without hyphens are referred to with all lowercase letters. For example, border is referred to as `border`, border-color is referred to as `borderColor`, and font-size is referrred to as `fontSize`.

The following example uses JavaScript syntax to define styles for tags, classes, and ID attributes. This code performs the same function of defining styles as standard CSS syntax located between <STYLE>...</STYLE> tag pairs.

```
<SCRIPT LANGUAGE="JavaScript1.2">
<!-- HIDE FROM INCOMPATIBLE BROWSERS
document.tags.H1.color = "red";
document.tags.H1.fontSize = "24pt";
document.classes.level1.color = "black";
document.classes.level1.fontFamily = "serif";
document.ids.biggreenline.color = "green";
document.ids.biggreenline.fontFamily = "arial";
document.ids.biggreenline.fontSize = "24pt";
// STOP HIDING FROM INCOMPATIBLE BROWSERS -->
</SCRIPT>
```

Although Navigator allows you to define styles using JavaScript, you cannot change style values dynamically. You can use JavaScript code to change the value of a style after it has been rendered by a Web browser, but the change does not appear until the user resizes the screen.

Using JavaScript and Styles in Internet Explorer

The Internet Explorer document object model accesses the styles for selectors using the all property of the Document object. The **all property** is an array of all the elements in an HTML document. The all property is appended with a period to the Document object, followed by a period and the name of a specific CSS selector. You then append a period and the style property, followed by a period and a specific CSS property. The **style** property represents the CSS styles for a particular tag, class, or ID. The general syntax for referring to a CSS style in Internet Explorer is document.all.*selector*.style. *property*.

 tip

The all and style properties are available only in Internet Explorer.

As in Navigator, when you refer to a CSS property in JavaScript code in Internet Explorer, you remove the hyphen from the property name and convert the property to mixed case. The following code shows the JavaScript syntax for referring to CSS styles in Internet Explorer:

```
<SCRIPT LANGUAGE="JavaScript1.2">
<!-- HIDE FROM INCOMPATIBLE BROWSERS
document.all.H1.style.color = "red";
document.all.H1.style.fontSize = "24pt";
document.all.level1.style.color = "black";
document.all.level1.style.fontFamily = "serif";
document.all.biggreenline.style.color = "green";
document.all.biggreenline.style.fontFamily = "arial";
document.all.biggreenline.style.fontSize = "24pt";
// STOP HIDING FROM INCOMPATIBLE BROWSERS -->
</SCRIPT>
```

In Internet Explorer, you must use the styleSheets[] array of the Document object to define new CSS styles with JavaScript. The styleSheets[] array is somewhat difficult to work with, so it is recommended you define styles using CSS syntax within a <STYLE>...</STYLE> tag pair. You can, however, use JavaScript to dynamically change styles in Internet Explorer. When you change a style in Internet Explorer using JavaScript, the changes are displayed immediately in the browser, whereas in Navigator you must resize the screen.

CSS Positioning

In Section A, you used the <IMG> tag to create simple animations with JavaScript. The <IMG> tag is limited, however, in that the only type of animation you can perform with it is stationary. That is, an animation created with the <IMG> tag does not travel across the screen. Actually, there is no way to reposition an image on a Web page, unless you load a new HTML document from the server. A proposed extension to CSS technology is something called CSS positioning. **CSS positioning** is used to position or lay out elements on a Web page. Although still a proposed extension to CSS, CSS positioning is already supported in Navigator and Internet Explorer. Because of the Document object incompatibilities between the two browsers, however, you cannot write JavaScript code that works in both browsers. You must design your program for one browser or the other, or write two sets of code and execute the correct set depending on which Web browser is in use.

There are two types of CSS positioning: relative and absolute. **Relative positioning** places an element according to other elements on a Web page. **Absolute positioning** places elements in a specific location on a Web page. Relative positioning is mainly used for the design and layout of Web pages and is beyond the scope of this text. Absolute positioning is used with JavaScript to create full animation, among other purposes.

You usually add positioning to tags with inline styles. You can also use CSS positioning in a document-level style sheet. However, if you apply positioning to a tag, such as <H1>, in a document-level style sheet, then all instances of the <H1> tag in the document will be positioned in exactly the same place. In contrast, using positioning for IDs in document-level style sheets works fine. It is usually easier, however, to add positioning directly to an element as an inline style.

Several common CSS positioning properties are listed in Figure 7-31.

Property	Description	Values
position	Determines how an element is to be positioned	*absolute* or *relative*
left	The horizontal distance from the upper-left corner of the window	A value in pixels
top	The vertical distance from the upper-left corner of the window	A value in pixels
width	The width of the boundary box	A value in pixels
height	The height of the boundary box	A value in pixels
visibility	Determines if an element is visible	*visible* or *hidden*

Figure 7-31: Common CSS positioning properties

Navigator does not recognize CSS positioning for elements that are not container elements—that is, for elements without a closing tag. For instance, you cannot use CSS positioning on an <IMG> tag, since it does not include a closing tag. To maintain compatibility with Internet Explorer, elements that are to be positioned are usually placed within <SPAN>...</SPAN> or <DIV>...</DIV> tag pairs. The <SPAN> tag is used for applying formatting to sections of an HTML document, while the <DIV> tag breaks a document into distinct sections. Specific CSS positioning properties are placed inside the closing bracket of an opening <SPAN> or <DIV> tag.

The following code absolutely positions an image contained within a <SPAN> tag pair. The resulting image is displayed in a Web browser in Figure 7-32.

```
<SPAN STYLE="position:absolute; left:150; top:165">
<IMG SRC="sun.gif">
</SPAN>
```

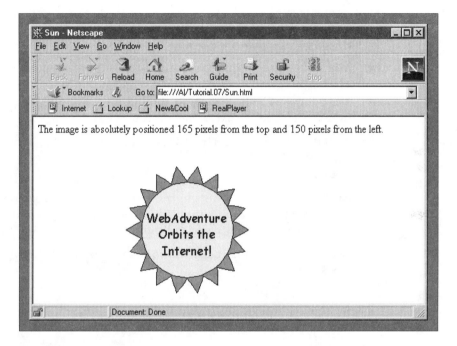

Figure 7-32: CSS positioning

Next, you will position two images in an HTML document. The images, named up.gif and down.gif, are located in the Tutorial.07 folder on your Student Disk. The up.gif file contains an image of a bird with its wings lifted, and the down.gif file contains an image of the same bird with its wings down. The Web page you create will contain the up.gif image twice and the down.gif image once. You will position the three images so the bird appears to be taking off.

To position two images in an HTML document:

1 Start your text editor or HTML editor and create a new document.

2 Type the <HTML> and <HEAD> sections of the document:

```
<HTML>
<HEAD>
<TITLE>Two Birds</TITLE>
</HEAD>
```

3   Type **<BODY>** to start the body section.

4   Add the following lines to create the first absolutely positioned image. The image, up.gif, is contained within a <SPAN>...</SPAN> tag pair. You use the STYLE attribute to absolutely position the image at 40 pixels from the left and 200 pixels from the top.

```
<SPAN STYLE="position:absolute; left:40; top:200">
<IMG SRC="up.gif">
</SPAN>
```

5   Add the following lines to create the second absolutely positioned image. The image, down.gif, is also contained within a <SPAN>...</SPAN> tag pair. You use the STYLE attribute to absolutely position the image at 250 pixels from the left and 80 pixels from the top.

```
<SPAN STYLE="position:absolute; left:250; top:80">
<IMG SRC="down.gif">
</SPAN>
```

6   Now add the following lines to create the third absolutely positioned image. The up.gif image is used again and is absolutely positioned at 480 pixels from the left and 10 pixels from the top.

```
<SPAN STYLE="position:absolute; left:480; top:10">
<IMG SRC="up.gif">
</SPAN>
```

7   Add the following code to close the <BODY> and <HTML> tags:

```
</BODY>
</HTML>
```

8   Save the file as **ThreeBirds.html** in the **Tutorial.07** folder on your Student Disk. Open the **ThreeBirds.html** file in your Web browser. Figure 7-33 shows the output.

Figure 7-33: Output of ThreeBirds.html

9 Close the Web browser window.

Next, you will learn how to create traveling images by dynamically positioning images with JavaScript. Because of the incompatibilities between Navigator and Internet Explorer, you will learn how to achieve dynamic positioning for each browser. First, you will learn about dynamic positioning in Internet Explorer.

Positioning in Internet Explorer

As you learned earlier, Internet Explorer allows you to use JavaScript to dynamically change CSS styles. Changes to the document's appearance are displayed immediately. Since CSS positioning is an extension to CSS, you can dynamically change an element's position on screen using the left and top CSS properties. For example, the statement `document.all.sampleimage.style.left = "3.00in";` moves an element with an ID of *sampleimage* three inches to the right by changing its left property to "3.00in". Combining the left and top CSS properties with a setTimeout() or setInterval() method allows you to create traveling animation.

As an example of CSS traveling animation in Internet Explorer, we are going to look at a simple animation of the birds you used in the last exercise. The program animates the two pictures of the birds using the setInterval() method with absolute positioning. Since the program only includes two frames in three different positions, it is not very exciting. However, it gives you a good idea of how to create traveling animation.

The code for the bird animation program is shown in Figure 7-34. Two Image objects, *up* and *down*, are created to hold each image file. Users click a Fly button to start the traveling animation. The onClick event of the Fly button's event handler calls the setInterval method, which executes the fly() function. The fly() function performs the animation using three `if` statements. Each `if` statement checks the value of a variable named position. If the position property is equal to 1 or 3, then the src property of the <IMG> tag named birdImage is changed to up.gif using the statement `document.birdimage.src = up.src;`. If the position property is equal to 2, then the src property of the <IMG> tag named birdImage is changed to down.gif using the statement `document.birdimage.src = down.src;`. Each `if` statement also changes the left and top properties of the absolutely positioned <SPAN> tag named bird, which contains the image. The position variable is then set to the next number: 2 or 3. After the third position appears, the position property resets to 1, and the animation starts over.

```
<HTML>

<HEAD>

<TITLE>Flying Bird</TITLE>

<SCRIPT LANGUAGE="JavaScript1.2">

<!-- HIDE FROM INCOMPATIBLE BROWSERS

var startFlying;

var updown = 0;

var horizontalPosition = 10;

var up = new Image();

up.src = "up.gif";

var down = new Image();

down.src = "down.gif";

position = 1;
```

Figure 7-34: Bird animation document

```
function fly() {

    if (position == 1) {

        document.birdimage.src = up.src;

        document.all.bird.style.left = 40;

        document.all.bird.style.top = 200;

        position = 2;

    }

    else if (position == 2) {

        document.birdimage.src = down.src;

        document.all.bird.style.left = 250;

        document.all.bird.style.top = 80;

        position = 3;

    }

    else if (position == 3) {

        document.birdimage.src = up.src;

        document.all.bird.style.left = 480;

        document.all.bird.style.top = 10;

        position = 1;

    }

}

// STOP HIDING FROM INCOMPATIBLE BROWSERS -->

</SCRIPT>

</HEAD>

<BODY>

<SPAN ID="bird" STYLE="position:absolute; left:40; top:200">

<IMG NAME="birdimage" SRC="up.gif" HEIGHT=200 WIDTH=200>

</SPAN>

<FORM>
```

Figure 7-34: Bird animation document (continued)

```
<INPUT TYPE="button" NAME="fly" VALUE=" Fly "
    onClick="startFlying=setInterval('fly()',500);">
<INPUT TYPE="button" NAME="stop" VALUE=" Stop "
    onClick="clearInterval(startFlying);">
</FORM>
</BODY>
</HTML>
```

Figure 7-34: Bird animation document (continued)

If you would like to see how the flying bird animation functions in Internet Explorer, a copy of the program named FlyingBirdIE.html is in the Tutorial.07 folder on your Student Disk. Remember that you can open this file only in Internet Explorer. If you open it in Navigator, you will receive an error message.

Next, to show how simple traveling animation is accomplished, you are going create an animation of the Earth revolving around the sun, for Internet Explorer. The coordinates of the orbit that the Earth will take are plotted in Figure 7-35. Note that the positions around the sun are not exact. In order to calculate exact positions, we would need a complicated formula to calculate the radius of the orbit. Also, note that smoother animation can be created by using more positions in the Earth's orbit.

Create the program even if you do not have a copy of Internet Explorer, since you will use the program later in this section when you learn about cross-browser compatibility.

To create the orbit animation for Internet Explorer:

1 Start your text editor or HTML editor and create a new document.

2 Type the <HTML> and <HEAD> sections of the document:

```
<HTML>
<HEAD>
<TITLE>Orbit</TITLE>
</HEAD>
```

3 Add the opening statements for a JavaScript section:

```
<SCRIPT LANGUAGE="JavaScript1.2">
<!-- HIDE FROM INCOMPATIBLE BROWSERS
```

4 To create a variable to track which of the 16 orbit positions is current, add the statement **position = 0;**.

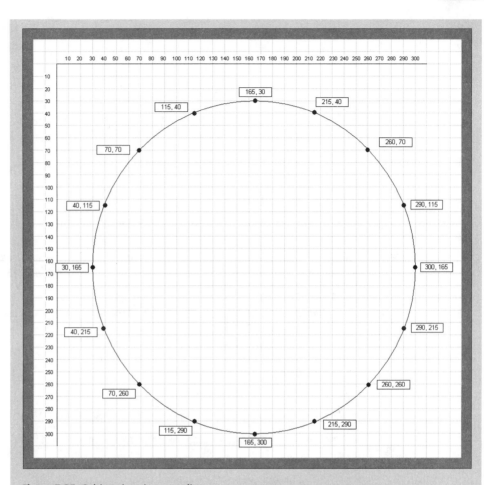

Figure 7-35: Orbit animation coordinates

5 Create the following array to hold the 16 positions corresponding to the left position of the image. The positions correspond to the first position in each set of positions plotted in Figure 7-35.

```
leftEarth = new Array(16);
leftEarth[0] = 165; leftEarth[1] = 215; leftEarth[2] = 260;
leftEarth[3] = 290; leftEarth[4] = 300; leftEarth[5] = 290;
leftEarth[6] = 260; leftEarth[7] = 215; leftEarth[8] = 165;
leftEarth[9] = 115; leftEarth[10] = 70; leftEarth[11] = 40;
leftEarth[12] = 30; leftEarth[13] = 40; leftEarth[14] = 70;
leftEarth[15] = 115;
```

6   Create the following array to hold the 16 positions corresponding to the top position of the image. The positions correspond to the second position in each set of positions plotted in Figure 7-35.

```
topEarth = new Array(16);
topEarth[0] = 30; topEarth[1] = 40; topEarth[2] = 70;
topEarth[3] = 115; topEarth[4] = 165; topEarth[5] = 215;
topEarth[6] = 260; topEarth[7] = 290; topEarth[8] = 300;
topEarth[9] = 290;
topEarth[10] = 260; topEarth[11] = 215; topEarth[12] = 165;
topEarth[13] = 115; topEarth[14] = 70;
topEarth[15] = 40;
```

7   Add the following orbit() function, which cycles the image of the Earth through the sixteen positions of the leftEarth and topEarth arrays. Each position is tracked by the position variable. The orbit() function will be called using a setInterval() method from the onLoad event handler in the <BODY> tag.

```
function orbit() {
    document.all.earth.style.left = leftEarth[position];
    document.all.earth.style.top = topEarth[position];
    ++position;
    if (position == 16)
        position = 0;
}
```

8   Add the following code to close the <SCRIPT> and <HEAD> sections:

```
// STOP HIDING FROM INCOMPATIBLE BROWSERS -->
</SCRIPT>
</HEAD>
```

9   Add the following opening <BODY> tag, which uses the setInterval() method to execute the orbit() function with the onLoad event handler.

```
<BODY onLoad="setInterval('orbit()',200)">
```

10   Type the following <SPAN> section, which contains and positions the image of the sun:

```
<SPAN STYLE="position:absolute; left:95; top:95">
<IMG SRC="sun.gif">
</SPAN>
```

11   Add another <SPAN> section to contain and initially position the image of the Earth. Since we will be animating the Earth using CSS positioning, the <SPAN> section is given an ID of *earth*.

```
<SPAN ID="earth" STYLE="position:absolute; left:165;
    top:30">
<IMG SRC="earth.gif">
</SPAN>
```

12 Type the closing **</BODY>** and **</HTML>** tags.

13 Save the file as **OrbitIE.html** in the **Tutorial.07** folder on your Student Disk. If you have a copy of Internet Explorer, open the file and see if the animation functions properly. Figure 7-36 shows the program output in Internet Explorer as it appears before the animation begins.

Figure 7-36: OrbitIE.html document in Internet Explorer

14 Close the Web browser window.

Positioning in Navigator

Navigator does not use CSS positioning for dynamic animation. Instead, you must use layers. **Layers** are used in Navigator to arrange HTML elements in sections that can be placed on top of one another and moved individually. You can still use CSS positioning with Navigator, but not for traveling animation. Although layering is not part of the CSS protocol, you need to understand layers to be able to create animation that functions in Navigator. Layering is a large topic that deals not only with animation, but also with other HTML design issues in Navigator. However, we will only discuss the aspects of layering that relate to animation.

You create a layer in an HTML document using a <LAYER>...</LAYER> tag pair. You use LEFT and TOP attributes of the <LAYER> tag to specify an initial position for a layer. You can also include the NAME attribute in a <LAYER> tag.

JavaScript accesses each <LAYER> tag using a Layer object. The **Layer object** contains several properties and methods for manipulating layers in JavaScript. The two methods of the Layer object that create traveling animation in Navigator are the moveTo() method and the offset() method. The **moveTo() method** moves a layer to a specified position, and it accepts two arguments. The first argument represents the number of pixels from the left of the window, and the second argument represents the number of pixels from the top of the window. The **offset() method** moves a layer a specified number of pixels horizontally and vertically from its current position. The offset() method also accepts two arguments. The first argument represents the number of pixels to move horizontally, and the second argument represents the number of pixels to move vertically.

You refer to a specific layer in JavaScript by using its position in the layers[] array or by using the value assigned to the <LAYER> tag's NAME attribute. As with other arrays in JavaScript, such as the forms[] array, layers are assigned to the layers[] array in the order in which they are encountered by the JavaScript interpreter. To refer to the first layer in a document, you use the statement `document.layers[0];`. However, it is usually easier to refer to a layer using the value assigned to its NAME attribute. For example, to refer to an array named animation, you use the statement `document.animation;`. Each layer contains its own Document object that you must also include in order to refer to a layer's elements; you use the Document object twice. For example, to change the src property of an image named myImage on a layer named animation, you use the statement `document.animation.document.myImage.src = "new_image.jpg;"`.

Figure 7-37 displays the same bird animation document you saw in Figure 7-34, but modified for use with Navigator. The displayed image is changed in the fly() function using the statements `document.bird.document.birdimage.src = up.src;` and `document.bird.document.birdimage.src = down.src;`. A single statement within each `if` statement uses the moveTo() method to move the layer named *bird*, which contains the image.

```
<HTML>

<HEAD>

<TITLE>Flying Bird</TITLE>

<SCRIPT LANGUAGE="JavaScript1.2">

<!-- HIDE FROM INCOMPATIBLE BROWSERS

var startFlying;

var updown = 0;

var horizontalPosition = 10;
```

Figure 7-37: Bird animation document modified for use with Navigator

```
var up = new Image();
up.src = "up.gif";
var down = new Image();
down.src = "down.gif";
position = 1;
function fly() {
    if (position == 1) {
        document.bird.document.birdimage.src = up.src;
        document.bird.moveTo(40, 200);
        position = 2;
    }
    else if (position == 2) {
        document.bird.document.birdimage.src = down.src;
        document.bird.moveTo(250, 80);
        position = 3;
    }
    else if (position == 3) {
        document.bird.document.birdimage.src = up.src;
        document.bird.moveTo(480, 10);
        position = 1;
    }
}
// STOP HIDING FROM INCOMPATIBLE BROWSERS -->
</SCRIPT>
</HEAD>
<BODY>
<LAYER NAME="bird" LEFT=40 TOP=200>
<IMG NAME="birdimage" SRC="up.gif" HEIGHT=200 WIDTH=200>
</LAYER>
```

Figure 7-37: Bird animation document modified for use with Navigator (continued)

```
<FORM>

<INPUT TYPE="button" NAME="fly" VALUE=" Fly "
    onClick="startFlying=setInterval('fly()',500);">

<INPUT TYPE="button" NAME="stop" VALUE=" Stop "

    onClick="clearInterval(startFlying);">

</FORM>

</BODY>

</HTML>
```

Figure 7-37: Bird animation document modified for use with Navigator (continued)

tip

If you would like to see how the flying bird animation functions in Navigator, a copy of it named FlyingBirdNavigator.html is in the Tutorial.07 folder on your Student Disk. Remember that you can open this file only in Navigator. If you attempt to open it in Internet Explorer, you will receive an error message.

Next, you will modify the orbit program so that it functions in Navigator. As with the Internet Explorer version, create the program even if you do not have a copy of Navigator, since you will need it when you learn about cross-browser compatibility.

To modify the orbit animation program so that it functions in Navigator:

1 Open the **OrbitIE.html file** in your text editor or HTML editor and immediately save it as **OrbitNavigator.html** in the **Tutorial.07** folder on your Student Disk.

2 In the orbit() function, replace the two statements that modify the left and top properties of the <SPAN> tag for the Earth image with the following single statement. The new statement uses the Navigator moveTo() method to change the position of the earth layer, which you will add next:

```
document.earth.moveTo(leftEarth[position],
    topEarth[position]);
```

3 Replace the <SPAN> section for the Earth image with the following layer tags:

```
<LAYER NAME="earth" LEFT=165 TOP=30>
<IMG SRC="earth.gif">
</LAYER>
```

4 Save the document. If you have a copy of Navigator, open the document and see if it functions correctly. Figure 7-38 shows the program output as it appears in Navigator before the animation begins.

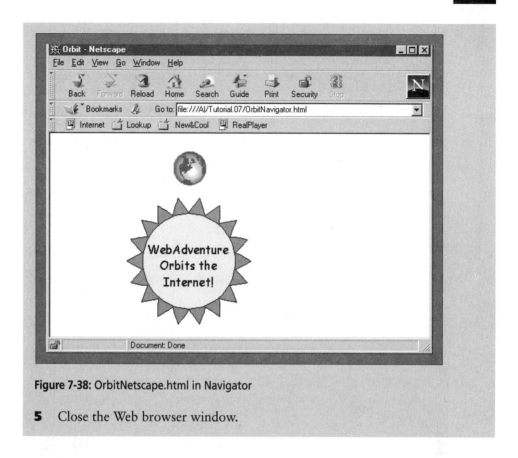

Figure 7-38: OrbitNetscape.html in Navigator

5 Close the Web browser window.

Cross-Browser Compatibility

People and companies want to attract visitors to their Web pages, and they want their Web pages to be as appealing and interesting as possible. About 46 percent of Internet users use Navigator, about 42 percent use Internet Explorer, and about 12 percent use some other browser. If developers were forced to choose a single Web browser, then a significant portion of Internet users would not be able to visit their Web sites. Many developers try to create DHTML code that runs equally well in either Navigator or Internet Explorer. However, creating true cross-browser-compatible DHTML files is a difficult task that requires a strong knowledge of both Microsoft's and Netscape's Document Object Models. In addition, you must write code that runs statements appropriate for the user's Web browser.

An easier solution than trying to pack Microsoft- and Netscape-compatible code into the same document is to create two separate documents, one for each Web browser. You can then use a "master" document that checks which browser is running when users open the file. After the master document learns which browser is running, it opens the appropriate Web page. You check which browser is running using the appName property of the Navigator object that you learned about in

Tutorial 5. If the appName property returns "Netscape," the master document opens the Netscape version of a file. If the appName property returns "Internet Explorer," the master document opens the Microsoft version of a file.

The program in Figure 7-39 opens a browser-specific version of the flying bird animation program. The onLoad() event handler in the <BODY> tag calls a checkBrowser() function. The checkBrowser() function uses the appName property of the Navigator object to see which browser is running, then uses the `document.location.href;` statement to open the correct file.

```
<HTML>

<HEAD>

<TITLE>Flying Bird</TITLE>

<SCRIPT LANGUAGE="JavaScript1.2">

<!-- HIDE FROM INCOMPATIBLE BROWSERS

function checkBrowser() {

     if (navigator.appName == "Netscape")

          document.location.href = "FlyingBirdNavigator.html";

     else

          document.location.href = "FlyingBirdIE.html";

}

// STOP HIDING FROM INCOMPATIBLE BROWSERS -->

</SCRIPT>

</HEAD>

<BODY onLoad="checkBrowser()">

</BODY>

</HTML>
```

Figure 7-39: Program that opens a browser-specific file after checking appName

Instead of checking the browser being used, many JavaScript programmers prefer to test which DOM is being used. You can test which DOM is being used by checking whether the Document object has a layers property or an all property. You can check for the layers and all properties using conditional statements such as if (`document.layers`) and if (`document.all`). For example, since only the Navigator Document object includes a layers object, the statement if (`document.layers != null`), which checks to see if the object is not equal to null, returns true if executed in Navigator and false if executed in Internet

Explorer. Similarly, since only the Internet Explorer Document object includes an all object, the statement if (document.all != null) returns true if executed in Internet Explorer and false if executed in Navigator.

The following code shows a version of the checkBrowser() function from Figure 7-39 modified to check for the all or layers objects.

```
function checkBrowser() {
    if (document.layers != null)
        document.location.href = "FlyingBirdNavigator.html";
    else if (document.all != null)
        document.location.href = "FlyingBirdIE.html";
}
```

> **tip**
>
> If you would like to find out more about cross-browser JavaScript techniques, visit Dynamic Drive at http://www.dynamicdrive.com and The Dynamic Duo at http://www.dansteinman.com/dynduo/.

Next, you will create a master document that opens a browser-specific version of the orbit program, depending on the browser in use. The document checks for the all and layers objects rather than the appName property of the Navigator object.

To create a master document that opens a browser-specific version of the orbit program, depending on the browser in use:

1 Start your text editor or HTML editor and create a new document.

2 Type the opening <HTML>, <HEAD>, and <TITLE> sections of the document:

```
<HTML>
<HEAD>
<TITLE>Orbit</TITLE>
```

3 Add the opening statements for a JavaScript section within the <HEAD> section:

```
<SCRIPT LANGUAGE="JavaScript1.2">
<!-- HIDE FROM INCOMPATIBLE BROWSERS
```

4 Create the following function to check which browser is being used. The function will be called from the onLoad event in the <BODY> tag:

```
function checkBrowser() {
    if (document.layers != null)
        document.location.href = "OrbitNavigator.html";
    else if (document.all != null)
        document.location.href = "OrbitIE.html";
}
```

5   Add the following code to close the <SCRIPT> and <HEAD> sections:

```
// STOP HIDING FROM INCOMPATIBLE BROWSERS -->
</SCRIPT>
</HEAD>
```

6   Type the following <BODY> tag that includes an onLoad event, which calls the checkBrowser() function:

```
<BODY onLoad="checkBrowser()">
```

7   Add the closing **</BODY>** and **</HTML>** tags.

8   Save the file as **OrbitMaster.html** in the **Tutorial.07** folder on your Student Disk. Open the **OrbitMaster.html** file from either Navigator or Internet Explorer to see if the correct version of the program opens. The name of the document that opens appears in the Address box in Internet Explorer or in the Location box in Navigator.

9   Close the Web browser window.

SUMMARY

- Cascading style sheets (CSS, also called style sheets) are a standard set forth by the World Wide Web Consortium for managing the formatting information of HTML documents.

- A single piece of formatting information is called a style.

- CSS styles are created using name/value pairs separated by a colon. The name portion of the name/value pair refers to a specific CSS style attribute known as a property.

- Inline styles determine the appearance of individual tags in an HTML document. You define inline styles using the STYLE attribute along with a string containing the name/value pairs for each style you want to include. Multiple properties are separated by semicolons.

- Document-level style sheets determine formatting for instances of a specific HTML element, such as the <H1> tag, and for specific CLASS and ID attributes.

- The CLASS attribute can be applied to any HTML tag, identifying various elements as part of the same class.

- The value of an ID attribute uniquely identifies individual tags in an HTML document.

- The tag, class, or ID to which specific style rules in a style sheet apply is called a selector.

- A regular class is used to define different style instructions for the same tag.

- A generic class is similar to a regular class, but it is not associated with any particular tag.

- There are three options for using JavaScript code to manipulate CSS: write code that functions only in Navigator, write code that functions only in Internet Explorer, or write both sets of code and execute the correct set depending on which Web browser is in use.

- The Netscape Document Object Model accesses the styles for selectors using the tags, classes, and ID properties of the Document object. The tag property provides access to the styles of tags in an HTML document. The classes property provides access to the styles of classes in an HTML document. The ID property provides access to the styles of ID attributes in an HTML document.

- When you refer to a CSS property in JavaScript code, you remove the hyphen, use a lowercase letter for the first letter of the first word, and use an uppercase letter for the first letter of subsequent words.

- The general syntax for defining a CSS style in Navigator is document.*tags, classes, or ids property.CSS selector.specific CSS property.*

- The Internet Explorer Document Object Model accesses the styles for selectors using the all property of the Document object. The all property is an array of all the elements in an HTML document. The style property represents the CSS styles for a particular tag, class, or ID attribute.

- The general syntax for defining a CSS style in Internet Explorer is document.all.*CSS selector.style.specific css property.*

- CSS positioning is used to position or lay out elements on a Web page.

- Relative positioning places an element according to other elements on the Web page.

- Absolute positioning places elements in a specific location on a Web page.

- Layers are used in Navigator to arrange HTML elements in sections that can be placed on top of one another and moved individually.

- The Layer object contains several properties and methods for manipulating layers in JavaScript.

- The moveTo() method moves a layer to a specified position.

- The offset() method moves a layer a specified number of pixels horizontally and vertically from its current position.

- Instead of writing Microsoft and Netscape code into the same document, it is easier to create two separate documents, one for each Web browser. You then write a "master" document that checks which browser is running and opens the appropriate file.

- Instead of checking which browser is being used, many JavaScript programmers prefer to check which DOM is being used. You test which DOM is being used by checking whether the Document object has a layers property or an all property.

QUESTIONS

1. The name portion of the name/value pair refers to a specific CSS style attribute known as a _____
   a. property.
   b. key.
   c. definition.
   d. style module.

2. _____ styles determine the appearance for individual tags in an HTML document.
   a. Tag
   b. Line
   c. Inline
   d. Instance

3. _____ style sheets determine formatting for instances of a specific HTML element, such as the <H1> tag, and for specific CLASS and ID attributes.
   a. Global
   b. Document-level
   c. Class
   d. Inline

4. The CLASS attribute _____
   a. contains a grouping of JavaScript functions.
   b. manages all the arrays within a given <SCRIPT>...</SCRIPT> tag pair.
   c. determines whether Internet Explorer or Navigator is the browser platform.
   d. identifies different HTML elements as part of the same class.

5. The value of an ID attribute _____
   a. contains a color identifier used for changing background colors.
   b. uniquely identifies individual tags in an HTML document.
   c. is a type of label used within JavaScript code.
   d. is only used with images in an HTML document.

6. The tag, class, or ID to which specific style rules in a style sheet apply is called a
   _____
   a. label.
   b. marker.
   c. indicator.
   d. selector.

7. A _____ class is used for defining different style instructions for the same tag.
   a. regular
   b. standard
   c. style
   d. JavaScript

8. A class that is not associated with any particular style is referred to as a(n)
   _____ class.
   a. irregular
   b. generic
   c. independent
   d. floating

9. What happens when you change the formatting of a style contained in a style sheet?
   a. Nothing. You must reload the HTML document from the server in order for the changes to take effect.
   b. All tags in the document that are associated with the style are automatically updated.
   c. Only the first instance of a tag associated with the style is automatically updated.
   d. You must right-click on each tag associated with the style and select Update from the shortcut menu.

10. Which of the following statements is true of JavaScript programs that manipulate CSS?
   a. JavaScript programs that manipulate CSS will run correctly on both Navigator and Internet Explorer.
   b. JavaScript programs that manipulate CSS written for Internet Explorer will run in Navigator, but JavaScript programs that manipulate CSS written for Navigator will not run in Internet Explorer.
   c. JavaScript programs that manipulate CSS written for Navigator will run in Internet Explorer, but JavaScript programs that manipulate CSS written for Internet Explorer will not run in Internet Explorer.
   d. You must write different sets of JavaScript code for each browser if you want to manipulate CSS styles.

11. How is the CSS property font-weight written in JavaScript?
   a. FONT-WEIGHT
   b. fontweight
   c. FontWeight
   d. fontWeight

12. When does a change to a style value using JavaScript code appear in Navigator?
   a. immediately
   b. after the HTML document is reloaded from the server
   c. after the user resizes the screen
   d. You cannot use JavaScript to change style values in Navigator.

13. How do you change the color style for the <H1> tag using JavaScript code in Internet Explorer?
   a. `document.H1.style.color = "red";`
   b. `document.all.H1.style.color = "red";`
   c. `document.all.H1.color = "red";`
   d. `document.H1.color = "red";`

14. When does a change to a style value using JavaScript code appear in Internet Explorer?
   a. immediately
   b. after the HTML document is reloaded from the server
   c. after the user resizes the screen
   d. You cannot use JavaScript to change style values in Internet Explorer.

15. _____ positioning places an element according to the positions of other elements on the Web page.
   a. Relative
   b. Absolute
   c. Inline
   d. Frame

16. _____ positioning places elements in a specific location on a Web page.
   a. Relative
   b. Absolute
   c. Inline
   d. Frame

17. Which properties are used with the STYLE attribute of inline styles for CSS positioning?
   a. left and top
   b. x and y
   c. horizontal and vertical
   d. x-axis and y-axis

18. Which HTML tag pairs are used exclusively by Navigator for positioning?
    a. <SPAN>...</SPAN>
    b. <DIV>...</DIV>
    c. <LAYERS>...</LAYERS>
    d. <POSITION>...</POSITION>
19. What method is—or what methods are—used in Navigator for positioning with JavaScript?
    a. the setAt() method
    b. the top() and bottom() methods
    c. the left() and right() methods
    d. the moveTo() method

 # EXERCISES

For the following exercises, locate the necessary images on the Internet or from a graphics program to which you have access. Create each program so that it functions with the Web browser you use most often: Navigator or Internet Explorer.

1. The Tutorial.07 folder on your Student Disk contains five images of a basketball: basketball1.gif through basketball5.gif. Animate the images so that the basketball appears to bounce up and down on the screen. Save the document as Dribble.html in the Tutorial.07 folder on your Student Disk.

2. The Tutorial.07 folder on your Student Disk contains three images of snowflakes: snowflake1.gif, snowflake2.gif, and snowflake3.gif. Use each image as many times as you like to create a snowstorm effect on a Web page. It should "snow" from the top of the screen to the bottom. Save the document as Blizzard.html in the Tutorial.07 folder on your Student Disk.

3. The Tutorial.07 folder on your Student Disk contains an image of a kangaroo, kangaroo.gif. Animate the image so that the kangaroo appears to hop up and down and across your screen. Save the document as Kangaroo.html in the Tutorial.07 folder on your Student Disk.

4. The Tutorial.07 folder on your Student Disk contains three images of fish: fish1.gif, fish2.gif, and fish3.gif. Use the fish images to create a fish tank in a Web page. The fish should swim across the screen from both directions. Use as many copies of the images as you think necessary. Save the document as FishTank.html in the Tutorial.07 folder on your Student Disk.

5. The Tutorial.07 folder on your Student Disk contains an image of a racecar, racecar.gif. Animate the image so that the racecar appears to drive around a Web page on an oval racetrack. Add buttons that start and stop the animation. Use several start buttons that "drive" the car at different speeds. Save the document as RaceTrack.html in the Tutorial.07 folder on your Student Disk.

6. The Tutorial.07 folder on your Student Disk contains an image of an airplane, airplane.gif. Create a Web page that includes the airplane image. Create several buttons that make the airplane fly. Create one button for takeoff, one button to land, another button that flies a loop-the-loop, and so on. Save the document as Pilot.html in the Tutorial.07 folder on your Student Disk.

JavaScript Reference

Comment Types

Line Comments

```
<SCRIPT LANGUAGE="JavaScript1.2" >
// Line comments are preceded by two slashes.
</SCRIPT>
```

Block Comments

```
<SCRIPT LANGUAGE="JavaScript1.2" >
/*
This line is part of the block comment.
This line is also part of the block comment.
*/
/* This is another way of creating a block comment. */
</SCRIPT>
```

Javascript Reserved Words

abstract	else	int	switch
boolean	extends	interface	synchronized
break	false	long	this
byte	final	native	throw
case	finally	new	throws
catch	float	null	transient
char	for	package	true
class	function	private	try
const	goto	protected	typeof
continue	if	public	var
default	implements	return	void
delete	import	short	while
do	in	static	with
double	instanceof	super	

Identifiers

Legal Identifiers

```
my_identifier
$my_identifier
_my_identifier
my_identifier_example
myIdentifierExample
```

Illegal Identifiers

```
%my_identifier
1my_identifier
#my_identifier
@my_identifier
~my_identifier
+my_identifier
```

Events

JavaScript Events

Event	Triggered When
Abort	The loading of an image is interrupted
Blur	An element, such as a radio button, becomes inactive
Click	An element is clicked once
Change	The value of an element changes
Error	There is an error when loading a document or image
Focus	An element becomes active
Load	A document or image loads
MouseOut	The mouse moves off an element
MouseOver	The mouse moves over an element
Reset	A form resets
Select	A user selects a field in a form
Submit	A user submits a form
Unload	A document unloads

HTML Elements and Associated JavaScript Events

Element	Description	Event
<A>...</A>	Link	Click MouseOver MouseOut
<IMG>	Image	Abort Error Load
<AREA>	Area	MouseOver MouseOut

(continued)

Element	Description	Event
<BODY>...</BODY>	Document body	Blur Error Focus Load Unload
<FRAMESET>...</FRAMESET>	Frame set	Blur Error Focus Load Unload
<FRAME>...</FRAME>	Frame	Blur Focus
<FORM>...</FORM>	Form	Submit Reset
<INPUT TYPE="text">	Text field	Blur Focus Change Select
<TEXTAREA>...</TEXTAREA>	Text area	Blur Focus Change Select
<INPUT TYPE="submit">	Submit	Click
<INPUT TYPE="reset">	Reset	Click
<INPUT TYPE="radio">	Radio button	Click
<INPUT TYPE="checkbox">	Check box	Click
<SELECT>...</SELECT>	Selection	Blur Focus Change

Primitive Data Types

Data Type	Description
Integers	Positive or negative numbers with no decimal places
Floating-point numbers	Positive or negative numbers with decimal places, or numbers written using exponential notation
Boolean	A logical value of true or false
String	Text, such as "Hello World"
Null	An empty value

JavaScript Escape Sequences

Escape Sequence	Character
\b	Backspace
\f	Form feed
\n	New line
\r	Carriage return
\t	Horizontal tab
\'	Single quotation mark
\"	Double quotation mark
\\	Backslash

Operators

JavaScript Operator Types

Operator Type	Description
Arithmetic	Used for performing mathematical calculations
Assignment	Assigns values to variables
Comparison	Compares operands and returns a Boolean value
Logical	Used for performing Boolean operations on Boolean operands
String	Performs operations on strings

Arithmetic Binary Operators

Operator	Description
+ (addition)	Adds two operands
– (subtraction)	Subtracts one operand from another operand
* (multiplication)	Multiplies one operand by another operand
/ (division)	Divides one operand by another operand
% (modulus)	Divides two operands and returns the remainder

Arithmetic Unary Operators

Operator	Description
++ (increment)	Increases an operand by a value of one
– (decrement)	Decreases an operand by a value of one
– (negation)	Returns the opposite value (negative or positive) of an operand

Assignment Operators

Operator	Description
=	Assigns the value of the right operand to the left operand
+=	Combines the value of the right operand with the value of the left operand, or adds the value of the right operand to the value of the left operand and assigns the new value to the left operand
−=	Subtracts the value of the right operand from the value of the left operand and assigns the new value to the left operand
*=	Multiplies the value of the right operand by the value of the left operand and assigns the new value to the left operand
/=	Divides the value of the left operand by the value of the right operand and assigns the new value to the left operand
%=	Modulus—divides the value of the left operand by the value of the right operand and assigns the remainder to the left operand

Comparison Operators

Operator	Description
== (equal)	Returns true if the operands are equal
!= (not equal)	Returns true if the operands are not equal
> (greater than)	Returns true if the left operand is greater than the right operand
< (less than)	Returns true if the left operand is less than the right operand
>= (greater than or equal to)	Returns true if the left operand is greater than or equal to the right operand
<= (less than or equal to)	Returns true if the left operand is less than or equal to the right operand

Logical Operators

Operator	Description
&& (and)	Returns true if the both the left operand and the right operand return a value of true, otherwise it returns a value of false
‖ (or)	Returns true if either the left operand or right operand returns a value of true. If neither operand returns a value of true, then the expression containing the ‖ (or) operator returns a value of false
! (not)	Returns true if an expression is false and returns false if an expression is true

Operator Precedence

- Parentheses (( ) [ ] .) *highest precedence*
- Negation/increment (! – ++ – typeof void)
- Multiply/divide/modulus (* / %)
- Addition/subtraction (+ –)
- Comparison (< <= > >=)
- Equality (== !=)
- Logical and (&&)
- Logical or (‖)
- Assignment operators (= += –= *= /= %=) *lowest precedence*

Control Structures and Statements

```
if (conditional expression) {
     statement(s)
}
if (conditional expression) {
     statement(s)
}
else {
     statement(s)
}
```

```
switch (expression) {
    case label :
        statement(s)
        break;
    case label :
        statement(s)
        break;
    ...
    default :
        statement(s)
}
while (conditional expression) {
    statement(s)
}
do {
    statement(s)
} while (conditional expression);
for (initialization expression; condition; update statement {
    statement(s)
}
for (variable in object) {
    statement(s)
}
with (object) {
    statement(s)
}
```

break A break statement is used to exit switch statements and other program control statements such as the while, do...while, for, and for...in looping statements. To end a switch statement once it performs its required task, you should include a break statement within each case label.

continue The continue statement halts a looping statement and restarts the loop with a new iteration. You use the continue statement when you want to stop the loop for the current iteration, but want the loop to continue with a new iteration.

Objects

This section lists the properties, methods, and events of the major JavaScript objects. Only properties, methods, and events compatible with both Internet Explorer and Navigator are listed.

Date Object

Method	Description
getDate()	Returns the date of a Date object
getDay()	Returns the day of a Date object
getFullYear()	Returns the year of a Date object in four-digit format
getHours()	Returns the hour of a Date object
getMilliseconds()	Returns the milliseconds of a Date object
getMinutes()	Returns the minutes of a Date object
getMonth()	Returns the month of a Date object
getSeconds()	Returns the seconds of a Date object
getTime()	Returns the time of a Date object
getTimezoneOffset()	Returns the local timezone offset in minutes from the current date and GMT
getUTCDate()	Returns the date of a Date object in universal time
getUTCFullYear()	Returns the four-digit year of a Date object in universal time
getUTCHours()	Returns the hours of a Date object in universal time
getUTCMilliseconds()	Returns the milliseconds of a Date object in universal time
getUTCMinutes()	Returns the minutes of a Date object in universal time
getUTCMonth()	Returns the month of a Date object in universal time
getUTCSeconds()	Returns the seconds of a Date object in universal time
setDate()	Sets the date of a Date object
setFullYear()	Sets the four-digit year of a Date object
setHours()	Sets the hours of a Date object
setMilliseconds()	Sets the milliseconds of a Date object
setMinutes()	Sets the minutes of a Date object
setMonth()	Sets the month of a Date object
setSeconds()	Sets the seconds of a Date object

(continued)

Method	Description
setTime()	Sets the time of a Date object
setUTCDate()	Sets the date of a Date object in universal time
setUTCFullYear()	Sets the four-digit year of a Date object in universal time
setUTCHours()	Sets the hours of a Date object in universal time
setUTCMilliseconds()	Sets the milliseconds of a Date object in universal time
setUTCMinutes()	Sets the minutes of a Date object in universal time
setUTCMonth()	Sets the month of a Date object in universal time
setUTCSeconds()	Sets the seconds of a Date object in universal time
toGMTString()	Converts a Date object to a string, set to the GMT time zone
toLocaleString()	Converts a Date object to a string, set to the current time zone
toString()	Converts a Date object to a string
toUTCString()	Converts a Date object to a string, set to universal time
valueOf()	Converts a Date object to a millisecond format

Document Object

Property	Description
alinkColor	The color of an active link as specified by the ALINK attribute of the <BODY> tag
anchors[]	An array referring to the document's anchors
applets[]	An array referring to the document's applets
bgColor	The background color of the document, as specified by the BGCOLOR attribute of the <BODY> tag
cookie	Specifies a cookie for the current document
domain	The domain name of the server where the current document is located

(continued)

Property	Description
embeds[]	An array referring to the document's plug-ins and ActiveX controls
fgColor	The foreground text color of the document, as specified by the FGCOLOR attribute of the <BODY> tag
forms[]	An array referring to the document's forms
images[]	An array referring to the document's images
lastModified	The date the document was last modified
linkColor	The color of the document's unvisited links, as specified by the LINK attribute of the <BODY> tag
links[]	An array referring to the document's links
referrer	The URL of the document that provided a link to the current document
title	The title of the document as specified by the <TITLE>...</TITLE> tag pair in the document's <HEAD> section
URL	The URL of the current document
vlinkColor	The color of the document's visited links, as specified by the VLINK attribute of the <BODY> tag

Method	Description
close()	Notifies the Web browser that you are finished writing to the window or frame and that the document should be displayed
open()	Opens a window or frame, other than the current window or frame, and is used to update its contents with the write() and writeln() methods
write()	Creates new text on a Web page
writeln()	Creates new text on a Web page followed by a line break

Form Object

Property	Description
action	The URL to which a form's data will be submitted
method	The method in which a form's data will be submitted: GET or POST
enctype	The format of the data being submitted
target	The window in which any results returned from the server are displayed
name	The name of the form
elements[]	An array representing a form's elements
length	The number of elements on a form

Method	Description
reset()	Clears any data entered into a form
submit()	Submits a form to a Web server

Event	Triggered When
onReset	A reset button is pressed or the reset() method is called
onSubmit	A submit button is pressed or the submit() method is called

Frame Object

Property	Description
action	The URL to which a form's data will be submitted
method	The method by which a form's data will be submitted: GET or POST
enctype	The format of the data being submitted
target	The window in which any results returned from the server are displayed
name	The name of the form
elements[]	An array representing a form's elements
length	The number of elements on a form

Method	Description
reset()	Clears a form without the use of a reset <INPUT> tag
submit()	Submits a form to a server without the use of a submit <INPUT> tag

Event	Triggered When
onReset	Executes when a reset button is selected on a form
onSubmit	Executes when a form is submitted to a CGI script using a submit <INPUT> tag or an image <INPUT> tag

History Object

Property	Description
length	Contains the specific number of documents that have been opened during the current browser session

Method	Description
back()	The equivalent of clicking a Web browser's Back button
forward()	The equivalent of clicking a Web browser's Forward button
go()	Opens a specific document in the history list

Image Object

Property	Description
border	A read-only property containing the border width, in pixels, as specified by the BORDER attribute of the <IMG> tag
complete	A Boolean value that returns true when an image is completely loaded
height	A read-only property containing the height of the image, as specified by the HEIGHT attribute of the <IMG> tag
hspace	A read-only property containing the amount of horizontal space, in pixels, to the left and right of the image, as specified by the HSPACE attribute of the <IMG> tag
lowsrc	The URL of an alternate image to display at low resolution
name	A name assigned to the tag
src	The URL of the displayed image
vspace	A read-only property containing the amount of vertical space, in pixels, above and below the image, as specified by the VSPACE attribute of the <IMG> tag
width	A read-only property containing the width of the image, as specified by the WIDTH attribute of the <IMG> tag

Event	Triggered When
onLoad	An image finishes loading
onAbort	The user cancels the loading of an image, usually by clicking the Stop button
onError	An error occurs while loading an image

Location Object

Property	Description
hash	A URL's anchor
host	A combination of the URL's hostname and port sections
hostname	A URL's hostname
href	The full URL address
pathname	The URL's path
port	The URL's port
protocol	The URL's protocol
search	A URL's search or query portion

Method	Description
reload()	Causes the page currently displayed in the Web browser to open again
replace()	Replaces the currently loaded URL with a different one

Math Object

Property	Description
E	Euler's constant e, which is the base of a natural logarithm
LN10	The natural logarithm of 10
LN2	The natural logarithm of 2
LOG2E	The base-2 logarithm of e
LOG10E	The base-10 logarithm of e
PI	A constant representing the ratio of the circumference of a circle to its diameter
SQRT1_2	1 divided by the square root of 2
SQRT2	The square root of 2

Method	Description
abs(x)	Returns the absolute value of x
acos(x)	Returns the arc cosine of x
asin(x)	Returns the arc sine of x
atan(x)	Returns the arc tangent of x
atan2(x,y)	Returns the angle from the x-axis
ceil(x)	Returns the value of x rounded to the next highest integer
cos(x)	Returns the cosine of x
exp(x)	Returns the exponent of x
floor(x)	Returns the value of x rounded to the next lowest integer
log(x)	Returns the natural logarithm of x
max(x,y)	Returns the larger of two numbers
min(x,y)	Returns the smaller of two numbers
pow(x,y)	Returns the value of x raised to the y power
random()	Returns a random number
round(x)	Returns the value of x rounded to the nearest integer
sin(x)	Returns the sine of x
sqrt(x)	Returns the square root of x
tan(x)	Returns the tangent of x

Navigator Object

Property	Description
appCodeName	The Web browser code name
appName	The Web browser name
appVersion	The Web browser version
language	The language, such as English or French, used by the Web browser
platform	The operating system in use
userAgent	The user agent

Method	Description
javaEnabled()	Determines whether Java is enabled in the current browser

Window Object

Property	Description
defaultStatus	Default text that is written to the status bar
document	A reference to the Document object
frames[]	An array listing the frame objects in a window
history	A reference to the History object
location	A reference to the Location object
name	The name of a window
opener	The Window object that opens another window
parent	The parent frame that contains the current frame
self	A self-reference to the Window object—identical to the window property
status	Temporary text that is written to the status bar
top	The topmost Window object that contains the current frame
window	A self-reference to the Window object—identical to the self property

Method	Description
alert()	Displays a simple message dialog box with an OK button
blur()	Removes focus from a window
clearTimeout()	Cancels a set timeout
close()	Closes a window
confirm()	Displays a confirmation dialog box with OK and Cancel buttons
focus()	Makes a Window object the active window
open()	Opens a new window
prompt()	Displays a dialog box prompting a user to enter information
setTimeout()	Executes a function after a specified number of milliseconds have elapsed

Event	Triggered When
onBlur	The window becomes inactive
onError	An error occurs when the window loads
onFocus	The window becomes active
onLoad	A document is completely loaded in the window
onResize	The window is resized
onUnload	The current document in the window is unloaded

Index